THE PENTAX WAY

FOCAL PRESS LTD,
31 Fitzroy Square, London W1P 6BH

FOCAL PRESS INC.,
10 East 40th Street, New York, NY 10016

Associated companies:
Pitman Publishing Pty Ltd, Melbourne.
Pitman Publishing New Zealand Ltd, Wellington.

THE ASAHI PENTAX WAY

The Asahi Pentax
Photographer's Companion

H. KEPPLER

Eleventh Edition
with Supplement

Focal Press Limited, London

Focal Press Inc., New York

🅑🅛 British Library Cataloguing in Publication Data

Keppler, Herbert
    The Asahi Pentax way.–11th ed.
    1. Pentax camera
    I. Title
    771.3′1   TR263.P4

ISBN 0 240 51018 6

First edition April 1966
First edition (U.S.A.) April 1966
Second edition February 1967
Reprinted July 1967
Reprinted October 1967
Reprinted March 1968
Second edition (U.S.A.) March 1968
Third edition January 1969
Third edition (U.S.A.) January 1969
Reprinted June 1969
Reprinted August 1969
Fourth edition January 1970
Reprinted October 1970
Reprinted February 1971
Fifth edition November 1971
Fifth edition (U.S.A.) February 1972
Reprinted April 1972
Sixth edition September 1972
Seventh edition 1973
Reprinted September 1973
Eighth edition May 1974
Reprinted December 1974
Ninth edition December 1975
Reprinted October 1976
Tenth edition January 1978
Eleventh edition with Supplement 1980

German Edition:
DAS ASAHI PENTAX BUCH
Verlag Die Schönen Bücher Dr. Wolf Strache.

Spanish Edition:
MANUAL PENTAX ASAHI
Ediciones Omega, S.A., Barcelona.

Italian Edition:
IL LIBRO ASAHI PENTAX
Editoriale Effe, Roma.

Printed and bound in Great Britain by
A. Wheaton & Co., Ltd, Exeter

CONTENTS

v

THE SLR PRINCIPLE

The 35 mm. eye-level single-lens reflex principle was undoubtedly one of the most convenient, logical and exciting
developments in the history of 35 mm. photography. You,
the user, can view your subject right through the camera's
own lens. You can see what the film sees. Your camera
preserves on film what you were seeing up to the instant of
exposure—whether a landscape using the normal lens or a
far distant nebulae with your camera attached to a telescope.
There, right before your eye, is the picture area. You can
note what is sharp, what is not sharp and what will actually
be included in the final negative or transparency. And no
matter how you use your camera, no matter what lens or
accessory is placed on it, you will continue to see as your
camera sees with no barrier between you and the subject.

Simple Focusing Methods

The simplest camera need be no more than a box with a
lens in front and a flat plane at the rear to hold the film. If
you point this simple camera at a bright object—a candle
flame—the simple lens will project an image of the candle
flame on the back of the box. You can make the image
sharper or fuzzier by moving the magnifying lens forward or
backward. This is the simplest and crudest type of focusing
system. You can easily see its failings. If you put film inside
the box and make the box light tight, you can't possibly see
whether the image is sharp or not since you can no longer see
the film plane without letting light ruin the film.

The simplest solution to this focusing problem is to mount
the lens on a small movable platform and mark various points
on the platform where a sharp image can be obtained for subjects at particular distances. As you focus on closer subjects
you must move the lens further away from the film plane.

Continue to make markings showing when the lens is in
position for a subject 3 ft. away, 5 ft. away, 10 ft. away up

to about 50 ft. away. You will probably find a point at which everything beyond 50 ft. looks sharp. This is called the infinity focus point.

Your marked platform is actually a focusing scale. If you could measure the distance of each subject from the camera every time with a tape measure and then set the lens to the scale properly, you would get sharp pictures. In practice, you have to resort to estimating the distance, which is not too accurate. However, scale focusing is common in simpler cameras.

Focusing Screens

Even the earliest camera designers realised that actual measurements or guesses were inconvenient or inaccurate. The earliest solution to the problem was the use of the ground glass back. By placing a piece of glass with a roughly ground surface behind the lens, a camera user could actually see the image projected by the lens. The lens could then be focused accurately until the subject was sharp on the ground glass. The ground glass could then be removed and the film put into the exact same plane. This is precisely how view cameras used in studios by professional photographers work today. They are not, though, convenient for all work.

Early Single-Lens Reflexes

A very logical solution to this problem was developed from the medieval camera obscura, later models of which were the first instruments to use the single-lens reflex principle. Light passed through a lens and was reflected upwards to a ground glass. Artists and draughtsmen placed tracing paper over the ground glass and traced the image.

Once suitable photographic materials had been discovered camera designers soon realised that a piece of film could be placed behind the mirror at a distance from the lens equivalent to that from the lens to the ground glass via the mirror. Moving the mirror out of the way lets the image fall on the film. That's just how single-lens reflexes work.

The first big single-lens reflexes were comparatively simple to use because you could view the image easily on the large 4 × 5 in., 9 × 12 cm., or 5 × 7 in. focusing screen. But as manufacturers made reflexes for smaller film sizes, it became more and more difficult to see images.

A few brave designers did try a single-lens reflex principle in a 35 mm. camera, but they met problems that seemed impossible to overcome. Even with a powerful magnifier, focusing was difficult on the tiny ground glass. In addition, the 35 mm. picture was horizontal. Suppose you wanted to make a vertical picture? In order to use the ground glass you would have to hold the camera vertically and view the image from the side. And the image would be upside down at that!

These problems prevented the widespread popularity of 35 mm. single-lens reflex cameras to any great extent until the 1950s. In 1950, the first real advance occurred. From Zeiss Ikon of Dresden came the Contax S—a 35 mm. single-lens reflex with a five-sided prism on top of the ground glass. You could hold the camera at eye level and see an unreversed, right side up, magnified focusing and viewing image. After you pressed the shutter release, though, the mirror flew up-wards, blacking out the view completely until you wound the film on for the next picture.

The Asahi Design

The Asahi Optical Co. Ltd., was founded in 1919. Today it is one of the world's leaders in camera and optical design. Asahi entered the photo field in 1923 when it commenced the manufacture of motion picture projector lenses. The first camera lenses were produced by Asahi in 1931.

However, Asahi's substantial growth in the photo industry began in 1951 when the Asahiflex 35 mm. single-lens reflex cameras were introduced. These were the first Japanese-made 35 mm. single-lens reflexes. Three years later Asahi announced a real breakthrough in reflex camera design—the instant-return mirror, which ended image blackout. Immediately after the shutter closed following exposure, the mirror swung downwards again into viewing position rather than remaining upwards blocking the view. Instead of a blackout after the release of the shutter, there was only a blink during the actual exposure.

Asahi Optical Co.'s main factory is located in Mashiko, Japan, which is north of Tokyo. It has another major factory in Itabashi, Tokyo. While some optical blanks and raw glass are purchased from outside sources, all grinding, polishing, assembly and lens design are done by Asahi.

While this brief history of popular camera design may give you some idea of just how important a part the Asahi com-

3

pany played in evolving the single-lens reflex design, let's see just what other features make the single-lens reflex the leading 35 mm. camera today.

First let's take a good look at that viewing system. The whole finder area of the Pentax is extremely bright. That's because of the very efficient optical system. Pentax cameras have used efficient optical systems from the very first and improved their finders down to the newest 35 mm. SLRs of today. Originally, 35 mm. eye-level reflexes produced a fairly dim image which became progressively dimmer towards the edges and corners of the viewing area. To overcome this, some SLR makers incorporated a large heavy condenser lens underneath the viewfinder prism. Pentax improved upon this by adding a so-called Fresnel lens, a flat plastic sheet below the prism incorporating concentric grooves which had ridges that produced the same effect as a large condenser but without the weight and thickness. As years went by and Pentax models were improved this so-called Fresnel screen (named after the inventor of the concentric ring substitute) became finer and finer so that the rings were barely noticeable in the Spotmatics, Pentax ES and K cameras. Later viewing systems incorporated an inverted condenser directly into the bottom of the prism itself, thus obviating the Fresnel rings completely. In addition, silvering the prism surfaces instead of using aluminium coatings further enhanced brightness.

To facilitate focusing, Pentax was among the first cameras to use central microprism spots. The microprism, incorporating many tiny optical pyramids, fractures the image into jagged pieces which appear to shimmer when images are out of focus. In focus, the images snap into sharpness. Later Pentaxes incorporated a split image rangefinder instead of a microprism. This feature, consisting of two semicircular opposing optical wedges in the middle of the focusing screen, causes an image to appear split in two pieces when out of focus. In focus, the two images realign themselves. More modern Pentaxes incorporate three focusing systems—a central split-image rangefinder, a microprism collar around the rangefinder and a full focusing screen outside. Some Pentaxes feature interchangeable viewing screens which allow the user many choices of focusing aids depending on his personal preference and the type of lens or optical system fitted to the camera.

4

FINDER SYSTEM

Here are the basic parts of the camera's interior. (Some Pentax cameras may have minor differences in their prism and condenser systems).

1. Five-sided prism.
2. Magnifying eyepiece.
3. Condensing lens.
4. Focusing screen.
5. Focal-plane shutter.
6. Rapid return mirror.

Early focusing screens were plain with no focusing aids at all. Microprism spots and split image range-finders were both helpful but use depended on subject and the preference of the camera owner. More modern viewing screens have central split-image rangefinders, microprism collars plus full focusing screens.

In modern focusing screens, the central split image rangefinder displaces bisected subject horizontally, microprism fractures image and outer focusing area blurs image when lens is out of focus (left). In focus, entire image aligns itself and snaps into sharpness (right).

Now let's turn to a very important part of any camera—the lens. Lenses for the Pentax have been designed for high quality. They are well finished, too, in handsome black satin with large, legible contrasting white or coloured numerals. Try the focusing ring. You'll find that it works with incredible smoothness. And check how closely you can focus with the normal 50 or 55 mm. lens—down to 18 in.

The very finest rangefinder cameras cannot approach this flexibility. Why? Because their finder systems are located on top of the camera body. At such close distances the finders see above the subject. This is known as parallax error. With the single-lens reflex you're looking right through the lens, so you see what you get.

All Pentax lenses (or Takumar as they were named until recent years) have anti-reflection coatings to minimise internal reflections and flare, but Asahi developed a superior coating for many of their lenses. This is a super multi-coating using a very special, precise, many-layered coating of high efficiency anti-reflection agents which allows the lens to transmit about 25 per cent more light than a conventional coated lens. The coating also reduces flare and unwanted internal reflections and produces unusually hard front and rear surfaces, less susceptible to scratching. The lenses are marked "SMC Pentax" (or Takumar), short for "Super Multi Coated", on the front ring.

One of the most important features of older Pentaxes has been the interchangeable screw thread lens mount. If you grasp the lens firmly and twist counterclockwise $2\frac{3}{4}$ turns, you can unthread and remove the lens. Starting with the KM, KX, K2 and K1000 cameras in 1975, Pentax introduced a more convenient, faster to change bayonet lens mount requiring only a 65° twist of the lens to fasten it or remove it from the camera. While screw thread Takumars are no longer being made, there are so many on the market it is certain they will continue to be plentiful for many years. Lens interchangeability allows you to place bellows units or extension tubes between the lens and camera body for very close photography. More important for some photographers is the possibility of interchangeable lenses. You can replace the normal lens with lenses of varying uses—telephoto lenses,

OLD AND NEW PENTAXES

Not everyone can own a new Pentax camera, and, luckily, Pentax cameras stand up well after many years' hard use, so there are many good old Pentaxes around in the hands of the original owners or purchased as used cameras. We'll start with the oldest models and work our way forward to today.

Older Models

Now to the camera models. The following are the models no longer in production.

Asahiflex I (Introduced 1951): This 35 mm. single-lens reflex had a waist-level-only viewfinder plus separate but non-focusing sports finder. The standard interchangeable lens in Asahi (not the present Pentax) thread was the 50 mm. *f*3.5 Takumar with preset diaphragm. The focal plane shutter offered speeds from 1/20 to 1/500 sec. plus T and B. The shutter was synchronised for both X and F flash. Film advance and shutter wind was by a single knob. Lenses from this camera can be used on present-day Pentax cameras with a special insert adapter. But the current lenses cannot be used on the Asahiflex I body.

Asahiflex IIB (Introduced 1954): Essentially the same as the original Asahiflex I, but the lowest shutter speed was 1/25 sec. instead of 1/20 sec. World's first instant-return mirror incorporated. Standard lens was 50 mm. *f*3.5 or 58 mm. *f*2.4 Takumar in Asahiflex thread with preset dia-phragm. These lenses can be fitted to current cameras with special insert adapter, but current lenses cannot be fitted to Asahiflex IIB body.

Asahiflex IIA (Introduced in 1955): Similar to Asahiflex IIB, but with additional slow shutter speeds of 1/2, 1/5, 1/10 sec. Lenses same as IIB.

Asahi Pentax (Introduced 1957): Completely new body de-sign with permanently mounted eye-level prism, rapid-wind lever, folding rapid-rewind crank, focal-plane shutter with speeds from 1 to 1/500 sec., separate slow-speed dial on front of camera, X and F synch., choice of 58 mm. $f2$, 55 mm. $f2.2$ or 58 mm. $f2.4$ Takumar lenses with preset diaphragm. New, larger Pentax thread mount.

Asahi Pentax S (Introduced 1957): Essentially same as Asahi Pentax but with nearer arithmetical progression of shutter speeds—1, 1/2, 1/4, 1/8, 1/15, 1/30, 1/60, 1/125, 1/250, 1/500 sec. instead of older 1, 1/2, 1/5, 1/10, 1/25 sec., etc. Lenses 55 mm. $f2.2$ or $f1.8$ Takumar.

Asahi Pentax K (Introduced 1958): Essentially same as Pentax S, but had top speed of 1/1000 sec., internally coupled semi-automatic diaphragm which closed to the pre-selected aperture automatically when the shutter release was pressed and reopened afterwards manually with a cocking lever. Camera had first central microprism focusing grid. Standard lens was 55 mm. $f1.8$ Auto-Takumar.

Asahi Pentax H2 (Introduced 1959): Similar to Asahi Pentax K but has top speed of 1/500 sec. with all speeds on single top, non-rotating (during exposure) dial, shutter cock indicator, 55 mm. $f2$ Auto-Takumar lens. Also sold under names of Asahi Pentax S2, Asahiflex H2, Heiland Pentax H2 (in U.S.).

Asahi Pentax S3 (Introduced 1961): Essentially same as Pentax H2 but has fully automatic diaphragm requiring no recocking to full aperture after exposure, top shutter speed of 1/1000 sec., standard lens 55 mm. $f1.8$ Auto-Takumar with fully automatic diaphragm. Sold in U.S. as Honeywell Pentax H3.

Asahi Pentax S2 (Introduced 1961): Modified version of model H2 with top speed of 1/1000 sec. While lens remained semi-automatic 55 mm. $f2$ Auto-Takumar, some S2 bodies had fully automatic diaphragm mechanisms in camera body similar to S3.

Asahi Pentax S1 (Introduced May 1961): Essentially same as S2 but with 55 mm. $f2.2$ Auto-Takumar, semi-automatic diaphragm. Some S1 camera bodies had fully automatic diaphragm mechanisms.

Asahi Pentax SV, Honeywell Pentax H3v in U.S. (Introduced 1962): Similar to S3 or H3, but with resetting film exposure counter, self-timer cocking wheel surrounding rewind knob, 55 mm. $f1.8$ or 55 mm. $f2$ Super Takumar lens.

Asahi Pentax S1a, Honeywell Pentax H1a in U.S.

Pentax, Pentax S: Older Pentax has slow speeds from 1 to 1/25 sec. on front shutter speed dial, fast speeds 1/25 to 1/500 sec. on main speed dial on top of camera. Pentax S has speeds from 1 to 1/30 sec. on front dial, 1/30 to 1/500 on main dial. Lens has pre-set diaphragm.

Pentax K: Slower speeds from 1 to 1/30 sec. on front speed dial, fast speeds from 1/30 to 1/1000 sec. on main speed dial on top of camera. Lens has semi-automatic diaphragm.

Pentax H2: All speeds 1 to 1/500 sec. on single dial on top of camera. Lens has semi-automatic diaphragm.

PENTAX PEDIGREE

1. Asahiflex (1951), known as Tower in U.S.: Waist-level finder, 50mm. lens. X-sync. only.

2. Asahiflex 1A (1953): Same as above but with X and F. sync.

3. Asahiflex 11B (1954), known as Tower 23 in U.S.: Instant-return mirror.

4. Asahiflex 11A (1955), known as Tower 22 in U.S. Separate slow speeds to $\frac{1}{2}$ sec. on front dial.

5. Original Pentax (1957), known as Tower 26 in U.S.: Eye-level pentaprism, rapid wind lever, folding rewind crank, larger Pentax thread mount, speeds from 1 to 1/500 sec.

6. Pentax S (1957): Same as Pentax above but with nearer arithmetical progression of shutter speeds. 55mm. *f*1.8 Takumar.

7. Pentax K (1958): Top shutter speed of 1/1000 sec. semi-automatic diaphragm mechanism coupled to new 55mm., *f*1.8 Auto-Takumar lens, microprism finder.

8. Pentax H2 (1959): also known as S2, same as K but all speeds on single, top, non-rotating dial, top speed 1/500 sec. but later S2 1/1000 sec., 55mm *f*2 Auto-Takumar.

9. Pentax S1 (1961), similar to H2 but with 55mm *f*2.2 Auto-Takumar.

10. Pentax Super S2 (Japanese market only): Similar to H2 but with top 1/1000 sec., fully automatic 55mm *f*2 Super Takumar.

11. Pentax S3 (1961), known as H3 in U.S.: Auto-manual control for automatic diaphragm mechanism, top shutter speed 1/1000 sec. 55mm., *f*1.8 Auto-Takumar.

PENTAX PEDIGREE

12. Pentax SV, H3v (1962); Similar to S3 but with self-zeroing exposure counter, self-timer, improved microprism, 55mm. f1.8 or f2 Super Takumar.

13. Pentax S1a, known as H1a in U.S. (1963). Top speed of 1/500 sec. Otherwise same as Pentax SV, H3v. 55mm., f2 Super Takumar.

14. Pentax Spotmatic (1964): New body and mechanism, re-positioned self-timer, pull-up knob backlatch, behind-the-lens exposure system, 50mm., f1.4 Super Takumar lens.

15. Pentax SL 1965: Same as Spotmatic but without metering system.

16. Pentax SP500, SP1000 (1971): Same as Spotmatic but no self-timer. SP500 has top 1/500 sec. only.

17. Pentax Spotmatic II (1971): Same as Spotmatic but with hot flash sync shoe and 50mm f1.4 or 55mm f1.8 Super Multi-Coated Takumar lens.

18. Pentax Spotmatic IIA (in U.S. and Mexico only) 1972: Same as Spotmatic II but with built-in Strobo-Eye for use with all Honeywell Remote/Auto Strobonar flash units.

19. Pentax ES (1972): Fully automatic exposure with electronically controlled shutter 1 to 1/1000 sec., manual speeds 1/60 to 1/1000 sec., 50 mm f1.4 Super-Multi-Coated Takumar, hot flash shoe atop prism, no self-timer.

20. Pentax ES II (1973): Same as ES but with self-timer, electronically controlled speeds to 8 sec., interior viewfinder blinds, shutter release lock.

21. Pentax Spotmatic F (1973): Similar to Spotmatic II but has full aperture metering, shutter release lock.

22. Pentax KM (current): bayonet lens mount, lenses marked "Pentax" instead of Takumar, plastic tipped wind lever, CdS metering system with needle visible in finder, self-timer, accepts screw thread lenses for manual operation by means of special adapter.

23. Pentax K-1000 (current): similar to KM but no mirror lockup, preview or self-timer. Has special 50mm f2 SMC Pentax lens.

24. Pentax KX (current): similar to KM but has centre-weighted silicon photo diode exposure meter system, shutter speeds, apertures visible in finder, shutter lock, film reminder slot on back, silver coated pentaprism.

25. Pentax K2 (current): similar to KX but no apertures visible in finder. Has metal blade electronically controlled shutter 8 sec. to 1/1000 sec., auto exposure control, also all manual speeds.

26. Pentax K2 DMD (current): first standard Pentax designed to accommodate motor drive. Otherwise same as K2 but has aperture readout in finder, exposure compensation warning, **extraneous light eyepiece blind, low battery voltage warning signal.**

27. Pentax MX (current): new compact body, same K bayonet mount as K cameras, shutter speeds 1 to 1/1000 sec., GPD center weighted metering circuit, LED meter readout in finder, shutter speeds, aperture visible in finder, plastic needle film takeup spool, provision for motor winder and motor drive.

28. Pentax ME (current): new compact body, K bayonet mount, auto exposure via electronically controlled metal blade shutter has speeds 8 sec. to 1/1000 sec., auto exposure compensation, GPD metering circuit, LED shutter speed indication in finder, **plastic film takeup spool, provision for auto winder.**

22/23

24

25

26

27

28

ACTION

Page 17 (top). You can often stop action without a very fast shutter speed. Here Leonid Bergoltsev needed but 1/60 sec. at f/2.8 to catch these Georgian dancers at the height of their leap.

Page 17 (bottom). The photographer used 1/1000 sec. to halt all action in the picture of a water skier. With a high contrast subject you may have to bias your exposure in favour of the light or dark area in the scene.

TWO LENS MONTAGE

Page 18. Starkly dramatic double print of man on ladder by Swiss photographer Kurt Lembachner is actually composed of two negatives montaged. The photographer shot scene with man and ladder using a 55 mm. *f*/1.8 and reshot with a 105 mm. *f*/2.8, then combined negatives on a single enlarging paper.

TELEPHOTO EXPOSURE

Page 19. Judging exposure with a long (500 mm.) lens can be difficult. Here the photographer exposed for a middle grey tone, thus the birds are in partial silhouette.

EXPOSING FOR FLESH TONES

Page 20. Richard Lukes here exposed for the most important area of the picture, the flesh tone, avoiding the influence of the bright background or dark shadowy rocks with his exposure of 1/125 sec. *f*/5.6.

Page 21. K. Niiyama avoided bright reflections from the water in the pool, and ensured correct tones with an exposure of *f*/8 at 1/250 sec.

LONG LENS ACTION

(Above). A 200 mm. *f*/4 Super-Takumar on Xharder Gaston's Pentax Spotmatic provided the ideal length for a tight cropping of a classic matador pass during a bullfight. The Belgian photographer shot at 1/250 sec. and *f*/16 on Kodak Tri-X Pan film.

CITY SCENIC

Page 23. An overall exposure reading produced a good negative of New York skyscrapers with 300 mm. *f*/4, Takumar.

EXPOSURE DILEMMA

Page 24. Should M. Yura use a fast shutter speed with his Pentax to stop action or a small aperture for depth of field? Luckily a compromise of 1/250 sec. at *f*/11 was possible.

Here are the features and
controls of the Sla and Hla
Pentax cameras.

1. Film counter.
2. Shutter release.
3. Shutter speed dial.
4. Rapid wind lever.
5. Prism housing.
6. Preview lever.
7. Folding rewind
crank.
8. Rewind knob.
9. Film indicator.
10. Neck strap lug.
11. Shutter cock indi-
cator.
12. Focusing mount.
13. Lens.
14. Diaphragm ring.
15. X flash terminal.
16. FP flash terminal.
17. Back lock.
18. Finder eyepiece.
19. Film chamber.
21. Film track.
22. Tripod bush or
socket.
23. Focal plane shutter.
24. Rewind button.
25. Film sprocket drive.
26. Take-up spool.
27. Film pressure plate.
28. Shutter release.
29. Depth-of-field scale.
30. Focusing scale.
31. Film Transport
indicator.

(Introduced 1962): Similar to SV or H3v but has marked top speed of 1/500 instead of 1/1000 sec., 55 mm. *f*2 Super Takumar lens.

Asahi Pentax Spotmatic or SP, Honeywell Pentax Spotmatic in U.S. (Introduced 1964): Behind-the-lens exposure meter system reading the illumination from the focusing screen. Standard lens is 50 mm. *f*1.4 Super Takumar.

Asahi Pentax SL: Spotmatic without the metering system.

Asahi Pentax Spotmatic II (Introduced 1971): Similar to the Spotmatic but is equipped with the new 50 mm. *f*1.4 or 55 mm. *f*1.8 Super-Multi-Coated-Takumar featuring a new multi-layered anti-reflection coating. The contact on the hot shoe is always switched off except when a flash unit is slipped into the shoe, thus preventing any accidental shock. There's a loaded film type indicator under the rewind knob.

Honeywell Pentax Spotmatic IIa (Introduced 1972): Available in U.S. and Mexico only, this model is same as Spotmatic II but has built-in Strobo-Eye electronic flash sensor for use with all Remote Auto-Strobonars made by Honeywell.

Asahi Pentax SP500, SP1000 (Introduced 1971): Same as regular Spotmatic but no 1/1000 sec. (on SP500) shutter speed and lacks a self-timer.

Asahi Pentax Spotmatic II Motor Drive: Motor-drive camera based on the Spotmatic.

Asahi Pentax ES (Introduced 1972): Automatic exposure camera with electronically controlled speeds 1 to 1/1000 sec., speed set visible in finder, manually controlled speeds 1/60 to 1/1000 sec., exposure-factor control dial.

Asahi Pentax ES II (Introduced 1973): Same as ES but has self-timer, shutter-release lock, automatically controlled electronic shutter speeds from 8 to 1/1000 sec., interior viewfinder blinds.

Asahi Pentax Spotmatic F (Introduced 1973): Similar to Spotmatic II but provides exposure meter readings at full aperture with Super Multi-Coated Takumar lenses.

Asahi Pentax KM (current): Similar to Spotmatic F but bayonet lens mount accepts K-mount Pentax lenses only for full-aperture behind-lens CdS cell circuit metering, but can be fitted with screw-thread S-type lenses from other Pentaxes for manual operation using K-mount adapter, hot sync shoe.

Asahi Pentax KX (current): Same as KM but has faster acting, more sensitive silicon photo diode metering circuit measuring centre weighted area of focusing screen, aperture, shutter speed settings visible in viewfinder, film box memo holder on back of camera.

Asahi Pentax K2 (current): Similar to KX but slightly smaller body, fully automatic exposure control similar to Pentax ES II with speeds from 8 sec. to 1/1000 sec., full manual control override, vertically running metal focal plane shutter, shutter speed only visible in finder.

Asahi Pentax K2 DMD (current): Similar to K2 but has provision for motor drive; also aperture readout in finder, exposure compensation warning in finder, extraneous light eyepiece blind, low battery voltage warning signal.

Asahi Pentax K-1000 (current): Similar to KM but has no mirror lock-up, depth of field preview, self-timer. Has special 50 mm. f2 SMC Pentax lens.

Asahi Pentax MX (current): Compact body camera using K-type bayonet of KM, KX, K2 cameras, Gallium Arsenide Phosphide Photo Diode centre weighted meter circuit, light emitting diode meter control in finder, shutter speeds, apertures visible in finder, shutter speeds 1 to 1/1000 sec., provision for auto winder or motor drive.

Asahi Pentax ME (current): Compact body auto exposure camera using K-type bayonet, GPD photo diode metering circuit as MX but with light emitting diodes in finder indicating auto shutter speed set, auto speeds with metal blade shutter 8 sec. to 1/1000 sec., provision for auto winder.

PENTAX ME AND MX

It should not have been too surprising to Pentax aficionados that Asahi in 1976 announced their intention of producing two extremely tiny single-lens reflexes of most advanced design. Asahi had introduced the first small eye-level single-lens reflex in 1957. Interest by photographers in an even lighter, less bulky, easy-to-carry camera system of camera body, lenses and accessories was bound to find a co-operative ear at Asahi Optical Company. Their ME and MX models were designed to combine modern technology, flexibility of purpose and ease of operation within a small size.

Other cameras in the family followed. The Pentax ME Super resembles the ME but in addition has manual shutter speeds and a few other features while the Pentax MV and MV-1 provide simplified controls for the novice.

The Pentax ME and MX were the first single-lens reflexes to make use of gallium arsenic phosphorus photo diodes as meter cells. The ME Super also has these cells. One on either side of the finder eyepiece reads a centre-weighted portion of the viewing screen. These cells provide reactions to light up to 1000 times faster than cadmium sulphide which had been the most common sensor material in single-lens reflexes. GPD cells have virtually no lag between the time the meter cells sense the illumination and the time they provide the exposure setting required.

They have better spectral sensitivity than silicon cells (used in the Pentax MV and MV-1), particularly by being virtually insensitive to the infrared, are less subject to variations due to temperature extremes and require far less current to activate their circuitry. Coupled with light emitting diodes, both GPD and silicon cells can provide lighted dot exposure information in the viewfinder which is more accurate, less subject to damage, and easier to see in any illumination than the more common meter needles. Most important, the drain on the two 1.5 volt batteries which power the circuits is quite low. The meter display can be used before and after the picture is taken with little worry of battery failure. Additionally, the Asahi engineers devised stabilizer circuits in these Asahi Pentax cameras to prevent the LED dots from flickering or showing more than one light at a time. The diodes give an instantaneous, precise reading of the exposure.

Common features in all ME and MV cameras include a unique magic needle loading system takeup spool with 15 white plastic rods through which the film leader can easily be slipped. There is no need to catch a film perforation on a gear tooth and no danger of film ripping during rewinding. Both cameras have very bright finders, thanks to new efficient means of silvering the finder systems. Magnification in the viewfinders is 0.95×, nearly life size, with a 50 mm lens. All cameras feature a precise, highly capable split-image rangefinder, plus a microprism focusing collar, plus a full-focusing, fine-grained viewfinder screen. All cameras but the MV have holders on the camera backs to hold the cardboard end of the film box as a reminder.

The cameras also have large and sturdy rewind cranks and knobs which are easy to grasp and operate. Lastly, but quite important: all cameras have the K bayonet lens mount introduced on the KM, KX and K2 cameras and can accommodate the entire series of Pentax SMC K mount lenses as well as the series of K mount M-compact lenses.

Loading the Cameras

Small, light cameras, the Pentax ME, ME Super, MV and MV-1 are $5\frac{1}{8} \times 3\frac{1}{4} \times 2\frac{3}{4}$ in. and weigh about 20 ounces ($31 \times 82.5 \times 67.5$ mm, weighing 570 g.) with the ultra compact 40 mm $f2.8$ SMC Pentax-M lens. The alternative 50 mm $f1.7$ or 1.4 SMC Pentax lenses are also light and compact.

To load the cameras, pull up on the rewind knob. The camera back will swing open. Place the film cartridge in the empty left-hand chamber, thread the film leader across the film plane to the takeup spool and push the leader end directly between any of the white plastic spool 'magic needles'. Make certain the sprocket holes of the film leader engage the sprocket teeth of the sprocket wheel right next to the takeup spool. Close the camera back and, using the rewind lever, take the slack out of the film by turning the lever in the opposite direction to the rewind knob arrow until the film is tight.

29

Set the film speed on the collar surrounding the rewind knob by grasping the outer ring of the collar, pulling upwards on the ring and turning to the numeral corresponding to the ASA rating of the film you have loaded. Black dots between the numerals indicate between settings for such film speeds as 25, 50, 125, 160 and 500. Check that the exposure compensation dial around the rewind knob of the ME and ME Super, or under the knob of the MV and MV-1, is indicating 1X. If not, reset it by turning the whole dial.

While winding film to the first exposure, set the shutter dial to 100X (125X on the ME Super) by pushing downwards on the white shutter dial release button and turning the dial itself to the X setting. You'll need two hands—one to turn the dial and one to press the button. By using the X setting, a non-electronic, mechanical speed, for winding the film to the first exposure, you will minimize battery drain and eliminate any possibility of accidentally making long exposures during winding. Advance the film with the rapid-wind lever and release the shutter until frame 1 appears in the frame counter, just in front of the wind crank hub. On the ME and ME Super, each time the shutter is wound, the small window behind the shutter dial scale will turn red to let you know that it is ready to fire. At the back of these cameras, near the top right edge, vertical orange stripes will jiggle back and forth in the window to indicate that the film has been loaded correctly and is being wound on the takeup spool properly. These stripes will also move during rewinding.

Exposure Meter

Turn the shutter dial back to the "auto" setting. While looking through the viewfinder, press in slightly on the shutter release itself—just a bit, not enough to release the shutter. If there are working batteries in the camera, you will see a red diode alight at the far left side of the viewfinder. If there is no red diode, the batteries are missing, are dead or are not making proper contact. With the edge of a coin, unthread the bottom battery cover in the "open" direction as indicated. Replace the two 1.5 volt silver oxide batteries (G13, S76E, MS76E, MS76H or the equivalent). Sometimes cleaning oxidation from the batteries will bring them back to working condition. Make certain the batteries face in the direction indicated in the battery chamber.

PENTAX ME, ME SUPER, MV AND MV-1 FEATURES

1. Exposure counter.
2. Rapid-wind lever.
3. Shutter release button.
4. Shutter setting index.
5. Shutter dial. ME Super has additional manual shutter speed control buttons.
6. (Hot shoe) flash contact.
7. Exposure compensation dial.
8. Film rewind crank.
9. Rewind knob/back release.
10. Film cassette chamber.
11. Self-timer (not on MV-1).
12. Lens release lever.
13. Lens alignment dot.
14. Focus ring.
15. Viewfinder window.
16. Film advance/rewind indicator (ME, ME Super only).
17. Sprockets.
18. Flash socket (not on MV or MV-1).
19. Power winder point (ME, MV-1 only).
20. Battery chamber.
21. Tripod/winder bush.
22. Shutter.
23. Film rewind button.
24. Film transport coupler (ME Super, MV-1 only).
25. Film take-up spool.
26. Pressure plate.
27. Back cover.

The orange stripes of the film transport indicator flicker on the ME and ME Super when the film is being properly transported, or rewound. Once film comes off take-up mechanism, flicker stills.

The self-timer on the ME, ME Super and MV-1 delays exposure by 4–12 seconds. Push down to set. To release, push up slightly on the lever.

Now when you press the shutter release, a diode should light.

Auto Operation of Pentax ME and ME Super

The Pentax ME and ME Super have a row of light emitting diodes in the viewfinder. Each is opposite a shutter speed which will be set by the automatic exposure system of the camera. You can select the shutter speed you wish by turning the camera's aperture ring. If there is insufficient illumination for the aperture you have set, the red dot opposite "under" will light. If there is too much illumination for a good exposure the dot opposite "over" at the top of the shutter speed scale will light. For hand-held pictures, you should use shutter speeds of 60 or greater. To stop action subjects, use a faster shutter speed such as 125 or more when possible.

While all the diodes of the Pentax ME are red, the diodes of the Pentax ME Super are colour coded to make proper choice easier. Speeds below 1/30 sec are indicated by yellow diodes warning that a tripod or other steady support is advisable. Speeds between 1/60 and 1/2000 sec (twice the fastest speed available on the ME) have green diodes indicating that the camera can be hand held. Red diodes are reserved for the over- and under-exposure warning signals.

You'll note that only one diode will light at a time with either camera. When the shift between speeds exceeds 50% of the next higher or lower speed the adjacent diode will light. However, the Copal 11-blade electronically controlled shutter of the ME and ME Super will actually set in-between speeds with great precision. In other words, although the diodes indicate only full marked increments of 1/60, 1/125, or 1/250 sec., the camera metering system will set continuously variable shutter speeds to provide the exact speed needed—1/68, 1/132, 1/277 sec., etc.

You needn't keep your finger on the shutter release to maintain exposure supervision. With the ME pull the wind lever out from the camera body 30° to operating position and then push in slightly on the shutter button. The LED dots will now remain on continuously until you shut them off by pushing in the wind lever itself. (Don't forget to do this when you are not using the metering system!) The ME Super has an improved meter turn-on system. Slight pressure

PENTAX ME, ME SUPER, MV AND MV-1 EXPOSURE SYSTEM

The film speed is set on the ME and ME Super by lifting up the dial, and turning it until the correct figure (ASA meter setting) shows in the centre of the window. The MV and MV-1 dials have no windows (far right). Instead you set index opposite the orange index mark.

The dashes between the figures indicate intermediate speeds. The MV and MV-1 scales have indexes that begin with 25.

To compensate for special conditions with the ME and ME Super, turn the dial a suitable amount one way or the other (from $\frac{1}{4}$x— for very dark backgrounds to 4x for very light). Make sure 1x is set for all normal scenes. The AV and AV-1 dials are similar but are located under the rewind knob. Match the compensation needed against the ASA index.

On auto, the shutter is set by the meter system to give a suitable speed. Press button and turn to L (lock), 100x (for flash) or B. MV, MV-1 have no locks. Note slightly different Pentax ME Super dial at right.

Shutter speeds are indicated in the ME by LED dots in the viewfinder. To alter the shutter speed, change the lens aperture.

1. Microprism collar.
2. Split-image focusing aid.
3. Under-exposure mark.
4. Shutter speed LEDs.
5. Shutter speed scale.
6. Mat focusing screen.
7. Over-exposure mark.

on the shutter release will light the diode display, but you do not need to keep your finger on the release. If you remove your finger, the display will remain lighted for approximately 20 sec. after which it will automatically turn itself off, thus preventing accidental battery drain.

Auto Operation of Pentax MV and MV-1

The auto exposure systems of the Pentax MV and MV-1 have been designed for camera owners who do not wish to learn about shutter speed controls but prefer a point-and-shoot camera with simple warning signals to indicate whether or not there is enough light to take a picture.

At the left of the MV and MV-1 viewfinder screens you will see a vertical transluscent panel. When you press the shutter release slightly, the panel will light with a green, red or yellow diode. The green diode means it's OK to go ahead and shoot. Red means the shot will be overexposed, and you should use a smaller aperture. Yellow indicates you should use a larger lens aperture if possible or, if not, a tripod or switch to flash. (For those who do wish to know what speeds these coloured diodes represent, they are: yellow, 1 sec. to 1/30; green, 1/30 sec. to 1/1000 sec.; and red, over 1/1000 sec.) To shift from one coloured diode to another, merely change lens apertures by turning the lens aperture ring. It's as simple as that.

The MV and MV-1 metering systems are activated by pressing slightly on the shutter release. However, you must keep your finger on the release to maintain the meter reading.

Keep your eye as close to the viewfinder eyepiece as possible when making exposures to prevent extraneous light behind the camera from entering the eyepiece and inflating the meter readings erroneously. If you wear glasses, it's advisable to purchase an eyecup for the camera to prevent such stray light leakage. When using your camera on a tripod or whenever you make exposures with your eye away from the finder, slip the black eyepiece blind (furnished with each camera) over the eyepiece.

Meter Coupling Range

While Asahi has provided the ME and ME Super with the minimum guaranteed range of exposure speeds possible with various ASA film settings (see chart at back of book), the

OPERATING ME, ME SUPER, MV, MV-1 AND MX

To load, push film leader between any two reels on the take-up spool. Wind on until the sprockets engage the sprocket holes top and bottom.

To change batteries, open battery compartment with a small coin. Put two silver oxide cells in the ME or ME Super holder, (+ showing) and replace it in the camera. Batteries are simply dropped into MV or MV-1 compartment.

To remind you of the film loaded, you can put your box top in the holder on the camera back.

The combined range-finder splits up part of the image, and makes the surrounding area shimmer. When in focus, the subject appears whole and unshaking.

To prevent large diameter lenses from coming into contact with the tripod head, insert the spacer ring (furnished with each camera) between tripod head and tripod socket of the camera.

cameras will commonly prove usable outside the range. For instance, you will probably be able to make exposures of 1 sec. or longer with films having an ASA rating of 400 or more even though the chart does not indicate this. Check out your own camera's shutter speed abilities at all ASA indexes even before you take any photos.

Additional ME, ME Super, MV and MV-1 Suggestions

The central split-image range-finder is surrounded by a microprism collar. Of course, you can focus on the ground-glass screen as well.

You can release the shutter in one of three ways: by squeezing gently, firmly and smoothly down on the shutter release button with your finger, by threading a cable release into the tapered thread of the shutter button or by using the self-timer on the front of the ME, ME Super and MV-1. The self-timer can be employed to allow you to get into the picture yourself or as a gentle release for long exposures when you have no cable release (but have placed the camera on a firm support). The self-timer can delay the shutter between 4 and 12 seconds depending on how far down you push the self-timer lever. To activate the self-timer, you just push up slightly on the same lever.

You may accidentally press the shutter release when you have the lenscap on and the shutter is wound. This, in effect, begins a long exposure in which the shutter may remain open. You can check this by looking through the camera. If the finder is black, you know the camera shutter is open. You must bring it back to closed as quickly as possible by pressing the white release button on the shutter speed dial (on the ME and ME Super) and turning the dial to the 125X or 100X setting. Then turn the dial back to "auto" if you wish to take pictures. With the ME or ME Super you can turn to lock to prevent such inadvertent firing again.

Besides using the setting for electronic flash with your flash connected to the hot shoe on top of the camera (or the 3 mm (PC) terminal on the left side of the ME or ME Super camera body), you can operate the camera mechanically with no battery or a dead one at 1/100X or 125X even though the camera's metering system and electronic control of the

PENTAX ME SUPER,
MV-1 AND MV FINDER
SYSTEMS

1. Split-image focusing
   aid.
2. Microprism collar.
3. Electronic flash LED
   indicator.
4. Manual mode LED
   indicator.
5. Overexposure LED.
6. Shutter speed LED.
7. Flash synchronization
   speed LED.
8. Shutter speed scale.
9. Matt focusing screen.
10. Underexposure LED.

Press the top button and
the speed increases up to
1/2000 sec. Press the lower button and the speed
decreases to 4 sec. Release
the button when the LED
glows besides the desired
shutter speed.

Select aperture and the
LED glows beside the speed
determined by the meter.
Separate LEDs warn when
the settings will result in
over- or underexposure
and whether the shutter
dial is set to manual.

1. Split-image focusing
   aid.
2. Microprism collar.
3. Normal exposure LED.
4. Flash-ready signal.
5. Matt focusing screen.

shutter is not working. Set the aperture to the right opening for 1/100 sec. or 1/125 sec. in accordance with the type of film you are using. (Most film comes with a paper instruction slip suggesting exposures for various subjects and lighting conditions.)

You can also compensate the automatic exposure for special subject or lighting conditions with the exposure compensation dial. For instance, if there is strong backlight behind your subject which might inflate the normal exposure reading, you can double or quadruple the automatic exposure by setting the dial to 2X or 4X. If you wish to halve or quarter the exposure, you can set $\frac{1}{2}$X or $\frac{1}{4}$X (see chapter on exposure for complete data on such variations from normal). Don't forget to turn the dial back to 1X when you are finished with the compensated exposures!

The ME Super has a finder warning signal to indicate that the exposure compensation dial is not set at 1X. A red diode opposite the top EF (for exposure factor) marking on the shutter speed scale will pulsate whenever the metering circuit is on. It will cease lighting when you return the dial to 1X.

The Pentax ME Super has a number of additional features and refinements not found on the other three cameras. These include the improved faster running Seiko MFC-E2 shutter with its top 1/2000 sec. speed (instead of the more common 1/1000 sec.), brighter viewing screen, lower shutter and mirror noise and vibration thanks to an improved air damper and, most important to many photographers, provision for manual speed control while maintaining metering ability.

To operate the ME Super with manual shutter speeds, press the exposure dial lock button and turn the dial from its auto position to M. When you press the shutter release slightly to activate the metering system, the green M near the top of the scale will light indicating you are operating manually. You will also note that one of the LEDs opposite a shutter speed is lit. The particular LED lit depends on your last use of manual speeds. The metering circuit "remembers" the last manual shutter speed set (even if you switch to the automatic mode) and will reset this speed as soon as you switch to manual.

To change manual speeds, you press one of two small rectangular buttons just to the left of the exposure mode dial. The button towards the front of the camera body will cause the shutter speeds and the indicating diodes in the finder to move upwards. By pressing the rear button, the speeds and diodes will descend. Simply depress the proper button and watch the diodes in the finder. When the manual speed diode you desire lights, remove your finger from the button.

How does the chosen manual shutter speed compare with the meter suggested speed? When your chosen shutter speed does not match the meter's suggested speed, either the over- or underexposure red diode will pulsate. If the top overexposure diode pulsates, you can match the suggested meter speed by pushing the front manual speed button. The manual speeds will begin to ascend in the viewfinder. When you have matched the meter's suggested speed, the red diode will go out. If you go too far, the lower, underexposure diode will pulsate and you should then push the rear button to achieve a lower shutter speed. By placing one finger on each button, you can quickly cause the manual speeds to move up and down either matching the meter's suggested speed or bracketing it above or below by one, two or more shutter speed variations. For instance, if you set the 60 manually and it causes both the under- and over-exposure diodes to go out, moving the speed to 125 with the front manual button will provide the equivalent of cutting the exposure in half. If you push the rear button, causing the 30 diode to light, you will double your exposure.

While the ME Super manual metering system is quite different from that on any other SLR, a little practice will allow you to master it easily. Remember, however, that you should either keep the shutter release pressed or repress it every 20 sec. or so to maintain the lighted diodes.

While the auto exposure compensation dial will probably provide you with sufficient exposure variations to handle most unusual lighting situations as explained in the chapter on exposure, there may be times when you will wish even more radical variations than the 1/4 to 4X compensation provides. That's when you'll use the manual shutter speeds. Many serious amateurs and pros also like to bracket exposures, shooting one according to the meter suggestion, then a second exposure at half that amount and a third at twice the suggested exposure. While this can be accomplished by the auto exposure compensation dial it is far swifter and more convenient to use the manual shutter speed controls.

Winder ME and ME II

One of the most popular accessories is the auto winder which attaches to the bottom of SLRs and automatically winds on the film after exposure. The Pentax winders, which fit only the ME Super and MV-1, not only provide automatic winding for single shots but can also be set to fire and wind continuously, thus allowing sequence photographs to be made.

Two winders are available and fit either the ME Super or MV-1. The older Winder ME requires 6 AA cells, has its main controls on the winder back and can fire up to 1.5 frames per second. The newer Winder II with all controls near the shutter release button allows remote control and can operate up to 2 frames per second.

The Winder ME has a bottom battery chamber with control panel at the back. To load 6 AA cells, pull back the spring-loaded ribbed catch on the bottom of the winder and pull down on the end of the battery compartment. The end will drop off, revealing cell compartments legibly marked as to the directions to insert the batteries. After loading, push the battery compartment cover in and upwards into place until you hear it click.

To load the 4 AA cells into the Winder II, press the side lock button. While holding it down, slide the battery cartridge out slightly and remove it. Insert alkaline energizer batteries (preferably, for greatest number of shots) or manganese alkaline batteries into the cartridge following the + and − indications inside the cartridge. Align the cartridge with the winder body. Slide the cartridge back and forth to make sure it is caught in the groove and then push it in all the way against the winder body until it clicks in place.

Attach either winder by first unthreading the film transport cap on the right end of the camera's bottom plate and rethreading the cover into the threaded storage receptacle for it on the battery compartment. Couple winder and camera together carefully. Fasten them by turning the knurled edge of the winder's connecting thumb screw until the screw of the winder tightens in the camera tripod bush and secures them solidly. Turn the C/S winder switch on the winder ME

POWER WINDER ME, ME II AND DATA BACK

The power winder ME or ME II fits directly to the bottom of the Pentax ME, ME Super or MV-1. It gives repeated single shots—or continuous shooting at about two frames a second.

1. Shutter release.
2. Film transport coupler.
3. Film rewind lever.
4. Drive cover holder.
5. Mounting screw.
6. Power contacts.
7. Motor function dial.
8. Guide pin.
9. Battery cover.
10. LED indicator.
11. Camera function switch.

Winder ME II is similar to Winder ME but has controls surrounding shutter release.

1. Auto/125x lever.
2. Release button.
3. Auto/125x indicator.
4. C/S dial.

back to "S". On the winder ME II the switch is on a dial on top of the grip. With every press of the rectangular release button on the winder's contoured vertical handle grip, the winder will release the shutter and advance film one frame. Slight pressure on the winder button will turn on the metering system. For continuous sequence pictures, turn the C/S switch to C. By holding down the release button the camera will fire up to 1.5 frames a second (2 frames a second on Winder II) until the end of the film. With the camera in automatic exposure operation, it's essential that the back switch (switch on the grip of Winder II) be set at the "auto" position. (When shooting flash at the mechanical 100X or 125X setting this same switch must be in the 100X setting or 125X with the Winder II.)

At the end of the roll, a special drag clutch will allow the motor to continue to operate, although more slowly, while preventing the film from being torn from the feed cartridge. The red warning light will remain on constantly if the C/S switch is on C and (of course) the rewind knob will cease to rotate. On the ME Super the film wind/rewind indicator orange stripes will no longer move. At this point turn the C/S switch to "off". Push the rewind lever upwards, then rewinding can be carried out normally. One set of fresh alkaline energizer cells should provide you with sufficient power to handle 150 rolls of 36-exposure film or the equivalent with the Winder ME, slightly less with the Winder ME II.

The Winder ME II can be operated by remote control. The winder grip top should first be removed with a finger nail. So that you won't lose the cap, fasten it to the remote release button of the accessory remote control cord. Plug the optional accessory remote cable into the remote terminal and tighten the collar. The button of the remote control cable will now operate in the same manner as the trigger release button on the winder.

There are a few additional hints that may help you operate the winder. When attaching it to an unloaded camera and making blank exposures using the rapid wind lever, the lever may not return to the proper position. If this happens, press the trigger release button once and then operate the camera normally.

If you use the self timer with the winder or if you use the

camera's shutter button and film does not automatically wind, press the winder trigger button to wind the film.

Do not turn off the C/S dial or remove the winder until the exposure is complete. Don't use the camera's B setting with the winder. If you do by accident, turn the shutter mode dial to the X setting and the shutter will close.

Using the Fully Coupled Flash

The ME, ME Super, MV and MV-1 can be fitted with special Pentax electronic flash units which automatically set the camera shutter to the proper X sync and provide flash information within the viewfinder. They cannot be fired accidentally before they have fully recycled following a flash exposure. During recycling, the camera will automatically revert to existing light auto exposure.

Both the Pentax AF200S and the AF160 are automatic flash units without connecting cables, and can also be used manually. The AF200S is powered by 4 AA manganese alkaline cells; the AF160 is powered by two. Insert the batteries into the flash unit after sliding open the battery compartment cover. Follow the + and − signs on the battery compartment. Replace the cover. Turn on the power switch. You should hear a faint whine which indicates that the unit is charging. Soon the ready lamp at the back of the unit should glow. When it takes more than 30 sec. for the ready light to go on, the batteries have insufficient power and should be replaced. After checking the flash, turn it off.

Slide the flash unit's foot into the hot shoe of the ME, ME Super, MV or MV-1. Tighten the knurled wheel above the shoe of the AF200S until the flash unit is securely fastened to the shoe. Set the ASA film speed index on the control panel of your flash unit. Now you must choose a suitable aperture and distance range. There are two ranges for both flash units. The AF200S provides a red colour coded range from 4.6 ft to 23.3 ft and a green range from 2ft to 11.5 ft. With 25 ASA film, the red range requires an aperture of $f1.4$; the green $f2.8$. At 100 ASA, the apertures are $f2.8$ and $f5.6$ respectively while 400 ASA allows apertures of $f5.6$ and $f11$. The AF160 has a green coded range from 1.6 ft to 13 ft and an orange range from 3.3 ft to 19.7 ft. With 100 ASA film, the green range requires an aperture of $f4$ while the orange range needs an $f2.8$ aperture. With 400 ASA film the apertures are $f8$ and $f5.6$.

The proper ranges and apertures can readily be seen on the control panel of the electronic flash units.

After setting the ASA index of the AF200S control panel, select the aperture and footage distance which is most appropriate for your picture taking. Colour coded horizontal bars at the 12 and 24ft markings will be adjacent to the proper apertures. Set the manual/auto switch at the back of the flash unit to the proper colour coded switch position. Set your lens to the suggested aperture. Turn on the flash unit with the on/off switch. Watch through the camera's viewfinder. In the MV and MV-1 finders, a red X diode will light when the unit is fully charged and ready to fire. In the Pentax ME Super finder, the green LED opposite 125X will light, indicating that the proper X sync shutter speed has been set, and the green M at the top of the shutter speed scale will begin to flash. Now you can take your flash picture. At close ranges, especially with high ASA film, the X in the MV and MV-1 and the 125X and M in the ME Super will light almost immediately after exposure. Both flash units have energy saving circuits which recycle very quickly at short flash-to-subject distances. At longer distances, it may take up to 6 sec. for the unit to recycle. During this period the camera exposure system will automatically revert to existing light auto exposure control and you can continue taking pictures without flash if you wish. When the flash has completely recycled, the flash signals will again light in the finder. You should be able to obtain upwards of 250 exposures with a fresh set of manganese alkaline batteries. When recycling time reaches 30 sec., discard the batteries and load the unit with new ones.

The units can also be used for manual flash. If the ME Super, MV or MV-1 is left on the "auto" setting, the finder signals will continue to operate, but you must then calculate your own flash guide numbers. After focusing, read the distance from your lens' focusing ring. Find this distance on the flash unit control panel and read off the proper aperture opposite. Set your lens to this aperture. Manual flash allows you to use the smallest possible aperture at every camera-to-subject distance for maximum depth of field. When the flash is used in the manual mode, however, the energy saving

SPECIALLY COUPLED ME SUPER AND MV-1 FLASH

1. Flash head.
2. Flash tube.
3. Flash sensor.
4. Battery compartment cover.
5. On/off switch.
6. Film speed setting.
7. Auto/manual selector.
8. Flash ready lamp.
9. Test button.
10. Fitting foot clamp.
11. Fitting foot.
12. Hot -shoe contacts.

Wide-angle (left) and telephoto adapters.

To open the battery compartment cover, push up on the finger grip and swing out the cover. Screw down the clamp to fix the flashgun in the accessory shoe.

1. Metre distance scale.
2. Lens aperture scale.
3. Film speed index.
4. Film speed setting button.
5. Tele adapter indicator.
6. Normal indicator.
7. Wide-angle indicator.
8. Distance scale in feet.
9. Tele adapter indicator.
10. Normal indicator.
11. Manual setting.
12. Auto/manual selector switch.
13. Auto setting.
14. Wide-angle indicator.

circuit is not operable and you will have full recycling time and the minimum number of total flashes.

The AF200S normally covers the angle of a 28 mm lens. Two AF200S accessories, wide-angle adapter AFW1 and telephoto adapter AFT1, provide efficient coverage for lenses down to 24 mm or up to 135 mm respectively. With the wide-angle attachments over the AF200S, a small amount of illumination is lost thus curtailing the maximum auto exposure distance and requiring a slightly larger aperture. With the tele attachment, you gain distance and can use a slightly smaller aperture. Instead of finding your proper aperture and distance with the long horizontal bars on the control panel, you will see two short bars, red and green, marked W and T for wide-angle and tele. Use these setting indicators instead of the long bars.

If you use the wide-angle and tele attachments for manual flash, halve the ASA index for the wide-angle attachment and double it for the tele attachment to calculate the proper guide numbers.

When using other, non-fully coupled electronic flash units on the Pentax ME, ME Super, MV or MV-1, the exposure mode dial should be set to the X position and the directions with the flash unit should be followed. The Pentax AF160 and AF200S can be used on cameras other than the ME, ME Super, MV and MV-1 both in the automatic and manual modes. However, these flash units will not furnish any finder information as they do with Pentax cameras. Also, the cameras on which you fit the AF160 or AF200S must be set manually to the X sync settings.

Besides the winders for the ME, ME Super and MV-1, the fully coupled flash units for the ME Super and MV-1, many other accessories are available. The ME, ME Super and MV-1 have removable backs which can be replaced by a special back, the Dial Data ME. This back will allow you to print the year, month and day the photo was taken on a corner of the picture frame. Alternatively, technical data such as aperture, speeds, numerals and letters can be imprinted.

Pentax MX

Let's turn to the Pentax MX, a non-automatic mechanical cloth-shutter camera just slightly bigger and heavier than the ME. The MX has been designed not only for the serious amateur who prefers to control his own exposures completely, but also for professionals requiring bulk film backs, motor drives and interchangeable screens.

The basic styling of the camera resembles the Pentax ME and, as explained, it has the same type of film loading, focusing and metering centreweighted system. The viewfinder also has the same focusing screen as the ME. It has a shutter release lock lever directly in front of the release button and a shutter cock reminder window next to the lock.

The metering controls of the MX are completely different from those of the ME, ME Super, MV or MV-1. You set the ASA index, 25 to 1600, in the window inset within the top shutter speed dial by pushing in the ASA film speed release button on top of the dial and turning the outer ring. Now, push in the shutter release slightly while looking through the viewfinder. One of the diodes at the right of the finder screen should light. If not, check, remove and replace the batteries on the bottom of the camera as explained with the ME. The battery compartment cover has a plastic holder into which you can slip the batteries.

With fresh, working batteries, again look through the finder while pushing the shutter release slightly. Directly above the picture area you will see the aperture you set reflected from the lens barrel itself (if you are using Pentax lenses). To the right within the picture area you will see a transparent plastic semi-circle with the shutter speeds marked in black. The actual speed set is at centre, while the next higher and lower speeds are above and below the centre numeral. To the right of this semi-circle are five LED dots —green in centre indicating metered exposure, orange above and below indicating $\frac{1}{2}$ f-stop over and under exposure, and red diodes on the outer edges indicating 1 f-stop or more over and under exposure. Turn the aperture ring and/or the shutter speed dial until the green diode lights (unless you wish deliberate over or under exposure of $\frac{1}{2}$ f-stop. In this case, stop at an orange dot). At the instant the exposure reaches more than 50% greater or less than the diode indication, the light will switch to the next diode. Therefore, at the moment your orange diode switches to red you know your exposure variation is 1 f-stop. The diode display will remain on if you pull out the rapid wind lever 20° and then push in slightly on the shutter release. Don't forget to turn off the metering circuit by pushing the wind lever home after use.

Unlike the Pentax ME which has a continuously variable electronic shutter control, the MX uses an all-cloth mechanically-operated shutter that provides just the set shutter speeds on the shutter dial. However, all shutter speeds will remain completely operable even if the batteries which power the metering system are dead or missing. The X sync speed for electronic flash is 1/60 sec. marked in orange on the shutter speed dial. Unlike the ME, the MX also has FP flash synchronization. By attaching a sync cord to the FP flash terminal on the left side of the camera body, FP class flashbulbs can be used at speeds from 1/60 to 1/1000 sec.

Focusing Screens

The focusing screen of the MX is interchangeable with other screens having other focusing aids such as cross hairs for scientific photography, etched lines for aligning architectural or copy work, measures marks for specialized applications, plus other variations of split-image rangefinders and microprisms. Each accessory screen comes with a tweezer-like pincette to aid in screen change. Remove the camera lens and, with the pincette, pull the screen retaining pin forward. This is located at the front top centre of the mirror chamber behind the foam cushioning material. The focusing screen frame and focusing screen will now drop down into the mirror chamber. You can remove and replace the screen using the pincette to grasp the tiny extending lip on the front edge of the focusing screen. After replacement, use the pincette to press the frame back up again beneath the prism until a distinct click is heard. Do not attempt to use your fingers or you may damage the mirror surface or dirty the screen.

Self-timer

The self-timer of the MX can be set by moving the lever on the right front of the camera downward. A full 180° provides approximately 15 sec., while smaller movements allow upwards of 8 sec. To release the self-timer, push inwards on the small button which will become visible when the self-timer lever is pushed downwards. The self-timer lever also

TELE PORTRAITS
Page 41. A long lens is good for portraiture provided you employ a fast shutter speed to minimize camera shake. M. Kondo used a fast film and 1/500 sec. at f/4.5 with his 300 mm. f/4 Takumar.

Page 42. With this equipment M. Kondo took another portrait.

INDOOR STUDY
Page 43. Bounce light on a backdrop was used by Glavco Cortini.

PEARL DIVER
Page 44. Compare her torso and foot to see the distortion used by K. Toshida for this effective shot.

FROZEN TEAR
Page 45. In order to use 1/500 sec. speed Ong Kim Leong used maximum aperture f1.8, and focused precisely on the tear itself.

MAKING BACKGROUND COUNT
Page 46. Backgrounds are often best out of focus, but this straw hut was essential to Vic Franzoni's study of mother and child.

LONG LENS FOR ANIMALS
Page 47. A long lens is helpful in bringing animals close when you cannot approach them yourself. K. Suzuki used a 200 mm. Takumar.

QUICK CANDID
Above. The automatic diaphragm is ideal for grabbed shots. Joseph C. Collins used his 55 mm. Super Takumar with 1/125 sec. at f/11.

PENTAX MX FEATURES

The MX is a manually-controlled full-aperture metering camera.

1. Exposure counter.
2. Shutter release lock.
3. Shutter release.
4. Rapid wind lever.
5. Film speed dial.
6. X-sync accessory shoe.
7. Aperture display window.
8. Film rewind crank.
9. Rewind knob/back release.
10. Shutter speed dial.
11. Self-timer.
12. Lens release lever.
13. Lens mounting indicator.
14. Lens.
15. FP sync terminal.
16. X-sync terminal.
17. Neck strap lug.

The viewfinder display is unlike that of the ME.

1. Lens aperture set.
2. Mat focusing screen.
3. Microprism collar.
4. 1 stop over- or under-exposure warnings.
5. $\frac{1}{2}$ stop over- or under-exposure indicators.
6. Meter recommended exposure indicator.
7. Shutter speed indicator.
8. Split-image range-finder.

To set the film speed, depress the catch and rotate the shutter speed dial until the ASA figure appears in the centre of the cut-out.

To set the shutter speed, simply rotate the dial until the right indication falls against the triangular index mark.

acts as a depth-of-field preview control. Just push the lever towards the lens and the lens will close down to shooting aperture.

Tripod Mounting

Each Pentax MX is furnished with a plastic tripod platform ring. If you mount your Pentax MX on a tripod with a large platform head, the focusing ring may rub against the platform head, thus making focusing impossible. In such cases, insert the ring between camera and tripod. That gives you sufficient clearance for focusing control.

When mounting either camera on a tripod, be careful not to use a tripod thread which is too long or it may penetrate the bottom of the tripod socket of the camera and seriously damage the camera mechanisms.

Power Drives

Like the Pentax ME, ME Super and MV-1, the Pentax MX can be fitted with a motor winder, the Winder MX. While it attaches to the MX in the same manner as the ME Winders do to the other cameras, the winders are not compatible or interchangeable. The MX winder uses four AA cells. Controls are virtually the same as on the ME winder, but there is no auto-100X switch since the MX is not an automatic exposure camera. However, once attached, the motor operation is precisely the same as on the ME already described except that the top continuous mode winder speed is 2 frames per second rather than the 1.5 of the ME winder.

Besides the winder, the MX can be fitted with a 5 frames per second professional motor drive powered by nicad batteries or 12 cells. Also available are a remote control release, a 250-exposure bulk film magazine back, as well as a Dial Data back similar in design and construction (but not interchangeable with) that for the Pentax ME, ME Super and MV-1.

PENTAX MX POWER WINDER

1. Shutter release button.
2. Camera shutter release.
3. Power contacts.
4. Transport coupler.
5. Grip.
6. Battery cover.
7. LED indicator.
8. Motor function dial.
9. Mounting screw.
10. Drive cover holder.
11. Film rewind lever.
12. Tripod socket.

To load batteries, turn the lock wheel and open the cover. Put in four AA alkaline cells, following the diagram inside. Close the cover and turn back the lock wheel.

THE K SERIES
PENTAX CAMERA
AND LENS SYSTEM

The Pentax K series were the first Asahi cameras to have a 45 mm diameter, three-clawed bayonet lens mount instead of the 42 mm screw thread mount used on previous Pentaxes. The K mount allows lenses to be interchanged far more swiftly with but a 65° turn of the lens instead of the $2\frac{3}{4}$ turns of the screw (or S mount) cameras. All lenses then available in S mount were made available in K mount. Additional lenses such as the 50 mm $f1.2$, which require the larger 45 mm diameter mount of the K were added to the line. The K lenses are called "SMC Pentax" instead of "SMC Takumar" for the S-mount lenses. K-series cameras have a narrow black horizontal stripe across the pentaprism, and plastic-tipped film transport levers.

Lens Mounting

While the K lenses cannot be fitted to S series camera bodies, any screw mount Takumar lens can be accommodated on the K camera bodies by the use of a K lens adapter mount. However the S lenses will have to be used manually. The automatic diaphragm mechanisms will not couple to the K cameras nor will the exposure system hook up. S lenses, when used on K cameras, must be closed down to shooting aperture manually and exposure readings should be also made at shooting aperture. (However the S lenses when on the K2 camera will still produce fully automatic exposures at shooting aperture, as we'll see.)

To mount the lens, you can either visually line up the red mounting dots on the back of the lens and on the face of the camera, or you can match up the raised white dot on the lens with the black lens release lever on the camera body. Press camera and lens together and twist lens 65° clockwise until it locks in place with a click.

To remove the lens, press the release lever and turn the lens counter-clockwise. You can easily do this holding the lens with your left hand so that you press the release with the right side of your left forefinger.

Features of K2 and K2 DMD Models

At 144 mm (5.7 in.) the K2 and K2 DMD is 1 mm or .04 in. longer than the KX or KM cameras, its height from base-plate to top plate is 70 mm (2.75 in.) or 4 mm (.16 in.) lower than the KX or KM.

The Pentax K2 has an electronically controlled vertically running bladed metal type focal plane shutter. This Asahi–Seiko shutter is extremely accurate and allows electronic flash synchronization at 1/125 sec. to reduce the chance of ghost images forming in bright existing light.

The Pentax K2 DMD is virtually identical to the K2 but it can be fitted with a motor drive. Additionally it has an aperture scale in the finder indicating the f-stop set which the K2 does not. We will discuss the motor in another chapter.

The meter uses a centre-weighted silicon photo diode system with silicon detector cells on either side of the eye piece. They read the amount of illumination from the focusing screen through the pentaprism and automatically adjust the shutter speed for the correct exposure (depending of course on the aperture and ASA film speed set). The silicon cells generate current when exposed to light (instead of changing their resistance as do CdS cells). The current is amplified electronically, and the system uses two 1.5V silver oxide batteries located in the bottom plate of the camera. The major advantages of the silicon cell over CdS are its much faster response to changes in lighting conditions, principally in low light illumination, and its lack of memory. CdS cells, particularly when exposed to bright light and then used in a darker area, tend to "remember" the bright light and can give inflated readings unless allowed to rest for some time.

A further advantage of the K2 and KX cameras is that they provide a silver vacuum evaporate coated pentaprism which provides far brighter viewing, focusing and meter reading images than is available on Pentax KM, K1000 and older cameras.

Meter Operation

The meter is switched on by lightly depressing the shutter release button. If the film transport lever is in its normal position, the meter switches off again when the button is released. However, if the transport lever is pulled slightly away from the camera body, once the release button is pressed, the meter remains on until the transport lever is pushed back home. (It is most important to do this when the camera is not in use to avoid meter battery drain and possible exhaustion of the battery.)

Within the finder, the black meter pointer comes down the right hand shutter speed scale with alacrity to point to the approximate shutter speed which the camera will set automatically. If you have the shutter speed dial set to "automatic" you see a blue-green translucent pointer at the right superimposed over the black lettering "AUTO". However, you can alternatively select your own electronically timed shutter speed and override the automatic shutter speed control. Just push in the small button on the shutter speed dial and turn the dial to the shutter speed desired. Within the viewfinder, the translucent pointer moves to the shutter speed you select, while the black meter pointer continues to indicate the exposure the metering system recommends. You can either "match needles" and follow the meter's suggestion or use a higher or lower shutter speed for special exposure situations (see chapter on exposure).

Influencing the Automatics

With the K2 or K2 DMD camera, the manually set shutter speeds are all electronically controlled and you have a full range of manual speeds from 8 secs to 1/1000 sec. The shutter will operate only with properly functioning batteries whether in manual or automatic mode.

The K2 and K2 DMD can be adjusted to give you exposure compensating speeds even on automatic. On the left side of the camera lens mount is a scale in red and white on black marked 1/4, 1/2, 1X, 2 and 4. For normal auto exposure operation the 1X (marked in white) must coincide with a tiny red dot on the chrome ring directly in front of the scale. To change the scale to one of the other markings (for special exposure conditions) or to return the scale to 1X,

54

PENTAX K2 FEATURES

Here are the controls for the Pentax K2 and K2 DMD cameras.

1. Strap ring lug.

2. Frame counter.

3. Shutter speed dial.

4. Depth of field preview button.

5. X-sync accessory shoe.

6. Lens mounting guide.

7. Mirror lock-up lever.

8. Folded rewind crank.

9. Bevelled edge.

10. Shutter release and lock.

11. Self-timer.

12. Lens release lever.

13. Aperture indication window (K2 DMD only).

14. ASA setting ring and lever.

15. Threaded flash terminals.

16. Battery check button and light.

17. Hinged camera back.

18. Film type reminder.

19. Viewfinder eyepiece.

20. Rapid wind lever.

21. Battery compartment.

22. Tripod socket.

23. Rewind button.

Unlike any other Pentax camera, the K2 and K2 DMD features a compact Seiko metal focal plane shutter with five blades, developed jointly by Asahi Optical and Seiko. Its electronic control permits automatic exposure or individual manual speeds plus an electronic flash sync speed of 1/125 sec. Here you see the entire shutter unit and its mechanical and electronic control mechanisms.

grasp the two raised ribbed lugs on the same exposure adjustment and turn the ring to a suitable setting. In the Pentax K2 DMD which indicates the aperture set within the viewfinder, an orange filter covers the aperture window as a warning when exposure compensation is in use. Use the exposure index adjustment scale for automatic exposure when the lighting conditions which require special exposure will remain constant for a considerable number of exposures. Use the manual speeds when the need for a particular exposure adjustment is to be only for a few shots. In either case however, be sure to return the settings to normal automatic exposure operation afterwards.

More than 90 per cent of your picture requirements can probably be met with the camera in normal auto exposure mode. The centre-weighted system tends to compensate for unusual lighting situations if the main subject is centrally located. If the main subject is not near the centre, take the camera off automatic, make the reading of your subject and then set your shutter speed manually for this reading when you return to the original composition of your picture. However, I cannot emphasize strongly enough that you must check regularly to make certain the exposure adjustment index is reset finally at 1X and the blue-green pointer is on "automatic". Having either incorrectly set accounts for many of the exposure errors committed even by professionals.

Special note on the K2 DMD: when using the camera for automatic exposure while your eye is not viewing through the finder, there is danger of extraneous light entering the eyepiece causing inflated meter readings. The DMD has a built-in finder blind to shut out such light. This can be closed by dialing the shutter blind signal on the shutter speed dial.

Meter Range

In order for the K2 and K2 DMD meter to operate properly, you must of course set the ASA index of your film. The ASA scale from 8 to 6400 is located at the front of the camera on the right side of the lens mount as you look at the camera. Settings in between the engraved numerals are represented by black dots. For instance, there are two dots between the 16 and 32 ASA markings. The first represents 20 and the

MORE PENTAX K2 AND K2 DMD FEATURES

Mounting a lens can be done by touch alone. Just align raised lens mounting guide with lens release lever, join lens to camera body, twist lens clockwise.

Screw thread lenses can be mounted to K2 with K mount adapter ring.

Meter switch operation. With wind lever close to body, metering system remains on only while shutter release button is slightly depressed.

If wind lever is pulled away from body, metering system can be kept on by depressing shutter release button slightly and releasing it.

With shutter release button fully extended, meter circuit is off.

When pressing shutter release to activate meter but not take picture, make sure you press release only half-way down or shutter will be released.

Returning wind lever to body position automatically turns off meter circuit.

second you would use for ASA 25 film.

To set the ASA index, the exposure adjustment scale must already be set at 1X or the ASA scale cannot be moved. Once the adjustment scale is at 1X, push in the ASA scale release lever (at the bottom right of the camera lens mount) toward the lens. At the same time, turn the chrome ASA setting ring closest to the camera body using its two knurled surfaces. When the ASA set properly is opposite the red indicator release the lever and the ASA will be locked. (It's well worthwhile to check this scale regularly to make certain the ASA is correct.)

The metering system sets automatic exposures from 1/1000 sec. down to 8 sec. at any aperture or ASA index. Depending on the individual camera itself, shutter speeds well beyond 8 sec. are possible although not guaranteed. The system always sets exactly the speed it determines; it is not limited to normal steps as you are when you choose the speed manually.

When using your camera for very long exposures remember that many films need additional exposure compensation if speeds exceed a few seconds. This is particularly true of colour films. A chart of these compensations, usually in the form of additional exposure needed, can be obtained from the manufacturer of the film. However for any shots up to 3 to 5 sec. standard automatic exposure should yield satisfactory results.

While loading and unloading film is precisely the same as explained in the chapter on operating Spotmatics, and focusing and holding the camera as indicated in the chapter on operating new and old Pentaxes, the K2 and K2 DMD can also be furnished with a split image rangefinder in place of the standard microprism (in some countries of purchase). Some users find the split image more convenient because they can align the top half of the subject in the central split image rangefinder with the subject matter in the bottom half more easily than they can bring an image into sharp focus with a microprism finder. The author finds that this is true with many people having the need of strong eyeglass corrections. If both systems, split-image and microprism are available in your area, it's highly advisable to try both and select the one best for you.

PENTAX K2 OPERATION

For automatic exposure control, shutter speed dial must be set to "automatic". Scale at right hand side of focusing screen seen through finder will show green transparent indicator superimposed over word "auto". Thin black pointer indicates approximate shutter speed set by meter system.

When using manually set speeds, green pointer will indicate speed selected, here 1/500 sec. Black pointer indicates meter's suggested proper speed of 1/125 sec.

By turning shutter speed dial to 1/125 sec. you can "match" the black pointers' suggested speed and achieve proper exposure. You can also set speeds above or below the black pointer for special lighting conditions.

ASA film speed scale is on right side of lens mount (with camera facing you). However before you can set the ASA, you must make certain exposure factor scale on left side of lens mount is set to IX.

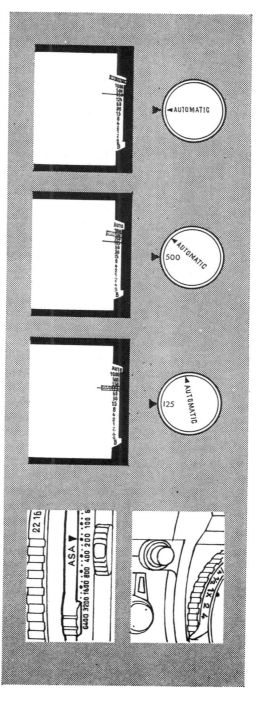

Additional Controls

There are some controls on the K2 and K2 DMD.

The K2 has a battery check button and indicator light at the rear of the camera. If the batteries are all right, pressure on the button will cause the light to go on. To interchange batteries, unthread the bottom battery housing cover with the aid of a coin edge in the cover slot. Remove the cover which has the battery clip holder attached to it. Replace batteries with two new Ever-Ready S76E or Mallory MS76H 1.5 volt batteries. Each should have its plus side facing out.

Electronic or regular bulb flash units can be connected to the K2 either through the hot shoe or by the two PC terminals located at the top right of the camera (with the camera facing you). These two terminals, normally covered by connected slip-on plastic plugs, are threaded for screw type connecting tips. These are not so subject to slipping off as are regular push-on PC tips. The shoe, which can accept most foot mounted flash units, has X sync only, suitable for all electronic flash to 1/125 sec. and for M, MF or FP bulbs to 1/15 sec. For FP bulbs, which can be used up to 1/1000 sec, the flash unit should be connected to the FP terminal at the edge of the camera.

The K mount lenses of the K2 and K2 DMD can be closed down to shooting aperture to preview the scene as it will look in terms of approximate depth of field. Press in the depth of field button just above the self timer. The lens will return to full opening when you remove your finger from the button. However do not attempt to make any exposure meter readings while you are pressing the button. Use it only for observing depth of field.

The self timer on the front of the camera works as follows: for full 9 second delay, push the arm counter-clockwise as far as it will go. The self timer is actuated when you press the shutter release. Shorter times can also be set by moving the arm to a lesser degree. If you decide not to use this mechanism once you have set it, just push the lever upwards again. It will operate via the clockwork mechanism but will not trip the shutter.

On the right side of the K2 or K2 DMD, close to the camera body (with the camera facing you) is a small lever

PENTAX KX FEATURES

Here are the controls for the Pentax KX camera.

1. Frame counter.

2. Shutter release and lock.

3. ASA film speed window.

4. Shutter speed dial.

5. Prism housing

6. X-sync accessory shoe.

7. Battery check button.

8. Threaded flash terminals.

9. Strap ring lug.

10. Self-timer lever.

11. Lens release lever.

12. Viewfinder eyepiece.

13. Film type reminder.

14. Lens mounting guide.

15. ASA film speed releasing pin.

16. Folded rewind crank.

17. Battery compartment.

18. Tripod socket.

19. ASA film speed window.

20. Rewind button.

which moves vertically. This is the mirror lockup lever. After focusing, you can lock the mirror in the up position by pressing the lever upward. The mirror remains locked upward until you move the lever downward. By locking the mirror during exposure you can minimise mechanical vibration for high precision photography such as photomicrography (through a microscope) or astronomical photography with a telescope. The mirror, incidentally, is oversize in the K2 to prevent mirror edge cutoff in the viewfinder, even when very long telephoto lenses are fitted.

At the rear of the K2 and K2 DMD is a film reminder memo holder. By inserting the box end of the film you have a quick indication of just what film is within the camera. The rapid wind lever, unlike that of other Pentaxes, is non ratcheted. A full single stroke of the rapid wind lever is needed to wind the shutter and advance the film.

In using the camera on automatic operation, you must set the lens aperture so that the shutter speed indicator needle within the viewfinder shows a speed between 8 sec. and 1/1000 sec. If the needle travels above 1/1000 sec. it's an indication that you should select a smaller lens opening. You can of course select whatever automatic shutter speed you wish by merely turning the aperture ring until that shutter speed is indicated by the black pointer in the viewfinder (provided that particular shutter speed and aperture combination is within the possibilities of the illumination under which you are working).

The K2 or K2 DMD camera provides fully automatic or manual exposure for any non-K-series lens or lens attachment such as a telescope, lens on bellows or microscope. The shutter speed registers in the viewfinder and changes as you change the aperture or lighting. Also, you can still switch the shutter speed dial to manual operation should you wish to.

When batteries are exhausted or absent in the K2, the camera's shutter will operate at 1/125 sec. no matter what speed is set. With the K2 DMD, the mirror will rise and shutter lock, warning you of the failure.

Features of the KX

The KX camera has the same silicon photo diode exposure meter system as the K2 but does not offer automatic expo-

PENTAX KX
OPERATION

Viewfinder shows aperture set in window at top of focusing screen plus shutter speed scale at right hand side. Green transparent pointer indicates actual shutter speed set, here 1/30 sec. Black pointer shows suggested proper speed as determined by metering system, here 1/125 sec.

By changing either lens aperture or shutter speed (as shown here) you can superimpose transparent and black pointers for proper exposure.

To turn on meter circuit, pull rapid wind lever away from camera body slightly and depress shutter release slightly. Meter will remain on until lever is pushed back against camera body. To lock release button, push lock lug forward as shown by small arrow.

Small reflecting window on front of prism housing transmits actual lens aperture set to viewfinder.

sure with its rubberized cloth, mechanically-controlled focal plane shutter. While it too has a full shutter speed scale within the viewfinder, you will note that the speeds are the more traditional 1 to 1/1000 sec. instead of from 8 sec. However the actual aperture you set on the lens is visible within the viewfinder at the centre top thanks to a reflecting prism system built into the front of the camera—a feature similar to that on the K2 DMD camera.

Operating the KX Meter

To switch on the meter, you must pull the rapid wind lever away from the camera body and press slightly down on the shutter release. The meter remains on until the wind lever is again pushed in to the camera body. Inside the viewfinder, the black meter pointer indicates the shutter speed suggested for any aperture set. To achieve proper exposure you can turn the aperture ring until the meter needles coincide. If you prefer you can change shutter speed or both. By selecting a speed either below or above the one recommended you can compensate for unusual exposure conditions as explained with the K2. In other words the KX match needle exposure system operates in a manner almost identical to that of the K2 when the latter camera is switched off automatic exposure and used manually with its meter.

To set the ASA film speed index, press down on the film speed indicator pin atop the rewind knob collar and turn the collar's outer ring until the proper ASA rating appears in the cutout window within the collar. In-between settings, marked by dots, can be adjusted properly as explained in the previous K2 instructions. The KX takes the same 1.5 volt batteries as the K2 and they can be interchanged in the same manner. The batteries, which operate the meter only and not the shutter, should last approximately 10 000 exposures or about one year. To check the batteries, press in the battery check button on the top of the camera between the prism and rewind knob while looking through the finder. If the black meter needle drops to 125 or lower the battery is all right.

The meter's exposure coupling range is not quite as broad as that of the F2. However with an ASA 100 film the meter couples properly at all settings except ƒ22 at 1/1000 sec.,

PENTAX KM AND K1000 FEATURES

Here are the controls for the Pentax KM camera.

1. Frame counter.

2. Shutter release.

3. ASA film speed window.

4. Shutter speed dial.

5. Prism housing.

6. X-sync accessory shoe.

7. Lens mounting guide.

8. Folded rewind crank.

9. Strap ring lug.

10. Depth of field preview button. (KM only).

11. Self-timer (KM only).

12. Lens release lever.

13. Viewfinder eyepiece.

14. Lens.

15. Rapid wind lever.

16. Threaded flash. (K1000 single X-sync terminal).

17. Battery compartment.

18. Tripod socket.

19. Hinged back.

20. Rewind button.

21. Meter needle in viewfinder.

a fairly rare brilliant light situation. However it's safe to assume that you will achieve proper exposure at all meter readings and exposure settings at which the two needles can be made to coincide.

Other KX features

When using non-K mount lenses with the K adapter, you have to match the needles for proper exposure by either turning the shutter speed dial or physically closing down the lens diaphragm.

The loading, handling and focusing of the KX are precisely the same as the K2, and the KX has a similar film box reminder holder at the back. Synchronization is similar except that the PC terminals are located at the front right of the camera body (as the camera faces you) and the top electronic flash sync speed is 1/60 sec., marked with a red X on the shutter speed dial. FP (focal plane) type flashbulbs however should not be used at speeds slower than 1/60 sec. The flash unit must be attached to the FP sync terminal. M, MF and FP bulbs can be handled up to 1/15 sec. at X sync.

The self timer operates in a slightly different manner on the KX. The arm must be turned the full 180° counter clockwise. It can then be placed into operation by pushing the small chrome lever (beneath the self timer arm) to the left. The self timer then operates the shutter after a 13 sec. delay. However once the self timer has been started it can be stopped in mid-point by returning the chrome lever to the up position. In this manner the timing can be varied from 5 seconds upward to 13 or the self timer can be stopped completely. If you decide you do not wish to use the self timer, take the picture without moving the chrome lever and then release the self timer mechanism with the lever following the exposure.

The depth of field preview lever of the KX is located in the same position as that of the K2, above the self timer, but it has one feature the K2 does not—a locking lever. After pushing in the depth of field button, you can lock it in position by pressing the lever at the base of the button 90° to the left or counterclockwise. Returning the lever upward releases the button. The purpose of the button like that of the K2 is to allow you to preview the approximate depth of field you will be able to record at any set shooting aperture.

Features of the KM and K1000

The Pentax KM and K1000, while using the same body shell and K bayonet lens mount as the Pentax KX, are probably closer to the classic Pentax Spotmatic camera concept than either the K2 or KX. While both offer full aperture metering and their CdS cells on either side of the eyepiece measure the average brightness of the viewfinder screen. The screen itself, the classic central microprism with full focusing area (or split-image rangefinder), shows a black needle indicator at the right side of the picture area with a plus sign at the top and a minus sign at the bottom. By changing shutter speeds, apertures, or both, the meter needle can be centred, thus obtaining proper exposure. Neither shutter speed scale nor apertures are visible in the finder. The view through the finder is slightly darker since the prism and viewing system is not silvered as is that of the K2 and KX. The focal plane shutter mechanism and its operation, lens changing, loading and unloading the camera, are the same as the KX just described. Neither the KM or K1000 have shutter release locks, battery checkers or film reminder tabs at the back of the camera. Both cameras have built-in photo switches which turn on the meter circuits when the lens caps are removed from the lenses, so it is important to keep the lenses capped when not in use to prevent battery drain.

While we have mentioned the absence of a battery checker in the Pentax KM or K1000, it is possible to check the condition of the 1.5 volt silver oxide battery (located in the bottom plate of the cameras as in the KX). Set your shutter speed dial to B and the ASA dial to 100. Observe the meter needle through the viewfinder. If the needle remains in the "up" position, your battery is all right. If the needle is anywhere else, replace the battery promptly.

There is one small operational procedure regarding setting the ASA film speed on the KM and K1000 which should be mentioned. On the KX, the ASA index scale surrounds the rewind knob. On the KX and K1000, it is within a window inset in the shutter speed dial. To set the proper numeral, simply lift up on the shutter speed dial collar and turn the collar until the ASA index becomes visible in the window. Then allow the collar to return downward.

In what way do the KM and K1000 cameras differ from one another? The K1000 has no depth of field preview lever, no self timer and only X synchronization for electronic flash at speeds of 1/60 sec. or slower or bulb flash at 1/30 sec. or slower. The KM has all of these features and offers both X and M flash sync similar to that available in the KX camera.

Both the KM and K1000 cameras can be handled and operated in the same manner as the KX, but care should be taken to observe the differences in the metering systems. The KX has a centre weighted system which favours central placement of the subject, while the two other cameras measure the average for the entire focusing screen. While making readings with all three from the same camera position will often provide identical exposure suggestions, the KM and K1000 may show slightly inflated readings when the principal subject is backlit. In such cases it's advisable to move in closer to the subject for a more accurate reading. On the other hand, in many scenics, the average reading of the K1000 and KM may be closer to the mark than the centre weighted reading. To make certain your exposures are as exact as possible, read the chapter on exposure.

There is a tendency to belittle the KM and K1000 cameras as to their abilities compared with the K2 or KX cameras. Nothing could be less fair. Both cameras are made to the same high precision, offer the same possible exposure ranges, the same excellence of optics. But by eliminating some extra features from these two cameras—features which have nothing to do with producing top-quality photos—Asahi has been able to offer high-quality picture-makers at most advantageous prices.

OPERATING THE PENTAX ES
AND THE ES II

The Pentax ES models were the first widely available electronically controlled SLR cameras in which the exposure was fully determined by a through lens meter which sets the correct shutter speed by means of highly accurate, shockproof, integrated circuitry. While these cameras have now been superseded by later models with bayonet lens mounts, the ES and ES II represent even today very advanced automatic exposure camera models well worth owning and using, quite capable of making photographs equal to those turned out by their illustrious successors.

The integrated circuits for automatic exposure control enable the whole electronic shutter system to withstand difficult temperature variations from −20° to +50°C, and make it more reliable. Moreover, the Pentax ES and ES II do not depend on specially-made lenses for automatic exposure. Literally any lens or lens accessory that you fit to the cameras from a high-magnification microscope to a superlong telescope can produce the same accurate, fully automatic exposure as the cameras' regular lens equipment. The meter system has no mechanical exposure limits. It can operate at any ASA index from 20 to 1600 and deliver proper exposures automatically at all apertures and shutter speeds, provided there is sufficient light for at least an 8-second exposure.

Basically, the camera bodies resemble the Spotmatic II, with all controls in approximately the same place and operation in the same manner. The ES and ES II have the same screw thread mount. But before we do anything else we have to insert the 6-volt silver oxide cells in the battery housing.

Unlike the Spotmatics or the SP500, which have battery housings on the bottom, the Pentax ES battery housing is on the left front of the camera (as you hold it facing you) close to the lens mount. Unscrew the cover of the battery housing and insert the battery. Make certain you get it in properly, with the minus terminal pointing inward.

The ES II uses four 1.5 volt cells. Open the battery cover on the bottom of the lens mount by shifting the cover-release pin to the right with a pin. Insert batteries as indicated on housing. Close cover.

How the Pentax ES Models work

Hold the Pentax ES or ES II to your eye. At the right edge of the finder, running vertically, is a shutter-speed scale from 1 to 1/1000 sec. on the ES; from 8 sec. to 1/1000 on the ES II. Although you will actually be setting your aperture on the lens first, the meter needle moves over the scale to keep you informed as to what shutter speed the meter is setting. To see how it operates, first set the proper ASA film speed of the film you will use in the small white cut-out window surrounding the rewind knob. By lifting up on the outer rim collar of the rewind-knob mount you can then turn the collar in either direction until the proper ASA film speed appears in the window. Then allow the rim to drop back in place. Next, turn the shutter-speed dial until the red arrow marked "Automatic" is opposite the indicator mark next to the dial on the top of the camera.

Now point the camera at a fairly bright subject and depress the shutter release ever so slightly. The meter needle will descend on the scale and indicate the shutter speed which will be set for the lens opening you are using. Unlike the Spotmatics I and II or the SP 500 (but like the Spotmatic F), the ES models allow you to view, focus and use your meter at full lens aperture.

If you want a slower or faster shutter speed, turn the lens aperture ring to a larger or smaller aperture and you'll notice that the meter needle will change position appropriately on the shutter speed scale in the viewfinder. However, the meter needle will respond much faster if you take your finger off the shutter release momentarily while changing aperture and then press the release again.

You may wonder why the meter needle within the viewfinder sometimes rests between marked shutter speeds. The speeds which are being set by the electronically controlled shutter are infinitely variable, from 1/1000 sec. to 1 sec. (and

PENTAX ES AND ES II FEATURES

Here are the controls for the Pentax ES cameras.

1. Film counter.
2. Shutter release.
3. Shutter speed dial.
4. Rapid wind lever.
5. Accessory shoe.
6. X-sync contact point.
7. Preview lever of lens.
8. Battery check button.
9. ASA film speed window.
10. Battery. compartment. Self-timer lever of ES II.
11. Aperture setting ring.
12. Focusing ring.
13. Flash terminals.
14. Stop-down lever.
15. Exposure factor control dial.
16. Rewind crank.
17. Rewind knob.
18. Viewfinder eyepiece.
19. Focal plane shutter.
20. Sprocket wheel.
21. Takeup spool.
22. Pressure plate.
23. Tripod socket.
24. Film plane rails.
25. Rewind button.

Here's what you see in the view-finder: Centrally, there is a microprism focusing circle surrounded by a fine focusing collar. You may however also use the outer areas for focusing if needed. At the right is your shutter speed indicator scale with pointer which will show you what shutter speed the automatic exposure system will select for any aperture you set on the lens.

To actuate the automatic exposure system, push down slightly on the shutter release button. The shutter speed indicator scale pointer will then swing downwards to show you the speed to be set.

actually beyond, to 8 sec., although these longer speeds aren't marked on the scale). The selection system is not simply setting fixed speeds of 1, 1/2, 1/4, 1/8, 1/15, 1/30 and so on; it is giving you the precise speeds. If the combination of lighting on the subject, the ASA film speed and the aperture you set requires 1/23rd of a second, that is what you get.

Overriding the automatic system

For general photography, you will set the click-stopped exposure factor control dial around the rewind knob at the red 1X setting. However, there are three alternate settings. To the right of the red 1X you will see a white 1/2X marking which you can use for such subjects as distant landscapes and scenics where standard exposure may result in overexposure. The 1/2X indicates that the camera will automatically cut the exposure in half when you take the picture. To the left of the 1X mark are the 2X and 4X settings, which actually cause the camera to double or quadruple the regular exposure. These are handy in moderate and heavy backlight situations, where there is much light from behind the subject pointing towards the lens. By using the 2X setting in moderate backlight and the 4X in heavy backlight, you can increase automatic-exposure sufficiently to get detail in your less well illuminated, backlit subjects. Since this dial is continuously variable, you can actually set exposure corrections between the markings for more precise exposure control.

Never use an aperture so large that the meter needle swings upward beyond 1/1000 sec. or downward below 1/30 sec. If the needle swings upward beyond 1/1000 sec., try a smaller aperture and get the needle down to 1/1000 sec. or below. If you don't, you will have an overexposed picture. If the needle swings below 1/30 sec. you will get proper exposure, but 1/30 sec. is generally considered the slowest shutter speed at which you should hand hold a camera unless you are a practised expert. For slow speeds use a tripod by all means or other firm support if you wish sharp photos.

Battery check

In the centre of the shutter-speed scale, within the viewfinder, you'll note a small cut-out segment adjacent to the 1/30 sec. marking. This is the battery-check indicator. If the battery or batteries are alive and well, the meter needle will deflect

FORM AND SHAPE
Above. Noting the interesting contrast yet similarity between the figure and guitar, Pell Holmstrom combined them neatly with a 28 mm. $f/3.5$ Pentax lens. Aperture with electronic flash was $f/16$.

SKATERS
Page 74. Bright light in foreground enabled M. Matsui to make an exposure of 1/60 sec. at $f/5.6$ using a 55 mm. $f/1.8$ lens.

BEATLE WATCHERS
Page 75. No biologists these youngsters, but fans of Beatle music. Corrie Meyer-Kattenburg used a 105 mm. $f/2.8$ Pentax lens at 1/125 sec. $f/2.8$ (*top picture*), then moved in for a closer look with a 55 mm. $f/1.8$ lens (*bottom picture*) but closed down to $f/5.6$.

BLACK AND WHITE
Page 76. To wash out the background, S. Yamazaki used intense bounce light on seamless backdrop, and exposed for the figure at $f/8$, 1/30 sec. with a 55 mm. $f/1.8$ Pentax lens.

BLACK AGAINST WHITE

Page 77. Antonio Cassera of Italy contrasted a high key nude study with a shaggy black dog using a Pentax SP with 55 mm. *f*/1.8 lens at *f*/8 at 1/60 sec.

NATURAL PORTRAIT

Page 78. With little light available, S. Miyano chose the slowest speed he could hand-hold safely—1/30 sec.—which allowed *f*/4 aperture, just enough to register both face, hands and sculpture in adequate focus. He used the 55 mm. *f*/2 Super Takumar on his Pentax K.

DECISIVE MOMENT

Page 79. Is maximum aperture and minimum hand-held shutter speed practical? Leo Qvennerstedt proves it is in this exciting available light picture of the birth of a baby made at 1/30 sec. $f/1.8$ with a 55 mm. $f/1.8$ Pentax lens. Here picture interest transcends any lack of sharpness.

CLOSE PORTRAIT

(Above). Swirling haired natural close portrait was actually made at 1/60 sec. at $f/8$ by Kjetil Moen of Norway using a Pentax SV and the ideal portrait lens, an 85 mm. $f/1.9$.

EXPOSURE CONTROLS FOR THE PENTAX ES and ES II CAMERAS

To set the ASA film speed, lift up the outer rim collar of the rewind knob, turn it in either direction until the proper ASA speed appears in the small cutout window, and then allow the rim to drop back into place.

For automatic operating make sure the shutter speed dial "automatic" pointer is set directly opposite the red arrowhead on the camera.

The Pentax ES II has a special setting which should be used when the camera is operated automatically away from your eye, such as on a tripod. Instead of setting the shutter speed dial to "Automatic with the arrow head, set it to "Automatic" opposite the red rectangle. This will close the viewfinder blinds preventing light from entering the finder and causing incorrect exposure. The ES camera is furnished with a slip-on black viewfinder cap which should be used in such cases.

To use manual shutter speeds or B (bulb) turn the shutter speed dial until the shutter speed you wish to set is opposite the red arrowhead on the camera.

When using most Super-Multi-Coated Takumar lenses, the stop down lever should remain in the down position.

If you wish to see your depth of field before taking a picture or you want to use non-SMCT lenses, push upwards on the stop-down lever.

For standard automatic exposure operation, the exposure factor control dial should be set at IX.

For special lighting situations where you need more or less exposure than the metering system would normally provide, grasp the outer ring of the control dial and turn it to 1/2X, 2X or 4X or in between, depending on the effect you wish to create.

to this cut-out or go beyond when the battery-checker button is pressed. This button is located atop the camera body, near the rewind-knob rim. However, I find the cut-out also useful for a quick check to see if I have a sufficiently fast speed to hand hold the camera. If the needle is at the cut-out I know I must take my chances or find a support of some kind for the longer exposure.

Manual shutter speed settings

Besides the automatic exposure operation already mentioned, users do have an alternative shutter-speed control. The camera may be taken off automatic exposure completely and operated with regular set manual speeds. Speed settings from 1/60 to 1/1000, plus B for extra-long exposures, are located on the shutter-speed dial. To use any of these, simply turn the shutter-speed dial to the shutter speed you wish. While on manual speed control the metering system is inoperative and the meter needle in the viewfinder will not indicate shutter speeds.

When taking a shooting-aperture reading with a Super Multi-Coated Takumar or using any other lens or lens system, push the switch on the left-hand side of the camera upward. Doing so will close down any Super Takumar, Multi-Coated or not, to the aperture set on the lens aperture scale. Now, when you press the shutter release slightly, the meter needle will show you the proper speed for that aperture. When you press the release all the way, the meter system will set this shutter speed for you automatically.

Care must be taken after using the stop-down switch to return it to the down position if you wish to resume regular full aperture metering.

Incidentally, if you release the shutter at "Automatic", with a lens cap on, or without lens, or with extension tubes, bellows, microscopes, telescopes or with other non-open-aperture metering lenses, the reflex mirror will remain up if you have not moved the stop-down lever *up*. To reposition the mirror to its normal position, just turn the shutter dial off "Automatic" or move the stop-down lever up.

By the way, if your batteries should perchance fail while you are out shooting (a very unlikely event if you change batteries every year, or after every 10,000 exposures), you can still

FEATURES OF THE PENTAX ES

The Pentax has an X-only sync contact, ideal for small cordless electronic flash units, built into the accessory shoe.

At the side of the lens mount on the camera body are two standard push-on PC flash terminals for flash units having sync cords. Use X for electronic flash and FP for focal-plane shutter bulbs.

On the Pentax ES make sure the 6-volt silver oxide cell is inserted properly with the minus terminal pointing inwards.

On the Pentax ES II, the battery compartment is located underneath the battery housing cover on the bottom of the lens mount. Open the cover by shifting the cover release pin to the right with a matchstick or similar object. Insert the four 1.5 volt silver oxide batteries facing the (+) and (−) marks inside the housing. Close cover by inserting the two cover hooks into the grooves shutting cover and pushing the battery housing lock pin back in.

To check the efficiency of the battery, press downward on the battery check button atop the camera while looking through the viewfinder The pointer on the shutter speed scale at right should swing downwards to the central cutout or a little further. If it doesn't, your battery needs replacing.

operate your camera by using the manual speeds, since the manual speeds do not depend on batteries at all.

Each Pentax ES comes with an accessory eyepiece cap which slides down over the finder eyepiece to prevent any light from entering the meter when you use the camera away from your eye. Remember to put it in place before taking a picture under these conditions. The ES II has a built-in view-finder shutter obviating the necessity of the accessory cap of the ES. Just rotate the ES II shutter-speed dial to the red-outlined rectangle and the interior shutter blind will close but still allow the camera to operate automatically.

The ES II has a few other differences we haven't covered before. There's a shutter-release lock lug next to the shutter-release button. Push it to the left, uncovering the red L, and the shutter becomes inoperative, preventing accidental exposure. Shutter speeds in the ES II finder are heavier and easier to see.

Both cameras have X-only hot shoe flash but have both X and FP sync terminals clearly marked on the camera's front.

Loading, focusing, operating the controls, etc., are broadly the same on the ES models as on other Pentax models.

OPERATING THE SPOTMATICS, SP500 AND SP1000

While there have been many Spotmatic camera models, all of them can be operated in a very similar manner. However, let's take a brief look at their differences first.

The original Spotmatic, now often referred to as the Spotmatic I, was Pentax's first behind-the-lens meter camera. The SP500 and SP1000 cameras are precisely the same as the Spotmatic I except that they do not have self-timers and the SP500 has a top speed of only 1/500 sec. instead of 1/1000 sec. As you can see, they are economy models of the Spotmatic I. If you own one, just follow all directions for Spotmatic I cameras.

The Spotmatic II is basically the same as the Spotmatic I, but has a hot sync shoe atop the prism which can be switched from X to FP sync or vice versa using the ring switch underneath the rewind knob. It has the 50 mm. $f1.4$ or $f1.8$ Super Multi-Coated Takumar. In the U.S. the Spotmatic IIa camera has an electronic flashing sensing device which we will discuss at the end of this chapter.

The Spotmatic F is similar to the Spotmatic II but allows you to make exposure readings through the lens at full focusing aperture provided a Super Multi-Coated Takumar lens is used. Older lenses do not have the necessary diaphragm coupling lever in the back which calibrates the meter to the maximum lens aperture. It has an X-sync only hot shoe but has a shutter-release lock lever around the shutter-release button.

A Pentax SL which is the same as the Spotmatic I but with no built-in metering system has been discontinued.

Hidden within the Spotmatic (but not the SL) body, at either side of the finder eyepice are two small highly sensitive cadmium sulphide cells which accurately measure the light transmitted through the prism from the surface of the Pentax focusing screen. These cells are connected to a mercury-battery-powered electrical circuit. By setting the proper shutter speed and aperture combination to centre a needle within the Pentax finder, the proper exposure can be obtained for any subject to be photographed—with normal lens, accessory lenses, scientific instruments, bellows, microscope or telescope. Here is how you operate the Spotmatic cameras (SL owners can follow the same steps except for instructions concerning the metering system):

Loading the Camera

Film is loaded precisely as previously described for older models with a single exception. To open the camera back of the Spotmatic, you need not pull out a side hinge. Instead, just pull up smartly on the rewind knob and the back will automatically swing open.

Opening the back also resets the frame counter to –2. When the rewind knob is pushed down again, you can close the back and advance film by alternately winding film and shutter and releasing the shutter until the first line after the zero appears in the frame counter (within the hub of the wind lever). This line indicates that you are ready for your first exposure. The frame counter will now continue to indicate the number of frames used and will change numbers every time film and shutter are wound.

To make sure that the camera is properly loaded and that the film is travelling through the camera correctly, tighten up the slack film using the folding rewind crank and turning it in the direction of the green R. Every time you advance film with the wind crank, the rewind crank should also turn, indicating that the film cartridge is paying out film.

Incidentally, take advantage of the film reminder dial around the rewind crank. Set it to "empty", "panchromatic", "colour daylight" (with the small sun) or "colour tungsten" (with the small bulb). The Spotmatic II and F dials are slightly different from that on the Spotmatic I. The II's dial has 20 and 36 exposure indicators in green (for tungsten type colour), white (black and white film), orange (for daylight type colour) and EMP for empty. The F's dial allows you to set it for 20 or 36 exposures and has a separate set of control lugs to provide a black-and-white symbol for black-and-white film, a red sun for daylight and a green bulb for tungsten film.

SPOTMATIC I, II, F, SP-500, SP1000 AND SL FEATURES

Here are the controls.
1. Film counter.
2. Shutter release F only has locking collar around release button.
3. ASA film speed window None on SL.
4. Rapid wind lever.
5. Hot sync shoe (Spotmatic II, IIa, F only).
6. Preview lever.
7. CdS meter switch Not on SL. On F this switch is preview lever only.
8. Focusing scale.
9. Rewind knob and crank.
10. Shutter speed dial.
11. Self-timer lever.
12. Rewind button.
13. Tripod bush or socket.
14. Lens.
15. Focusing mount.
16. Battery cover Not on SL.
17. Flash terminals.

To operate self timer push self timer lever counter clockwise. To start self timer push button shown.

To check Spotmatic I, II, SP500 and SP1000 battery life, turn shutter speed until its tiny index window shows red. With Spotmatic F, set shutter speed to B, turn ASA dial to 100. Turn on meter switch (not necessary on F) and view through finder.

If Spotmatic I, II, SP500 or SP1000 needle drops rapidly, battery is all right. Spotmatic F needle should rise to top of scale. If not, replace battery. Remove bottom cover by twisting coin in cover slot. Take out old battery. When inserting new battery, make sure that the plus side (+) is down towards camera except in Spotmatic F where plus (+) should be *away* from camera.

Checking the Battery

First, make sure the camera's mercury battery which powers the metering system is installed and working. Turn the camera over and look at its bottom plate. You'll see a small circular cover with a fairly wide slit. Use the edge of a coin in the slit to turn the cover in the direction of "open".

Insert the battery with the small + downwards, away from the cover (except in the Spotmatic F). Refasten the cover securely. The battery under normal circumstances will last up to two years, but it is advisable to check it occasionally.

Mercury batteries, unlike the standard alkaline cells used in flash and flashlights do not become weak slowly. They maintain power almost to the end of their life and then die quickly. To check battery, set the shutter speed dial at B and the film speed indicator at 100. Press upwards on the SW switch to turn on the meter circuit. If the battery is all right, the needle should fall rapidly towards the − (minus sign). In the Spotmatic F, the needle should rise. If the needle is anywhere near the centre, the battery should be replaced. For replacement, use a Mallory RM400R or equivalent except in the Spotmatic F which uses a PX-625. To be safe, keep an extra battery in your camera case or gadget bag.

Next, set the ASA film speed index in the small window within the shutter-speed dial. Just lift up the outer rim of the speed dial and turn this outer rim until the proper ASA index for the film being used appears opposite the red marker in the window.

Using the Meter

All meters in these Pentax cameras measure the total brightness of the entire ground glass. To turn on the meter, press upwards on the small lever at the left-hand side of the camera. The metering circuit is now "on" and the lens diaphragm closed down to whatever aperture you have set.

The Spotmatic F camera has a metering system which remains on at all times. To prevent battery drain, keep the lens cap in place except when the camera is in use. When Super Multi-Coated Takumar lenses are attached to the F camera, exposure readings are made at full aperture and you should not push the depth-of-field lever. However, when the SMCT lens is removed and replaced with any other lens or optical system, the camera automatically switches to make

Here are the electrical
and optical parts used in all
Pentax Spotmatic, SP500
and SP1000 cameras.

1. Ground glass.
2. Variable resistor.
3. Ground glass mask.
4. Pentaprism.
5. CdS cells.
6. Eyepiece.
7. Semi-fixed resistor.
8. Lens.
9. Diaphragm blades.
10. Rapid-return
    mirror.
11. Fresnel lens.
12. Galvanometer.
13. Switch.
14. Mercury battery.

When shutter speed and
aperture have been set
correctly for the proper
exposure, the meter needle
is centred exactly in the
dot within the viewfinder.

readings at shooting aperture—like other Spotmatics. Then you push the preview lever upwards before making your reading.

At the right of the picture area you will see a small vertical cut-out section with a + at the top and a − at the bottom. A needle can be seen travelling within this area. Rotate either shutter speed dial or aperture ring until the needle is exactly centred between the lips of the small opening. If the needle swings upwards towards the + it indicates that you will be overexposed. If the needle swings down towards the −, the picture will not get sufficient exposure.

There are limits beyond which the meter needle cannot be made to centre properly. If you look at the triangular indicator of the shutter-speed dial of the Pentax Spotmatic I, SP500 or SP1000, you will see that it changes colour as you turn the dial itself. When the indicator is black, the meter is operational. When the indicator turns red, the meter is not operating within its limits. Check the extent of these limits in the Facts and Figures section for full particulars as to what settings can be used and which ones cannot for all cameras. You will see from the table that if you have an ASA 100 film you can use any Spotmatic I shutter speed from 1 sec. to 1/1000 sec. with any aperture that will centre the needle properly. The total range of the aperture settings possible depends on the lens being used. Note, however, that there is an area of exposure from ASA 400 to 3200, from B to 1/4 sec. which cannot be used even though the shutter-speed indicator may not turn red.

With all cameras except the Spotmatic F, the view through the finder dims as you close down your lens aperture to centre the meter needle. While it isn't necessary to reopen the lens to full aperture before taking a picture, you may want to do so to get a brighter viewing image or to refocus more easily. To do so you push down on the SW switch on the side of the camera. The meter will turn off and the lens reopen fully. However, if you don't need to recompose or refocus, you can shoot while at stop-down aperature. The SW switch will return to the down position automatically after exposure, which means you will have to press it upwards again for the next shot if you wish to check exposure again.

With the Spotmatic F you focus at full brightest aperture and take the meter reading at the same time with no need

To open camera back for loading, pull upwards sharply on the rapid rewind knob.

To set film ASA index for the Spotmatic's meter system, pull upwards on outer ring of shutter speed dial, turn until proper ASA index appears in cutout window, then let ring fall back into place.

Set shutter speed by turning shutter speed dial in either direction.

Turn focusing mount until image becomes sharp on microprism grid and surrounding fine focusing collar.

Turn on Spotmatic's meter circuit by pushing upwards on meter switch. On Pentax Spotmatic F, you push the switch only when *not* using Super Multi-Coated lenses.

While looking through viewfinder, turn aperture setting ring until meter needle within finder is centred.

Press shutter release to take picture.

to stop down the lens—provided you are using a Super Multi-Coated lens. With all other lenses or attachments, such as bellows or extension tubes, you will have to make your readings at shooting aperture as explained by pushing upwards on the depth-of-field lever (which isn't labelled SW on the Spotmatic F). Unlike the other Pentaxes, the lever will not return downwards automatically and must be moved manually. However, you will find using the Spotmatic F far more convenient.

The SW switch should not be kept on unless you are actually making a meter reading. Leaving the switch in the "on" position causes loss of mercury battery life. You can tell whether the Spotmatic I's meter is on by looking at the SW switch. If a small red dot indicator is showing on the switch, the meter circuit is in operation. If there is no red dot, the meter is off. Of course, you can also tell by looking through the finder to see whether the needle moves from the zero point when you aim the camera at a bright light source.

On some early models the meter needle remained in the central position when the meter was switched off. On current models the meter needle position is towards the minus mark when the meter is switched off.

Special Subjects

While the two cadmium sulphide cells reading the focusing screen will generally give you an accurate exposure meter measurement for both your colour and black-and-white work, some reasonable thought must be given to special picture-taking situations in which an overall integrated exposure may not be best.

When some specific part of a subject within the picture frame is of prime importance, and this area is of a brightness different from that of the rest of the picture area, a special exposure reading technique must be used. Instead of taking a reading from camera position, approach closer to your subject so that only the area of importance is visible through the finder. Make a proper exposure reading by centring the needle while viewing the subject from this close-up position. Then return to your regular camera position and make your picture using the same exposure you obtain when close-up.

Quite often it will not be possible for you to approach close to your subject. In such cases, you can make a substitute reading from a subject closer at hand which is in the same light as the subject. For facial tones, the palm of your hand makes a good substitute. Just be certain that it is in the same type of lighting as the real subject.

Because the Spotmatic meter reads through the lens, you can use this ability to advantage to make a precise close-up reading from a distance if you have a longer than normal focal length lens. Instead of approaching closer to your important subject area, change to a longer lens which just frames the important area. Now take a meter reading and set your camera accordingly. Then change back to the shorter focal length lens.

The behind-the-lens meter reading system works equally well for any lens or accessory to which the camera is attached. For instance, the metering system will instantly tell you the right shutter speed for any bellows extension and close-up lens, for a microscope or telescope. As you change the aperture of your accessory, the meter will also change its reading. Then you can recentre the needle to the correct exposure by turning the shutter-speed dial.

When shooting small objects at close distances or when you use the Spotmatic cameras for astro-photography, some additional thought must be given to altering the exposure. The main subject may be only a small part of the whole picture area and may differ in brightness. If it is darker than the rest of the picture you must give more exposure than the meter recommends. If it is lighter, you give less. The amount by which you open up or stop down your lens must depend on individual circumstances. Sometimes it may be possible to take a close-up reading from a substitute object similar in tone, but even that can never give a completely reliable reading. It is advisable to make two or three exposures around the estimated correct one.

There is one danger which you should avoid for most accurate exposure readings. The two meter cells face forward to read the light coming through the lens via the mirror and the pentaprism. But a certain amount of additional illumination can also enter the finder system through the eyepiece. This is particularly true if the major illumination for the picture is exceedingly strong and is right behind the photographer. Quite often this light is brighter than the subject itself.

If the photographer does not keep his eye as close as possible to the eyepiece, thereby excluding extraneous light, an inflated meter reading can result. This does represent somewhat of a problem for eyeglass wearers who cannot get their eye right up to the finder window. Moreover, eyeglasses themselves may pick up additional light and transmit it through the finder. Eyeglass wearers may eliminate this if it becomes a serious problem by using the Pentax clip-on prescription eyepice. This consists of a rubber eyecup and a small lens adapter. The eyepice can be slipped over the finder window. For best results, however, eyeglass wearers should have their eyeglass prescriptions ground to fit the small adapter ring of the clip-on eyepiece. Opticians can accommodate eyeglass wearers in this manner if the clip-on eyepiece is brought to them. You can then have your exact prescription mounted in the eyepice. Whenever it isn't needed, of course, the eyepiece and eyecup can be slipped off the camera instantly.

The Honeywell Spotmatic IIa

As mentioned before, the Spotmatic IIa is identical in all features to the Spotmatic II except that it has a Honeywell Strobo-Eye remote sensor for automatic electronic flash built right into the side of the camera. The sensor automatically measures the light reflected from the flash and turns off the flash when the required amount of illumination has been reached. Unlike other automatic flash systems, it can be used for on or off camera flash or bounce flash. Here's how you operate it: Connect a standard PC flash sync cord to the Remote Honeywell Auto/Strobonar and to the camera's X sync terminal or flash sync shoe (with the control set for X sync). After pulling up the rewind knob, set the inner dial around it to the film's ASA index (ASA 25 to 400). For any automatic flash unit you have a choice of three possible apertures with any given film. Turn the outer dial until the ASA index is opposite the range indexes and note the aperture recommended. The triangle index mark indicates the largest aperture of the range, the circle, the middle aperture, while the square represents the smallest aperture. The smaller the aperture used the shorter your maximum automatic exposure range. You can check the range with the dial on the back of your electronic flash unit. When in doubt you can test flash the unit. A green light will go on if you are in proper range. Although the ASA film-speed dial only goes up to 400, you can use faster films. If the film is double speed (ASA 800), set the dial to 400 but use apertures one f-stop smaller than is indicated. For an ASA 1600 film, you would use apertures two f-stops smaller than indicated.

OPERATING NEW AND
OLD PENTAXES

Although the writers of instruction manuals which accompany cameras have the best of intentions, the writings and suggestions often leave much to be desired. While these booklets do form the useful function of getting a camera owner off on the right foot by showing him the controls and explaining how to operate them, they often do not give the hints and tips that only much use with a camera can reveal. If our suggestions here differ somewhat from those in the instructional booklets or the advice given by your camera dealer, please accept our apologies. We will attempt to draw on our years of experience in practical shooting with the Pentax and also the experience of many professional photographers who have been using it. Sometimes our ideas and the ideas of the instruction book won't coincide. In that case, you be the judge.

Holding the Camera

Let's start from scratch. How do you hold the camera? This might seem a very academic question. However, if you do hold the camera the way you see it held in the instruction booklets, you'll find that you must change hands continuously as you focus and then shoot. It is best to find one position which gives you a firm, shake-free grip that need not be changed while the camera is at eye level.

Unfortunately, users' physiognomies are different. The ideal shooting position for one user may not suit the next. The size of your hand, your nose, whether you are right or left eyed, right or left handed has much to do with camera holding.

Let's assume you have now read the instructions that came with your camera, you have tried all the controls, enjoyed yourself by trying to focus on everything in sight—in short given your camera a full dry run. Now you are ready to learn how best to use it. Here are a few camera-holding positions you should try. Adapt and alter whichever seems to suit you best.

WOODLAND SCENIC

(*Above*). Bright sunlight filtering through the trees gives this photo of two children in the woods an almost fairy tale appearance. A Pentax SP with 50 mm. $f/1.4$ lens was used by Pedro Luis Raoto of Argentina at 1/125 sec., $f/22$.

FISHERMEN'S FESTIVAL

Page 98. The excitement of a watery carnival was caught by J. Matsunaga using a 55 mm. $f/2$ Pentax lens at 1/125 sec. $f/8$.

WIDE ANGLE BALLOON

Page 99. Balloon, although close to earth was captured in its entirety with 28 mm. $f/3.5$ lens set at $f/6.3$, 1/250 sec. by George Harvar. of the U.S. using a Pentax SP.

SPORTS AND GYMNASTICS

Pages 100–1. Even 1/500 sec. shutter speed used by S. Suyama failed to halt all action, but A. Shimazaki used a motionless instant with 1/60 sec.

BANDSMAN

Page 102. Traditional street band drummer in Italy was photographed by Adamo Zilio with Pentax SP, 50 mm. $f/1.4$ lens, 1/60 sec. at $f/11$.

SPEED AND DEPTH

Page 103. Only a very fast film could allow G. Konig to shoot at 1/1000 sec., to freeze the action yet maintain $f/11$ for good depth.

ACTION STOPPED AND NOT

Page 104. (*Top*). Using 1/30 sec. K. Sasaki made action-like blurs of karate boxers. (*Bottom*). To arrest action Kondo shot at 1/250 sec.

This is a position that seems to work well with small-boned, right-handed, right-eyed people, but it may still work for you if you don't quite fit into such a specialised category:

Place the camera on the palm of your left hand with thumb and forefinger grasping the knurled focusing ring. Grasp the right side of the camera with your right hand, keeping your thumb on the tip of the rapid-wind lever and your right forefinger on the shutter-release button. Draw your arms in towards your body and raise the camera to eye level. Use your left arm as the camera support and your right hand as the directional arm which points the camera. Focus with your left thumb and forefinger and press the shutter release with your right forefinger. If you are right eyed you should be able to focus, wind and release the shutter without shifting your hands. Find this awkward? Then try an alternative hold:

Instead of resting the camera in your left hand, grasp it firmly with your right directional hand, making this the support hand as well. Now grip the focusing ring between left thumb and forefinger but allow the camera body to leave your left palm. You can focus, advance and shoot now without changing finger position.

Here's a third alternative: Keep the grip on the camera with your right hand but turn your left wrist around so you are now grasping the focusing mount with your left thumb and forefinger but from above the lens instead of below. Again try operating all shooting controls without changing your grip.

One of these positions should do the trick for you. If you are left-eyed, you will have to move the camera slightly from your face when winding film and shutter in order to clear your nose.

Why are the three positions of holding the camera listed in the order given? Because the first is the most stable—with one hand acting solely as camera support; the second the next stable with the working hand holding the camera but the left hand offering two-point support from below. The last position, gripping the lens from above with the left thumb and forefinger obviously offers less stable support.

With any position, however, try to press the camera to your forehead for additional support. Of course, if you wear glasses this is not possible.

105

While one of the three positions will probably suit you for shooting horizontal pictures, you'll also want to take vertical pictures. The best position evolved by professional photographers it to cradle the left side of the camera in the palm of the left hand. Grasp the focusing ring with the thumb and forefinger of the left hand. Now bring the right hand over the right side of the camera so that the thumb hits the end of the rapid-wind lever and the forefinger is over the shutter release. Again, this will allow you to focus, view, shoot and advance film without changing your finger position.

Focusing

Now let's try focusing with your new position. You will find that you cannot possibly turn the focusing ring the full 270° from nearest focusing to infinity without moving your focusing thumb and forefinger several times as you twist the focusing ring. However, you will find that most subjects do stay within certain focusing zones—portraits from 18 in. to six or so ft., middle-distance scenes from 6 to 25 or 35 ft., and scenics or landscapes between 35 ft. and infinity. Therefore once you have the general range of your subject material you will be able to take one grip on the lens mount and not be forced to alter it as your subject moves back and forth.

Now let's try focusing on some objects outdoors or in your own room. Don't pick out a book jacket or a picture on the wall. These are easy to focus and are on a single plane. If you intend to use your camera mostly for copying work, this will do nicely, but if you intend to photograph three-dimensional objects by all means try to find a willing one, animate or inanimate. Of course, a human being is ideal.

Although you will probably want to use your camera under all lighting conditions, first practice under fairly good light. Practice and experience will inevitably allow you to focus with almost equal facility under more trying lighting conditions.

Unless you happen to hit on the exact focusing distance, the scene in your finder will look rather blurred, or shattered if your camera has a microprism focusing spot. If it is equipped with a split-image rangefinder, the two halves will not line up, indicating that the lens is out of focus. Take a picture in this manner and you'll get almost the same blur as you see—almost because if you use a smaller lens aperture

HOLDING THE PENTAX

While there are countless ways that the Pentax can be held, here are several tried and true methods. Adopt or adapt the one best for you.

Cradle Pentax on palm of left hand with thumb and forefinger operating focusing mount. Use right hand to direct camera, release shutter.

Hold camera with right hand. Grab focusing mount between thumb and forefinger.

If neither of the first two methods suits you, try holding camera in right hand, grasping focusing mount between thumb and forefinger of left hand at right angles to the camera.

For verticals, cradle end of Pentax in palm of left hand, grasp focusing mount between thumb and forefinger. Use right hand to direct and steady Pentax, release shutter.

Far right is good solid stance for steady picture taking. Place feet comfortable distance apart, draw elbows into body for maximum support.

than maximum aperture for shooting you will achieve slightly better sharpness even for out-of-focus images. We'll see just how this works and how we can put it to use later when we investigate depth of field.

Now as you move the focusing ring back and forth, you'll note that the image seems fuzzier or the split image is further apart when you twist the ring in one direction and sharper or closer as you move it in the other direction. Keep moving it towards the sharpest image. Some years ago there was much controversy over whether it was best to move the focusing ring swiftly or slowly. It was difficult to decide on the exact point of sharpest focus. With the microprism or split-image focusing aid, this is no longer a problem. You can move the focusing ring as slowly and precisely as you wish. When the image you are focusing upon is in correct focus, you will see it "snap" into absolute sharpness. When the image is out of focus it will seem to shimmer and appear blurred and broken up into two pieces. When it stops shimmering and becomes one single needle-sharp object you have pinpoint-sharp focus.

What should you focus on? We'll discuss this later when we examine how to photograph various types of subjects. Right now, just focus on whatever is the most important element in your picture. In a portrait, focus on the eyes. In a landscape, focus on the principal point of interest.

Releasing the Shutter

Now that your camera is pointed at the subject and you have achieved sharp focus, let's release the shutter. Releasing a shutter properly is akin to firing a pistol or rifle on a firing range. It must be so gentle and so easy that the camera is not jarred at all. If someone is watching you shoot, he should not be able to see any indication that you are actually taking the picture. Only your slightly arched right index (or middle finger if you find it easier) should move. And it should move so slowly and smoothly that it's undetectable.

Although there has been much talk in the past about whether it's best to hold your breath when shooting or whether you should take a deep breath and then let out some of it, most such talk is academic. As more and more pictures are taken of subjects in action, and more and more depends on the instant when the subject is ready, it becomes evident that the photographer rarely has the advantage of

OPERATING
OLDER MODELS

When shooting with the Pentax H2, advance film and wind shutter with single stroke of rapid wind lever. Set shutter speed dial, select shooting aperture by turning click stop aperture ring. Pull down cocking lever to open lens to full focusing aperture. Focus Pentax H2 and shoot.

When shooting with the Pentax K, advance film and wind shutter with single stroke of rapid wind lever. Set shutter speed using fast speed dial on top of camera or slow speed dial on front of camera. When using slow speeds, top dial must be set to 30. Select shooting aperture by turning click stop aperture ring. Pull down cocking lever to open lens to full focusing aperture. Focus Pentax K and shoot.

When shooting with the Pentax S, advance film and wind shutter with single stroke of rapid wind lever. Set shutter speed using fast shutter speed dial on top of camera or slow speed dial on front of camera (with top dial set at 30). Select shooting aperture by pushing in and turning click stop aperture ring. Open lens fully with rear aperture ring. Focus lens. Close down aperture to preset stop. Press shutter release.

dictating the exact shooting moment. Therefore he must be ready at all times, breath and all. Many professional photographers allow themselves to breathe easily—perhaps more slowly than usual so that their chests won't cause the arms supporting the camera to move any more than necessary. At the moment of exposure they merely freeze their breath control, whether inhaling or exhaling, while the shutter release is pressed. After shooting, they resume regular breathing.

How should you stand to take a picture? With your feet spread out a comfortable distance to give yourself a good solid support. Remember you may want to swivel your body to follow a subject, point your camera up or down, lean slightly one way or the other. Adopt a stance which will allow you to do all these things without changing foot positions. After a while, this will come to you naturally.

Now squeeze off a few pictures, changing subjects several times. From here on, proficiency in focus and ability to hold a camera steady depend on practice. You now know all there is to it mechanically. If you think that steadiness and precise focus are not important at all times remember that most unsharp pictures taken at all speeds and lens openings are generally the result of camera unsteadiness and improper focus, not subject movement.

Setting the Controls

Let's get acquainted with the other external controls, the shutter-speed dial and aperture ring. In order to set these, you must bring your camera down from eye level so you can see the speed dial and aperture ring on the lens. With many of the new Pentax models you can adjust controls while looking through the finder. With some Pentaxes, the camera is fully automatic and you need only set the aperture control. The metering system will set the speed.

With other Pentaxes you will want to set controls in the fastest and most convenient way possible. Here's how many professionals do it. If you bring the camera down from your eye still grasped in right and left hand, move your left thumb and forefinger from the focusing ring closer to the body where you can grip the aperture control ring. Then move the right thumb and forefinger so they are gripping the shutter speed dial. You can now set the two controls almost simultaneously. However, you can hold the whole

PENTAX CARRYING CASES

Collapsible soft case allows neckstrap to be fastened to camera body lugs. Removable front and top piece can be crushed and stuffed handily into a pocket.

Hard leather case was furnished for older cameras, has its own neckstrap attached to sides of case. Bulkier front and top piece is usually removable but is not collapsible.

Short soft case fits around camera and lens, permits the user to operate the camera without removing it from the case. Lens with regular cap in place remains exposed. Shutter release and wind plus finder can be exposed for operation by unsnapping top side section of case. Shutter noise is minimized while protection from rain, snow, moisture, dust is maximized. Short cable release is furnished with case. Short soft case is not available for all models.

If desired, most front and top pieces of cases can be removed by turning them so that they disengage from slotted swivel snap.

camera in one hand and set all controls with the other but this does slow up camera operation. Caution: it's best to set the aperture ring from underneath so that you don't move the preview lever by error.

Aperture setting is easier than on lenses of different makes. All Pentax and Takumar lenses have diaphragm scales turning in the same direction. Note that you can set lens apertures not only on the marked settings but also on the in-between dots which indicate half full *f*-number settings. This allows the Asahi lenses to be set with far greater exposure accuracy than lenses with only full *f*-stop markings. You'll also note that all settings are click-stopped—that is they have small click detents which prevent the settings from changing after you've set them. This also is true for the shutter-speed settings. The shutter-speed dial can also be continuously turned in any direction to move to the proper shutter-speed setting. With other cameras, you often must move the shutter-speed dial in one direction or you may find that you cannot turn the shutter-speed dial continuously.

Carrying the Camera

We've been discussing camera holding with the bare camera. While the camera is certainly easier to hold with no case, most users will want to shoot pictures with the case on so that the camera will receive maximum protection. There are two distinct types of camera case. Both allow the owner to use the camera without removing it from the case. Both are furnished with sturdy neckstraps. The strap for the soft ever-ready case fastens to the split rings attached to the eyelets of the camera. You can remove the case for film loading without taking off the neckstrap. The neckstrap remains on permanently.

The advantage of a permanent strap is obvious. Whenever the camera is in use, with case or without case, you can have the strap around your neck to protect the camera from slipping from your grasp. This is a design Asahi pioneered. The hard leather case has a strap attached to the case itself.

This most common case furnishes the best protection for your camera. It consists of a camera body holder with tripod anchor screw and a front and top flap which can be unsnapped and lowered for picture taking. On some cases, the front flap can be snapped off completely for convenience. Often the front flap can be swiveled around when lowered. If the front flap cannot be removed, be careful when shooting not to allow the flap to obscure the lens partially. Although you may not notice it through the viewfinder, a tiny edge of the case front covering the lens can cause a blur over part of the negative image.

In attaching the camera to the case make sure the tripod screw is attached securely.

While the ever-ready camera case remains the best all-around protection for your camera, many amateurs and most professionals do not use such cases. They feel the cases are hindrances, since they must be opened before use. While opening, a valuable picture may be lost. Instead, they carry their cameras, naked, by the neck straps. The disadvantage, of course, is the high incidence of damage that such carrying engenders. A good compromise is to keep the camera in the back part of the case but remove the front flap when travelling anywhere you might wish to take pictures.

Some neckstraps are adjustable and some are not. If you have an adjustable strap, it's advisable to keep it fairly short so that the camera will rest on your chest when you're not shooting, not on your stomach. This length is also best for carrying the camera over your shoulder since your arm and elbow will serve as protection for it. When you turn there is less danger of the camera swinging out with considerable force and being damaged by hitting something. The shortened strap also allows you to use the strap for additional support when shooting. You should be able to wrap the strap around your arm and wrist until it pulls tight and helps hold the camera at eye level.

Loading the Camera

Now let's see how to load the camera with film. There are many ways that this can be done. Here is the technique we've found most efficient and foolproof. Open the back of the camera. This can be done on older models by pulling down on the sliding latch on the left side of the camera. On the more recent Pentax cameras, simply pull upwards on the rewind knob.

Then pull upwards on the rewind handle so that the film cassette can be dropped in the empty film chamber with the film end (the leader) lying across the film channel left to right. Now hold the camera so that the end with the empty film chamber is pressed toward your body, the prism housing is at the left and the open back cover is away from you. Draw sufficient film from the 35 mm. cassette so that you can easily slip the end of the leader into one of the slits in the take-up spool. Push the leader end in as far as it will go.

Now advance the film by alternately winding with the wind lever and releasing the shutter until the take-up spool tightens the film leader across the sprocket wheel. Make sure the sprocket teeth engage the sprocket holes. With the thumb of your right hand turn the take-up spool by its milled edge until the film is tightly wound on the spool. Close the camera back.

Before advancing film to the first exposure take this little precaution used by almost every professional photographer: once the back is closed, take up the slack in the film cassette by rewinding the film until it is tight. Use the folding rewind crank to do this. You can then use the rewind knob as an indicator that the film is properly threaded in the camera and is actually advancing. Every time you wind the film and shutter using the wind lever, the rewind knob should also turn. If it does not, film is not travelling inside the camera body. This means that the film leader has probably slipped out of the take-up spool slot.

Now you're ready to advance film for the first picture. Except on early models, you need not set the frame counter. When you close the camera you will see that the frame counter on top of the wind knob registers at two dots before zero. Advance the film by winding the lever and releasing the shutter three times—until you reach the first vertical line after the zero marking. You are then ready to take the first exposure.

With earlier models having no automatic frame counter, loading is exactly the same. However, when you close the camera back and take up the slack with the rewind crank, advance the film using the wind lever and shutter release three times. Then turn the frame counter with your fingers to the No. 1 marking. From this point on, both auto resetting and manual frame counters will register each exposure automatically as the camera is wound.

You can always tell when the shutter is wound and ready

LOADING OLDER PENTAXES

On older Pentaxes, pull down latch on left side of camera with your finger, On newer models, pull rewind knob smartly upward, Back will swing open,

Pull up on rewind knob and insert film cartridge into chamber. Return rewind knob to original position after inserting cartridge.

Thread film leader into take-up spool slot. Push end in as far as possible.

By operating rapid wind lever and releasing shutter, wind on film until full width of film lies over sprocket wheels and sprocket holes on both edges engage sprocket wheel teeth.

Close back. Push latch back to original position, if necessary.

With wind lever and shutter release, advance film until frame counter on wind lever hub registers first indicator line after 0.

On older Pentaxes without auto resetting frame counter, close camera and advance film three frames. Then turn frame counter dial to first line after 0 with finger.

for an exposure. There's a small indicator hole adjacent to the shutter-speed dial. When the indicator inside is red, the camera is ready for shooting. When the indicator is blank you must wind film and shutter before taking a picture.

Unloading

After the last exposure—12, 20 or 36, depending on the length of film you're using—you must rewind the film into its cassette. Do not open the camera until the film is rewound or the light will get at it and ruin your pictures.

Many people find that they can actually make one or even two additional exposures on a roll of film provided they have loaded the camera carefully. It is quite all right to try this provided you are careful when winding the film. After the last officially indicated exposure (12, 20 or 36) wind the film and shutter with the wind lever very gently and carefully. Stop instantly if you feel any additional tension on the wind level. Tension indicates that you have reached the end of the roll. Don't force the lever further or you may cause the film to detach itself from the cassette spool. If this happens you will have to unload the camera in complete darkness or ruin your entire film. However, if you're careful you should be able to squeeze out at least one additional exposure on nearly every roll of film.

To rewind the film, press in the small button on the bottom of the camera, unfold the rewind crank and turn it in the direction of the arrow on top of the rewind knob. It's advisable not to rewind too swiftly or you may generate some static electricity on the film which could cause static markings. However, you should still be able to rewind a 36-exposure roll within about a 20-second period.

There has been much discussion as to whether the film should be wound back into the cassette completely or whether the leader end should stick out as it did before shooting. Most professionals prefer to wind the film into the cartridge completely so that the film cannot be mistaken for an unused film. You can rewind it either way quite easily. While rewinding, put your ear close to the camera. Listen carefully. You will hear a pronounced click and feel less tension on the rewind crank as the film leader is at last pulled free from the take-up spool.

If you want the end of the leader to stick out, remove the film immediately at this point by re-opening the back of the camera, pulling upwards on the rewind knob and turning the camera so that the film will drop into your hand (which is easier than keeping the camera right side open and trying to pick the cartridge out with your fingers). If you want to wind the film all the way back into the cassette, just continue rewinding after the leader has pulled loose from the take-up spool. When there is virtually no more tension on the rewind crank as it revolves, the film has been completely withdrawn into the cartridge. Open camera back and remove film.

COLOUR FILMS

More and more 35 mm. camera owners today are discovering the delights of colour photography. While only a few years ago, photographers were primarily interested in black-and-white pictures, today the swing is toward colour.

The addition of colour even to a rather drab subject certainly heightens the interest in the picture. And while it's pleasant to be able to take out one's wallet and show small colour photographs of friends or family, there is probably no greater thrill than to project a bright colour transparency on to a good-sized screen for an appreciative audience.

Colour Negative Film

In 35 mm. photography there are two main types of colour film. If you are primarily interested in having colour prints, a negative colour film is the preferable material to use. Used properly and developed either by you or a commercial processor, the colour negative looks something like the black-and-white negative except that the various parts of each picture frame are oddly coloured in the complementary colour to the actual colour of the subject you photographed. When printed (and again this is something you can do at home, although it's more complicated and needs more precise technique than black-and-white) the colours resume their true, original nature.

Colour prints can be made from transparencies as well as from colour negatives, but they are sometimes more expensive. Even prints from colour negatives cost sufficiently more than black-and-white prints to make negative colour users rather chary of having every negative printed in colour. If possible, it's advisable to have the colour negative film processed and then to have black-and-white prints made. From these you can pick out the best shots for colour printing.

Perhaps the least expensive way to see your colour negative results is to have a contact sheet or contact strip made in colour. This is a long contact print, same size as your 35 mm. negatives. While the quality is certainly not

WHAT COLOUR FILM?

Colour films are either reversal films, which produce a transparency, or negative films, which produce colour negatives. Which is best?

Reversal films produce one colour transparency of each picture. Duplicate transparencies are generally inferior to original and are costly. Colour prints are slightly more expensive than prints from negative film.

Negative colour films produce a colour negative of each picture. From this negative either black-and-white or colour print can be made at less expense than with reversal film. However, making a transparency is an additional extra charge. Transparencies from negative colour film generally do not have the quality of the original transparency from reversal film. However, negative film has more exposure latitude than transparency film, can produce surprisingly good colour prints or slides even if original shot was substantially over or under-exposed.

THE COLOUR ILLUSTRATIONS

Page 121: Soft diffused light prevented any harsh shadows from falling on this study of a boy and his toy stuffed bear. Photographer Brendan Doyle of Ireland used a 50 mm. $f/4$ Macro Takumar lens on his Pentax S3. His exposure was 1/60 sec. at $f/5.6$. Note how simple background in almost same tonal range as subject's sweater and toy gives photo an almost pastel quality.

Page 122: A rainy day in a small French village offered Guiseppe Lonardi an excellent picture possibility of photographing two children sharing a single umbrella. Although the rather poor light prevented the photographer from using any aperture smaller than $f/4$ with his Pentax and 50 mm. $f/1.4$ lens, that aperture was sufficient for a surprisingly good amount of sharpness from foreground to background. The 1/30 sec. shutter speed was sufficient to stop almost all movement from the rear save for a tiny blur in the girl's right galosh.

Page 123: Brightly coloured patterns can be found in everyday life if you look for them. Here the photographer, peering down from an office window, found the intriguing colours in a car park across the street.

Page 124: Achieving good figure studies requires much practice in posing, in lighting and in model selection. Here a seamless red studio backdrop eliminates any distractions from the contours of the model.

Page 125: Shooting from inside out, Veli Nurminen of Finland posed the young man carefully in a doorway for a classical colour silhouette. His exposure of 1/250 sec. at $f/5.6$ with a 50 mm. $f2$ lens on his Pentax H2 was for the outdoor scene. Note how very much the bright coloured liquid in the glass held by the subject adds to the photo. The photographer focused on the figure in the doorway but the out of focus building outdoors does not detract from the picture.

Page 126: Close-up pictures of small figurines can easily be made with the Pentax in any of four ways: with close-up lenses over the camera's own lens, with a lens on an extension tube; with a lens on a bellows unit or with the 50 mm. $f4$ Macro Pentax lens. Focal length is quite important in choosing lenses for close-ups. When shooting three-dimensional objects such as this figurine, a slightly longer than normal lens will prevent, or at least minimize, any perspective distortion that close working distance with a shorter lens might possibly cause.

Page 127: Macrophotograph of an ant can be accomplished easily with a Pentax. A full set of extension tubes or long bellows draw plus a fairly short focal length lens provide sufficient bigger than life magnification. The normal 50-55 mm. Pentax lens makes an excellent copying and close-up lens for such work.

Page 128: Harsh, direct late afternoon sun crosslit Canadian fishing and hunting guide's face, warming it slightly. Note how cross lighting picks out all the details. The 105 mm. $f2.8$ Pentax lens was stopped down to $f8$ and the shutter speed was 1/125 sec. Subject was actually sitting in stern of small boat controlling an outboard motor while photographer shot from amidships.

what you should expect if the pictures were printed individually, a contact sheet or strip is sufficient to allow you to examine your colour negatives to see which you wish to use for colour prints.

Can you get good black-and-white prints from colour negatives? Yes, you can. However, for most accurate rendition, special enlarging paper is necessary. If you're interested, ask your photo dealer about it.

Besides having the ability to produce either colour prints or black-and-white prints directly, negative colour films have another important feature. They usually have far more exposure latitude than do transparency films in that they do not form the final picture and a certain amount of correction can be carried out in printing. Some of the negative colour films actually seem to have just about the same seven-stop latitude as black-and-white films. This means that some error in exposure calculation is allowable with little loss of colour print quality. A great deal of error can be tolerated with somewhat greater loss of quality—usually heavier, muddy colours.

Most negative colour films can be used in any kind of lighting, except domestic tungsten lighting. Ideally, they are usually designed for use with clear flashbulbs or something between that light and daylight, but as we have mentioned before, a certain amount of correction can be made in printing. You can safely use daylight, electronic flash, blue or clear flashbulbs without a filter. With photoflood lighting it is advisable to use the appropriate filter and with ordinary household lighting a filter is absolutely necessary for correct colour rendering. The laboratory printing machines can just about manage the correction for photofloods but not for ordinary tungsten light. Daylight, electronic flash and blue flashbulbs give light of a similar quality and it is usually possible to mix them in the same shot. But you must never mix any of these types of illumination with photoflood or tungsten lighting. You can use them on the same roll of film, but not in the same shot.

Transparency Colour Film

The most widely used and popular 35 mm. colour films are the transparency types which, after processing, yield a positive colour transparency which can be viewed with a hand illuminator or can be projected on a screen with one of the many projectors available on the market today. The cost of the film often includes the cost of the processing. After taking your pictures, you simply mail the film (in the mailing bag supplied) to the processor, who returns your slides, generally mounted in cardboard or plastic for projection. If they are returned in strips, it's a simple matter to obtain suitable mounts and mount the transparencies yourself.

The cost of producing slides is much lower than the cost of obtaining colour prints from each frame of a negative colour film. And you can, of course, have prints made from the slides. There are many different transparency colour films available which cover the film speed range almost as completely as do black-and-white films. And, like the black-and-white films, the slower-speed colour films yield the best quality—brightest colour and least graininess—while the superfast colour films do allow pictures under poor lighting conditions but at a price—loss of brightness and increased graininess.

Besides the possible increased cost of making colour prints there are other drawbacks to transparency films. Your exposure with any transparency-making reversal film (a film which yields a positive image rather than a negative one) must be extremely accurate. Instead of the vast latitude of black-and-white film or even of negative colour film, most transparency colour films yield only a latitude of about one full f-stop over or one full f-stop under the proper exposure. Beyond this range, your picture will look washed out, lacking colour, if overexposed, or too dense if underexposed.

Unfortunately there is no practical norm which you can follow as to when your shots are exposed exactly right since so much depends on how you intend to view the slides. Generally the brighter the projector and the smaller the projected image, the denser and less exposed should be the colour slide. Colour slides with average colour and brightness quite often look pale and sickly when projected by the exceptionally bright and efficient modern 35 mm. projectors. You will have to establish your own exposure norm depending on your own equipment. Of course, the correct ASA film speed rating should be used until you see what results you get.

Since there is so little exposure latitude in colour trans-

FILM LATITUDE AND GRAININESS

The best pictures are always made when you expose the picture correctly. But how far from the proper exposure can you stray and still get adequate results?

In black-and-white film, the amount of permissible error is 7 full f-stops (3½ on either side of correct exposure) as shown on the Pentax clip-on meter. With colour reversal film, the latitude is but two full f-stops (one on either side of correct exposure). Colour negative film has a latitude similar to black-and-white film, however.

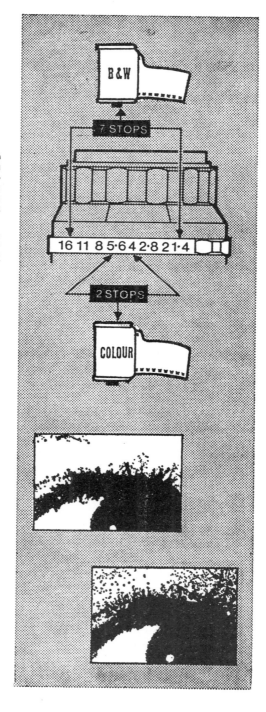

Does a fine grain film always yield the most apparent sharpness? Not necessarily. Here fine grain film produces more fine detail in eye (above). However, less fine grain film (below) appears to produce sharper image because grain clumps have sharper edge. Films which give such apparent extra sharpness are said to have higher acutance.

parency films, you should use exposure meter readings. In determining exposure if there is a range of brightness between highlight areas and shadow areas of more than two f-numbers, it's advisable to favour the highlights and if necessary underexpose the shadows. While dark shadows lacking detail are acceptable in colour slides or prints, washed out highlights with no detail are very disturbing.

There is another important consideration you face when shooting 35 mm. colour transparencies—colour balance. Unlike colour negative film, which can be altered in colour during printing, it is nearly impossible to alter transparency film colour selectively after it is exposed. Since all colour transparency films are carefully designed to render colours correctly under specific lighting conditions, any variations away from these conditions must be corrected in shooting by the use of the proper filters.

Film manufacturers have done their very best to make proper colour balance easy for 35 mm. camera owners. Many film makers have two types of colour film—one for daylight and one for artificial light.

With photoflood lamps, you should use artificial light type (or Type A film). You can use daylight film with the appropriate filter but only at the cost of appreciable loss of film speed. A special Type B film is available for use with high-powered studio lamps. Quite often you will want to use flash with your daylight film. In that case you should use electronic flash or blue-coated bulbs. If you use clear bulbs you must use a filter over the camera lens.

Until rather recently, only complicated charts were available to help you pick the right filter to match the light source to the film. However, we've included a helpful nomograph in the Facts and Figures Section at the back of this book which can quickly give you the proper filter for virtually any type of colour film and any type of illumination. We would suggest you check the types of films you intend to use most and the illuminations you will most often encounter and purchase the necessary filters immediately. When you are actually shooting, it's too late to think about the filters you need. Asahi make excellent filters, although not all you may need. Always ask first for a filter made by the maker of your lens—Asahi.

If you are in any doubt, take your camera and lens to your

photo dealer and he will see to it that you purchase the filter you need and that it threads properly into the front of your lens.

Although proper filtration is generally recommended for best colour results, you will be surprised at the colour you can get using the illumination around your own home. One of the joys of owning a fine 35 mm. camera with a fast lens is the possibility it offers to shoot colour by existing light at home and elsewhere indoors. You will, of course, need large apertures and fairly slow shutter speeds (and a fairly high-speed colour film). You won't get accurate colour rendering because no colour film is balanced for ordinary tungsten light, but Type A or B or negative colour film can give quite pleasing results.

Make careful exposure meter readings of your subject matter. Keep subjects fairly close to your light sources—a person reading by a table lamp is a good example. Try to use light from white frosted bulbs or light from lamps whose shades are fairly close to white. If you don't, the colour of the shade or bulb will overlay all the colours in your picture.

Slide Projectors

Now a word about projection equipment. There are many excellent machines on the market in nearly every price category. The simplest machines with low powered illumination are generally manually operated—you put one slide at a time through them by hand. These projectors are comparatively inexpensive but quite compact. They have the additional advantage of being simple in construction so there is little mechanically that can go wrong (aside from the projection bulb burning out once in a while).

From these machines you can pick your way upwards through semi-automatic machines that take slide trays. You can leave your slides stored right in the trays. At the top of the list are the very comprehensive fully-automatic remote control projectors that allow you to focus them at a distance or focus automatically.

The choice depends on your pocketbook, need of extra conveniences and the amount of brilliance you require. The larger you intend to project your slides, the better should be the machine.

Before leaving the subject of colour photography we must point out one unfortunate failing. As of the present time, few dyes used in colour transparencies are near permanent. The colours in both types of materials are liable to fade in time. This doesn't mean that they *will* fade. It does mean that they *may* fade. Aside from keeping both prints and transparencies away from heat and light when not being viewed, there is little you can do to prevent possible fading.

Colour photography nevertheless represents perhaps the most exciting challenge that photography has to offer.

While having as many colour prints made as you wish offers no problem (except a monetary one), you may wish to have colour slide copies made. These can be made by most colour labs but you will find it an easy and less expensive matter to make them yourself at home. The Pentax equipment available is simple. You can usually make better copies yourself than you will receive if you let a regular photo-finisher do the work for you. All the information you need to select the right equipment can be found in the chapter on slide copying (see page 278).

BLACK-AND-WHITE FILMS

The problem of choosing and using the right black-and-white films correctly is extremely important in 35 mm. photography. With the tiny $1 \times 1\frac{1}{2}$ in. negative format there is little room for error in film choice. Unfortunately for the novice there seems to be a virtually endless choice of films by many manufacturers.

Film Speed

It's most easy to divide the available films into types by their film speeds. Basically films with a low film speed are considered to be slow and need more exposure than films with a higher film speed. The standard indications of film speed now in use are those approved by the American Standards Association (ASA) and the German Deutsche Industrie Norm (DIN).

ASA film speeds are directly proportional to the sensitivity of the film. A film having an index of 100 needs for correct exposure just half the amount of light that is necessary for a film with an ASA rating of 50. These rating are supplied by the film manufacturers who have tested their films for speed using a very precise technique as outlined by the American Standards Association.

With DIN scales, each increase of three numerals represents an arithmetic doubling of film speed. Thus a film with a 21 DIN rating is twice as fast as a film with an 18 DIN rating. The scale is logarithmic. Since the ASA scale is now in most common use, we will use it only here. However, a conversion scale is printed in the back of this book for those with films or exposure meters in other film speed settings.

We'll divide all films into four groups according to speed.

GROUP 1: VERY SLOW (finest grain) ASA 16–ASA 25.

GROUP 2: GENERAL PURPOSE (medium slow, very fine grain) ASA 32–ASA 64.

GROUP 3: GENERAL PURPOSE (medium fast, finest grain) ASA 80–ASA 200.

GROUP 4: HIGH SPEED (least fine grain) above ASA 200.

You can usually classify films by examining the boxes in which the film is packed. Many manufacturers list the speeds on the container. Others include it in the instruction booklet. Practically each major film maker produces one film in each group, except perhaps Group 1. Which brand within a group is best must remain a matter of personal choice although we suggest that at least at first you choose major brands. Now let's see how the groups differ and which films should be used for what purposes.

Choosing the Right Film

Which group is the best for all-round shooting? We'd suggest Group 3 as first choice. These provide amazing combinations of speed, exposure, latitude, lack of graininess and ability to produce crisp photographs. It's quite often almost impossible to tell pictures made with these films from photographs made with films in Group 2 *provided the Group 3 films are developed properly*. Group 3 films can easily handle outdoor scenes yet give you sufficient speed to cope with many difficult low-lighting conditions.

The choice of the next most important group depends very much on the type of pictures you take. If you want to be able to make natural-light photographs under poor conditions and yet come up with some very good negatives, Group 4 is your best bet. There is quite a variance in film speed within the group. For best results with acceptable sharpness and graininess we suggest you use films with speeds no higher than 400 ASA. Films with higher ratings should be reserved for subject material which is just impossible to handle with slower film. With the super-fast fast films print quality will undoubtedly suffer. With proper care, however, the moderate fast films from ASA 200 to 400 can yield surprisingly good results.

The very careful workman desirous of all the quality that the 35 mm. film size can provide will undoubtedly be drawn to Group 2. These films are obviously meant to be used in bright light. Results when used carefully and processed properly can be amazing and almost impossible to tell from much larger sized films than 35 mm. These films can exploit the fine qualities of the Pentax lenses to the fullest degree.

Group 1 films do permit fantastically fine negatives capable of incredibly great enlargements of over 20×. However, unless such gigantic enlargements are contemplated (such as photomurals) the extreme loss of speed in Group 1 (as compared to Group 2) would preclude their use.

You'll actually find that the greatest differences in quality characteristics are not between Group 1 and Group 2, or Group 2 and Group 3, but between Group 3 and Group 4. Fast films are special-purpose films and should not be used for general purposes. Undoubtedly, however, as films and developers improve, the differences between film groups will become less.

Film choice cannot be separated really from exposure and processing. These two considerations can make or break the quality of your black-and-white negative just as much as the actual choice of film.

Exposure Latitude

What can an average black-and-white film capture in terms of the subject? Although black-and-white films do vary according to Speed Group (and films also vary from one manufacturer to another) most modern black-and-white films can reproduce a subject with a brightness range of about 7 f-numbers. So if your meter reads an exposure of 1/300 at f2 in the shadows, and 1/300 at f16 in the highlight areas, all the detail between these two extremes can be registered on the film. While a straight enlargement or print cannot possibly reproduce all this detail, a good print maker can preserve nearly all of it by careful print manipulation. This is quite an amazing range and should serve as a great comfort to those photographers who are not quite sure of their ability to decide upon the correct exposure.

However, don't let this very great film latitude delude you into thinking that any exposure between the two extremes will ensure a good negative. Proper exposure always yields the best negative. The further you depart from correct exposure the poorer your negative becomes. Both underexposure (not allowing enough light to strike the film) and overexposure (too much light hitting the film) will cause trouble even though you may get printable negatives.

When you overexpose, your negative becomes quite dense. An overexposure of your principal subject material of but one f-stop can actually cause an increase in graininess which may be visible on your print. More overexposure also dulls sharpness and causes loss of detail.

Making an error in the opposite direction is also costly. At one time it was thought that a slightly underexposed, thin negative yielded the best print. With today's films, it doesn't. Thin or underexposed negatives must be printed on a very contrasty paper. Contrasty paper tends to emphasise the graininess. For best prints with least graininess it's advisable to produce negatives easily printable on normal Nos. 2 or 3 grades of printing or enlarging papers.

Are there any special tricks in the use of exposure meters when shooting black-and-white pictures? Very few. Since the use of meters does vary so, it's advisable to follow the instructions which are provided by the meter manufacturer quite carefully.

All Pentax meters—built into cameras and hand-held— have very complete instructions. See chapter on the Pentax Exposure Meters.

Developers—Special and Otherwise

A word of warning. You will quite often hear of photographers "pushing" film speeds in order to use films in poor lighting conditions. They set their meters not to the official ASA film speed ratings but, instead, to much higher, inflated readings. These photographers then attempt to compensate for this underexposure by using special developers. Often much of the supposed gain in film speed is illusory. Since black and white films do have so very much latitude, a certain amount of underexposure is possible, particularly in low lighting conditions. Negatives exposed in this manner can yield good prints. However, careful tests of "pushed" film processed in the so-called speed developers indicate that no more than about $1\frac{1}{2}$ f-stops of true speed can be gained even with the best of them.

What developer should you use with black-and-white films? Certainly your first choice should be the developer recommended by the manufacturer of the film. Quite often the name of the recommended developer will appear in the instruction sheet which is packed in the film. If you wish to experiment with other developers after you have become familiar with the film manufacturer's product, well and good.

WHICH B & W FILM?

Choose your film to fit the subject whenever you can. The faster ASA speed films do show graininess to a greater extent than the slower films. As speed increases, resolution and contrast decrease.

Use film in this group for fine copying work, subjects to be made into giant enlargements or murals.

Use film in this group for bright outdoor scenes, landscapes and intricate detail where sharpness and resolution are essential in the final print.

Use film in this group for shooting action where you need a fairly fast shutter speed to halt movement.

Use film in this group under poor lighting conditions where it would be impossible to take a picture without it.

But in making fair evaluation tests always run a dual test with two rolls of film. Shoot both rolls under similar conditions. Then develop one roll in the new developer and one roll in the manufacturer's developer. Then compare the negatives and prints made from them.

Aside from choice of film, proper exposure and processing, what other considerations will improve black-and-white picture quality? Let's take a better look at this elusive quality we call sharpness.

What is Sharpness?

Sharpness is not a very exact term. Do we mean lack of graininess, crisp outlines of the subject? More detail? Perhaps some of all of it. What, for instance, is graininess?

Actually the small sandpaperish texture we see in a "grainy" print is not the effect of individual silver grains at all. It is rather the effect of the clumping together of these grains. The individual grains are much too small to see with the naked eye. The individual grains and the grain clumps are much smaller in fine-grained, slow films, than in high-speed, fast films. At one time it was thought that the size of the grain clumps and only the size of the grain clumps governed the sharpness of the picture. Today many more factors appear involved.

Sensitometrists have found that it isn't so much the size of the grain clumps which is the most important factor in determining picture sharpness—it is rather the sharpness of the grain clumps. That is, if grain clumps have soft, indistinguished edges, the picture tends to lack crispness no matter how fine the grain. Even when graininess is greater the picture will *appear* sharper if the grain clumps have sharply delineated edges. The ability of a film to delineate these grain clumps sharply is termed the acutance of a film. When a film is said to have high acutance, the technician is merely indicating the film's ability to produce a sharp picture, not necessarily the film's graininess characteristics. Actually specific tests have been worked out which allow technicians to measure the acutance of a film.

What does the difference between graininess and acutance mean in practical terms? Simply that at average viewing distance some of the more modern, faster films which have very good edge sharpness characteristics may appear to be sharper and crisper than some of the fine grained films. Of course if you go right up to the enlargement and examine the print for resolution of fine detail you will find that the slower fine grained film reproduced the detail to a greater extent than the faster films. However, at ordinary viewing distances the film with more graininess but more acutance may look sharper.

Perhaps sand forms a good analogy. Sand grains with smooth round surfaces, well worn by time and water, are certainly fine grain. But does it look as crisp as coarser grained sand with rough edges? A mosaic at a proper distance may appear far sharper and crisper than a painting even though every line in the painting is crisp and the painting as detailed as the human hand can make it.

Producing the Print

We'll discuss printing and enlarging only briefly since it's really a whole field in itself.

Unless you actually do your own developing and printing and enlarging, you will not know what fabulous pictures can be made with your Pentax camera. Unfortunately, all too often owners of first-class cameras simply drop their exposed film off at a photo store and let the photo store processors develop and make snapshot-sized enlargements of each picture. These prints, often made by production line machinery, are inexpensive comparatively, but give you no more than a tiny inkling of what is really contained in the negative. Many amateur photographers have come to accept these pictures as the most they could expect from their fine 35 mm. cameras. Those who do their own processing and enlarging at home do know what can be done in black-and-white—the wonderful huge enlargements that can be made with all the fine detail.

If you simply cannot in any way find it possible to do your own processing and printing, by all means try a first-class professional laboratory, if and when you have a picture you really prize. While such a lab cannot possibly interpret the printing of the picture as you could yourself, you will get a result far superior to the small snapshot. Perhaps a few glimpses of what your negative really holds will inspire you into taking up developing and printing.

EXPOSURE

Whether you have ever used a camera or not, you have probably heard about exposure. You may know that a film which is not exposed to enough light will give you an underexposed picture while a film which is exposed to too much light will produce an overexposed picture. Obviously the ideal is perfect exposure. If there were but one single setting on a camera which produced perfect exposure, this might be simple. However, there are many possible perfect exposures depending on your subject, what is the most important element in your subject and just what type of a picture you wish to create.

Although proper exposure is often thought of as the product of the film's speed, shutter speed and lens aperture, another control is inextricably connected to the problem—focus. These four factors will determine at all times the effects that can be achieved with any given subject matter.

Film Speed

We'll start with film speed. Let's briefly examine what we mean by fast films, slow films and medium speed films. When using either colour or black-and-white, slow films generally need more light to record a picture than do fast films.

In other words, if you use a slow film, you will have to allow more light into the camera with either a slower shutter speed or a larger lens opening than you would with a fast film. You probably know that a large lens opening means that you will have a very shallow zone of sharp focus and a slow shutter speed means that any movement of your subject (or of the camera) will cause a blurring of the picture. Fast films allow smaller lens openings and faster shutter speeds. You can also take pictures in poorer lighting conditions. Why not use fast films all the time? Because the faster films usually have inferior quality—poorer colour rendition in the case of colour films and more graininess in the case of both colour and black-and-white. You should not choose a film any faster than you really need.

Shutter Speed

Now let's discuss shutter speed. In most cameras with leaf shutters which open and close centrally like an iris of an eye, the concept of shutter speed is visible. When you use a fast shutter speed, you can actually see the shutter opening and closing quite swiftly. With the focal plane shutter, the action is quite different. The shutter travels at a constant speed at all settings from 1/30 sec. to 1/1000 sec. The secret is in the size of the open slit between the shutter blinds. At high speeds the slit is narrow; at low speeds the slit is much wider. A narrow slit passes little light and so produces the equivalent of high shutter speeds. A wide slit passes more light and thus produces the equivalent of a slower shutter speed. The actual full shutter action of the slit travelling from one side of the film area to the other is far longer than the higher shutter speeds set on the camera. The amount of time it takes the full slit to cover a specific point on the film plane governs the shutter speed.

When do you use fast shutter speeds and when do you use slow speeds? Fast shutter speeds stop movement. They minimize any motion of the camera and cameraman and also minimize movement of the subject. It would again seem logical to use fast shutter speeds at all times, but you can't. Fast shutter speeds allow little light to hit the film as compared to slow shutter speeds. If the amount of light hitting the film is low, you must compensate for this by allowing more light in during the short exposure. You can only do this by using a large lens opening.

Lens Apertures

So we come to the theory and use of lens apertures. You can see the difference between a large aperture and a smaller one by looking through your viewfinder. Set the lens aperture ring to a fairly small opening—f8 or f11. Now press the preview lever, if your Pentax camera or lens has one. The view through the finder becomes much dimmer because the lens opening has closed down. If you turn the camera around so that you can look through the front of the lens, you'll see the smaller aperture formed by the iris diaphragm blades.

When looking through the finder with the smaller aperture,

the view is dim, but you do get more sharpness in depth—near and far objects before and behind the plane of focus appear sharper than when the lens is wide open. This is the proof that you do get more depth of field or a deeper zone of sharp focus at smaller lens openings.

You may wonder just what relationship the so-called ƒ-stops have to the lens openings. The ƒ-stop is a ratio obtained by dividing the focal length of the lens by the actual measured diameter of the aperture of the lens. Low ƒ-numbers mean large apertures; high ƒ-numbers indicate small apertures. Thus, ƒ8 is a smaller aperture than ƒ4. On Pentax lenses each marked ƒ-number is twice the value in light-gathering power of the next number: ƒ4 lets in twice the light of ƒ5.6, for instance.

Small lens openings, as we've seen, allow you more depth of field (zone of sharp focus). You get more foreground sharpness in front of the object that you focus upon and more background sharpness behind it. In addition, all lenses deliver their best performances at apertures smaller than maximum. Therefore you usually attempt to use smaller lens openings for the most sharpness. But at the same time, you are also trying to use the fastest shutter speed to get more sharpness by stopping movement. This is much like a tug-of-war game. When you increase one element, you lose some of the other. Every exposure is a compromise based on decisions you must make about the light level and how you want to treat your subject.

Exposure Aids

Many years ago there was no definitive aid to setting the shutter speeds and apertures correctly for your camera. At best you followed the small printed slip of instructions which accompanied your film. These instructions gave specific lens openings and shutter speeds for various lighting conditions (such as 1/30 sec. at ƒ11 in bright sun). While this might be enough for the average snapshooter with a simple camera, it certainly was highly unsatisfactory for owners of quality cameras. Suppose you didn't want to use 1/30 sec. but wanted to use 1/500 or 1/1000 sec. to stop the action of a soccer game? Suppose the light wasn't exactly bright sun but there seemed to be a slight haze? Suppose the subject

HOW FOCAL LENGTHS COMPARE

While there are many different reasons for using various focal length lenses, one of their primary purposes is to change the size of the subject and the angle of view. Here are the important Pentax focal lengths used in turn on the same subject from a fixed camera position. From left to right, pictures were made by Pentax lens in the following focal lengths: 18 mm., 28 mm., 35 mm., 50 mm., 55 mm., 85 mm., 105 mm. and 135 mm. Note the unusual perspective of the 18 mm. semi-fisheye.

Above, left to right, we have 200 mm., 300 mm., 400 mm., and 500 mm. Below is an enlargement of a picture made with 1000 mm. Compare this with the first 18 mm. photo on the preceding page.

A LONG LOOK

(*Above*). Down the track, right at the photographer—only he is far away, behind the 1000 mm. Pentax lens. A 1/500 sec. stopped action, fast film allowed *f*/16 for depth of field. (*Below*). Unable to approach these elephants, Gordon Warsberg used a 500 mm. lens at *f*/16 with a 1/250 sec.

WIDE ANGLE SCENIC

Too many photographers simply use their wide angle lenses to take in a greater view of far distant subject material. Actually it is most important to consider the foreground and middle ground area. If it is barren, a wide angle lens will make it look more so. The Piazza San

Marco in Venice, famed for its pigeons, provided an excellent study in both width and depth for an 18 mm. Pentax semi-fisheye. Note extreme depth of field even at f/11 from pigeons in foreground to building in background. Curving lines of buildings is typical of the distortion produced with this lens.

GRAND PRIZEWINNER

Page 150 (*top*). Winner in Asahi's International Photo Contest was the famous Max Jacoby picture showing the crowd out to greet U.S. president, John F. Kennedy, on his visit to Berlin. Jacoby used a 135 mm. *f*/3.5 Pentax lens and made the exposure at 1/250 sec. *f*/9.

MULTIPLE EXPOSURE

Page 150 (*bottom*). Alix Jeffry of the United States photographed the subjects singly using a 35 mm. *f*/3.5 lens on his Pentax SP, full aperture at 1/30 sec. He then carefully combined the images in printing.

RHYTHM PATTERN

(*Above*). By reprinting negatives of two girls many times on a single piece of enlarging paper, Joesf Helmers of Belgium has produced a fascinating rhythmic pattern. Original photos were made at 1/125 sec. and *f*/11 using an 85 mm. *f*/1.9 lens on a Pentax SP camera.

AT THE ZOO

Page 152. This Penguin was on one side of barrier. Photographer K. Niiyama was on other. A 135 mm. *f*/3.5 Pentax lens brought them fairly close together. Exposure was *f*/11 at 1/125 sec.

were wearing very light clothes? The number of possible variables which would make the directions on the instruction slip questionable in terms of reliability were practically endless.

A more scientific means of determining correct camera settings was needed—a method which could offer you a wide variety of possible exposure choices depending on your shutter speed and aperture requirements.

Pentax offers three excellent modern metering systems— the fully automatic exposure camera models with built-in meter making a reading right through the lens, semi-automatic cameras, also with through-lens metering, and special spot meters which allow you to make accurate exposure readings even from tiny subject areas at a distance —such as actors on a stage.

Asahi has employed three separate types of through-lens metering systems in their cameras: cadmium sulphide, silicon photo diode and gallium arsenide phosphide photo diodes (called CdS, Spd and GPD for short). You will find a description of the metering system within your camera in the chapter describing your model. However, it is important to learn the assets and limitations of the three systems in order to make better exposures with them.

The oldest circuitry employs CdS photo resistor cells on either side of the viewfinder eyepiece to measure the light from the viewing screen. Most cameras which have such cells are set for the proper exposure by centring a meter needle within the viewfinder, using the shutter speed and aperture controls. Pentax cameras having CdS cells usually average all the light from the screen. CdS cells are quite accurate even in very poor light. They have one disadvantage in that they have a memory. Here is how it might affect you. If you are taking pictures in bright light and then suddenly switch to a dark location, the CdS cells tend to "remember" the brighter light for some time and may give you an inflated low light reading. Therefore, if your cameras do have CdS cells, they should be protected against possible inadvertent exposure to very bright light when the camera is not in use by keeping the lens cap in place. If the camera is operated in bright light, the CdS cells should be given a few minutes to recover before they are used to measure light in a darkened area.

Spd cells are equally sensitive as CdS but they do not have

any memory problem. Even if you do make readings in very bright light, they are capable of immediate use in low existing light conditions. They respond to light changes up to 1000 times faster than CdS.

GPD cells operate much like Spd cells, but are completely insensitive to infra-red rays while Spd often are not. When photographing a sunset over a sandy beach scene, Spd cells might respond improperly, causing underexposure. Spd cells all have special filters designed to eliminate infra-red rays, but they are not always 100 per cent successful.

Using Exposure Meters

If you watch most people make an exposure reading, you will see that they always stand at camera position, point the meter or camera in the general direction of the subject and then use this camera position reading to find the amount of light reflected from the scene. This is a hazardous and not always accurate method of determining exposure. Let's try to develop a better one.

First, before taking any reading, check the film box or instructions to find the film speed. This essential information will probably be given in either ASA (American Standards Association) or DIN (Deutsche Industrie Norm) ratings or both. Set your camera's ASA dial or meter calculator to this rating before you do anything.

Now check the description of your camera model in this book to see whether your camera's through-lens meter reads an average of the entire picture area or, as most of the more modern Pentaxes, it is centre weighted and therefore gives more emphasis to the centre of the picture area.

Both metering systems are equally capable of providing proper exposures, but the centre weighted metering system allows you to take more accurate readings of specific subject areas even from camera position and also tends to minimize backlight problems where an averaging meter might provide an inflated reading caused by the bright backlight around the main subject. No matter which type of metering system your camera does have, the following metering suggestions will result in more exposure accuracy.

For scenes with average tonal range in which there is no marked difference between highlight and shadow brightness, use an overall reading from camera position.

For scenes with bright highlights and deep shadows, make close-up exposure readings of the darkest and brightest subject areas and take the average between them as the proper setting.

When you want to emphasize the dark areas of a scene with bright highlights and deep shadow, take readings from darkest and middle tones. Use average between them.

When you want to emphasize the highlight areas in a similar scene, make readings of highlights and middle tones. Use exposure mid-way between.

When shooting pictures of a landscape with pronounced sky area, tilt your camera or meter downwards slightly to prevent bright skylight from inflating the reading.

When you are standing in a different light than the subject, try to approach closer for a more accurate reading.

With a sidelit subject, take readings of highlight and shadow areas. Average them. If you wish one or the other to dominate, alter exposure accordingly by taking readings of dominating tone and middle tone, then using average.

For subject backlit, approach close and take reading blocking out extraneous light from behind the subject.

For a silhouette, point meter at light—sky, sun, etc.—beyond subject. Use this reading.

For water scenes, take reading from palm of your hand in the same light. Use this reading to avoid inflated exposure caused by reflection of light from water.

For shooting extreme close-up pictures or copying documents, take a reading from a neutral grey card (available from your photo retailer). Place card where subject would be and in same light. If you don't have a grey card, try using the palm of your hand. Make certain shadow of meter doesn't fall on the palm of your hand. Also get meter sufficiently close so it will measure your hand and your hand only.

Making special area exposure meter readings with the fully automatic exposure Pentax cameras can be done quite easily. For most subjects, of course, the exposure automatically set with the camera on standard automatic exposure settings will suffice. However, when you do wish to use a special reading such as those we've described, simply make the reading and note in the viewfinder and on the aperture scale the suggested settings. Now move back again to actual shooting position and use the exposure compensation dial or the manual shutter speeds to achieve just the exposure that you want.

Choosing the Right Setting

Once you have accurately measured the light, you will see on your meter scale or dial an embarrassing choice of riches. You don't have just one possible exposure setting, you have a whole series. If, for instance, your meter indicates 1/30 sec. at f11, you will also note from the meter that you can use 1/60 at f8, or 1/125 at f5.6, or 1/250 at f4 and so on.

All of these are exposures of equal value. As the shutter speed gets faster, the lens opening gets larger. Therefore, the same amount of light hits the film, no matter which pairing you choose.

Occasionally you will find that a separate meter does *not* give you a clear-cut, marked exposure indication. For instance, the meter may suggest 1/125 half-way between f4 and f5.6. But that's no problem here. You simply set your lens aperture ring mid-way between the two lens openings and you'll find that there is a built-in click stop setting to take care of just such in-between readings.

But which of the many varieties of exposure settings should you choose? Until recently the general rule was to use a fairly small lens opening—f11 or f16 where possible, instead of f1.8, f2.8, and to compensate for this by using a slower shutter speed.

This, of course, gave you far more sharpness in your picture from foreground to background. You can see this by examining the depth of field scale on your Pentax lens. Note how the large aperture markings on the depth of field scale—f1.8, f2, f2.8—are right close together. They delineate the near and far boundaries of the acceptable sharpness on your focusing scale opposite. But look at the markings for f11 or f16. See how much further apart they are. When you compare them with the focusing scale you see that far greater depth of field is possible for these small openings.

For many years great depth of field was thought to be most advantageous in photography. It meant the subject focused upon was sharp and so was a good deal of territory in front of and behind the subject. However, photographers have been rethinking the problem of shutter speed versus lens

METERING METHODS

Simply pointing the camera in the direction of the subject from camera position does not necessarily yield the right reading. Here are some techniques which you should use for best exposure. For average scenes a reading from the camera position is usually quite accurate. However it's advisable outdoors to point the meter or camera slightly downwards when taking the reading to exclude excessively bright sky.

When parts of the subject are in shadow and part in bright light, make a close-up reading of each area; use a mean average of the two for your exposure.

Always take a close-up reading of your principal subject if you can for best exposure. This is most important when any amount of backlight is present. Get close enough to your subject to make an accurate reading without including extraneous backlight. If you want a silhouette, however, expose for backlight only.

Often you won't be able to get close enough to your subject for a close-up reading. If you can hold the palm of your hand in the same type of light as the subject, you can read your palm and get an accurate reading of the fleshtone of your subject. For general scenes a better substitute is a neutral grey card available from many photo dealers.

Watch out for arches or other foreground shieldings which may give you an erroneous reading of your more distant subjects. If necessary, move forward to exclude unwanted foreground.

openings. Many now feel that the old ways were not necessarily best.

By using a small lens opening and getting a great deal of depth you do register much foreground and background sharply. Is this good? Many photographers think that the rest of the picture when delineated sharply actually detracts from the viewers' concentration on the main subject. They also point out that a picture with sharpness, foreground to background, is directly opposed to the natural way we see subjects. When our eyes focus upon a subject, objects in front of and behind this plane are out of focus. Therefore the small lens opening often distorts the picture we should see with our naked eye. A larger lens opening which showed the main subject sharp but renders the rest of the scene softly is far closer to seeing reality.

Further, after much study, many professionals discovered that much unsharpness in pictures made with good equipment comes from the use of an inadequately fast shutter speed. A slow shutter speed can emphasize not only movement of the subject but also movement of the camera. And with more and more present-day camera owners concentrating on moving subjects and more and more photographers disregarding the tripod except when absolutely necessary, a faster shutter speed would certainly seem advantageous. Therefore, many photographers today advocate the reverse of the old-school teaching. They suggest a fast shutter speed to stop action of subject and movement of camera user, and a larger lens opening to throw the distracting matter around the subject out of focus.

Of course, there will always be exceptions to the rule— pictures where you will deliberately want sharpness from foreground to background or photographs where you will want a slow shutter speed to show a blurred action, indicating speed. However, only by actually trying faster shutter speeds and larger lens openings and then comparing the pictures you make in this manner with the small aperture, slow shutter speed variety, will you be able to make up your own mind about the controversy.

Previewing the Picture

Almost all Pentax cameras provide a method of previewing the picture at actual shooting aperture. In the screw thread

Super Takumar lenses of the now discontinued screw thread mount Pentaxes, a depth of field preview lever, in the form of a half-moon, allowed the lens to close down to shooting aperture when the lever was moved to the manual position. Additionally, later cameras including the Spotmatic Pentaxes all incorporated a stop down preview lever on the camera body itself (which also turned on the metering system). Beginning with the K bayonet mount lens cameras, the SMC Pentax lenses no longer had depth of field preview levers. Instead, the function was completely taken over by a control on the camera body itself. However, there still are a number of tele and special purpose lenses which do not have automatic diaphragm controls. With such lenses the apertures must be closed down by hand both for exposure readings and for previewing depth of field.

Of course, what you see is an approximation of your real depth of field. You are only looking at a small ground glass magnified about 5×. Some areas will appear sharper on the ground glass than when they are enlarged on a print or on a projection screen. If it's essential to know exactly how much sharpness you are getting, you will find the depth-of-field scale on the lens more accurate and the depth-of-field tables usually supplied with each lens even more so. But the depth-of-field preview lever can be a very practical "in the field" tool.

With the more modern bayonet mount Pentax cameras, the depth of field preview button automatically returns to the "off" position when finger pressure is removed. However, with older cameras and the Super Takumar lenses, remember to reopen the lenses to full focusing aperture after previewing for maximum focusing and viewing brightness.

This preview facility is useful because it is always best to focus when possible at full lens opening. At maximum viewing aperture your picture is at its brightest and depth of field is at its smallest. This means that as you focus, the picture will "snap" in and out of focus with much more alacrity than with smaller apertures. At first it may seem puzzling as to why this is an advantage. Wouldn't it really be better if you used a small lens opening where the image seemed in focus over a greater range? The key to the answer is in the word "seemed". Actually, no matter what aperture you use, critical sharpness is only maintained in the precise plane on which you focus. The so-called depth of field is an area in depth before and behind the subject where sharpness is *considered* acceptable. Sharpness falls off slowly in front of and behind the plane of focus. At the point where we consider the picture no longer to be acceptably sharp, we place the limits of the depth of field. Therefore to pick and focus upon that important plane of critical sharpness you should always focus at maximum aperture where the plane of critical sharpness can be determined most easily.

Matching Settings to Subject

Now let's get back to those peculiarities of choosing the right shutter speed and aperture from that large series of possible shutter speeds and apertures. There is no set rule as to which set of equal exposures you use. You must choose your exposure settings to match your picture-taking conditions. Often this requires very good judgment—the type of judgment no automatically-operating camera will ever be able to do all by itself.

Obviously when you are faced with a subject in movement, you should immediately use the fastest shutter speed possible. However, there is a danger in carrying this to extremes. Is 1/1000 sec. or 1/500 sec. at f1.8 or f2 really a more intelligent choice than 1/250 sec. at f2.8 or f4? The answer, of course, is no. You should reserve the very large apertures of f1.8 or f2 for those low-lighting conditions where only such apertures will make picture taking possible.

The reasons: first there's the depth-of-field problem again. The depth of field at maximum or nearly maximum aperture is so perilously shallow that any slight error in focus or movement of the subject in depth will produce a picture without acceptable sharpness. In addition, no lenses for any modern 35 mm. cameras—not even the Pentaxes—deliver their very best sharpness at maximum apertures. These apertures should be thought of as a reserve—like knowing your car can do 125 miles per hour. Use only when absolutely necessary.

For average picture taking it's advisable to use lens openings smaller than f4 or—stretching things a bit—f2.8. You will find the f5.6 to f8 or f11 range a very good one. Now for the speed problem.

HOW TO USE
DEPTH OF FIELD SCALE

You can check your approximate depth of field at any time by glancing at the depth of field scale on your lens. If, for instance, you are focused upon a subject at about 8¼ feet away, the depth of field scale on your normal lens will look much like that below. Simply read the depth of field between the two lens aperture indicators. For instance, if you were using an aperture of ƒ16, depth of field would extend from 5 ft. to 30 ft. However, if you were using ƒ4, depth of field would be but 7 to 10 ft.

Much nonsense has been written about shutter speeds. You probably have seen or heard of many charts and tables ostensibly telling you just what shutter speeds you need to halt certain actions. The speed set depends on the type of action, the direction the subject is travelling and the distance the action is away from the camera. The error of such a table can easily be discovered by examining the problems of photographing a man running. His body may be moving at one specific speed forward which can be stopped at the speed suggested by the table. But his arms and legs must certainly be moving at a far greater speed. A locomotive may also be moving at a specific speed, stoppable by a certain shutter speed setting. But the wheels are actually revolving at a faster speed.

What we are discovering is that most objects in motion do not have a single stoppable speed but, instead, a number of motions at different speeds.

We can also dispense with the belief that it is possible to use a slower shutter speed when the subject is at a distance. It is true that the subject will look less blurred if you produce only a small print, but if you make enlargements to give the same-sized image from the two different viewpoints, you will get precisely the same amount of blur. In colour, of course, if you project all your slides at the same magnification, the more distant viewpoint will give an apparently sharper image—but the subject will be much smaller.

On the other hand, a subject moving directly across in front of the camera will be blurred to a greater degree than a subject which is moving diagonally across or is heading straight for or away from the camera. However, you can stop movement of the subject comparatively simply by moving (panning) the camera so as to keep the subject in the same position in the viewfinder. You follow your subject as a hunter might follow a flight of ducks. Pan smoothly with the camera held steady in the hands. Move the body at the hips and fire as you pan. Don't stop panning as you release the shutter.

Shooting Action

What's the right shutter speed to use? Why, the fastest you can, of course, depending on the film you have, the lighting conditions and the necessary lens opening. When shooting

162

action, with a single subject in movement, such as a child, try to keep your aperture no larger than $f4$.

When shooting action such as football or hockey you may needs a small lens opening to get enough subjects sufficiently sharp in the picture. Your choice: more sharpness because of a smaller lens opening or more stopping power because of a greater shutter speed? The higher shutter speed at the expense of sharpness in depth is probably the right choice in nearly every picture-taking situation, particularly where your shooting distance is rather long, as it may be at sports events. But don't overdo it and open the lens further than $f2.8$.

Let's turn from action to two other types of general subject material—portrait and general scenes. How should they be handled in terms of proper exposure selection?

Settings for Portraits

In portraiture it might also be assumed that the most sharpness from front to rear of the subject is required. But this is not necessarily so. If you examine the depth-of-field scale on your lens or the tables that accompanied your lens, you'll note that depth becomes far less at close focusing distance—such as portraits—than it is in medium or distant shots. Therefore, in order to register a portrait head in sharp focus from nose to back of ear, for instance, it is essential to use a very small aperture—$f16$ is none too small. Unless you have a great deal of light or you are using a rather fast film, a small aperture will probably require a lengthy shutter speed. This may mean $1/30$ sec. or even more—$1/15$, $1/8$ or longer. At such slow shutter speeds, a tripod is really needed to assure sharpness. And your subject must certainly remain quite still. The combination of added paraphernalia plus the necessity of requiring your subject to freeze in a pose generally produces a very static picture unless you're working with a professional model used to posing.

Professional 35 mm. camera users who specialize in portraits have been slowly weaned away from the small aperture and now think nothing of lens openings of $f4$, $f5.6$ or $f8$ for really good technically high-quality portraits. They feel that the human eye sees a person more like a lens with a large opening than a lens with a small one. When you talk to a person, you generally look them in the eye. Other parts of their head, nose, ears, become far less important and actually are unsharp unless you shift your gaze right to them. Modern-day 35 mm. portraiture often calls for just such an approach —pinpoint focus on the eyes. You'll be surprised in a head-on portrait how very little the sharpness of nose or ears matters. It's essential that your plane of sharpness be highly detailed. The rest of the subject surprisingly takes care of itself.

A larger lens opening, of course, means that you are able to use a higher shutter speed. It is no longer necessary for your subject to remain absolutely motionless. And you won't need a tripod either. With your camera and subject relaxed, you have a far better chance of a natural and more exciting portrait.

Lastly, let's consider general scenes and landscapes briefly in terms of focus and exposure. Here, too, quite often you may be misled into thinking you need a small aperture when you don't. Many a landscape subject really has no close subject matter and could actually be shot at full aperture as far as depth of field is concerned. However, since we do know that no lens produces its best results at full opening, a small aperture is recommended. But there's no reason why a landscape can't be photographed at $f4$ or $f5.6$. Don't use a small aperture just because you've always heard that small apertures are employed in landscape pictures! Of course, if you have a subject in the foreground or are attempting to frame your distant scene with near foliage, you should use a smaller lens opening which will register both foreground and background sharply. However, it's quite obvious that it may be most intelligent to think in terms of a large aperture and high shutter speed at all times and modify this depending on the subject matter instead of thinking the other way around—slow shutter speed and small lens opening —as most photographers have been doing almost since the advent of photography.

We've discussed what should be the largest aperture normally required—$f2.8$. How about shutter speed? What is the most advantageous range for picture taking? Many photographers feel that the 1/125 sec. is almost the ideal compromise since it can stop a good amount of action, it does minimize camera movement and yet it's not so high that you may need a very large maximum lens opening. It's wise at all times to remain above 1/30 sec. when hand-holding a camera. At slower speeds even the photographer's breathing or the tiny movement of a subject will pause the picture to lose sharpness. It is true that many professional photographers do pride themselves on the ability to hand hold very slow shutter speeds and produce sharp pictures, but the percentage of photographers who really can do this is small and the number of successful shots that these photographers can make in this manner is also minute.

You can see now why we stressed the importance of focus in this chapter in exposure. Focus pinpoints what you and your camera are viewing while the exposure settings determine the depth behind and in front of the critical focus and also govern what can and cannot register in your picture. We'll go into this more critically in the individual chapters on black-and-white and colour film.

Using Depth of Field

There are a few tricks of the trade in focus however which can make picture taking easier and give you more sharpness for any exposure. One is the intelligent use of depth of field. As we've seen, at any aperture there is a certain amount of acceptable sharpness in front of and behind the main subject (which we call the zone of sharp focus or the depth of field). The smaller the lens opening, the more the depth of field. The closer the subject, the less depth of field. And we have seen in the chapter on lenses that focal length also is directly connected with depth of field.

Surprisingly, even very few professional photographers use depth of field properly. Most waste it. Actually if you don't need it in one spot, you can sometimes transfer it to another where you do need it. Here's how this works.

Supposing you are photographing a man standing at 15 ft. from the camera. If you focus on him, the depth-of-field scale on your lens (for more exact figures, consult the depth-of-field table that came your your lens) will indicate a depth of field from about 10 ft. to 35 ft. In other words, anything between these two distances will appear in adequate focus. Let's say you have a beautiful landscape in the background. Of course, the depth-of-field scale will indicate that the background won't register sharply. However, by shifting the depth of field you can achieve sharpness in the background with little sacrifice to your main subject. Here's how you'd go about it in this case. Instead of keeping the main focus at 15 ft., shift the focusing ring on your lens to approximately 35 ft. (slightly over 30 ft. or under 10 metres will do nicely). Now look at the depth-of-field scale on your lens. It will show that everything between the original 15 ft. setting and infinity will be adequately sharp. You then have both main subject and landscape background in adequate sharpness within the depth of field. All you've really lost is the depth of field you had in front of the subject which you were not using. Always keep in mind that you can shift your main critical point of focus to either end of the aperture markings on the depth-of-field scale—if you need extra sharpness beyond the normal depth of field—provided you won't mind losing sharpness at the other scale end. You will, of course, lose some slight sharpness of the main subject if you do this. As explained before, only one plane in the picture—that on which the camera is actually focused—will be critically sharp. If you do intend to shift depth of field, then you must accept a loss of critical main subject sharpness in return for a gain in overall picture sharpness. With a little practice using your depth-of-field scale on the lens you'll be able to make adjustments, if and when necessary, quickly and correctly.

There is still another possible shifting of the depth of field which can be used. This involves the so-called hyperfocal distance. If you are taking a picture of a landscape, you may find yourself focusing at infinity or nearly so. By consulting your depth-of-field scale on the lens you can quickly establish the nearest point of your depth of field for any lens aperture. But what is your far point? Theoretically it extends beyond the infinity marking. This, of course, is useless depth. Photographically there's nothing beyond infinity. You are possibly wasting valuable sharpness in your depth of field. You can shift the infinity marking of your lens from the centre focus mark to the depth-of-field scale aperture you intend to use. You thereby gain much more depth of field in the foreground (see diagram overleaf).

If you originally were focused on infinity, you can shift your focus to the far point of depth of field at the aperture you're using. Then everything from half this distance to infinity will be in focus. This distance at which you set your lens to get such depth is called the hyperfocal distance.

PROPER USE OF DEPTH OF FIELD

Here are two examples illustrating how you can shift your depth of field so it does more work for you.

A. Here you have focused upon a main subject at 15 ft. The depth of field in front of subject is wasted because there is no useful subject material. However, the landscape behind is out of focus, outside the depth of field.

B. By changing your focus setting so that the 15 ft. distance is at the near depth of field mark instead of at centre point, you have now shifted your depth of field so that it extends from your main subject backwards to infinity, thus producing an adequately sharp background.

C. Here's another case of misused depth of field. You have focused your camera at infinity for a landscape. But much of your depth of field is lost beyond the infinity point.

D. By shifting the infinity setting on the focusing mount until it coincides with the near depth of field mark on your lens aperture scale, you have also shifted your depth of field into a more useful position. Depth now extends from 15 ft. to infinity.

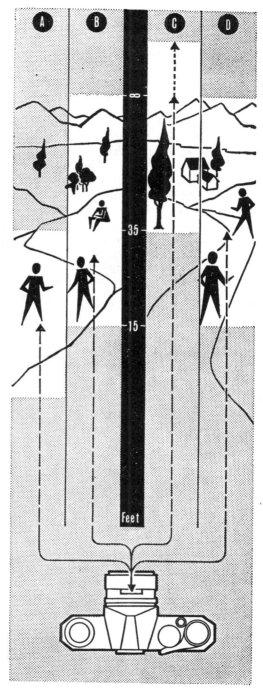

Let's take an example. If you are using $f11$ and have your lens focused at infinity, your near point of focus on the depth-of-field scale would be roughly about 30 ft. Now if you line up that 30 ft. marking with the centre line of the focusing scale, you will see that the infinity marking is still within the depth of field (on the left-hand side of the $f11$ aperture marking on the lens' depth-of-field scale). But look what you've gained on the right-hand side. Your nearest point of sharpness is about 15 feet. By shifting the focusing scale and using the hyperfocal distance you've increased the depth of field from 30 ft. to infinity to 15 ft. to infinity.

While this aspect of depth of field may be slightly difficult to grasp at first, some work with the depth-of-field scale on practical problems should make it quite clear. When there doesn't seem to be enough depth of field or sufficient zone of sharp focus, don't give up. If you can't use a smaller lens opening, try shifting the zone as you want it. (You can often gain far more sharpness by shifting the focus and thus the depth of field than you can by attempting to use a slightly smaller lens aperture. And you don't have to sacrifice shutter speed at all.)

Brightness and Contrast

Before we leave the subject of general exposure, there are a few considerations that you should keep in mind when choosing exposure and when operating a meter.

Correct exposure is always easier to determine for flatly lit subjects. You need not worry about highlight detail or shadow detail. Slight errors in judgment are not necessarily fatal. However, as brightness range in the picture increases (the difference in measurable illumination between the darkest part of a picture area and the brightest) troubles in determining exposure begin.

Unfortunately no film is capable of registering the brightness range that you can see with the human eye. As you scan a brilliantly lit scene, the iris of your eye can automatically accommodate for brightness change by opening up further to show you detail in dark shadows and then closing down when you look at a brightly lit area. If you switch your view quickly and don't give the irises in your eyes time to accommodate to the new lighting condition, you will momentarily experience the same problem your camera has many times

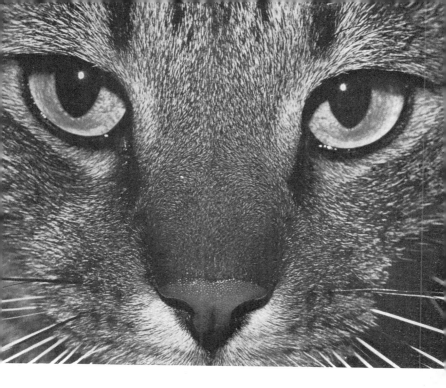

EXTENSION TUBE CAT

(*Above*). Flash, slightly above the cat (named Oscar) highlighted the furred facial textures. A No. 2 extension tube allowed R. Anthony Lovatt's 55 mm. *f*/2 Pentax lens to focus sufficiently close for this feline portrait. Even so, the photo represents but ½ of the original negative area. Note that with a simple flash set-up only one highlight appears in each eye, a number of such highlights are confusing and look unnatural, especially with animal subjects.

SEA HORSE

Page 170. Although the standard lenses of most Pentax cameras permit pictures to be made at a minimum of 18 in., it isn't sufficient for extreme close-ups. H. Inoue Fukuoka used extension tubes and electronic flash to make this close-up of a sea horse. His 55 mm. *f*/1.8 Pentax lens was closed down to *f*/16. When photographing subjects in a tank from the outside, it is advisable to place the lens right up against the glass to avoid troublesome reflections. On nearly all lenses the flange protrudes further forward than the lens surface and so there is no risk of damage to the optical surface when using this technique. Furthermore the side of the glass tank can be useful for steadying the camera where no alternative support is available.

NORMAL LENS ALONE

(*Above*). A bird in the hand is easily captured on film with the close focusing normal 55 mm. *f*/1.8 Pentax lens at its minimum 18 in. setting. Ennio Citta used 1/250 sec. to make certain the subject and hands would not be blurred but had to sacrifice depth of sharpness in the hand with an *f*/4 aperture, in order to base the exposure on the subject itself. A small dark subject in relatively bright surroundings needs special care with exposure. A general meter reading would be only a basis to work from, the lens would then be opened two stops or so to achieve good detail in the feathers. But care must be taken to focus accurately with such a small depth of field.

EASY WATER DROPLETS

Page 172. Freezing droplets of water is actually very simple if you have Pentax extension tubes and the necessary electronic flash unit to stop all movement. Just drop a small object into water and shoot the picture. Timing only takes practice. K. Kurata's 55 mm. *f*/2 Pentax was attached to extension tube Nos. 2 and 3. His exposure was at *f*/16.

FROSTY CLOSEUP

Page 173. Crystalized frost on a window in winter was the subject of Peter Millan's closeup made at *f*/16, 1/60 sec. with a 55 mm. *f*/1.8 Pentax lens.

MACRO PHOTO

Page 174. For extreme closeups of insects, a bellows unit is very useful. Here an insect's multi-faceted eyes are caught with a 50 mm. *f*/1.4 Super-Takumar lens set at *f*/22 for maximum depth of field (which is very shallow in closeup work). The electronic flash unit was manoeuvred to obtain proper exposure so that the small aperture could be maintained.

CATERPILLARS

Page 175. Special lighting isn't always necessary or closeups of insects. N. Miyazaki photographed these larvae with his 55 mm. *f*/2 Pentax lens at *f*/8. Shutter speed was 1/30 sec.

WINDOWLIGHT

Page 176. Sunlight through a kitchen window illuminated this day lily for James Gianelos. His wife held a piece of black paper from a box of printing paper behind the flower to serve as a backdrop. Exposure with a *f*/2.8 Pentax lens on extension tubes was *f*/22, 2 sec.

permanently, an inability to really see detail in what's in front of you. Perhaps the most usual illustration of this is in your discomfiture on entering a darkened cinema from the daylit street. If there is no attendant to light your way, it is an appreciable time before you dare go in search of a seat.

As we'll see in the two chapters on black-and-white and colour film, there are specific limitations as to the brightness range that a film can encompass. In the case of black-and-white film, the range is rather wide. Only by special print manipulation can you get on to printing paper all the high-light and shadow detail that is inherent in a wide brightness range negative. However, by careful exposure you can get an amazingly detailed negative with today's films under surprisingly contrasty conditions. The trick of reproducing it is in the printing. However, when exposing for colour you will not be nearly as fortunate. Colour films simply do not have the ability to reproduce colours correctly in a great range of brightnesses. It's necessary to make your choice as to what part of the brightness range you wish to render most correctly and then take a close-up reading of this area if possible.

In this chapter we've given you the exposure basics for both colour and black-and-white which will allow you to handle most normal picture taking situations adequately. The problem of exposure is understandably a large and almost never-ending one. Every roll of film you expose will teach you more for future shooting.

USING FILTERS

Filters are a very useful aid in black-and-white photography. They can emphasise certain colours in a picture by making them darker or de-emphasise colours by lightening them. Perhaps the most well-known use for filters is to bring out clouds. Actually the filters generally used for this purpose— yellow, green, orange or red, don't really "bring out the clouds". They darken the blue sky so that the contrast between sky and clouds can be seen.

The best way to learn the proper use of filters is to understand what they do. It will then be an easy matter to put this knowledge to useful work.

Black-and-white films must translate all the colours in a scene into shades of grey—with pure white at one end of the scale and black at the other. Today's panchromatic (sensitive to all colours) films do a very remarkable job of this. However, two problems can still exist. There are some colours which the films do not render properly. Secondly when rendering colours into shades of grey, some colours which contrast with others when you can actually see the colour, are very similar in brightness and therefore are rendered as almost the same shade of grey. Filters can often help alleviate both conditions.

Except for grey neutral-density filters, whose function is simply to absorb light of all colours, filters are made in various colours. They may take the form of a sheet of coloured gelatin sandwiched between two pieces of optically pure glass or glass dyed in the mass.

What the Filter Does

The colour of the filter determines just what colours will pass through to your camera and what colours won't. Filters always transmit strongly the colour of the filter itself. A red filter transmits red, green transmits green, yellow transmits yellow, etc. While transmitting its own colour the filter also holds back (or absorbs) other colours. A red filter holds back blue or green, a green filter holds back red and blue, a yellow filter holds back blue. The deeper the colour of the filter the more strongly it acts. As a result, all filters for black-and-white pictures lighten the tone of the print of objects of the filter colour and darken the tone of colours they hold back.

Filter Factors

Coloured filters cut down the amount of the total light striking the film, so an increase in exposure must be made to compensate. Each filter has a filter factor which determines the proper exposure compensation. Filter compensation is not necessary with Pentax cameras having through-the-lens metering systems. The meter automatically gives you the correct exposure. The following applies to Pentaxes when using separate meters. Filter factors tell you specifically how much more exposure you must give. For instance, most medium yellow filters have a factor of 2. This indicates that you must double the normal exposure. Instead of using an aperture of $f11$ without a filter, you would use $f8$ with the filter. Many exposure factors are in fractions such as 1.3, 1.4, 1.5, etc. Of course it's almost impossible (and impractical) to make such minute adjustments. For practical photography just take the factor to its nearest full or half number: 1, 1.5, 2, 2.5, etc.

You needn't change aperture. You can instead alter shutter speed. With a factor of 2, cut the speed to one-half. With a filter factor of three, cut the speed to one-third or to the nearest appropriate setting. A third and perhaps the easiest way of dealing with filter factors is to alter the ASA rating of your exposure meter setting. If you are using a film with an ASA rating of 160 and you have a filter with a factor of 2, cut the ASA rating to 80. If the factor is 1.5, use an ASA setting of 125. If the factor is 3, use an ASA setting of 50.

If you find this arithmetic too difficult, turn to the Facts and Figures section at the back of the book. There you'll find tables giving the most often used filters along with the recommended filter factors and amounts of exposure increase.

Choosing Filters

What filters should you own? A look in any filter catalogue or a trip to the photo store will reveal an almost endless number. It's best to start out with one or two and then add other filters when and if needed.

The basic black-and-white film filter for all photographers is usually the medium yellow. Its principal function is to make clouds stand out by darkening the sky slightly. But even on cloudless days it will prevent the sky portion of your picture from looking grey and washed out. It will also darken water and bluish shadows. Other objects are seldom affected at all by the medium yellow filter's action.

The second most important filter is probably the light green. Not only will it darken blue slightly but it tends to make faces slightly darker and less washed out. It lightens the green in foliage and grass.

A medium-red filter will probably be your third choice. This adds a startling dramatic quality, making blue skies almost black and also darkening foliage appreciably. It is not recommended for portraiture since it will make skin tones quite chalky. It's extremely handy at the seashore if you have whitecaps since it will darken the water measurably, making the white foam stand out.

The Asahi company provide many of the filters you will need. Each threads securely into the front of your Pentax lens. However, you may want to purchase additional filters. If so, be sure to take your camera lens to your photo dealer when the filter is fitted. Always insist on filters which thread directly into the front threads of the Pentax lens or filter adapter rings which also thread into the front of the lens.

With adapter rings, you purchase one ring and then can place non-threaded filters right into the adapter where they are held in place by a retaining ring which threads securely into the adapter ring. Under no circumstances purchase any lens accessories including filters which simply push on the front of your lens. These can easily drop off and become lost. More important, they will scratch the fine finish of your Pentax lens mount.

UV and Polarizing Filter

Two other important filters should be mentioned. The UV or Ultra-Violet haze-cutting filter holds back ultra-violet light rays only, in sunless scenes, preventing, or at least limiting, haze in the picture. Unlike all other filters for black-and-white photography, the UV has no filter factor at

WHAT FILTERS DO

Here is the complete spectrum of colours as seen by your eye, by ordinary panchromatic film and by various filters plus the pan film. Yellow filter darkens blue and violet. Light green makes green (such as foliage) much lighter. Note dark red appears almost black. Orange filter lightens orange and yellow, red slightly, makes green slightly darker, darkens blue and ultra-violet measurably. Strong red filter makes red and orange nearly white, has almost same effect on yellow. Blue is very dark, green almost black. Strong green filter makes red appear black, darkens orange, violet and blue, lightens green and yellows.

all and requires no additional exposure increase. Many photographers leave it over their lens permanently for lens protection. The UV filter can never harm your picture. It can only help.

The last filter of importance is the polarizing filter. It is one of the few filters which has important functions in both black-and-white and colour photography. It works like no other filter.

Light, when travelling, vibrates in all directions. However, in certain instances light from a blue sky or from reflections vibrates in one plane only. This light is said to be polarized. By turning the polarizing filter you can either let through all of these light polarized rays or you can block them out partially or completely. You can thus darken blue skies to any degree you wish or eliminate partially or completely unwanted reflections—as from water or glass—simply by turning the polarizing filter until the sky darkens appropriately or the reflections disappear or lessen.

Although the polarizing filter does darken skies or water and may eliminate reflections, it does not alter the tonal rendition of black-and-white pictures or the colour in colour shots. The polarizing filter will also cut through haze.

There is no set filter factor for polarizing filters. Much depends on the degree of polarization achieved. It's advisable to check the instructions accompanying the polarizing filter before attempting to use the filter. Usually, however, the increase will vary between 2× and 4×.

Polarizing filters work outdoors only when the sun is actually shining. The filter will then darken the sky which is 90° away from the sun. If you make your thumb and forefinger into an imitation pistol as children do, then point your forefinger at the sun, your thumb will scribe a band in the sky indicating the maximum degree of polarization.

When a polarizing filter is used to minimize or eliminate reflections from a shiny surface such as glass or still water, it will have its maximum effect when the light source and camera angle are approximately 30° from the surface. Light source and camera must be opposite each other. Metal surfaces with reflections cannot usually be handled by a polarizing filter unless a polarizing filter is actually put over the light source itself as well as the camera's lens.

Fortunately, you can see the exact results of a polarizing

filter through your Pentax viewfinder and judge for yourself when you have maximum polarization effect.

TAKUMAR LENSES AND
SUPER MULTI-COATING

The quality of Asahi's lenses for Pentax cameras has always been among the finest in the world. However, in 1971 Asahi introduced a major advance in optical design and manufacturing. This is the now famous Super Multi-Coating. Here's what it's about.

Although we normally think of a glass lens surface as transmitting all the light that hits its surface, that's not what happens. A certain amount of the light instead is reflected backwards again and isn't transmitted at all. Most optical glass today, if left untreated, reflects about 7 per cent. However, it isn't just the light loss that affects the final picture. Since most lenses today consist of many elements—7 in the case of a 50 mm. $f1.4$ and as many as 15 in a zoom lens—the total amount of reflection from all surfaces when added together is considerable. A 7-element lens might transmit only 41.8 per cent of the light while the zoom might only transmit 17.5 per cent. In addition the reflected light bouncing around inside the lens itself often reaches the film in the form of ghost images and a general loss of brightness and contrast of the main image.

Lens makers now use anti-reflection coatings on all optical glass-to-air surfaces to cut down the reflection. With such coatings a dramatic improvement can be noticed. Surface reflection is cut to 1.7 per cent and the 7-element lens can transmit 81.4 per cent of the light while the 14-element zoom transmits 66.3 per cent. However, in many situations, particularly in back-lighted scenes or brightly illuminated areas, distinct reflections are still caused on the film and loss of contrast and colour can be noted, caused by what is commonly called "flare".

Asahi's exclusive Super Multi-Coating combats this by the use of seven ultra-thin anti-reflection layers using several kinds of rare elements. Reflection from a surface is cut to 0.2 per cent. A 7-element lens transmits an amazing 97.6 per cent of all light while the 14-element zoom lens shows an incredible brightness increase of over 50 per cent more than a single-layer coating, bringing transmission up to 95.3 per cent. Ghost images virtually disappear, contrast increases immensely, colours are richer. In addition, Super Multi-Coating allows maximum light transmission for all wavelengths of light while cutting off ultraviolet rays like a UV filter. A Super Multi-Coated Pentax lens requires no lenshood and no UV filter. All Asahi lenses now being made have this great optical advance. Every lens so coated is marked "SMC", which stands for Super Multi-Coated.

Since the first Asahiflex in 1951, Asahi has used six different names to identify its lenses, based on changes in mechanical features, lens coatings and lens mounts. They are as follows.

Takumar: Used from the Asahiflex through the 1957 Pentax S, these screw thread lenses have what is known as 'preset' mechanisms. Before taking a picture, you set the preset ring to the aperture you wish to use. You can then view and focus the lens at full aperture for maximum brightness and focusing ease. When ready to take your picture, you turn the lens diaphragm manually and it will stop automatically at the already set 'preset' aperture. After exposure, you can reopen the lens again fully by hand if you wish. These lenses can be used on all screw thread lens mount Pentaxes and even on K mount cameras with K adapters, but you must make your exposure meter readings manually at stop down aperture if your camera has a built-in meter.

Auto-Takumar: Beginning with the Pentax K in 1958 and continuing through the Pentax H2 of 1959, Asahi employed a more convenient diaphragm mechanism called 'semi-automatic'. You no longer need set the lens aperture you wished on a preset ring. You set it directly on the aperture ring. After you finished viewing and focusing at full aperture and pressed the shutter release, a spring within the lens mount automatically closed down the lens to your desired aperture, actuated by a collar within the camera body which pressed a metal rod on the back of the lens itself. After exposure you 'recocked' the lens to full aperture again by pressing down on a lever attached to the lens mount. These lenses could be used manually on older Pentaxes except the Asahiflex. The lenses also fit all newer screw thread Pentaxes with which the automatic diaphragm mechanism also works. However, with any through-lens metering camera, the lens must be used manually for determining readings.

With a K adapter the lenses will also fit the K and later cameras, but must be used completely in a manual mode.

Super-Takumar: Beginning with the Pentax S2 of 1961 and continuing until the 1964 Spotmatic I, Asahi used a fully automatic diaphragm mechanism. When you pressed the shutter release, the lens automatically closed down to your predetermined lens opening. Directly after exposure, the lens automatically reopened to full aperture with no need of recocking. These lenses work manually on older Pentaxes (except the Asahiflex) up to the Pentax S. On Pentaxes K through H2, they may work by closing the aperture at shutter release and reopening either during film wind or when pressure is removed from the shutter release (or sometimes they may not work at all!). On later Pentax screw thread lens cameras, the automatic diaphragm mechanism will operate properly but all meter readings must be made at stop down aperture. They will also fit K mount and later cameras with a K adapter but must be used only in the manual mode.

SMC Takumar: Beginning with the 1971 Spotmatic II and continuing through the Pentax ES II and Spotmatic F of 1973, Asahi introduced Super Multi-Coated lenses with a mount quite similar to the Super Takumars except that an additional lever at the back provided full aperture metering on Pentax ES, ES II and Spotmatic F cameras (but not on the Spotmatic II or previous cameras, on which they must be used the same way as Super Takumars). SMC Takumars can be fitted to K mount cameras with a K mount adapter but can only be operated manually.

SMC Pentax: By 1975 KM, KX, K2 and K1000 cameras Asahi introduced a full bayonet lens mount. These lenses cannot be fitted or used with screw thread mount Pentaxes. On K mount and later cameras, they provide full aperture meter readings and fully automatic diaphragms.

While the foregoing listing of Takumar and Pentax lenses seems simple in theory, it isn't so exact in reality. Many special lenses such as long telephotos, perspective control and some zooms continue to be marked 'Pentax' although they have preset or simply manual aperture diaphragms with which meter readings must be made at stop down aperture. In the lens listings, this is so noted.

While we shall only be listing the currently manufactured Pentax lenses, almost all except the new compact M lenses and the 50 mm. *f*1.2 Pentax are and have been available as screw thread Takumars for the older cameras and should be purchasable.

Those Pentax lenses marked with an 'M' in their name are compact lenses, small in size and light in weight—designed for the compact Pentax SLR cameras. However, they are equal optically to the larger lenses and can be used just as well on the non-compact Pentax cameras.

The "Normal" Lens

Lenses can be divided into five groups according to use: normal (with which the camera is originally furnished), wide angle, telephoto or long focus, special purpose and zoom. There are Pentax lenses of many different types which fit into all these categories. Let's start out with an examination of the so-called normal lens. The word "normal" refers to the lens' focal length—the distance between a point in the lens and the film when the lens is focused on infinity. A normal focal length lens on any camera is considered to be a lens whose focal length closely approximates the diagonal of the picture area produced on the film. With 35 mm. cameras, this actually works out to be about 43 mm., generally considered a little too short to produce the best angle of coverage and most pleasing perspective. Consequently, makers of 35 mm. cameras have varied their "normal" focal lengths between 50 and 58 mm. With early single lens reflexes the longer 58 mm. length was in general use. However, in recent years there seems to be a trend to slightly shorter focal lengths which produce a greater angle of view. Current Pentax models use both 50 and 55 mm. focal length lenses. As explained, the 55 mm. lens does produce a life-size viewing image through the finder. The 50 mm. image is slightly smaller.

Normal lenses don't just vary slightly in focal length. They also differ in maximum aperture. The Asahi company has, in years past, produced normal lenses with apertures of *f*3.5, *f*2.4 and *f*2.2. However, present lenses are faster, allowing more light through—*f*2, *f*1.8, *f*1.7, *f*1.4 and *f*1.2. There is a full *f*-stop of actual speed between the *f*1.4 and *f*2 lenses. The *f*1.8 is roughly 1/2 stop between *f*1.4 and *f*2. The *f*1.2 is 1/2 stop faster than *f*1.4. For all practical purposes the optical ability is the same with any of them at similar apertures. In terms of choice, the 50 mm. ƒ1.4 or ƒ1.2 produces a brighter viewing image than the ƒ1.8 or ƒ2. Since it does have a larger aperture, it has a shallower depth of field and therefore offers a snappier-to-focus image with less depth of field. Most important, of course, is the ability of the lens to gather more light for picture-taking. The ƒ1.4 or ƒ1.2 can produce a better exposed negative under very poor lighting conditions (where maximum aperture is needed) than can the other two lenses.

The present normal focal length lenses available on cameras are:

40 mm. ƒ2.8 SMC Pentax-M, 5 elements in 4 groups, 56° picture angle, graduated in both metres and feet to 0.6 m. and 2 ft., ƒ22 minimum aperture, 49 mm. accessory size, dimension 63 mm. dia. × 18 mm. length (2 7/16 in. × 15/16 in.), weight 110 g. (3.88 oz.).

50 mm. ƒ1.2 SMC Pentax, 7 elements in 6 groups, 46° picture angle, graduated in both metres and feet to 0.45 m. and 1.5 ft., ƒ22 minimum aperture, 52 mm. accessory size, dimensions 65 mm. dia. × 48.5 mm. length (2 9/16 in. × 1 15/16 in.), weight 385 g. (13.48 oz.).

50 mm. ƒ1.4 SMC Pentax, 7 elements in 6 groups, 46° picture angle, graduated in both metres and feet to 0.45 m. and 1.5 ft., ƒ22 minimum aperture, 52 mm. accessory size, dimensions 63 mm. dia. × 41.5 mm. length (2 7/16 in. × 1 5/8 in.), weight 265 g. (9.28 oz.).

50 mm. ƒ1.4 SMC Pentax-M, 7 elements in 6 groups, 46° picture angle, graduated in both metres and feet to 0.45 m. and 1.5 ft., ƒ22 minimum aperture, 49 mm. accessory size, dimensions 63 mm. dia. × 37 mm. length (2 7/16 in. × 1 7/16 in.), weight 238 g. (8.4 oz.).

50 mm. ƒ1.7 SMC Pentax-M, 6 elements in 5 groups, 46° picture angle, graduated in both metres and feet to 0.45 m. and 1.5 ft., ƒ22 minimum aperture, 49 mm. accessory size, dimensions 63 mm. dia. × 31 mm. length (2 7/16 in. × 1 3/16 in.), weight 185 g. (6.53 oz.).

55 mm. ƒ1.8 SMC Pentax, 6 elements in 5 groups, 43° picture angle, graduated in both metres and feet to 0.45 m. and 1.5 ft., ƒ22 minimum aperture, 52 mm. accessory size, dimensions 63 mm. dia. × 39 mm. length (2 7/16 in. × 1 1/2 in.), weight 221 g. (7.74 oz.).

55 mm. ƒ2 SMC Pentax, 6 elements in 5 groups, 43°

picture angle, graduated in both metres and feet to 0.45 m. and 1.5 ft., f22 minimum aperture, 52 mm. accessory size, dimensions 63 mm. dia. × 39 mm. length (2 7/16 in. × 1 1/2 in.), weight 227 g. (7.95 oz.).

The normal (50–55 mm.) choice of focal length lens is the best compromise yet worked out for most picture taking needs. Physically it's small. Optically, it is very well corrected. In practical terms it can handle almost any picture-taking situation with good flexibility, be it scenic or close-up. It can focus closer than two feet without any additional accessories. Many have found that the lens fills every need and have never investigated the other lenses available. They should. The experience of at least trying other lenses is very enjoyable, even if you don't (or can't) purchase every single one of them.

The slightly shorter 40 mm. f2.8 represents a most desirable compact lens. When mounted on a compact camera, lens and camera can actually be slipped into a pocket. The 'M' designated lenses, as already stated, are designed primarily for the smaller cameras but can be used on all K mount cameras. The f1.2 is a triumph in optical design, bringing you fine sharpness in an ultra speed lens capable of splendid results in low existing light conditions. While an f1.4 lens today represents a standard, the Pentax owner not needing such speed can save money, size and weight with one of the smaller aperture, f1.7, 1.8 or 2 lenses.

Wide-Angle Lenses

Selecting the first additional lens is always difficult. Should it be a wide-angle, long-focus (or tele) lens? This depends much upon the type of pictures you plan to take. If you specialise in general scenes, group shots, interiors and other pictures where you don't wish to approach too close to a subject but want to get more into the picture than the normal lens gives you, the wide-angle lens is certainly the one you should consider first. Why did we specify "where you don't wish to approach too close to a subject?" Because of a very interesting optical phenomenon—apparent perspective distortion —which is more pronounced with wide-angle lenses than with others as we'll see a little later.

If you decide up a wide-angle lens just how wide a lens should you choose? It might seem logical to get the widest possible. While this certainly would cover a greater subject area than a less wide lens, there are definite disadvantages to the very wide lenses and reasons why a moderate wide-angle lens is a better choice.

As the angle covered by the lens becomes wider and more subject matter appears on the negative area, the images themselves become smaller on the negative or transparency. If a greater angle of view is to be accommodated it can only be done if all the objects within the negative area are smaller in size. And the wider the lens the smaller the objects.

While subjects are becoming smaller, other optical events are happening. Wide-angle lenses make depths appear far greater. In other words, a tree behind a man will appear smaller and at a greater distance when shot with a wide-angle lens than when shot with a normal or longer lens. You can illustrate this easily by photographing a person in front of a tree with a normal lens. Now replace the lens with a wide-angle lens. Move into the person until his body is the same size on the viewing screen as it was with the normal lens. Take another picture. The tree in the picture will appear much more distant and smaller although the body remains the same size. Many lens buyers who wish to photograph distant scenics do purchase very wide-angle lenses to get more into their scenics only to find that the distant mountains have now become so small they are almost invisible.

We are not attempting to discourage you from buying and using a wide-angle lens, but buy it for the right reasons. A wide-angle lens helps most in showing more middle-distant objects—groups and interiors as we mentioned.

Perhaps the best all-round focal length for general wide-angle use is the 35 mm. It covers an angle of 63° as compared with the 55 mm. normal lens' 43°. The next question, of course, is "How fast a wide-angle lens do you need?" Wide-angle 35 mm. SMC Pentaxes come in two speeds.

Inverted Telephoto Wide-Angle

The most common wide-angle is the 35 mm. $f2.8$ SMC Pentax, but there is also an $f2$ which is a full f-stop faster

DIAPHRAGM MECHANISMS

Fully Automatic: SMC Pentax, Super Takumar and SMCT lenses allow you to (1) select the aperture you wish; (2) focus at full aperture for maximum brightness. When you press the shutter release the lens will automatically close to your pre-selected aperture (3) and then reopen automatically to full aperture after the exposure is made.

Semi-automatic: All Auto Takumar lenses allow you to (1) select the aperture you wish. You then must use the cocking lever (2) to open the lens diaphragm fully for maximum brightness in focusing. You can then focus at full aperture (3). When you press the shutter release, the diaphragm will automatically close to your pre-selected aperture and remain closed (4).

Preset: Most Takumar lenses allow you to (1) select the aperture you wish. You can then focus at full aperture for maximum brightness (2). When you are ready to take a picture, you turn the preset ring until it stops, which will close the lens down to your selected aperture (3). You can then take the picture (4). The diaphragm will remain closed until you reopen it manually.

Manual: Some Takumar lenses have no preset mechanism. Instead you focus at full aperture for maximum brightness (1). You then manually close the lens down to the aperture you wish (2) and press the shutter release (3). The diaphragm will remain closed until you reopen it manually.

than the $f2.8$. However, the $f2$ is also far larger in physical size.

While the additional speed of the $f2$ may be extremely valuable to many photographers for use in low light, the large aperture also has an additional advantage. Wide-angle lenses are undeniably harder to focus than longer lenses. The short focal lengths have far greater depth of field at any given aperture and subject distance than the longer lenses. As a result it can be more difficult to find the exact plane of sharpest focus when focusing a wide-angle lens. However, the wider the maximum aperture, the shallower is the depth of field. If you view through the 35 mm. $f2$ Pentax you will quickly see that it is a faster and easier focusing lens than the $f2.8$. The subject "snaps" in and out of focus far more precisely than with the $f2.8$ lens.

Undoubtedly, the much higher cost of the 35 mm. $f2$ Pentax will be a criterion as to which lens you may buy. For ease of focusing and versatility the $f2$ is preferable.

Though the 35 mm. can be considered the "standard" wide-angle lens, a slightly wider angle for those who want it is provided by the 28 mm. $f2.8$ SMC Pentax-M and $f2$ SMC Pentax, while the 30 mm. $f2.8$ should prove useful for all photographs needing an in-between angle—for small room interiors, for example.

The current wide-angle lenses are:

35 mm. $f2.8$ SMC Pentax-M, 6 elements in 6 groups, 62° picture angle, graduated in both metres and feet to 0.30 m. and 1 ft., $f22$ minimum aperture, 49 mm. accessory size, dimensions 63 mm. dia. × 35.5 mm. length (2 7/16 in. × 1 3/8 in.), weight 174 g. (6.14 oz.).

35 mm. $f2$ SMC Pentax-M, 7 elements in 7 groups, 62° picture angle, graduated in both metres and feet to 0.30 m. and 1 ft., $f22$ minimum aperture, 49 mm. accessory size, dimensions 63 mm. dia. × 42 mm. length (2 7/16 in. × 1 5/8 in.), weight 205 g. (7.18 oz.).

30 mm. $f2.8$ SMC Pentax, 7 elements in 7 groups, 72° picture angle, graduated in both metres and feet to 0.30 m. and 1 ft., $f22$ minimum aperture, 52 mm. accessory size, dimensions 63 mm. dia. x 39.5 mm. length (2 7/16 in. × 1 9/16 in.), weight 215 g. (7.52 oz.).

28 mm. $f2.8$ SMC Pentax-M, 7 elements in 7 groups, 75° picture angle, graduated in both metres and feet to 0.30 m.

and 1 ft., f22 minimum aperture, 49 mm. accessory size, dimensions 63 mm. dia. × 31 mm. length (2 7/16 in. × 1 1/4 in.), weight 156 g. (5.5 oz.).

28 mm. f2.8 SMC Pentax, 9 elements in 8 groups, 75° picture angle, graduated in both metres and feet to 0.30 m. and 1 ft., f22 minimum aperture, 52 mm. accessory size, dimensions 62.5 mm. dia. × 69 mm. length (2 7/16 in. × 2 11/16 in.), weight 423 g. (14.8 oz.).

While the foregoing are considered the most useful all round wide-angle focal lengths, optical developments in the 1950s led to the perfection of an even wider angled group of lenses. These provide incredible coverage for narrow, short, camera-to-subject spaces. In addition, because of their ability to produce apparent distortion of close subjects, making them appear far larger than more distant objects, these lenses are prized for producing unusual creative pictures. While the early 20 and 21 mm. wide angles were incredibly bulky, today's are far smaller. Additionally, modern optical designers have been able to give us even wider angle lenses down to 15 mm. For those who want a bridging lens between the ultra wides and the 28 mm. focal lengths, we now have the 24 mm. focal length which today many photographers prefer to the 28 mm.

24 mm. f2.8 SMC Pentax, 9 elements in 8 groups, 84° picture angle, graduated in both metres and feet to 0.25 m. and 0.79 ft., f22 minimum aperture, 52 mm. accessory size, dimensions 63 mm. dia. × 41.5 mm. length (2 7/16 in. × 1 5/8 in.), weight 194 g. (6.79 oz.).

20 mm. f4 SMC Pentax, 12 elements in 10 groups, 94° picture angle, graduated in both metres and feet to 0.25 m. and 0.8 ft., f22 minimum aperture, 58 mm. accessory size, dimensions 63 mm. dia. × 57 mm. length (2 7/16 in. × 2 1/4 in.), weight 300 g. (10.5 oz.).

18 mm. f3.5 SMC Pentax, 12 elements in 11 groups, 100° picture angle, graduated in both metres and feet to 0.25 m. and 0.79 ft., f22 minimum aperture, built-in filter wheel with UV, Skylight, Y2 and O2 filters, dimensions 63 mm. dia. × 61.5 mm. length (2 7/16 in. × 2 2/16 in.), weight 328 g. (11.48 oz.).

15 mm. f3.5 SMC Pentax, 13 elements in 12 groups, 111° picture angle, graduated in both metres and feet to 0.3 m. and 1ft., f22 minimum aperture, built-in filter wheel with

UV, Skylight, Y2 and O2 filters, dimensions 80 mm. dia. ×
81.5 mm. length (3 1/8 in. x 3 3/16 in.), weight 550 g.
(19.25 oz.).

Long-focus and Telephoto Lenses

Why do you need a longer than normal focal length lens?
Many may think that the longer lens is simply used for
bringing distant objects closer. Actually this is only one of
many important uses for longer than normal lenses. For
instance, slightly longer than normal lenses—from 85 to
135 mm.—are often used for portraiture. Because these focal
lengths are longer than normal, you can actually go further
from your subject and yet produce the same size image on
the negative. By shooting from a slightly greater distance,
you can avoid apparent perspective distortion which makes
near objects appear over large as compared with far objects.

In portraiture this is extremely important. For instance, if
you shoot a portrait of a person looking into the camera
from less than 3 feet, there is a good chance that the person's
nose, which is closest to the camera, will appear far too large
in comparison with the face. Ears may appear too tiny.

While this state of perspective may be quite true in reality
if you do approach that close to a person and look at them,
your own ability to see in three dimensions renders the view,
large nose and all, in proper perspective. A camera which
reproduces a view on a flat plane cannot do this.

To correct the apparent distortion so that the face becomes
more acceptable, we use a longer lens and stand further away
from the subject. We now have a portrait with quite an
acceptable nose.

Longer lenses take care of other apparent perspective distortions—the hand with cigarette which appears too large
through a normal or wide-angle lens will return to apparent
proper perspective with a longer lens used further away.
The foot crossed but pointed toward the camera will also
appear more normal from the more distant viewpoint with
a slightly longer lens.

Of course, what we are really requiring the longer lens to
do is to compress depth for us—push in the nose which
appears too large until it is rendered more acceptable. And
the distant viewpoint that the long lens makes possible pro-

WHICH LENS?

By changing lens focal lengths and subject distances you can change the comparative size of objects within a picture. By changing focal lengths you only change image size.

Sign in close foreground and building in background appear like this when shot with 35mm wide angle lens.

With 50mm lens and increased camera to subject distance to keep sign at same size, building size increases and depth decreases.

Photographer now changes to a 200mm lens and again backs away from sign until it appears equal size to that above. Building in background looms far larger and distance to building appears far shorter

From same distance as 200mm picture above, photographer switches to a 50mm lens. Immediately all subject material becomes smaller. But note that size relationship between sign and building are the same.

Shifting lenses again, this time to a 35mm, at the same distance as above, the image becomes smaller but there still is no change in relative sign-building size.

With 135mm lens, background appears to interfere with head.

By shifting to shorter 35mm lens and decreasing subject distance to maintain same size as main figure, background shrinks and appears further off where it is less distracting.

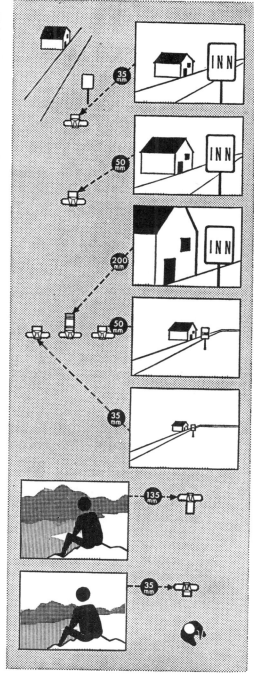

duces such compression with all subject matter in depth—just the opposite effect to that of the wide-angle lens which seems to stretch depth. With a longer lens, a street photographed down its length will appear shorter. Cars on the street will appear close together. This is known as foreshortening distortion.

While the words "foreshortening distortion" do sound rather ominous, they really aren't. Foreshortening often aids picture taking. Mountains which seem too small and distant to your eye appear larger and more dramatic in the picture. Subjects in middle distance seem larger and closer. The picture elements seem more compact. The photograph gives the impression of being more tightly composed.

How much foreshortening distortion is good and how much is too much? This is a matter of personal choice, and unless you have a good number of different focal lengths at your command, you will have to accept whatever foreshortening your own longer-than-normal focal length produces.

This, of course, brings us back to the problem of selecting a first longer-than-normal focal length lens.

Many camera owners do make an initial mistake of attempting to get the longest lens possible on their first purchase. While such lenses can be very impressive and they do have the ability of bringing distant scenes closer—with some difficulties as we shall see—the medium telephoto or long focal length lens is far more versatile for general photography.

Telephoto Lenses

While the differences between a telephoto and long focal length lens should mean little to the photographer in terms of practical use, you may still wonder what the difference is. The difference is optical. "Long focal length" indicates that the distance between the middle of the last lens element and the film is approximately equal to the focal length of the lens. Therefore a 135 mm. long focus lens will extend nearly 135 mm. from the rear lens element to the film plane.

By today's physical lens standards, that's a rather lengthy lens barrel. Most lens makers, Asahi included, have successfully reduced the size of long focal length lenses to $\frac{1}{2}$ or, in some instances, even $\frac{1}{3}$ their former length by employing telephoto optical designs. A telephoto lens consists of a lens element group at the front which converge the light rays strongly, plus a lens element group at the back which lessens the convergence. By employing these positive and negative lens groups, the back focus (or actual distance from last lens element to film plane) can be shortened considerably while maintaining the same focal length. A tele lens design is bound to be more complicated and therefore more expensive to manufacture.

Because the medium telephoto lens is so important in photography today Asahi offers 6 lenses in 5 focal lengths between 85 and 150 mm.

The 135 mm. focal length deserves prime mention. It is classically the general purpose moderate tele for single lens reflexes and best fills the needs for a lens which brings objects quite close—reaching out and pulling in the very distant objects with more convenience that longer lenses. The 120 mm. f2.8 SMC Pentax bridges the gap between 100 and 135 mm. with a very compact close-focusing optic, making it an ideal compromise lens with high speed.

The 135 mm. length is also excellent for portraiture since it does minimise apparent perspective distortion. Its limitation, however, is one of minimum camera-to-subject distance. Quite often it's not possible in the confines of a home to get into the picture all the elements because of the necessary great lens-to-subject distance.

The 150 mm. SMC Pentax is a close rival of the 135 mm. Giving a slightly larger image, it is faster, smaller, lighter in weight and just as easy to handle.

120 mm. f2.8 SMC Pentax, 5 elements in 4 groups, 21° picture angle, graduated in both metres and feet to 1.2 m. and 4 ft., f32 minimum aperture, 52 mm. accessory size, dimensions 62.5 mm. dia. × 74.5 mm. length (2 7/16 in. × 2 15/16 in.), weight 355 g. (12.43 oz.).

135 mm. f2.5 SMC Pentax, 6 elements in 6 groups, 18° picture angle, graduated in both metres and feet to 1.5 m. and 5ft., f32 minimum aperture, 58 mm. accessory size, dimensions 67.5 mm. dia. × 85.9 mm. length (2 11/16 in. × 3 3/8 in.), weight 470 g. (16.45 oz.).

135 mm. f3.5 SMC Pentax-M, 5 elements in 5 groups, 18° picture angle, graduated in both metres and feet to 1.5 m. and 5 ft., f32 minimum aperture, 49 mm. accessory

size, dimensions 62.5 mm. dia. × 65.7 mm. length (2 7/16 in. × 2 11/16 in.), weight 276 g. (9.74 oz.).

150 mm. *f*4 SMC Pentax, 5 elements in 5 groups, 17° picture angle, graduated in both metres and feet to 1.8 m. and 6 ft., *f*32 minimum aperture, 52 mm. accessory size, dimensions 62.5 mm. dia. × 96 mm. length (2 7/16 in. × 3/4 in.), weight 338 g. (11.83 oz.).

For some photographers the smallish maximum aperture and the minimum focusing distance of 5 or 6 ft. may seem a handicap. Quite often a larger maximum aperture is wanted for shooting pictures with existing low light indoors. Often apertures of *f*2 or larger are needed. The 85 mm. *f*1.8 SMC Pentax is for just such purposes. Its slightly longer than normal focal length minimises apparent perspective distortion of close subjects, allows you to remain a respectable distance from your subject while still filling your picture frame well and gives you an extremely large maximum aperture. With the very short minimum focusing distances there are few lenses to equal them for available light photography.

While the 85 mm. *f*1.8 SMC Pentax is pre-eminent for existing low-light photography, undoubtedly the professional photographers' favourite all-round focal length lens is the 100 mm. SMC Pentax-M, an incredibly compact and light, close-focusing optic which many photographers prefer as a 'normal' lens to a 50 mm. With its double focal length it is ideal for portraiture, preventing apparent perspective distortion. Its longer focal length provides tighter cropping and composition from the same camera to subject distance as the 50 mm.

85 mm. *f*1.8 SMC Pentax, 6 elements in 6 groups, 29° picture angle, graduated in both metres and feet to 0.85 m. and 2.75 ft., *f*22 minimum aperture, 52 mm. accessory size, dimensions 64 mm. dia. × 56 mm. length (2 1/2 in. × 2 3/16 in.), weight 331 g. (11.59 oz.).

100 mm. *f*2.8 SMC Pentax-M, 5 elements in 5 groups, 24.5° picture angle, graduated in both metres and feet to 1 m. and 3.3 ft., *f*22 minimum aperture, 49 mm. accessory size, dimensions 62.5 mm. dia. × 55.7 mm. length (2 7/16 in. × 2 1/4 in.), weight 225 g. (7.88 oz.).

The Really Long Lenses

Lenses from 35 mm. to 150 mm. focal lengths have always

been considered the standard range for most Pentax owners. But the ease with which the Asahi Pentax can be fitted with longer lenses plus the constant cutting of weight and bulk of all lenses has made it no longer necessary to use tripods at all times even with the longer lenses. It's not unusual today for an amateur to shoot sports from his seat in the stands while hand-holding a 300 mm. lens, or to use a 200 mm. lens to photograph children jumping off a diving board.

Prices of such long lenses, once astronomic and almost beyond the scope of the average amateur photographer, have dropped to a point where they are not prohibitive—although, of course, good tele or long focal length lenses such as the Takumars are still not inexpensive.

Why a longer than 150 mm. lens? For just such subjects as the two we've described. The long lens allows you to photograph objects which you cannot approach closer. The long hand-held and tripod-mounted lenses for 35 mm. cameras have revolutionised bird photography.

The problem, as always, in selecting focal lengths is just how long a lens should you contemplate. The answer depends on your own personal needs.

Asahi has aided the outdoor photographer willing to sacrifice great maximum aperture in return for a considerable decrease in lens size and weight. There are alternative versions of the lens in the 200 and 300 mm. focal lengths, while even the 400 mm. lens may be hand-held.

Looking through a 200 mm. or longer lens in a Pentax is an experience. It's your first real glimpse of the telescope qualities of a long lens. You can capture on film objects and detail not readily visible to your naked eye.

Surprisingly enough, the 200 mm. lens, besides being a splendid lens for bringing middle-distance images extremely close, is a remarkably flexible lens for distant scenes. As stated elsewhere, many photographers become quite disappointed when using normal or wide-angle lenses whenever they try to shoot widespread landscapes. All parts of the landscape become so small and insignificant that little of the grandeur of the original scene remains.

With a 200 mm. lens, you can select interesting parts of a large scene, magnify them with the 200 mm. lens and then photograph them with more clarity and detail than you were able to see.

The lens also remains a fine outdoor candid portrait lens. Few subjects believe the photographer can be so far away and still take crisp closeups. This is particularly true with the 200 mm. ƒ4 SMC Pentax-M which weighs only 14 oz. and is more compact than many shorter focal length lenses produced by other manufacturers.

Because the 200 mm. ƒ4 SMC Pentax-M and the 200 mm. ƒ4 SMC Pentax-M are light and small, they have no tripod socket. If you do wish to use them on a tripod, you can attach the tripod to the socket on the camera body itself. Most such lenses are too heavy to allow this and must have their own tripod socket. There is no danger, however, with these lenses.

200 mm. ƒ4 SMC Pentax-M, 6 elements in 5 groups, 12° picture angle, graduated in both metres and feet to 2 m. and 6.5 ft., ƒ32 minimum aperture, 52 mm. accessory size, dimensions 63.5 mm. dia. × 111 mm. length (2 7/16 in. × 4 3/8 in.), weight 405 g. (14.18 oz.).

200 mm. ƒ4 SMC Pentax, 5 elements in 5 groups, 12° picture angle, graduated in both metres and feet to 2 m. and 6.5 ft., ƒ32 minimum aperture, 58 mm. accessory size, dimensions 65 mm. dia. × 137 mm. length (2 9/16 in. × 5 3/8 in.), weight 516 g. (18.06 oz.).

Probably one of the most convenient lens lengths for sports and animal photography is the 300 mm. It's manageable hand-held or it can be used on a tripod. The 300 mm. ƒ4 for the Pentax has the added advantage of being remarkably fast for such a long lens and so will allow you to shoot tele shots even under rather poor lighting conditions.

300 mm. ƒ4 SMC Pentax, 7 elements in 5 groups, 8° picture angle, graduated in both metres and feet to 4 m. and 13 ft., ƒ32 minimum aperture, 77 mm. accessory size, dimensions 85 mm. dia. × 188 mm. length (3 3/8 in. × 7 3/8 in.), weight 942 g. (32.97 oz.).

Before we hit the tripod-only long lenses, there is one more Pentax specially designed so that it, too, like the 200 mm. ƒ4 and 300 mm. ƒ4 Pentaxes, can be hand-held, if and when desired. While furnishing a surprisingly large maximum aperture, the 400 mm. ƒ5.6 SMC Pentax is still sufficiently small and light for non-tripod use. The tripod socket ring which allows the camera to be used for either horizontal or vertical pictures, can be removed when the lens is used hand-held.

400 mm. ƒ5.6 SMC Pentax, 4 elements in 4 groups, 6°

picture angle, graduated in both metres and feet to 8 m. and 27 ft., $f45$ minimum aperture, 77 mm. accessory size, dimensions 85 mm. dia. × 277 mm. length (3 3/8 in. × 10 7/8 in.), weight 1,240 g. (43.4 oz.), manual diaphragm operation.

There are two extremely long focus lenses at the big end of the Pentax lens scale. Both are designed for tripod-only operation since they are far too bulky and heavy to be hand-held. Such very long lenses have specialised applications such as photographing rocket firings from a safe distance, astro-photography, extremely long distance photography (when weather conditions warrant it), special sports events.

The 500 mm. $f4.5$ SMC Pentax is quite fast in maximum aperture for its length. It therefore provides a bright focusing image. It has a smooth double helical focusing mount like shorter Pentax lenses plus a built-in lens hood. This fast, easily-handled lens is prized by news and sports photographers.

500 mm. SMC $f4.5$ Pentax, 4 elements in 4 groups, 5° picture angle, graduated in both metres and feet to 10 m. and 35 ft., $f45$ minimum aperture, 52 mm. accessory size threads at the rear, dimensions 126.5 mm. dia. × 440 mm. length (4 15/16 in. × 17 5/16 in.), weight 3,330 g. (116.6 oz.), manual diaphragm control.

The 1000 mm. $f8$ SMC Pentax is double the focal length of the 500 mm. yet it still has a very focusable maximum aperture of $f8$. Because of the vast size and weight of this lens, a special tripod is furnished with it as well as wooden cases for both tripod and lens.

It might seem strange that a tripod should accompany the lens. However, with such extreme focal lengths the slightest tremor of the camera and lens—even if a very high shutter speed is used—will cause a loss of sharpness. The tripod furnished holds the lens in perfect balance with camera attached and provides the extreme rigidity needed. The tripod provides full camera movement, both vertically and horizontally, and allows the lens plus camera to be turned 90° for horizontal and vertical pictures.

The focusing mechanism is quite different from that of the 500 mm. Pentax—two rack and pinion wheels which move the entire camera body back and forth.

1000 mm. $f8$ SMC Pentax, 5 elements in 5 groups, 2.5°

picture angle, graduated in both metres and feet to 30 m. and 100 ft., f45 minimum aperture, 52 mm. accessory size threads at the rear, dimensions 143 mm. dia. × 738 mm. length (5 5/8 in. × 29 1/16 in.), weight 5,250 g. (183.8 oz.), manual diaphragm control.

There is now a more modern, far lighter and more compact alternate to the 1000 mm. f8 SMC Pentax all-glass lens in the 1000 mm. f11 SMC Pentax Reflex, a catadioptric lens, similar to an astronomical telescope, in which the light enters the lens front through a correcting plate, is then reflected forward by a precision-ground reflecting mirror to a tiny secondary mirror attached to the centre of the correcting plate. This mirror again redirects the light backwards through a clear hole in the main mirror to the camera body. By reflecting the light backwards and forwards in this manner the total length of the needed lens barrel is cut immensely. While reflex lenses have many advantages, including far closer focusing than comparative focal length all-glass lenses, they do have what some photographers feel are disadvantages. They have but one single aperture. If a smaller opening is needed to satisfy the exposure, neutral density filters must be used to cut the light. These of course can do so, but they do not increase depth of field as would a smaller lens aperture. Additionally, out-of-focus highlights in the photograph, instead of appearing simply as round circles, become round doughnuts with black holes in the middle, a phenomenon caused by the secondary reflecting mirror in the centre of the correcting plate. While many photographers have used these doughnuts or rings for added interest in their pictures, such rings are not natural and do not exist in the subject. Some other photographers may find them annoying.

1000 mm. f11 SMC Pentax Reflex, 6 elements in 4 groups, 2.5° picture angle, graduated in both metres and feet to 8 m. and 26.24 ft., 52 mm. accessory size threads at the rear, built-in filter wheel with 1X, 2X, 2.8X, 4X neutral density filters, skylight, Y48 yellow, O56 orange, R60 red filters, dimensions 119 mm. dia. × 248 mm. length (4 11/16 in. × 9 3/4 in.), weight 2,300 g. (80.5 oz.).

The Zoom Lens

We now come to an extremely interesting type of lens—the zoom. Anyone who has watched sports coverage on television

THE ADVANTAGES OF SUPER-MULTI-COATING

In present day optical glass, if left uncoated (A), about 7% of the light is reflected back from each side of a glass surface and does not reach the film. This reflection can be reduced by 75 per cent by applying a thin magnesium fluoride coating on the lens surface (B). This technique, used by most lens makers since World War II, can reduce reflection to 1.7% of the total light hitting the surface. With Super-Multi-Coating however (C), the amount of reflection is reduced to only 1/35 of that of an uncoated element. Total reflection is therefore cut to as low as 0.2% of the light.

Super-Multi-Coating improves light transmission and flare elimination in zoom lenses tremendously. Here we see a 14-element zoom lens. Without any lens coating (A), only 17.5% of the light would finally reach the film. With regular single coating of magnesium fluoride (B) about 66.3% of the light reaches the film. Asahi, using Super-Multi-Coating is able to transmit up to 95.3% of the light to the film or 50% more brightness than a standard single coating.

Now let's see how Super-Multi-Coating improves a standard normal focal length lens of 7 elements. With no coating (A), only 41.8% of the light reaches the film. With magnesium fluoride coating (B), 81.4% of the light gets to the film. Super-Multi-Coating (C) allows 97.6% of the light to reach the film.

has seen the advantage of the zoom lens. From a fixed camera-to-subject distance, a zoom lens seems to allow you to travel towards the subject area—or away from it if you start close. The zoom is actually a continuously variable focal length lens covering an infinite number of possible focal lengths between a minimum zoom and maximum zoom focal length.

In order to qualify as a true zoom, the lens must maintain focus throughout the zoom. That means if a zoom lens is once focused upon a subject, you can zoom to any focal length without the necessity of refocusing. This is important since there are so-called zoom lenses which are not really zoom lenses at all. They must be refocused at all different focal lengths. These are really multiple focal length lenses, not zooms.

While the zoom concept is not new, the successful application to the high standards of still photography is. Zoom lenses have many more lens elements than do ordinary lenses. Some of these move within the lens during the zoom thereby changing the focal length. To compensate for this lens element shift other elements must also move to maintain optimum sharpness. Until lens coating became practical for all lenses, such zoom lens designs were known but were not usable. The internal reflection from so many glass surfaces plus the light loss made the theoretical designs impossible in practical terms. The optical glass available was also inadequate for the high refraction indexes needed.

Even with the advent of coating and the use of high-refractive-index glass, most zoom lenses left much to be desired. Definition if good at one focal length was poor at others. Lens faults such as pincushion distortion (where straight lines at the edge of the picture area bow in) or barrel distortion (where lines bow out) were considered normal for zoom lenses. There was also lens flare showing as loss of contrast and distinct image separation with bright objects. Many zoom lenses suffer somewhat from such faults even today—but not the SMC Pentax zooms.

These lenses at any focal length and aperture equal the performance of most single focal length lenses.

The Pentax zooms cover a very wide range of focal lengths. All operate in what today is considered the most convenient manner: a single generous-sized control collar provides zooming by pushing and pulling the collar forward or backward while the same collar focuses the lens as you turn the collar. This so-called 'single-touch' system eliminates the need to shift back and forth between separate zooming and focusing controls used in the so-called 'two-touch' systems.

The advantages of a zoom lens are many. You can achieve the precise picture cropping you wish from a fixed camera to subject position by merely changing zoom focal length. The zoom, by taking the place of a number of standard focal lengths generally carried, makes it unnecessary for you to carry or interchange such lenses. For action subjects, you can continue to follow the action, keeping it in focus, near and far, without changing lenses to do so. Lastly, many interesting creative effects can be achieved by zooming during a long exposure.

The disadvantages of zoom are that, physically, even the smallest is considerably bulkier and heavier than any of the single focal length lenses that they replace. Secondly, the closest focusing distances of each, while satisfactory at long focal lengths, is often too distant for such usages as portraiture when the zoom is set for shorter focal lengths. For instance, if you used an 85 to 210 mm. zoom, it would focus down only to 3.5 m. or 12 ft., quite sufficient for 210 mm. But at a portrait-making focal length, around 100 to 135 mm., these minimum distances would be far too great for a close portrait which might require a 1 m. or 3.3 ft. close focusing distance, quite possible for the 100 mm. $f2.8$ SMC Pentax-M lens. When buying a zoom, always keep its close focusing ability in consideration.

The last disadvantage of a zoom is the relatively small maximum aperture. Zooms have speeds of $f3.5$ or smaller. If you intend to use the lenses indoors in poor light, this aperture might not be sufficient. An $f3.5$ lens cannot perform as well in poor light as an $f2.8$ or faster.

Can you substitute a single zoom lens for various focal lengths? Yes, if the advantages listed outweigh the disadvantages. However, you may wish to compromise. For instance, if you do intend to shoot pictures in low light, an 85 to 210 mm. $f3.5$ may be sufficient for your other work if you also buy a 85 mm. $f1.8$ SMC Pentax just for low light photography.

The Pentax zooms can be divided into three types: general purpose (45 to 125 mm.) which incorporate most of the focal lengths in general use: 50, 85, 100, and nearly 135; moderate tele (85–210 mm.) including most tele lengths such as 85, 100, 120, 135, 150 and 210 mm., and superlong tele (135–600 mm.) providing single tele lengths of 135, 150, 180, 200, 300, 400, 500 and 600 mm.

For general use the 45 to 125 mm. length will be the most helpful; for sports actions and candids, 85 to 210 mm. might be your choice, while the 135 mm. to 600 mm. length is excellent for professional sports photography where the lens can be placed on a tripod and the action followed.

The first two lenses can be hand-held easily, but the third needs a tripod. Between the two 85 to 210 mm. zooms the $f3.5$ represents a later design, not only providing greater light gathering power but also shorter maximum physical length and closer minimum focusing.

45–125 mm. $f4$ SMC Pentax Zoom, 14 elements in 11 groups, 50.5° to 20° picture angle, graduated in both metres and feet to 4 m. and 13 ft., $f22$ minimum aperture, 67 mm. accessory size, dimensions 69 mm. dia. × 127 mm. length (2 11/16 in. × 5 in.), weight 612 g. (21.42 oz.).

85–210 mm. $f3.5$ SMC Pentax Zoom, 12 elements in 11 groups, 29° to 12° picture angle, graduated in both metres and feet to 1.9 m. and 6.23 ft., $f32$ minimum aperture, 67 mm. accessory size, dimensions 76.5 mm. dia. × 207.5 mm. length (3 in. × 8 3/16 in.), weight 1,050 g. (36.75 oz.).

85–210 mm. $f4.5$ SMC Pentax Zoom, 11 elements in 10 groups, 29° to 12° picture angle, graduated in both metres and feet to 3.5 m. and 12 ft., $f32$ minimum aperture, 58 mm. accessory size, dimensions 67.5 mm. dia. × 217.5 mm. length (2 11/16 in. × 8 9/16 in.), weight 739 g. (25.87 oz.).

135–600 mm. $f6.7$ SMC Pentax Zoom, 15 elements in 12 groups, 18° to 4° picture angle, graduated in both metres and feet to 6 m. and 20 ft., $f45$ minimum aperture, 52 mm. accessory size thread at rear, dimensions 105 mm. dia. × 582 mm. length (4 1/8 in. × 22 15/16 in.), weight 4,070 g. (142.5 oz.).

Special-purpose Lenses

The 17 mm. $f4$ SMC Pentax Fish-Eye at first glance would

seem simply to be wider than usual wide-angle lenses. However, it is more than that. Unlike general purpose lenses, it has pronounced barrel distortion at the picture edges—that is the centre of straight lines bow out like a barrel while the ends of the lines curve inwards. The closer you get to the picture edges the more pronounced becomes this bowing.

Besides being able to cover an amazing angle for ultra-wide angle pictures, the barrel distortion can produce interesting effects in the hands of the creative photographer. Since you can see right through the lens using the Pentax finder, you can produce just the effects you wish by careful choice of viewpoint and subject matter.

17 mm. $f4$ SMC Pentax Fish-Eye, 11 elements in 7 groups, 180° picture angle, graduated in both metres and feet to 0.2 m. and 0.66 ft., $f22$ minimum aperture, built-in UV, yellow and orange filters, dimensions 64.5 mm. dia. × 34 mm. length (2 1/2 in. × 1 5/16 in.), weight 234 g. (8.19 oz.).

The normal focal length macro lens, specially computed for high resolution and mounted in a focusing mount allows focusing to a life size 1:1 image ratio. Such lenses have become popular among single lens reflex users. By limiting the maximum aperture to a moderate size, very high correction for optical faults can be made. In addition, an extremely flat field can be maintained which means that flat subjects can be copied at close range with excellent, even sharpness from centre to corners.

Such macro lenses need not be used only for specialised work. In their universal focusing mounts they can focus from the extreme close-up position right to infinity.

The 50 mm. SMC $f4$ Pentax-M Macro is suitable for high resolution normal photography and specialised close-up and copying work as well—all without any special accessories or adapters. In addition, the lens can be used on an enlarger.

Photographers desiring the highest standards of definition and colour correction at the expense of a larger maximum aperture may wish to consider the Macro-Takumar as their primary standard lens. Certainly for copying work, nature close-ups or scientific applications, it is ideal.

50 mm. $f4$ SMC Pentax-M Macro, 4 elements in 3 groups, 32° picture angle, graduated in both metres and feet to

0.234 m. (0.77 ft.), magnification 1:2, 49 mm. accessory size, dimensions 63 mm. dia. × 42.5 mm. length (2 1/2 in. × 1 11/16 in.), weight 160 g. (5.6 oz.).

Another macro lens, the 100 mm. *f*4 SMC Pentax-M Macro, is double the focal length of the 50 mm. *f*4 yet provides the same ability to focus from infinity to half life size. Because it is double the focal length, it can produce the same size image as the 50 mm. but at twice the film plane to subject distance. This means that the user can be twice as far away from difficult-to-photograph objects such as live insects and yet produce the same size image as with the 50 mm. lens. The extra focal length is important to still-life photographers too, such as those who make flower photographs. When shooting three-dimensional subjects at close range, there is less danger of apparent perspective distortion —closer parts appearing overly large as compared with the more distant ones. Flower photographers generally prefer a longer length lens for their close work and in the 100 mm. length they have an ideal one. Like the 50 mm. *f*4 SMC Pentax-M Macro, the 100 mm. *f*4 is highly corrected for definition, colour and linear distortion. For those who already have a standard 50 mm. lens on their Pentax and have hesitated to buy a second lens in the same focal length such as the 50 mm. *f*4 Pentax-M Macro, the lens will provide a length suitable not only for close-ups but also for general photography where a 100 or 105 mm. lens would be called for.

100 mm. *f*4 SMC Pentax-M Macro, 5 elements in 3 groups, 24.5° picture angle, graduated in both metres and feet to .45 m. and 1.48 ft., *f*32 minimum aperture, 49 mm. accessory size, dimensions 64.6 mm. dia. × 77.5 mm. length (2 1/2 in. × 3 1/16 in.), weight 355 g. (12.43 oz.).

However, there is still another method of operating the Pentax which allows you to focus continually from infinity to close-up—an equipment which produces an even greater close focusing image size than does either the 50 or 100 mm. *f*4 Pentax-M Macro lens. The 100 mm. *f*4 Bellows SMC Pentax is specially designed in a short mount to fit on the Pentax Auto-Bellows or Bellows Unit. With the bellows compressed, the lens can focus on infinity. With the bellows at maximum extension, you can achieve 1.62 magnification of the subject with the Auto-Bellows or 1.4 with the Bellows

Unit. However, it isn't simply the additional magnification that makes the Bellows-Pentax important. The Bellows-Pentax, like the 100 mm. *f*4 SMC Pentax-M Macro, is twice the focal length of the 50 mm. *f*4 Pentax-M Macro. You can achieve the same image size with the Bellows-Pentax as with the 50 mm. *f*4 Pentax-M Macro, but at a greater camera-to-subject distance. In photographing small live animals this is a great advantage of course. In addition you do get less apparent perspective distortion with three-dimensional objects with the Bellows-Pentax since you can remain further away from your subject.

Since the Bellows-Pentax has no scales except an aperture ring, the magnification and exposure factor scales have been engraved on the chrome bellows track of the Bellows Unit and on the removable scale of the Auto-Bellows. The Bellows-Pentax itself is specially designed, like the Macro Pentaxes, to produce extremely high definition with a very flat field, meaning that you can achieve good sharpness from picture centre to picture corner.

100 mm. *f*4 SMC Pentax Bellows, 5 elements in 3 groups, 24.5° picture angle, closest focusing distance at maximum bellows extension 22.17 in., *f*32 minimum aperture, 52 mm. accessory size, dimensions 60 mm. dia. × 40 mm. length (2 3/8 in. × 1 9/16 in.), weight 186 g. (6.51 oz.).

Anyone who has ever tried to photograph buildings with a 35 mm. camera has encountered the frustrating problem of converging vertical lines. In order to encompass an entire building or buildings (or a reasonable portion), it is often necessary to point the camera upwards. When the picture is produced, either as a negative or transparency, the buildings appear to be falling over backwards because their vertical edges converge.

There are several ways to combat this problem. If you have a negative, black-and-white or colour, some measure of correction can be had by tilting the enlarging easel or negative carrier (if physically possible) in the opposite direction of the tilt. The enlarger lens must be used at a very small aperture to provide sufficient depth of focus for such a tilt. Unfortunately, sometimes the tilt is too much for such correction or the final photograph is a transparency in which the buildings are destined forever to be falling over backwards.

P.W. 11—L

Owners of press and view cameras have long had recourse to the proper optical remedy. By first placing the camera back parallel to the buildings to be photographed and then raising the front standard with lens upward, parallel to the camera back, they have been able to encompass all the building(s) without tilting the camera upwards, therefore eliminating all converging lines.

Today, owners of Pentax cameras have a versatile wide-angle lens which provides the exact same movement as the view camera to prevent the need for tilting the camera. Using such a lens, converging lines can often be eliminated or at least minimized. This is the 28 mm. SMC f3.5 Pentax Shift lens.

The secret of the lens's success lies as much in its mount as in the optics. The entire lens assembly when mounted to a Pentax can be shifted 11 mm. parallel to the camera body at 30° intervals throughout the full 360° rotation. A large rotatable collar provides 12 click shift positions from o to 11 mm. It is only necessary to line up the camera with its back parallel to the buildings to be photographed and then shift the lens in the direction of the convergence. This can easily be seen on the camera's focusing screen. It is quite possible to shift in small increments while watching the view until the converging lines straight completely. The lens, of course, can also be used as a standard wide angle.

A shift lens has two other possible uses. By taking one photograph with full shift in one direction and a second photograph with full shift in the opposite direction, two photographs can be made which can be joined together for a perfectly matched, wider-than-normal 35 mm. panoramic view. Secondly, if you are photographing artwork which has a reflection when the camera is placed directly in front of the subject, it is possible to reposition the camera to the side of the artwork and then move the shift lens towards the artwork. You can then get the same angle of view and perspective as if the camera was in front of the art, but the reflection can often be eliminated completely.

28 mm. f3.5 SMC Pentax Shift, 12 elements in 11 groups, 75° picture angle, graduated in both metres and feet to 30 cm. and 1 ft., f32 minimum aperture, preset diaphragm, metering by stop down method, maximum shift 11 mm., 360° lens rotation with 12 stops at 30° intervals, built-in

Y-48 (yellow), O-56 (orange), Skylight filters; built-on gelatin filter holder, dimensions 80 mm. dia. × 92.5 mm. length (3 2/16 in. × 3 5/8 in.), weight 611 g. (21.39 oz.).

PENTAX ACCESSORIES

The most important accessories are fully described and their operation explained in the appropriate chapters, but there are a few other extremely useful items of which you should know.

Right-Angle Finders

Although the Pentax does not have an interchangeable view-finder—because the designers feel that a fixed, fully-enclosed prism has closer tolerances and is more dust-proof—there is often a need for viewing at waist level. This is provided by Right-Angle Finders which slide into grooves behind the pentaprism eyepiece and provide all the advantages of a waist-level finder plus a few others. Not only do they produce a brilliant magnified image of the entire focusing screen for horizontal shots, they can also be swivelled around for waist-level vertical photographs. This can't be done with an ordinary waist-level finder. The eyepieces of the finders is adjustable.

The Right-Angle Finders are especially useful for viewing subjects where it is inconvenient or even impossible to get behind the camera for ordinary eye-level prism viewing. If you have the camera on a copying stand or are taking pictures on or near the ground, such a finder is very convenient. They are also handy for candid photography. Since the finders operate at 90°, you can face in one direction but take pictures in another.

The most advanced right-angle finder for any Pentax camera is the Refconverter II and Refconverter M. Refconverter II, designed for K series cameras, provides a waist-level image which is seen correct right to left, meaning that all scales in the finder can be read easily and action followed conveniently through the finder. (Similar finders made for other cameras usually show images reversed as in a mirror, quite an inconvenience.) The Refconverter M is similar to the II but is designed to fit the Pentax ME and MX eyepiece.

PENTAX ACCESSORIES

Stereo attachment for Pentax provides two stereo images on each 35mm standard 24 × 36mm frame. Viewer holds mounted stereo slide.

Right angle finder allows Pentax to be used at low angles, for close-ups, on copy stands or other positions where it's inconvenient to view and focus directly through the prism finder.

Rubber eyecup slips over eyepiece, eliminates stray light from causing reflections on eyepiece, inflated exposure readings.

Magnifier offers 2X magnification for critical focusing.

Film magazine allows bulk film to be loaded into the Pentax without danger of scratching.

Dummy lens attaches to front of 200, 300mm Pentax and Takumar lenses, allows pictures to be taken at right angles thanks to an internal mirror.

Additionally it has a built-in 2× magnifier which is brought into the optical system by moving a small lever.

A less expensive finder in which the image is reversed right to left is available for K cameras as the Refconverter. However, it is only recommended for K cameras with no scales in the finder such as the K1000 or KM.

Focusing magnifier

For critical work at eye level, you may wish to enlarge the image seen in the viewfinder. This will allow you to focus with more precision. The Magnifier or Magnifier-M slides into the eyepiece grooves and offers a 2× enlargement of the central portion of the focusing screen. It is hinged so you can flip it out of the way instantly to view the entire screen area. Additionally, it accepts the SMC eyepiece correction lenses, Magnifier-M is for the MX and ME Pentaxes while the Magnifier fits the K series cameras.

Correction Lens Adapter & Lenses

For those Pentax users who need eyepiece correction before they can view and focus properly, there is a Correction Lens Adapter in two versions, plain for K series cameras and M for MX' and ME cameras. (Similar adapters have been available for older Pentaxes.) The adapter slides in grooves over the finder eyepiece.

Correction lenses to fit the adapter are available in 8 different diopter strengths: −5, −4, −3, −2, −1, +2 and +3 diopters. However, the Pentax viewing system itself has a diopter strength between −0.5 and −1. Therefore, should you need a correction of +2 diopters, you should purchase a +3 diopter correction lens (+2 − [−1]). Add the diopter correction lens strength to that of the viewfinder to get the total correction.

Eyecup

Eyeglass wearers often find that extraneous light reaches the camera eyepiece, causing reflections and perhaps inflating the meter reading. The Eyecup M (for M cameras) and Eye-cup II for K series cameraas shields the finder from such dangers. Many non-eyeglass wearers find it handy as well.

Film Cassette

The Asahi Film Magazine provides the Pentax owner who wishes to load his own bulk film with a precision all-metal film cassette. It comes apart quickly for loading and yet snaps together positively to prevent accidental opening when loaded with film. The Pentax film cassette can also be used in other 35 mm. cameras.

Lens Covers and Camera Caps

Rear Lens Covers are available to protect the rear of Pentax lenses when they are not attached to the camera. These simply bayonet directly on to the back of each lens.

Caps for the camera body bayonet into the front lens mount of the camera. Whenever the camera body is carried or stored without lens, the cap should be used to prevent dust, dirt or moisture from entering the camera body.

Mirror Adapter

A 90° mirror adapter screws into the front part of the 200 mm. *f*3.5 Takumar, the 200 mm. *f*4 Super-Takumar or SMC Pentax lens and the 300 mm. *f*6.3 Tele-Takumar. It contains a 45° reflex mirror which enables the user to "shoot round corners". The front of the adapter has a dummy lens. The viewing screen image when using this adapter is upright but reversed left to right. Maximum aperture is reduced to *f*5.6 and a slight increase in exposure is necessary.

Stereo Adapter

The Asahi Pentax Stereo Adapter set consists of the Stereo Adapter and Stereo Viewer. The Stereo Adapter fits the front frame of the Pentax 50 mm. or 55 mm. lens for taking stereo colour pictures (reversal colour/colour slides). The Stereo Viewer is for viewing the stereo colour slides.

When using the Stereo Adapter with a Pentax camera having a through-lens metering system, there is no problem in determining exposures, as the meter reads the exact amount of light coming through the Stereo Adapter and the taking lens. When using this adapter with a non-TTL camera, open up the diaphragm by a half stop to give optimum exposure.

Dial Data Backs

Both the Pentax MX and ME can be fitted with Dial Data Backs which are readily interchangeable with their standard backs. However, since the two cameras are of different body construction, the backs are not interchangeable between them. The Dial Data Backs allow the date or other information to be printed directly on the photograph as the picture is being taken. The built-in light is powered at the instant of exposure by three 1.5 volt silver oxide batteries. A light emitting diode flashes at the moment of printing to confirm the data recording. A battery check diode flashes when the B.C. button is depressed to insure sufficient battery voltage.

The Dial Data Back has three dials. The left dial is engraved with white numerals for the years 1976–1986 (76–86). The central dial has the months 1–12 and the right dial the days of the month (1–31). Additionally, the dials can be programmed, left to right, for recording the aperture, shutter speed or letters of the alphabet (A–M) and the frame number shot (0–36). In order to balance the exposure of the data and the picture, it is necessary to set the ASA index control on the Data Back for ASA 25–50 or 64–400. The data is imprinted in a corner of the picture where it will not interfere with the subject. The Dial Data Back on the Pentax ME can be seen on page 217.

Data MX Backs

The Pentax K2 DMD and a slightly modified Pentax MX can both be fitted with a Data MX Back readily interchangeable with their regular backs. However, neither the regular Pentax K2 nor MX can be so fitted. The special modified camera bodies must be so purchased originally. The camera bodies both have light-shield metal plates built into the film plane of the camera which can be moved into position or out when desired. When in position, the shield blocks out exposure from the lower right-hand corner of the film plane (upper left-hand corner of the photograph). In this blacked-out square the Data Back can print in the face of a clock indicating the exact time and date the picture was taken,

216

PENTAX DATA BACK

1. Data recording unit.
2. Film speed setting (ASA).
3. Battery check lamp.
4. External battery socket.
5. Battery check button.
6. Watch.
7. Battery chamber cover.
8. Terminals for cordless connection.
9. Shield plate.
10. Shield plate dial.
11. Data recording aperture.

To insert a new battery, remove the battery chamber cover by sliding in direction indicated by arrow. Insert a 6v silver oxide battery to match diagram at base of battery chamber. (Vinyl tape rests underneath battery for ease of removal later.)

The shield plate should be lowered into position as shown. The small square corner corresponds to the top left-hand corner of your viewfinder.

To remove the watch, raise watch grip, then turn to the left until it stops. Lift out. To replace, insert into compartment to match red dots. Turn to right until it stops and lower watch grip.

To wind watch, rotate arm back and forth as with ordinary watch. To set time, pull arm out one notch, then rotate. Pull arm out as far as it will go to change the date.

Set the ASA ring to the same film speed as that of the film currently in use. Colour film speeds of 64, 80 and 100 ASA are set at the 64-100 position. For Fujicolor F II 400, set ASA ring to the black and white 100 ASA position. Incorrect setting may result in over or under-exposure of the watch image, making if difficult to see.

plus additional data in the centre of the dial. Alternatively, the clock face can be removed and replaced with a circular all-data memo plate. One six-volt silver oxide battery powers the Data Back. To balance the clock face exposure and picture exposure, it is necessary to set the ASA index of the film on a dial atop the Data Back. There are four settings: three for black-and-white film (ASA 100, 200 and 400) and one for colour (ASA 64–160). LEDs flash to confirm the imprinting of data at each exposure and to indicate battery strength when the B.C. button is pushed. Electric coupling to the camera is done internally.

The Data Backs can be used for ordinary picture-taking or for scientific purposes where time, date or picture-taking information at the instant of exposure are necessary. By rotating the shield plate dial on the camera's focal plane with the ball of a thumb, the shield can be lowered and photographs made without data or the black corner.

THE PENTAX MOTOR DRIVE
SYSTEMS

The possible uses and conveniences of advancing film by motor instead of rapid wind lever, and automatically releasing the shutter for sequence photography, have multiplied considerably in recent years. While only a few years ago a motor drive for a 35 mm. camera was considered somewhat esoteric and only to be used by specialized professional photo technicians, motor drive cameras have found their way more and more into everyday photography for professional and amateur alike. Sports enthusiasts have discovered that a motorised camera lessens the chances of missing the peak action. Any continuing action such as a horse jumping over a fence or a diver springing from a board to the water below can be photographed in precisely timed, equally spaced photographs, thanks to a motor drive. The photographer can concentrate purely on exposure and focus. Botanists can do time-lapse studies of a flower opening by arranging for the motor to advance film and release the shutter at long prescribed intervals.

Certainly the advent of the simple inexpensive motorized winders such as those for the Pentax ME and MX cameras indicate the interest even by new camera buyers in automating their camera film advance systems. We have already covered these simple motors when discussing the cameras. In this chapter we will explain the motor drive systems which provide greater flexibility than the winders and often much higher speeds or, more correctly, additional frames shot per second.

There are three basic Pentax Motor Drive systems. The first has been designed for special models of the standard Pentax cameras. The earliest was available for the Pentax Spotmatic camera, then the Spotmatic II, while a slightly altered version now fits the Pentax ES II, Spotmatic F and Pentax KX cameras. Again, let me stress that the regular models of these cameras cannot be fitted or altered to accept the motor drive. The motor drive will only connect with those camera models specially manufactured for it that have the necessary electrical and mechanical couplings on the bottom of the camera body.

The second motor drive system, the Motor Drive MD, is for the Pentax K2 DMD camera. All K2 DMD cameras manufactured can accept the MD motor, but the standard K2 camera cannot.

The third motor drive system is the Motor Drive MX which is designed exclusively for the Pentax MX camera.

We will first discuss the Motor Drive System for the Pentax camera special models of the ES II, Spotmatic F and Pentax KX cameras. The Set 36 consists of a camera (Asahi Pentax ES II Motor Drive, Spotmatic F Motor Drive or Pentax KX Motor Drive) plus a motor drive unit II, 3 m. power cable, battery grip II with terminal cap, NiCad battery type 10/500 FZ, charge pack and battery checker. There are optional accessories such as a relay pack, power and timer.

If the standard 36 exposures of a normal film cartridge are insufficient for your needs, Set 250 provides the same equipment as Set 36 but adds a special 250-exposure bulk film magazine, cartridge loader and coupler. There are two versions of the bulk film back, Model IIF for the KX and Spotmatic F, and Model IIE for the Pentax ES II. They are not interchangeable.

Setting Up

To attach the motor drive unit, simply unthread the slotted cover on the end of the camera's bottom plate by turning it clockwise, attach the unit to the bottom of the camera and lock the two together using the knurled knob of the motor drive unit. To make sure that the drive and camera are correctly locked together and that the film wind mechanism meshes properly with the motor, slowly cock the rapid wind lever of the camera and depress the shutter button.

To attach the battery grip, turn the C/S wheel on the grip to the green dot and thread the grip to the base of the motor drive unit using the knurled knob of the grip. Make sure that the electrical contact of the grip fits properly into the hole of the motor drive unit. The grip can be loaded either with

MOTOR DRIVE MX

1. Trigger release button.
2. Grip.
3. Remote control socket.
4. Motor drive.
5. Battery grip mounting screw.
6. Battery grip M trigger release.
7. Battery grip M.
8. Exposure counter dial.
9. Bulk film back terminals.
10. Film rewind release.
11. Battery grip mounting screw.
12. LED.
13. Motor drive C/S dial.
14. Motor drive mounting screw.
15. Battery grip M C/S dial.
16. Remote control socket.
17. 3 m power cable M.
18. 10 m power cable M.

POWER PACK M

19. Main power pilot lamp.
20. Trigger button.
21. Timer knob.
22. Timer pilot lamp.
23. Remote control terminals.
24. Main power switch.
25. C/S switch.
26. Battery charge switch.
27. Timer-on switch.
28. Timer start switch.
29. Remote control socket.
30. DC terminals.
31. Fuse.
32. AC socket.

eight penlight size cells in a battery holder which will yield about 1500 exposures, or a rechargeable nickel cadmium battery—YUASA 10/500FZ (Japan), EVEREADY 10/BH500 (U.S.A.) or DEAC 10/500DKZ (Europe)—which offers about 2000 exposures per charge. We'll discuss NiCad batteries a little later.

Loading and Shooting

Load your camera as you would an ordinary camera and make two blank exposures to bring the camera's frame counter to 1. Make sure that the rewind knob turns when you throw the rapid wind lever, indicating that the film is running through the camera properly. Now turn the disc in the base of the motor drive unit and set the drive's own exposure counter to the number of frames you wish to expose. The counter is of the subtracting type. When it reaches zero, the unit will switch off automatically.

Next, turn the switch on the battery grip to S for single shots or C for consecutive sequence photography. With the switch at S, the camera exposes one frame when you press the grip's trigger button and winds automatically to the next frame when you release pressure. At C setting, the camera continues to fire frame after frame, up to 3 frames per second at 1/1000 sec., as long as you maintain pressure on the trigger button. After the last exposure, depress the film rewind release button of the motor drive unit and rewind the film with the folded rewind crank of the camera. You don't have to keep your finger on the rewind release button after you press it in once.

Use speeds 1/60 to 1/1000 sec. for consecutive sequence firing. With the Pentax ES II, 1/30 can be your slowest speed if the camera is operated in its auto exposure mode. For slower speeds, set the motor drive to S for single exposure. For either Bulb or Time exposures, set the control wheel on the back of the motor drive to B and the C/S switch on the grip to S. For time exposures, turn the C/S switch to "off" while pressing the trigger button. This keeps the shutter open. To close it, simply turn the C/S switch back again to S.

When the batteries are weak or near discharge, the exposure rate slows down slightly.

K2 DMD MOTOR DRIVE OPERATION

To mount the motor, open it up and fix it by the captive screw. Attach the battery grip below it in the same way.

Shoot off two blank exposures to wind on the fogged film, and set the counter for the number of frames on the film. The motor stops when the counter falls to zero.

The camera fires from either of the trigger release buttons. The C/S dial setting determines whether you set single or multiple exposures. Top: single shots, bottom I fps.

The battery grip C/S switch, with its central "off" position controls the battery grip trigger operation. The rate is still controlled on the motor dial (S gives 2 fps).

The battery pack (which can also be used remotely) holds 12 AA cells. To withdraw the battery holder, press the release slide.

A few words of warning: when using either the Spotmatic F or KX Motor Drive cameras at slow shutter speeds for single frame exposures, keep your finger pressure on the release button until the exposure is completed. If you don't, the motor drive will advance in mid-exposure and ruin your picture. Secondly, if you don't intend to use the camera for a few days, release the cocked shutter of the camera, using the camera body's own shutter release. This will untension all components and prolong the life of the spring mechanisms.

Cold Weather Operation

If you intend to operate the motor drive in cold weather, detach the battery grip when not in actual use and keep it warm in your pocket. It might be advisable in continuous cold weather to keep the battery grip in a warm place and connect it to the motor drive with various lengths of connecting cords which are available. In this manner the camera can be operated by remote control up to about 33 ft. distance. However, because of the increase resistance in the connecting cord, a separate relay pack or power pack is needed for greater distances.

When using the Pentax motor drive unit in cold weather be careful of sudden temperature changes. Wipe all parts to avoid condensation and wipe the nickel cadmium battery if one is used, before insertion in the battery grip.

Battery Checking and Charging

To check the amount of charge remaining in the nickel cadmium battery, insert the plug of the battery checker into the side socket of the battery grip with the grip's C/S dial set to C. The battery can still be operated if the checker's dial reads between 10 and 12. If below that, replace the battery or recharge. Don't use the battery checker for longer periods than 10 seconds or it will overheat.

To recharge the NiCad battery, set the C/S dial of the battery grip to the green dot, screw the fastening knob of the battery grip into the threaded hole of the charge pack, check to see that the contact of the battery grip makes contact with that of the charge pack and plug the charge pack cord into an AC outlet. Charging time is 14 hours but the unit can be

MX MOTOR OPERATION

To set the motor, remove the cover from the MX camera baseplate, and store it on the motor.

Attach the motor below the camera.

Mount either the Battery Grip M or the NiCd Battery Pack M below the Motor Drive.

Shoot off two blank exposures to wind off the fogged film before setting the counter to the number of frames on the film.

Select continuous (C) or single shots (S) and you can release the shutter with either of the trigger releases.

left charging up to 24 hours without harm. The average NiCad battery will last for a minimum of 100 recharging cycles. For best results, recharge the battery at temperatures above freezing but below 40°C. (104°F.).

Attaching the Bulk Film Magazine

All operating instructions for the Set 36 apply also to the Set 250. However, to use the 250 bulk film back you must first remove the camera's hinged back. Open the camera and swing out the back. Insert the small screwdriver supplied between the back cover hinge and the light seal from the inside of the back. Push the screwdriver towards the camera's base plate to unfasten the front shaft of the hinge. Now detach the top portion of the back. Detach the bottom portion by sliding in towards the camera's base plate. (When you want to replace the camera's regular back, just reverse these directions.)

To attach the bulk film magazine, turn the magazine's cartridge locking knob completely to the "open" position. Depress the set button and at the same time push the set lever with the white plastic roller to erect the camera's body retainer plate. Attach the camera body to the magazine by pressing the body and magazine together, making sure that the camera's film take-up chamber matches the film take-up chamber of the magazine. Check that all light seal edges of the magazine are properly set in the grooves of the camera body. Be careful during the entire procedure not to touch the thin film guide plate located over the film roller.

To lock camera and magazine, press the film rewind side of the camera body to the other side of the magazine. The camera and magazine will lock with a snap. Now return the locking knob to the "close" position to lock magazine and body completely.

Te remove the magazine, open the film cartridge locking knobs, push the set lever while depressing the set button to erect the camera's body retainer plate and lift the film rewind knob of the camera body. Disengage the film rewind side of the camera body from the magazine.

Using the Magazine Without Motor Drive

You can use the bulk film magazine and Spotmatic motor drive camera without the motor drive if you wish by attaching

MOTOR DRIVE K2 DMD

1. Aperture read-out window.
2. Trigger release.
3. Motor drive grip.
4. Motor drive MD.
5. Remote control socket.
6. Battery grip trigger release.
7. Battery grip.
8. Exposure counter set dial.
9. Exposure counter.
10. Rewind release lever.
11. Rewind release lock.
12. Remote control socket.
13. Motor drive C/S dial.
14. Battery grip C/S dial.
15. 3 m power cable M.
16. 10 m power cable M.

NiCd BATTERY PACK

The Battery Pack fits both K2 DMD and MX Motor Drive.
17. Power contacts.
18. Release button.
19. C/S dial.
20. Attachment screw.
21. Attachment screw slot.
22. Remote control socket.

the special coupler to the base of the camera body. Insert the threaded portion of the coupler into the receptacle on the base of the camera itself, making sure that the coupler's gears mesh properly with the gear of the magazine. Fasten the coupler by turning its knurled knob counter clockwise. Now cock the camera using the rapid-wind lever.

Attaching Motor Drive and Battery Grip

Attach the motor drive unit to the camera body and the battery grip to the motor drive unit as with Set 36. To activate the exposure counter of the bulk magazine, however, you must connect the outlet on the left rear of the motor drive unit with that on the bottom of the take-up side of the magazine using the exposure counter cord.

Loading Bulk Film Cartridge

To open the magazine and remove the bulk film cartridge for loading, first turn the locking knobs of the magazine to the "open" position. With your fingernail, pull out the magazine lock back. Pull away the back cover using the nipple, being careful not to drop the magazine back cover which is now completely detached. You can now remove the film cartridges from the film chambers by pulling out the release knobs.

The cartridges can be disassembled by pressing the round release button and turning the inner tube until the cut edge comes under the protrusion. You will now have three parts: film take-up spool, inner tube and outer tube.

Although you may wish to load the film cartridge in another way, you'll find the furnished filmwinder most convenient. With it you can use a standard 100 ft. bulk film spool and at one time load up to 33 ft. for 250 exposures.

To operate the loader, first pull out the winder handle and turn it so you can set the exposure counter dial to the number of frames you wish to load into the cartridge. The loader will automatically stop winding after this set amount has been loaded. The counter is conveniently marked in luminous paint for ease of operation in the dark.

In the dark, remove the bulk film from its can and place the bulk film spool on the rear wheel of the loader. To detach one of the rims of the reel, turn it counter-clockwise while holding the other rim. Place this reel on the shaft of

MOTOR DRIVE MX OPERATION

The Motor Drive C/S dial controls the motor rate whichever trigger you use. S: single shots. H: 5 fps. L: 0.5 fps. Intermediate settings are available. Note that on slow shutter speeds, the rate slows down as required.

The Battery Grip C/S switch affects the shooting mode when you use the Battery Grip Trigger. Its central portion also switches off the power. With the battery grip dial set to S, and the Motor Drive dial set to S, the motor operates as on the 'high' setting.

The NiCd battery pack also has its own dial, which works in the same way.

At the end of the film, operate the rewind release knob to allow the film to be rewound in the normal way with the camera's rewind crank.

On a tripod or copy stand, the Battery Grip M must be used at a distance through a Remote Cord M.

the winder and place the take-up spool of the cartridge on the other shaft. Erect the film holder and let it fall to the other side. Now pull the film over the sprocket gears and insert the leader end into the slit of the take-up spool. Cut the leader end to allow easy insertion into the slit.

Don't attach the film leader end to the take-up spool with tape because the film is not rewound after all exposures have been made. It is completely taken up on to the take-up spool of the bulk film back.

Push the film holder down so that the film perforations engage with the sprocket gears. A magnetic button keeps the film holder down in its working position.

Using the winding handle, wind the film until it stops automatically. After cutting the film, put the remainder of the bulk film back into its can. Remove the loaded take-up spool and reassemble the cartridge.

Insert the take-up spool into the inner tube and place in the outer tube. Turn the inner tube in either direction until it locks with the outer tube.

Loading Cartridges into Magazine

To load the bulk film magazine with the empty cartridges, drop the cartridges into the film chambers with the outer protrusion of the cartridges downwards. Turn the cartridges so that the two end protrusions drop properly into place. Push back the release knobs and reinstall the magazine back by reversing the procedure for removal. Turn the locking knobs to the "close" position.

To insert a loaded cartridge, place it in the film chamber and push back the release knob. Pull out about 10 inches of the film leader and insert the end into the slit of the other cartridge's take-up spool. Roll the film around the take-up spool about three times, emulsion side in, and check to make sure the film end is now secure on the take-up spool. Assemble the cartridge and insert it into the other chamber making sure that the sprocket gears of the camera body properly engage with the film perforations. Push back the release knob and place the magazine back on the camera as already explained.

Setting Exposure Counter

To set the film magazine exposure counter, make five blank exposures manually using the camera's rapid-wind lever to

MOTOR DRIVE
SYSTEM FEATURES

Here are the major operating parts and accessories for the Pentax Motor Drive 250 Set.

1. Back cover lock of bulk film magazine.
2. Film cartridge locking knob.
3. Set button.
4. Set lever.
5. Camera body retainer plate.
6. Film cartridge locking knob.
7. Bulk film magazine.
8. Motor drive unit.
9. Cordless battery grip.
10. Trigger button.
11. Back cover of film magazine.
12. Connector plug for film magazine exposure counter.

13. Bulb switch dial.
14. Battery grip attaching knob.
15. C/S (consecutive/single) switch dial.
16. Film magazine exposure counter.
17. Connector plug for film magazine exposure counter.
18. Motor drive unit exposure counter.
19. Film rewind release button of motor drive unit.

Soft leather case

advance film. Wind the lever again for the sixth exposure. Pull out the release knob and turn the exposure counter knob clockwise until the index points to the number of frames you wish to shoot. If there are fewer than 36 exposures remaining, you can set the counter to 0.

Checking Film Transport

The film is moving correctly if both release knobs of the film magazine turn clockwise when you wind film manually, using the rapid-wind lever, or if you use the motor drive unit. If both knobs are not moving the film leader is probably not secure on the take-up spool and you should rethread it.

Partial Unloading

You can remove just those frames you have already shot whenever you wish by first making five or more blank exposures to protect those frames already exposed. You can then open the magazine, cut the film and remove the cartridge with the exposed film. In rethreading the remaining film, you must reshape the leader edge and reload as if you were again placing fresh film in the magazine.

Automatic Switch-off

There is an automatic switch-off mechanism near the take-up cartridge within the magazine which will turn off the motor drive unit when all film has passed through or when the counter is at 0. Therefore the motor drive unit cannot be operated with the bulk film magazine unless there is film passing through the magazine.

Relay Pack Connections

The accessory relay pack allows the Pentax motor drive unit to be operated at distances greater than 33 ft. (the limit for simple cord connection), to be powered by a 12 volt DC source such as a car battery, and to trip the shutter release in a number of ways for trick photography, surveillance work or nature photography.

When using the loaded battery grip with the relay pack, connect the "Batt" socket with the remote control socket of the battery grip using an extension cord. Now connect the "Motor" socket with the remote control socket of the motor

HOW TO ASSEMBLE SET 36 MOTOR DRIVE UNIT

Remove threaded bottom cover by turning it clockwise using a thin coin edge in the cover slot.

Attach the top of the motor drive unit to the base of the camera by turning fastening knob to the right. Secure tightly.

Slowly cock camera's rapid wind lever and depress shutter release button to assure correct coupling of film winding mechanism.

With C/S switch at green dot, attach battery grip top to base of motor drive unit with protruding thread. Turn knob to right to secure.

HOW TO ASSEMBLE SET 250 MOTOR DRIVE UNIT

With camera back fully open, insert screwdriver (supplied) between back cover hinge and light seal. Push screwdriver toward's camera's base plate to disengage front shaft of hinge. Detach bottom portion in same manner. (Reverse procedure to re-install back.)

Camera back may now be removed.

To attach bulk film magazine, depress set button near fully opened film cartridge knob. Push set lever and erect camera body retainer plate.

Align film takeup side of camera with film takeup side of magazine. Magazine's light seal edges must be properly set in camera body grooves.

Push film rewind side of camera body to other side of magazine. Magazine will lock to camera body with snap. Return locking knob to close position.

To use motor drive camera and film magazine without motor drive unit, attach coupler to base of camera body.

drive unit. To activate the camera and motor drive unit, you can either press the trigger button of the relay pack or use the battery grip button.

By attaching extension cords to the two remote control terminals of the relay pack and touching them together, the camera can also be made to fire and advance film. By using these two extension cords as the connection for various tripping devices, the relay pack can be used to set off the camera in all sorts of novel ways—when an animal enters a trap, when a door or window opens, etc.

On the back of the relay pack is a C/S switch. Operate it and the trigger button in the same way you operate these controls on the battery grip.

Power Pack Operation

The accessory power pack performs all the functions of the relay pack and will in addition run the motor drive from a 50–60 cycle AC line of 110, 120, 200, 220 or 240 volts and act as a battery charged. When ordering the unit specify the voltage of the AC line on which it will be operated.

When using the power pack's DC input terminals to connect it to a 12 volt DC source, be sure that the AC input and "Batt" sockets are plugged off. When attaching the loaded battery grip to the power pack, keep the power pack switch "off". When using the power pack with other 12 volt DC sources, you can keep its switch either "on" or "off". The pilot lamp won't light in either case.

To use the power pack as a relay pack, follow all directions given previously for the relay pack. To use it as an AC pack, connect the AC input socket to an AC outlet. Connect the "Motor" socket with the remote control socket of the motor drive unit. When the power pack switch is turned on, the pilot lamp will light indicating that the power pack is in operation. Now operate as you would the relay pack.

To use the power pack to recharge your NiCad battery in the battery grip, connect the NiCad battery-loaded grip with the "Batt" socket of the power pack. Connect the AC input socket with an AC line outlet and turn on the switch. The pilot light will go on and charging will begin. Charge for the same time as indicated with the regular battery charger already described. However, you can still run your motor drive unit from the power pack while charging the battery.

FEATURES AND ACCESSORIES

For exposures other than B or T, set bulb switch at arrow (1) and C/S switch (3) at S. For B (bulb) exposure, set bulb switch at B (2) and C/S switch (3) at S. For T (time) exposure, set bulb switch at B (2) and C/S switch (3) at S.

Battery loader accepts 8 penlight cells readily available in many countries. Approximately 1500 exposures can be made on one set.

To check battery, plug checker (1) into side socket of battery grip. Set C/S dial (3) to C (which also means "check"). Good battery should read 10-12 in black area. When recharging ni-cad battery, set C/S switch (3) to green dot.

To set film magazine exposure counter, make 5 blank exposures manually, cock rapid wind lever for 6th shot, pull release knob downwards, turn exposure counter knob clockwise until index points to num-ber of exposures you wish to make.

Film roller in magazine near takeup cartridge auto-matically switches off motor drive unit after film has run over roller.

To remove film cartridge turn locking knobs to open position, pull out edge lock with fingernail and pull back cover away using nipple.

Keep a good grip on back cover which is now completely separated.

Pull out release knobs and remove film cartridges from film chambers.

To insert film cartridges, drop them into the film chambers with the pro-truding outer lip down.

While operating the power pack, if the pilot lamp does not go on, the fuse may have burned out. You can check the conditions of the fuse easily by removing the fuse cover.

Remote Control Operation

Either the relay pack or the power pack must be used if you wish to control the motor drive unit at a distance of more than 33 ft. First connect the motor drive unit with the relay or power pack using the extension cord. Then connect the pack being used with the battery grip, the 12 volt DC power source or the AC outlet using the power pack. Connect the remote control terminals of the relay pack with the extension cord. By using a small switch at the end of the extension giving intervals between 5 and 60 seconds, 2 and 60 minutes cord or shortcircuiting the cord by bringing its two wires together, you can cause the motor drive unit to operate.

The length of the extension cord from the motor drive unit to the relay or power pack must not exceed about 33 ft., but the extension from either pack to the switch can be up to 20,000 ft. depending on the amount of resistance within the cord. The maximum permissible resistance of the extension from pack to switch is 365 ohms.

A radio control unit is available for remote control of the motor drive system. Its receiver connects with the radio control terminals of the power pack. The transmitter sends signals from about 1500 ft. (outdoors on flat ground) to operate the motor drive unit, change the C/S switch of the power pack and check whether the camera shutter is operating correctly.

Timers for Time-lapse Sequences

Three different AC powered timers are available to activate the motor drive unit through the relay or power pack at any preset time interval. There are second, minute and hour timers and 1 and 24 hours respectively. When ordering, specify the intervals required and the working AC voltage. All timers can be used either for 50 or 60 cycle operation. Each timer has an AC outlet at the rear to connect flood or other light sources for photographic illumination up to a maximum of 600W.

By turning the rotary switch at the bottom left of the timer to Position 1, only the rear AC outlet is switched on. At

Position 2 the timer is also switched on. After you have set the needle of the timer dial, the remote control terminals at the back of the unit automatically activate the motor drive unit when the dial reaches zero after each elapse of the set time.

At Position 3, the timer is switched on and the AC outlet cuts in two seconds before shutter release so that your subject is lit automatically. The lights are switched off again after each exposure.

At the bottom right of each timer is a reset button which allows you to reset the timer to the preset time before the timer reaches the zero mark.

There are two pilot lamps on the front of the timer. The left-hand lamp lights when the AC outlet is switched on. The right-hand lamp is illuminated when the timer is switched on.

K2 DMD Motor Drive

The Motor Drive MD II for the Pentax K2 DMD camera makes provision for standard 36-exposure cartridges only. No 250-exposure bulk film back is available. However, a Data Back MD can be fitted for imprinting data directly on the film frame as it is being shot.

To attach the MD Motor Drive to the K2 DMD, rotate the tripod socket screw of the motor clockwise so that the screw threads into the socket and fastens motor and camera together securely. Now set the C/S switch to the green dot "off" position and attach the Battery Grip M to the Motor Drive MD with the battery grip's tripod screw. An alternative to the Battery Grip M (which operates on 12 AA-size penlight batteries) is the NiCad Battery Pack M. This provides a more compact combination since the NiCad battery pack fits horizontally under the motor rather than fastening vertically. The NiCad pack has the advantage, too, of being rechargeable. The penlight cells must be disposed of after they become weak.

Load the camera, Set the C/S dial of the battery grip or NiCad pack to "S". Make two blank exposures, using the trigger release of the motor drive. If, instead, you use the rapid wind lever on the camera, there's a chance that the camera shutter release button may lock. If this happens, you can release the shutter by pressing the trigger release. If the exposure counter reads zero, however, the motor drive will stop. In this case, move the exposure counter setting dial in the direction of the white arrow on the back of the motor.

After you've made your blank exposures, reset the exposure counter to read the number of exposures you intend to shoot —usually 20 or 36 depending on whether you've loaded a 20- or 36-exposure roll. Remember that the motor will always stop when the counter reaches zero.

You can fire the motor drive with either the trigger release on the front motor drive grip or the trigger release on the battery grip. If you are using the motor drive trigger release, set the C/S dial of the battery grip to C or S. However, if you set the battery grip dial to the green dot, the motor will be switched off and you won't be able to fire it from motor drive grip trigger.

With the battery grip or NiCad pack C/S dial set to either C or S, you can set the motor drive C/S dial to C for continuous sequence shots or to S for single shots. On C, you can adjust the firing rate. If you turn the dial counter-clockwise all the way to the right-hand end of the orange band, you can make exposures at 2 frames per second with shutter speeds between 1/60 and 1/1000 sec. If you move the dial to the left-hand end of the orange band, you will achieve 1 frame every 2 sec. With a mid band setting the camera will deliver 1 fps. The dial can also be set anywhere in between.

The battery grip C/S dial does not have such a choice of firing speeds.

When you use the trigger release on the battery grip set to S, you will get single exposures. When you set the battery grip dial to C, the actual firing rate will be controlled by the position of the motor drive C/S dial. If the motor drive C/S dial is set to S but you fire the camera from the battery grip or NiCad pack with its dial set to C, the frames per second speed will be 2. The firing rate is adjustable for all camera shutter speeds between 1 sec. and 1/1000 sec. However, between 2 and 8 seconds, the film will be advanced immediately as soon as the shutter closes.

It might seem highly unnecessary to complicate matters by having two C/S dials, one on the motor and another on the battery grip or NiCad pack. However, the grip or NiCad pack can be removed from the motor and used as a remote control by attaching either a 3 m. or 10 m. power cable from the remote control socket of the MD motor drive to the socket of the battery grip or NiCad pack. The C/S dial of the grip or NiCad pack can then operate the motor at a distance with the C/S dial on the motor drive itself previously set for whatever continuous firing speed you wish.

A word of caution when using the B setting of the shutter speed dial with the motor in operation. No matter where the C/S dial is set, the shutter will not close until you remove your finger from the trigger release. During this exposure, the batteries within the camera are powering the shutter action and thus draining. It is therefore not advisable to use long B exposures since the total life of the camera battery is 15 hours. This battery-powered B exposure when the motor is used differs radically from B exposures using the K2 DMD camera alone. With the camera alone, the B is purely a mechanical shutter speed and requires no battery power.

To change batteries in the battery grip, slide the battery holder lock of the battery grip toward the white arrow on the holder. When replacing the dead batteries with new ones, make certain that the batteries are inserted into the holder in the proper plus and minus orientation as per the diagram on the battery holder. You can tell easily when it is time to change batteries. The speed of the motor advance will drop. However, one single set of batteries should power up to 40 rolls of 36-exposure film. If alkaline energizer batteries are used, up to 100 rolls can be run. With the rechargeable nickel cadmium battery pack, you will be able to shoot up to 40 rolls of film on one charge. For information on life of the NiCad battery pack and instruction on recharging, turn to the following pages on the Motor Drive MX which uses the same NiCad battery pack.

Coming back to the K2 DMD and its Motor Drive MD, we still must remove the film from the camera at the end of the film. Depress the rewind lever lock button. Hold it in and push the rewind lever itself in the direction of the arrow. Now you can release the rewind lever and rewind film into the original cartridge using the unfolded rewind crank. If you can't get the rewind lever to budge, unfasten the Motor Drive MD and depress the rewind button on the bottom of the camera itself before rewinding.

Motor Drive for Pentax MX

The Motor Drive MX, which operates only in conjunction with the Pentax MX camera, provides single exposure operation, sequence photographs up to 5 fps, operation with standard 20- or 36-exposure cartridges or by means of the 250-exposure bulk film back, and much greater picture-taking capacity.

Three separate power sources are available. There's a standard Battery Grip M which operates on 12 AA-size penlight cells. With alkaline energizers some 100 rolls of 36-exposure film can be powered before battery exhaustion. The NiCad Battery Pack M fits beneath the motor horizontally, forming a much more compact camera–battery combination. It weighs some 20 per cent less than Battery Grip M and can expose up to 40 rolls of film on one 6-hour charge. The Pack M can be recharged some 300 times before it need be replaced. Thus cost is considerably less than batteries over a long period of operation. Power Pack M operates from AC mains, and has a built-in timer for interval or time-lapse photography. It is the most economical power supply.

To attach the Motor Drive MX, remove the Camera Body Film Transport Coupler Cap by rotating it counterclockwise with the edge of a coin. To avoid misplacing the cap, thread it directly into the screw thread receptable designed for it atop the motor drive platform. Fasten motor drive and camera securely to each other by threading the attachment screw of the motor into the camera's tripod socket and tightening it.

Before attaching Battery Grip M, make certain the grip's C/S switch is turned to "off" by aligning the two green dots. Then thread the Battery Grip M attachment screw into the motor's tripod socket. Fasten securely by rotating the screw clockwise.

If you are using the NiCad Battery Pack M instead of the Battery Grip M, thread the pack into the motor with the edge of a coin by twisting the grooves of the screw head until the pack is securely fastened to the motor drive.

After loading the Pentax MX with film, shoot two blank photos to bring fresh unexposed film into the film plane— as you would normally without the motor drive. Rotate the Exposure Counter Dial of the motor drive clockwise to the number of exposures you intend to shoot. We'd suggest you use the rapid wind lever and shutter release of the camera itself to check on the proper loading of the camera. If the camera has been loaded properly, the rewind knob will rotate each time you advance film.

Now set the C/S dial of the Battery Grip or NiCad Pack to S for single exposures or to C if you wish continuous film wind and automatic shutter release. When the motor is not in use, keep the switch at "off" with the two green dots aligned. This will prevent accidental firing.

You can either fire the camera plus motor drive by using the Trigger Release atop the Motor Drive Grip itself or the Trigger Release on the Battery Grip. If you have attached the NiCad Pack, you'll find a release button at the back of the pack.

If you wish to use the Trigger Release Button on the Motor Drive MX Grip, set the Motor Drive's C/S dial to S for single exposures, H for high-speed consecutive shots, L for low-speed consecutive shots or anywhere between H and L that you need. At shutter speeds of 1/60 to 1/1000 sec., the Motor Drive MX will run at top speed—5 frames per second—when the C/S dial is set to H. And at 0.5 fps when the dial is set at L. If you use speeds of 1/30 sec. or slower, the fps will correspond to the shutter speed set, no matter how the C/S dial is set between H and L.

If you use the Trigger Release Button of the Motor Drive MX Grip, the setting of the C/S dial on the Battery Grip is of no importance since it will be overridden by your controls on the motor drive itself. The method of firing, single or continuous, is always controlled by the C/S dial of the unit you are using to fire. If you use the B setting on your shutter speed dial, the shutter will remain open as in a T or time exposure. You can then complete the exposure by turning the shutter speed dial to any speed faster than 1/8 sec.

When you use the Battery Grip's Trigger Release Button, the Battery Grip C/S dial will control single or continuous pictures. However, the actual speed of continuous firing will be determined by the setting between H and L on the Motor Drive's C/S dial. If the Motor Drive's C/S dial is set to S and the Battery Grip or NiCad Pack dial is set to C, you will get high-speed continuous firing just as if the motor's dial was switched to H.

P.W. 11—N

Following the last exposure, the Motor Drive will lock to prevent the film end from being torn from the film's supply spool. To rewind film, slide the Film Rewind Lever leftwards and then push it upwards. This will push in the camera's own rewind button. Now rewind film with the rewind crank as you would if the motor drive was not attached.

If you wish to use the MX Motor Drive on a copy stand or tripod, it cannot be attached with the Battery Grip M in place. Either a 3 m. or 10 m. power cable must be attached between the motor drive and the battery grip so the camera and drive can be mounted on the tripod or copy stand and operated remotely by the Battery Grip. The NiCad pack can be used similarly but can be allowed to remain on the motor drive if convenient, since it can be fastened directly to a tripod or copy stand through its bottom tripod socket. Even if you let the NiCad pack remain fastened to the motor drive, the camera can still be fired remotely by attaching the accessory 3 m. Remote Trigger Connector into the Motor Drive MX's Remote Control Socket. To operate the motor, simply bring the two contacts at the end of the connector together. This same method of remote control can be used with the Battery Grip M. The distance at which the camera can be operated by remote control can be extended over two or three hundred meters (600 to 1000 ft) by attaching ordinary household two-lead electrical cable to the Remote Trigger Connector M.

Batteries are loaded into the Battery Grip M in the same manner as described with the Standard Pentax Motor Drive System. The NiCad Battery Pack M however requires some special attention for optimum efficiency. When it is in use and the film transport gets sluggish, the pack should be recharged using the accessory Charge Pack M or the Power Pack M (which we will be discussing later). To recharge the Pack M, insert the plug of Charge Pack M into the remote control socket of the NiCad Battery Pack M with the groove face of the plug facing up. Use the lock ring to hold the plug in place. Connect the Charge Pack M to the AC mains by means of the wall plug. Set the C/S Dial of the NiCad Pack to either C or S. The red charge lamp should now go on, meaning that charging has started. A full charge will take 6 hours. Overcharging beyond 8 hours should not be undertaken. While the pack can be recharged some 300 times before before discarded, maximum NiCad battery life is about 3 years regardless of whether the battery is used or not. After the 3 years or 300 charges, consult your Pentax dealer who can arrange to have the NiCad battery replaced in the Battery Pack M.

When recharging, the ambient temperature range during the recharging should remain between 0–40° C (32–104° F). At higher temperatures, full battery charge will not be reached. Also, charging the battery at excessively high or low temperatures shortens battery life. Temperature and humidity conditions are also important when storing the Battery Pack. 10–25° C (50–77° F) is ideal. High humidities are to be avoided. Following a long period of non-use, do not attempt to operate the motor drive with the NiCad Pack until the battery has been recharged. If the battery is not in regular use, it should be taken out and recharged at least once every other month or battery life and performance will be curtailed.

If you must use your motor drive in low temperatures, your NiCad or penlight cell batteries will not be efficient. To obtain maximum efficiency use fresh penlight cells or a just-recharged NiCad battery pack. If possible, keep the batteries warm until just before you will need them.

The Power Pack M is a most versatile instrument with multiple uses. It can be used as an AC power source, as a 5 to 120 sec. timer and intervalometer, as a 12–15 volt DC power source, as a remote control power source or as a recharger for the NiCad Battery Pack M (in which case the regular accessory Charge Pack M is not needed).

To use Power Pack M as an AC power source, fasten either the 3 m. or 10 m. power cable between the Motor Drive MX Remote Control Socket and the Remote Control Socket or Power Pack M. Remove the cap from the power pack's AC socket at the rear of the power pack and attach the AC cord, securing it in place with the knurled metal locking ring. Plug the AC cord into an AC wall outlet.

When you switch on the main power, the main power pilot lamp will light. You can operate the motor drive either with its own C/S Trigger Release Button or that on the Power Pack M, but remember to set the C/S switch to the proper position on the unit being used to trigger the camera.

When operating the Power Pack M as a timer, the C/S switch position is of no importance. Set the timer knob for the time delay you wish or between shots. The setting can be at the marked 5 to 120 sec. intervals or anywhere between. When the timer switch is set to "On" the red timer pilot lamp will illuminate. When you set the timer start switch to "Start", the camera shutter will be tripped after the number of seconds dialed on the timer knob. After 50 per cent of the timing interval selected, film will automatically be advanced and, at the set time dialled, the second exposure will be made. This will be repeated automatically until the timer start switch is set to "Stop" or the end of the film is reached.

You can use the Power Pack M as a power source for 12–15 volt DC current (the same as an auto battery). At the rear of the Power Pack M are two DC terminals which can be connected to a 12–15 volt, 2 ampere or more, DC input. When connecting the input, make certain the plus and minus terminal designations are properly observed. With a 12 volt source, the film transport will be rather slow and the fps exposure will drop.

When you are using a DC power source, the main power switch should be set to "DC–ON". The main power pilot lamp will not light, however. All operations with the Power Pack M can be carried out on DC as on AC, but the timer cannot be used.

To recharge the NiCad Battery Pack M with Power Pack M, connect a 3 m. power cable from the remote control socket of the NiCad Battery Pack M to that of the Power Pack M. Set the Battery Charge Switch to "Bat. Charge". Charging will take from 10 to 15 hours.

You can fire off two motor-driven Pentax MX cameras simultaneously by connecting remote control trigger connectors to each camera and then shorting the contacts by connecting the plus (+) terminals of one lead to the minus (−) terminals of the other lead. Of course, both motor drives must have been connected to a power source.

The back cover of the Pentax MX camera can readily be interchanged with Magazine Back MX. This cordless connection provides up to 250 exposures with bulk film.

THE PENTAX EXPOSURE
METERS

Two of the more important accessories for users of the earlier Pentaxes without meters are the two separate exposure meters. The clip-on meter is designed to fit the S1, H1, H1a, S1a, S3, H3, SV and H3v cameras.

Attaching the Clip-on Meter

To attach the clip-on meter to your camera, you depress the two release levers on either side of the meter eyepiece and slip the meter over the prism housing. You then release the levers and the meter locks in place. To lock the coupling, rotate the meter shutter speed dial until the coupling pin on the bottom of the meter dial couples with the slot in the camera's shutter speed dial.

To use the meter, you must first set the ASA index for your film on the film speed setting collar. Hold the ribbed film speed dial firmly between your right thumb and forefinger so it doesn't turn. Make sure the white dot is upwards where you can see it. Now with your left thumb and forefinger rotate the shutter speed dial of the meter. As it rotates, you will see that the white dot will change ASA indexes with a positive click for each setting. Continue turning the shutter speed dial until the proper ASA setting is opposite the white dot.

The meter has a three-way switch on top marked L (for low light), H (for high light) and "Off".

To turn on the meter, rotate the switch to the H position and point the meter towards the subject. If there is insufficient light to move the needle indicator on top of the meter to the first broad black stripe on the meter needle dial, turn the meter off again and rotate the switch in the other direction to L. However, never set the "L" for low light setting until you have found that the "H" for high light scale is not usable. If bright light hits the meter cell while it is in the low light position, the cell can be permanently damaged or at least temporarily made unable to measure low light illumination accurately.

Reading the Meter

To make a reading, turn the shutter speed dial of your meter to the setting you wish to use, note the position of the needle indicator on the scale and read off the recommended aperture opposite the appropriate broad black or chrome band. Set the camera's lens to this aperture and you're ready to make a picture.

In the "off" position, the meter needle indicator should line up with the short black line at the right of the meter needle scale. If it does not, you can readjust "zero point" by turning a small zero readjust screw on the back of the meter.

Changing the Battery

You can check battery life in an instant. At the hub of the light level switch is a small green button. When the button is pressed, the meter needle should swing over the meter scale to a green scale marking. If it does, the battery is usable. If it does not, the battery needs to be replaced.

On the underside of the meter you will find a circular battery hold-down cover and arm. Swing the arm to the side, off the cover. Replace the battery with a Mallory 625 or similar mercury battery.

The Asahi Spot Meters

The Pentax Spotmeters made by Asahi rank among the most accurate and useful exposure measuring instruments in the world. These are the Asahi Pentax Spotmeter V (the latest model) and the Digital Spotmeter. These meters, unlike the built-in through-the-lens camera meters, do not produce a reading of the entire picture area. Instead, they accurately measure a spot of only 1° of arc—from any distance from the subject.

The spot meter is particularly useful when long-focus lenses are used. With it you can make an extremely accurate reading of a distant object—an on-stage performer right from your theatre seat, a boat far out in the ocean. You need not attempt to take close-up readings by approaching close to the subject or finding an appropriate substitute nearby. It can

246

CLIP-ON METER FEATURES

Here are the features of the Pentax clip-on and coupled exposure meters.

1. Shutter speed dial.
2. "Low", "High" and "Off" switch.
3. Battery check button.
4. Needle indicator.
5. F/stop scale.
6. Light window.
7. Film speed dial.
8. Film speed setting.
9. Battery hold down.
10. Mercury battery.
11. Zero adjust screw.
12. Camera attachment clips.
13. Shutter speed coupling pin.
14. Release lever.
15. Film speed index mark.

Here are the features of the earlier clip-on meter.

1. Shutter speed dial.
2. "Low", "High" and "Off" switch.
3. "Low" light position.
4. "Off" light position.
5. Aperture scale.
6. "High" light position.
7. Needle indicating scale.
8. Needle indicator.
9. Light window.
10. Film speed setting.

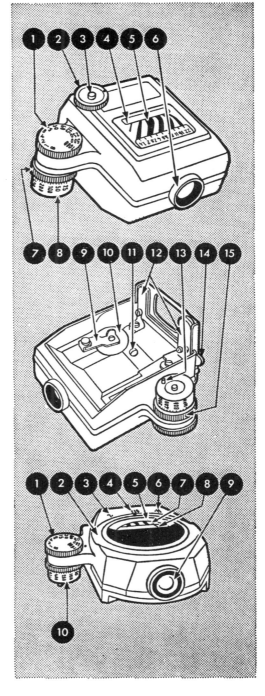

also take readings from very small objects, such as a tiny flower a dozen feet away. Moreover, it gives you an accurate check on the relative brightness of all objects within the picture area, which can be useful if you are afraid that the brightness range of a scene may be too great for accurate colour reproduction.

The spot meter consists of a one-piece body with attached handle made out of high-impact, crack-proof plastic. At the back of the housing is an eyepiece which allows you to view the scene through the lens at the front of the meter. When you hold the meter to your eye you will see a right-side-up rectangular viewing image of 21°. In the centre of the field you will see a small engraved circle. This 1° circle is the area actually measured by the spot meter.

Using the Spotmeter V

The actual operation of the Spotmeter V is relatively simple. Hold the meter to your eye by grasping the handle. Turn the adjustable eyepiece until you can see the engraved scale within the meter clearly. Don't try to look *through* the meter at a scene. Instead, concentrate your eye focus *on* the scale engraving itself. Point the meter at the subject to be measured. Place the centre measuring ring directly over the most important or representative area of the subject. Depress the metering button. The meter needle within the finder will climb to a point on the meter scale. (Note: Earlier Spotmeter models had both a high and low light scale. If the meter needle did not respond on the high scale, you pressed the low light scale button. The Spotmeter V is more convenient, having one single elongated scale.)

The calculator dial for the spot meter is located on the left side. First set the ASA or DIN film speed index in the two central curved film speed windows. To do this, push on the two metal nipples so that the inner calculator dial rotates to the proper ASA setting. Now turn the outer ring to match the light level number read by you against the white triangular pointer at the bottom of the calculator dial. You can now read all the possible *f*-number and shutter speed combinations on the outer rings on the top of the calculator dials. Any of the couplings will produce correct exposure. The entire dial is marked in full *f*-numbers and mathematical

METER ANGLE COVERAGE

Discontinued clip-on Pentax meters cover a 40° angle of view which is just slightly less than the angle seen by the normal lens of the camera. Pentax cameras featuring averaging behind-the-lens meter see a 46° angle of view duplicating the exact angle of the 50 mm. lens. However, this metering angle varies with each different focal length fitted to the camera. The Pentax behind lens meter always covers the same angle of view as the lens fitted. The Pentax Spot Exposure Meters cover a very narrow angle of 1° to give you pinpoint exposure accuracy of even a tiny area at a great distance.

shutter speed progressions, but there are in-between markings indicating 1/3 f-numbers as well. In low light, when the meter scale is difficult to read, press the scale illuminator button on the side of the meter.

A spot meter must be used with much thought. If it is, it will certainly yield the best exposed pictures, particularly with colour transparency films where exposure must be extremely accurate.

The single meter reading made from one part of a subject will seldom be sufficient in actual shooting unless the single object read has a brightness the same as the rest of the picture area. To use the meter fully, take a reading of the brightest area in which you wish to hold high light detail. Then make a second reading in the shadow area in which you wish to hold detail. Use the calculator dial to find the proper exposure for each of these areas. In black-and-white photography, films can generally handle any brightness range up to 7 full f-stops. In other words, should the shadow reading suggest 1/30 at f2 and the high light reading come to 1/30 at f16, an exposure of about 1/30 at f5.6 will give you a negative adequately exposed through the whole range. Negative colour film would probably find this a little too much and it would be advisable to bias your exposure towards the end of the scale in which you wish to obtain most detail. Colour transparency film can handle the brightness range, but only at the expense of true colour rendering. Here it is advisable to bias your exposure towards the high light reading unless the shadow colours are of vital importance.

The spot meter has a usable shutter speed range from 4 minutes to 1/4000 sec. and an aperture range from f1 to f128. It can handle films from ASA 6 to ASA 6400. The silicon photo diode cell circuit is powered by three G-13 batteries. Older model Spotmeters used one 1.3 volt mercury battery (Mallory RM640, Eveready E640 or equivalent) and one 9-volt dry battery (Mallory M 1604, Eveready 216 or equivalent).

Checking the Battery

To check battery life, hold the meter to your eye and press the small button marked "B" above the light metering button. The meter needle should swing over to a short black

1. Objective lens.
2. Zero adjustment screw.
3. Battery checker button.
4. Light metering button.
5. **Adjustable eyepiece.**
6. **Shutter speed scale.**
7. **Diaphragm scale.**
8. **DIN scale.**
9. Index for DIN scale.
10. ASA scale.
11. Index for ASA scale.
12. Light level scale.
13. Index for light level scale.
14. Battery housing cover.
15. Outer ring for matching light level.
16. Film speed setting plate.
17. Nipple for turning inner disc.
18. Scale illuminator button.

When using meter, place small central spot over area to be read. In bright light read needle on top H scale. In low light read lower L scale. Horizontal bar beneath lower scale is battery check indicator.

In older Spotmeters, to replace mercury battery, unscrew battery housing cover (14) with a coin. When replacing mercury battery, make sure + side is up. To replace the dry battery, unscrew the strap retainer (19) and turn lever (18) in direction of the arrow. **Housing will then open and battery can be removed. When inserting new dry battery make sure it makes correct contact with + and − terminals.**

With Spotmeter V, unscrew slotted base cap with coin edge. Insert three G-13 batteries in cap holder as indicated on inner side of cap with all '+' signs facing away from cap. Retighten cap.

horizontal line two-thirds of the way across the meter scale if the batteries are all right. If the needle does not swing fully, the batteries should be replaced.

Digital Spotmeter

Asahi's most advanced meter is the Digital Spotmeter, a highly pocketable 1° spot reading silicon photo diode cell instrument featuring a light emitting diode digital readout visible in all lighting conditions. Like the Spotmeter V, the Digital Spotmeter features an eye-level pentaprism finder system in which a central circle representing the sensitive metering area can be seen on a viewing screen similar to that found in a Pentax camera. However, there is no scale or needle located on the screen. After focusing the finder by rotating the eyepiece adjustment lock ring until the centre circle appears sharp, squeeze the metering button and check the sharpness of the digital readout in the finder. If it is not sharp, readjust the lock ring to a midway point so both circle and digital display are sufficiently sharp to be read easily. Next, hold the rubber eyepiece frame so it does not rotate and lock it into place by rotating the eyepiece adjustment lock ring clockwise until it stops.

Match the ASA of the film you are using at the top front of the meter's lens mount with the green ASA index mark by rotating the ASA shutter speed dial. Hold the meter to your eye. Press the metering button while covering the subject you wish to be read with the circle. The reading will appear at the bottom part of the screen as a digital number representing the exposure value (EV). If a single dot appears after the digital number it indicates an additional 1/3 EV number. Two dots indicates 2/3 an additional EV number. For instance, if you see a digital number 8 and two dots, the reading with be EV 8 2/3.

To translate this EV number into useful shutter speed and aperture combinations, you again return to the scales on the meter lens mount. Line up the EV you read with the IRE standard index triangle at the rear of the lens mount. Both the IRE scale and EV scale are coloured orange. You can then select any of the shutter speed and aperture combinations directly ahead on the shutter speed and aperture scales. Suggested spot meter uses already explained in the directions

PENTAX DIGITAL SPOTMETER

1. Objective lens.
2. Trigger switch.
3. Grip.
4. Film speed index.
5. Film speed scale (ASA).
6. Shutter speed scale.
7. Aperture scale.
8. IRE standard index.
9. Film speed/shutter
9. Film speed/shutter
   speed ring.
10. Aperture/exposure
    value ring.
11. Exposure value scale.
12. IRE scale.

When using the meter, place the central spot over the area to be read. The digital scale below the viewing image shows the exposure values (EV). The figure alone is the exact EV. One or two dots following indicate one 1/3 or 2/3 more; thus the diagram shows EV $13\frac{2}{3}$.

To charge the battery, remove the battery chamber cover with a coin. Insert the 6v battery plus side undermost.

for the Spotmeter V apply equally here and should be read before you attempt to use the Digital Spotmeter. ASA, shutter and aperture scale ranges of the two Spotmeters are identical although the Digital meter is slightly more sensitive, being able to read a measuring range of EV 1–20 as opposed to the Spotmeter V's 1–19.

The Digital Spotmeter is powered by a single 6 volt silver oxide battery located underneath a slotted screw-off cover at the bottom of the handle. The battery should be inserted plus side down. If the digital readout fails to light when the metering button is pressed, replace the battery.

COPYING AND CLOSE-UPS

The closest focusing range of the 50–55 mm. Pentax or Takumar lens is about 18 in., measured from the film plane of the camera. While this itself is remarkably close for a normal camera and lens with no special attachments, many will want to make pictures at even closer range.

The single-lens reflex is the ideal close-up camera. With its reflex focusing finder, you can clearly see exactly what will appear on the film whether you are making a close-up portrait or a photograph through a microscope.

Although there seems to be much mystery surrounding the making of close-ups, technique can be as straightforward or as complicated as you wish. If you have fairly ordinary close-up needs, you may need nothing more than a simple close-up lens over your regular camera lens. For great magnification with extreme sharpness, more advanced techniques are necessary. However, they are not complicated once you understand the basic mechanics.

Close-up Equipment

Let's begin with the simplest type of close-up. You have a subject—a flower, a map to be copied, a page from a book which you would like to reproduce. You focus your 50–55 mm. lens at the subject. But even at its closest focusing distance the image on the finder is far too small.

The easiest way to make it larger is to thread a close-up lens to the front of your normal lens. This close-up lens is a low-powered magnifier which lightly shortens the focal length of your normal lens. By shortening the focal length while maintaining the same film place to lens distance you get the effect of a closer-focusing lens. The stronger the close-up lens, the closer you can focus.

The special Pentax Close-up Lenses provide focusing ranges of from $8\frac{1}{2}$ in. (with the normal lens's focusing mount fully extended) to $18\frac{1}{2}$ in. (with the camera lens's focusing mount set at infinity). There are two strengths of close-up lenses for the Pentax normal lenses, plus four additional close-up lenses for the longer Pentax focal lengths. Full specifications can be found at the rear of this book among the charts and tables. However, you can also use non-Pentax close-up lenses; they are readily available from your photo dealer. Generally speaking, a +1 lens focuses from 20 in. to 38 in.; a +2, from 13 to 20 in.; a +3, from 10 to 13 in.; a +4, from 8 to 10 in.; a +5, from $6\frac{1}{2}$ to 8 in.; a +6, from 6 to $6\frac{1}{2}$ in.; a +8 at 5 in. and a +10 at 4 in. The focusing distances are not dependent on camera lens focal length. No matter what lens you use on your camera, subject distance with the same close-up lenses remain the same. Naturally, the area covered varies with the local length of the lens and the image size will be greater with the lens of longer focal length.

Greater magnification can be obtained by using longer focal length camera lenses with the close-up lenses. This is not recommended, however, since longer lenses do not provide good sharpness with close-up lenses.

Close-up lenses have one great advantage over other methods of making close-up pictures. You need make no alteration in your exposure calculations when you've attached a close-up lens.

Close-up lenses do have a disadvantage. They tend to cause a loss of definition when compared to photographs made with your camera lens alone. The amount of sharpness lost depends on a number of factors; quality of the close-up lens, strength of the close-up lens, aperture used, focal length of the lens used, quality of the camera lens over which the close-up lens is placed.

The stronger the close-up lens, the more loss of quality in your picture. If possible it's advisable not to use close-up lenses stronger than +3.

Do not use a large aperture when using close-up lenses. Instead use an aperture of $f8$ or smaller, if possible. The larger apertures tend to produce rather unsharp pictures with close-up lenses.

The close-up lens magnifies the image through the camera's taking lens. The better the camera's taking lens, the better will be the product of the camera lens plus close-up lens combination.

Loss of sharpness when using close-up lenses is most often apparent in the corners and edges of the picture area.

COPYING WITH YOUR PENTAX

Copy Stands III and IIIp offer you greater freedom of camera movement. Both have a sliding camera support arm with focusing rail mounted on to a column The column of Copy Stand III is mounted on a flat base. An accessory clamp lets you fit it to a table. Copy Stand IIIp has a longer two-part column, and packs into a case—which also forms the baseboard. The base can also hold a camera, lens and extension tubes.

To set up the copy stands first mount the column securely. Then select arm height and lock the arm. Fit the focusing rail to the arm. Mount the camera on the focusing rail.

The closest film-plane to the baseboard distance is 302 mm on Copy Stand III and 261 mm on Copy Stand IIIp.

For snapshots, or any type of close photography where quality is not so much of an essential, close-up lenses can provide a simple, efficient, compact and inexpensive way to make close-up pictures.

The alternative to the close-up lens is lens extension—extending the focusing range of the camera lens by actually moving the lens physically further away from the film plane of the camera. To do this the camera lens must be removed from the camera body. Either a rigid extension tube or tubes, variable extension tube or a variable bellows unit is then inserted between lens and camera body. The further away you move the lens from the film, the greater the magnification of the image on the film.

Macro and Micro

There are three terms you should know and be able to distinguish between in close-up photography. The simple close-up, macrophotography and photomicrography. You will hear these terms often, unfortunately misused more than not. The differences between them are relatively simple.

Close-up photography includes all pictures made at distances closer than the normal close focusing.

Macrophotography is the process of taking larger than life size pictures of a subject. That does not mean larger than life size pictures in an enlargement. It means that the actual size of the image on the film itself must be as large as or larger than the object itself.

Photomicrography begins and macrophotography ends when the image on the film is 10 times or greater than the size of the object itself.

We, therefore, have close-up photography from a lens's close focusing distance to a life size image, macrophotography from life size image to ten times life size image, and photomicrography when the image is any bigger.

Magnification

In close-up photography it is not correct to talk in terms of camera-to-subject distance to indicate the size of the image on your negative or transparency. A long focal length lens will produce a larger image from the same distance than a shorter focal length lens. However, lenses of different focal

CLOSE-UP LENSES OR BELLOWS?

With close-up lenses, power of close-up lens (usually in diopters) determines front-of-lens-to-subject distance. Note 50 mm., 100 mm., 200 mm. lenses all must be used as same 4 in. distance with +10 close-up lens. However the longer the camera lens the more magnification through the same close-up lens. No exposure increase is necessary but there will be a decrease in sharpness with powerful close-up lenses when used on longer than normal local length camera lenses.

By inserting extension bellows between camera body and lens, much more flexibility is available. Distances are now measured from focal plane to subject and are usually greater than with close-up lenses. Because magnification can now be altered by bellows extension and lens interchangeability, more control can be exercised over subject perspective because you can vary camera-to-subject distance. Note 50 mm. picture far left resembles 50 mm. plus close-up lens shot above. However, same size image can be produced with 100 mm. lens at greater distance (centre) with less apparent depth between dice. With 200 mm. lens (right) far greater distance can yield same size image with even more depth flattening. Sharpness of original lens is maintained but additional exposure must be given.

lengths can produce images of the same size if the camera-to-subject distance is varied.

In close-up photography, therefore, a term having a more common base than distance was needed. The common term used is magnification.

If the image on film is precisely the same size as the actual object we say the magnification is 1. If the image size is only half the size of the subject the magnification is .5. If the image size is only 1/10 the size of the object the magnification is .1.

When images become larger than the actual subject we obtain magnification like this: images twice as large as the subject 2, four times as large as the subject 4, etc.

These numbers once understood are simple to apply. If you are ever in doubt as to what the magnification is, you need do nothing more than put a measuring rule at the picture area and check how much of it appears in the Pentax's viewfinder, keeping in mind that the Pentax negative roughly measures $1 \times 1\frac{1}{2}$ in. or 24×36 mm. If you see a full $1\frac{1}{2}$ in. across the frame, you have a life-size 1×; if you see $\frac{3}{4}$ in., you have 2× magnification.

These numbers are quite important since the additional exposure increase needed when using bellows extension or extension tubes for close-up and macro work are directly related to the magnifications.

Exposure Adjustment

There's a very good reason why additional exposure must be given when the lens is extended beyond its normal close focusing point. The amount of light transmission of a lens for a 35 mm. camera falls off, like all light, as the square of the distance. Ordinary f-number light transmission is based on the amount of light effectively delivered to cover the format of a 35 mm. negative. However, as a lens is moved further and further away from the film plane, it not only enlarges the image cast on the film plane, but also spreads the illumination further. The 35 mm. negative area in the centre is no longer getting the same amount of transmitted light even though the lens's physical aperture remains the same. To compensate for this loss of illumination, additional exposure must be allowed. Before the through-lens metering systems used today in all SLR cameras, it was necessary to compute the additional exposure needed from the extension distance of the lens from the film. With all the Pentax cameras offering through-lens metering, the built-in meter will measure the exact light through the extension. If you own one of the auto exposure Pentax cameras it will automatically give you the correct shutter speed exposure for almost any extension. With old Pentaxes having no through-lens meters, the exposure increase must be taken into consideration. The Pentax bellows units are clearly marked with the magnification factors and necessary exposure increases. The extension tubes are also specifically calculated for exposure increase based on the amount of magnification.

While various extension tube sets have been made for the screw thread Takumar lenses, there are two sets of tubes in bayonet K mount. The Auto Extension Tube Set K consists of three tubes: No. 1 is 12 mm. long, No. 2, 19 mm. and No. 3, 26 mm. These tubes provide fully automatic diaphragm coupling and open aperture metering to the Pentax K mount cameras. A second extension tube set K, consisting of a 9.5 mm. No. 1 tube, 19 mm. No. 2 tube and 28.5 mm. No. 3 tube have no internal automatic diaphragm coupling or full aperture metering. Obviously, the Auto Extension Tube Set K is far more convenient to use. Tubes of either set can be used singly or combined within the sets to offer extended close-up ability. For instance, with a 50 mm. Pentax lens, No. 1 tube of Auto Extension Tube Set K provides magnification to .38×, but, combined with No. 2, to .75×. When all three tubes are used together, even greater magnification is possible. However, it is not advisable to use the $f1.2$ or $f1.4$ lens at greater than 1× magnification unless the lens is reversed on the tubes, using a reverse adapter, or loss of sharpness with result.

Complete tables of magnifications, areas to be covered, film-to-subject distances and exposure factors for various focal lengths of Pentax lenses can be found at the end of this book in the Facts and Figures section.

Besides the two extension tube sets, there are two longer single extension tubes also with automatic diaphragm and full aperture metering couplings. One is 50 mm. and the other 100 mm. The charts include information for use of these with various lenses also.

By glancing at the charts you will quickly see that the longer the lens used on any given tube, the less the magnification. For maximum magnification the shorter focal length lenses are preferable. For instance, with Nos. 1 and 2 tubes, a 135 mm. lens produces .34 magnification, while a 35 mm. lens produces .47 magnification with No. 1 alone.

Fixed length extension tubes have the disadvantage of providing only a very limited range of magnification from the camera lens' own close focus to infinity setting. However, Pentax also manufactures a Helicoid Extension Tube K which works like a standard extension tube of 26.5 mm. but can be extended by turning its helicoid mount to a length of 46.5 mm. With a 50 mm. $f1.4$ Pentax lens, for instance, it can provide magnifications of from .52 to 1.06 continuously. Its disadvantage is the lack of any internal auto diaphragm or full aperture meter coupling. Full information on its abilities when used on various Pentax lenses can be found in the back of this book in the Facts and Figures section.

We cannot give unqualified indorsement to the short focal length lenses as best for close-up results, however. The shorter lenses must be used quite close to the subject as compared to the longer lenses. This closeness can cause apparent perspective distortion in three-dimensional subjects, that is, the closest parts of the subject will look over large as compared to those parts more distant from the camera. Longer lenses get around this trouble to a greater extent by allowing you to maintain a greater camera-to-subject distance. The normal 50 to 55 mm. lens with which your camera is equipped makes an adequate close-up lens with tubes or extension bellows. The special Macro-Pentax lenses are better.

Increasing exposure to compensate for extra lens extension with non through lens meter Pentaxes is simple as long as you have the necessary magnification factors or exposure increase factors in table form. There are two basic ways to use these factors. You can either divide the ASA index of the film you are using by the exposure factor and read your meter directly or you can multiply the shutter speeds you intend to use by the exposure increase factor. For instance, if you were using a film with an ASA index of 100, and were using auto extension tubes Nos. 2 and 3 together with a 55 mm. Takumar lens, you would see that an exposure increase factor of 3.8 is recommended. It would, however, be close enough to divide the 100 index by 4 and set your meter's ASA index scale to the resulting 25. The meter would then indicate proper exposure for this combination of extension tubes. However, you could instead alter the shutter speed. In other words, if your meter was set at ASA 100 and called for a shutter speed of 1/125 sec., you could multiply the speed by 4 and shoot at 1/30 sec. Both methods of using the exposure increase factor would yield proper results with the No. 2 and 3 tube combination.

While the extension tube set represents the most compact and least expensive method of extending the lens for close-up work, it does have definite limitations. The three tubes used together do have a rather limited magnification. To get greater magnifications, more extension would be necessary. Adding a second extension tube set is possible but rather awkward in terms of the number of tubes which must be threaded together.

The other disadvantage of extension tubes is the fixed magnification. In order to increase magnification you must change tubes or use more than one. Some magnification alteration is possible by using the lens's own focusing mount in conjunction with the Helicoid Extension Tube K, but all tubes are still limited in range flexibility.

Using the Bellows

The Pentax bellows units offer an excellent solution to the problem. After placing the camera body at one end of the bellows and the camera lens at the other, you can increase magnification continuously by drawing the bellows out further and further. There are presently two models, the Bellows K and the Auto Bellows K with double cable release to operate diaphragm and shutter simultaneously. The Auto Bellows K is slightly longer than the Bellows K and has a lens reversing system and improved construction. The necessary magnification and exposure factors are engraved on the chrome metal bellows guide rods. You do no more with the 50 or 55 mm. Pentax lens than note the position of the lens mount and read the proper increase and magnification at that point right from the rod.

While the use of extension tubes is limited because they do not produce great magnification, the bellows units have a limit in the other direction. Auto Bellows K has a minimum extension of 38 mm. which means that with the 50 mm. Pentax lens it has a minimum magnification of .73. For less magnification with the normal lens but greater magnification than with the lens as used regularly in the camera, you must revert to one of the extension tubes. Bellows K has a minimum extension of 32 mm.

For both bellows, however, there exists a remarkable lens, the 100 mm. $f4$ SMC Pentax Bellows lens. This lens is mounted in a special short barrel. When bayoneted into the bellows unit, the 100 mm. $f4$ Bellows lens provides continuous focusing from infinity (with the bellows almost fully compressed) to 1.4× magnification at maximum bellows extension with the Bellows K and 1.32× with the Auto Bellows K.

This means that you can use the same lens and camera to take ordinary distance pictures yet quickly increase bellows extension whenever required for extreme close-ups. The 100 mm. $f4$ Bellows Pentax is specially computed to give excellent centre-to-corner definition for close-ups. It has a preset lens diaphragm which allows you to focus at full aperture yet close down to shooting aperture quickly. The lens is completely described in the chapter on lenses.

The Asahi Bellows should not be confused with other types of bellows units which are often available. The Asahi Bellows are very rigid, extra sturdily made units which provide maximum close-up flexibility.

Let's start with the small, compact and simple to use Bellows K. If you only plan on taking close-ups occasionally or need a unit you can actually hand hold and carry with you easily, the Bellows K should fit the bill ideally. It is composed of a removable bayonet Pentax mount at the rear, the bellows proper, the front lens mount whose position is governed by a large wheel at the left and a locking wheel on the right, and the bellows rod on which the front lens mount rides. Remove the lens from your camera. Mount your camera lens to the front of the bellows, and your camera body to the rear by removing the rear ring attaching it to the camera and refastening it to the bellows. The bellows rod is marked on one side with the magnification factors for a 55 mm. lens and marked in millimetres of extension on the other. By observing the millimetres extension for any subject you can then look up the proper exposure factor or magnification for

AUTO-BELLOWS K FEATURES

Here are the features of the Pentax Auto-Bellows:

1. Rear board.
2. Magnetic seat for scales.
3. Bellows.
4. Lens lock release button.
5. Index for scales.
6. Lens mount.
7. Cable release socket
8. Gear rail.
9. Stopper screw.
10. Clamp knobs.
11. Tripod position shift knob.
12. Red dot.
13. Clamp screw B.
14. Extension knobs.
15. Clamp knob.

Two magnification scales are provided. One is for the 50mm lens; the other, for the 55mm lens, also has a millimetre calibration for lens extension.

The double cable release allows the lens diaphragm to be closed down first and then releases the shutter.

any lens in the directions accompany the Bellows K or use the magnification and exposure scale at the back of this book.

The Auto Bellows K, although larger and heavier, is a far more versatile unit which will allow you to maintain fully automatic diaphragm connections so you can view and focus at full aperture as you would with the camera lens mounted directly on the camera.

To attach it to your lens and camera, first loosen the set clamp screw at the rear of the bellows and remove the rear lens board ring. Remove the lens from your camera and attach the ring in its place. Attach the ring, now mounted on your camera body, to the back of the bellows and tighten the clamp set screw. Attach the lens to the front of the Auto Bellows. To extend the bellows, rotate the extension knobs and tighten the clamp knobs on the other side when you have the extension length you wish. Always remember to loosen these clamp knobs before changing the extension. Once you have the bellows extension you want and decide you wish to maintain this exact magnification, you can focus or refocus by moving the now fixed bellows extension and camera. To do this you move camera bellows and lens backwards or forwards in relation to the subject, using the tripod positioning knob located on the undercarriage of the bellows.

Two scales are provided with the Auto Bellows, one for the 50 and one for the 55 mm. lens. They are engraved on both sides for normal lens use and for use when you reverse the lens, as we'll explain. They fit atop the bellows and stay in place magnetically. For accuracy, you must set the focusing ring of your lens to infinity. Also set the preview lever of the lens to automatic position.

To take advantage of the fully automatic diaphragm, you'll need the double cable release provided with the bellows. Attach the cable with the red ring to the socket on the side of the front board of the bellows and attach the other cable to the release of the camera body itself. By pressing the release button of the double cable you can cause your lens at the end of the bellows to close down to shooting aperture and then the camera shutter to operate. To adjust the release so this will operate properly, loosen the ring at the red marked end of the cable and adjust the plunger so that the diaphragm will close down before the shutter is released. Tighten the ring after adjustment.

While operation of the bellows in normal position will be quite satisfactory for most of your picture taking situations, you will get better definition in macrophotography by reversing the lens and using it backwards on the Auto Bellows K. To reverse the lens, first remove the stopper screw at the very end of the bellows tracks. Now, while holding tight to the screw on the front board, loosen the bellows clamp screw. Separate the bellows from the front board. Loosen the front plate clamp knob and remove the board from the front end of the bellows. Reverse the front board and lens and attach them in reverse position to the rail rod. Fix the front end of the bellows onto the front end of the lens and tighten the bellows clamp set screw. Rethread the stopper screw at the end of the bellows track. When using the magnification scale rods, be sure to place them in the reverse position. Note that you can still operate the automatic diaphragm of the lens and camera using the double cable release although the tripod socket on the front board will be on the opposite side of the bellows. If you need additional magnification, more than is provided by maximum bellows extension, you can use a shorter focal length lens or add extension tubes between the front of the bellows in unreversed position and your lens in reverse position, using the reverse adapter. However, the double cable release automatic diaphragm mechanism will not operate with the extension tubes in place.

For optimum results in macrophotography, try using the SMC Pentax-M Macro lens or SMC Pentax Bellows lens. For extreme close-ups, wide angle lenses used in reverse are often quite good and helpful.

Warning: Don't use Super Multi-coated Takumar lenses on the old discontinued Bellows II having the dual support rods. They may lock and require a repairman to remove them.

Copipod Copying Stand

For precision alignment, framing and sharpest close-up results, a rigid stand to hold the camera at the proper distance and angle is needed. The Copipod is Asahi's light, portable copying unit. It consists of four calibrated telescoping legs plus a lensboard with adapting rings for 49 mm. or 52 mm. diameter front threaded lenses. A flat leather carrying case is provided. With the four legs fully telescoped, the Copipod allows a normal 55 mm. lens to focus at its minimum 18 in. focusing distance.

When using a Copipod, remember not to use direct overhead lighting or the shadow of the camera plus Copipod itself will be thrown on the subject.

Copystand III, IIIP

There are two rigid copystands designed for precision close-up work. The Copystand III and IIIP differ only in that the III has a fixed stand while the IIIP has a longer two-piece vertical support column which can be disassembled and the entire unit fitted into a baseboard carrying case.

The Copystand III provides a film plane to subject distance of 790 mm. (31 in.) or shorter while the IIIP allows distances to 828 mm. (32½ in.). Both have a critical focusing range of 58 mm. (2.3 in.). With a 50 mm. lens, the III provides a maximum photographable area of 350 × 495 mm. (13.8 × 19.5 in.).

Additionally, a Table Clamp is available to allow the support column of the Copystand III to be attached to a table, desk or stand without the baseboard.

To assemble Copystand III, insert support column bottom into the column mount. Fasten, using the column clamp screw. Fit the arm on the support column and fasten it with the support column screw at whatever height you need. Fit the critical focuser into the two pins at the tip of the arm and use the critical focuser clamp screw to fasten it. To raise or lower the critical focuser, loosen the clamp lever and adjust with the critical focuser knob. After adjustment, remember to lock the clamp lever.

Place the Pentax camera body on the camera on the camera mount and fasten it with the camera clamp screw.

If you have the Copystand IIIP, remove everything from the carrying case, turn the case upside down and fasten the two halves of the case into a single baseboard, using the hooks and snaps on either side of the case. Thread together the two sections of the support column, and thread the bottom of the support column into the baseboard column mount. Attach arm, critical focuser and camera as with the Copystand III.

If you lower the copying arm as far as it will go and place

the critical focuser also at its lowest point, the closest film plane to baseboard distance that can be achieved is 302 mm. (12 in.) with Copystand III and 261 mm. (10.2 in.) with the IIIP. When you are using a 50 mm. lens on the III, subjects smaller than 9.3 × 14 cm. (3½ × 5½ in.) or 1:3.9 magnification cannot be photographed unless the critical focuser is attached upside down on the arm. The camera must then be attached to the stopper projection. (Without turning the critical focuser upside down, the minimum subject size possible with the Copystand IIIP is 7 × 10.5 cm. (2¾ × 4 in. or 1:2.9 magnification.) Make certain the camera and baseboard are parallel before photographing.

You can use the Copystand III for photographing larger subjects than possible on the baseboard by loosening the column clamp screw and turning the support column 180°. Relock the clamp screw. Now you can place the unit on a table but photograph over the edge from the floor. Make certain to place a heavy weight on the baseboard to prevent the unit from tipping over. With the Copystand IIIP, loosen the clamp screw, turn the arm 180° and lock again.

Either the regular Bellows or Auto Bellows can be attached to the Copystand III or IIIP by removing the critical focuser and attaching the bellows unit directly to the arm.

Exposure for Close-ups

Close-up exposure techniques require care and good judgment. With all modern Pentax cameras the meter reading, of course, is done directly through the lens, which does aid proper exposure considerably. However, equally good results can be obtained with a separate meter provided the meter reading is done properly. First, let's examine the classic method of obtaining a close-up reading from an ordinary hand-held exposure meter.

Most such meters read a fairly wide angle of coverage. generally an angle somewhat greater than the normal lens of your camera. For the most accurate reading possible, try to get the meter as close to the subject as you can without obstructing the illumination on the subject or casting a shadow on the subject yourself. This is particularly important when photographing a fairly small object in the midst of a field of a different brightness—a small insect on a white or black background, for instance. If the reading is made from a point too far away, the background will dominate the scene and give you an erroneous reading for the subject. The Pentax cameras with through-lens meters make certain you are getting exposure for the subject only, but even with these cameras you may find it necessary to adjust the readings when the background dominates the picture.

The best method of determining accurate close-up exposure with an ordinary hand-held, general-use meter is to make a substitute reading using on 18% neutral grey test card (available from photo dealers). This card provides a medium-grey surface which, when read by a meter, produces an exposure for normal subject material. You hold the card just in front of the subject, but in the same light as the subject, and take a meter reading from the card rather than from the subject.

The best accessory meter to use for close-ups is one of the Pentax Spotmeters which read a 1° central angle. With these you can easily make accurate readings of even the tiniest subjects and exclude all unimportant background material. No grey card is necessary. The Spotmeters are fully described in the chapter on the Pentax exposure meters.

If you have the CdS clip-on meter which fastens to the top of the older Asahi Pentax prism housing and engages the shutter speed dial, this meter cannot be used on the camera for measuring close-ups accurately. Instead, remove the meter and use it as an ordinary hand-held meter to get the proper close-up reading and then set the camera's controls accordingly.

There is one more method of calculating proper exposure for close-ups that owners of older Pentaxes have used successfully: making a meter reading through the prism finder of the light coming through the Pentax lens. This is rather a primitive duplication of the method used by the newer cameras which take a very accurate through the lens meter reading. Before using this exposure technique on an important subject, try the method out to see whether it will work for you.

Place the cell window of your CdS clip-on meter against the viewfinder of your camera. To make sure that no extraneous light is striking the CdS cell, fit the rubber correction lens adapter to the Pentax. Set the ASA index of your meter for the film you are using. Next extend the bellows or fasten the extension tube between camera and lens. Then focus on your subject until you are certain you have the right size image magnification you wish. Close down your lens aperture to shooting opening. Take the meter reading through the finder. Hold the meter as close to the eyepiece as possible and use the low light scale. Set the shutter speed dial of the meter so that the $f16$ black calibration of the meter's scale matches the meter needle dealing. Now read the correct shutter speed from your meter's shutter speed dial. Set your camera to this shutter speed and you are ready to shoot the close-up picture.

You can also try this system with other meters. Take a reading through the finder as already explained. But after setting the calculator dial, read the proper shutter speed opposite the $f1$ aperture marking on the meter calculator dial.

In the author's opinion, this technique, although far from exact and absolute, can furnish you with a general area of proper exposure. Once having calculated an exposure in this manner, take some pictures with slightly less exposure and others with slightly more to make sure you do get the picture. As you experiment more with the system, you will learn just exactly how far you can really trust it.

Lighting the Close-ups

Lighting small close-up objects is something of a problem. Large floods and spots are not only too big to squeeze into the tiny space between camera lens and subject, they also often produce far too much light and heat.

There are several worthwhile lighting alternatives. A 35 mm. slide projector with no slide usually makes an excellent light source. The concentrated projected light beam can be aimed with certainty. To cut down on the area illuminated, simply cut the proper cardboard mask and insert it in the slide holder. A small white cardboard, such as an index file card, can be used as a backup reflector on the opposite side of the subject. The light from the projector can strike the subject directly and also be reflected by the card. The diminutive high-intensity table lamps which make use of small bulbs similar to those used in automobile headlamps make excellent close-up light sources. In addition, you will find that their illumination seems to produce good colour results with both Type A and Type B tungsten colour films.

While tungsten illumination is probably the easiest to

handle in terms of seeing the effect on the subject and being able to calculate exposure accurately, it does have disadvantages with living subjects. It is bright and hot. For shooting pictures of moving objects—small animals or insects, for instance, electronic flash provides undeniable advantages. Whereas most extreme close-ups are shot at relatively slow shutter speeds, the very short duration of the electronic flash itself provides the ability to stop subject action.

It is quite possible to use electronic flash extremely close to your subject, while some auto exposure flash units do work as close as 2 feet from the subject. There are no practical rules governing proper manual exposure. You will simply have to experiment with a roll of film to see just what exposure would be proper with the flash unit in extreme close-up position. If there seems to be too much light you can cut down the illumination with one or more layers of white handkerchief over the flash head.

Electronic flash ring lights which fit around the outside of the lens provides very even and shadowless illumination for close-ups. Most such units come with full exposure directions for close-up use. When photographing very close, however, even these rings may produce a dark central spot in the middle of the picture area where the lens is located. In such cases the standard electronic flash head is probably preferable.

The direction of the light is particularly important in close-up photography. Front lighting is even but quite flat in character. It picks up little of the surface detail of three-dimensional objects although it is fine for non-textured two-dimensional copy work. Cross lighting at about a 45° angle is generally best for producing three-dimensional effects with highlights and shadows. Such shadows can be extremely confusing. One light should definitely predominate if the picture is to look normal. For such subjects as bas-reliefs, etchings or engravings, a rim light at almost 90° from camera position skimming the surface of the art work is effective in picking up the fine lines and reproducing them with the necessary contrast.

When copying two-dimensional surfaces such as the pages of a book, stamps, maps, etc., an opposite technique must be used to the one employed with three-dimensional objects. When shooting two-dimensional surfaces, lighting should be frontal and as even as possible. You can check evenness by measuring the light at the centre of the picture area and at

The adapter consists of a main tube (top), and fastener tube (bottom) with coupling ring.

The light-sealing tube replaces the microscope eyepiece when you do not wish to use it.

First withdraw the light-sealing tube, which is stored upside-down clamped in the fastener tube.

Unlock the breech-lock action coupling mount and remove the camera lens. Bayonet the main tube on to the camera, remove the microscope eyepiece, and clamp the fastener tube to the microscope draw tube. Replace the microscope eyepiece, or insert the light-sealing tube, and finally, couple the camera to the fastener tube and tighten the coupling ring.

the edges with a good exposure meter. There should be no more than a 25% fall off of illumination or the darkening will show up in the negative or transparency. The same light sources—projectors, high-intensity lights, electronic flash or ringlight—can be used, although there is no real need for the latter two. Usually a continuous light whose effect on the subject can be studied is preferable.

When photographing semi-glossy and glossy surfaces, manoeuvre the lighting so that no glare is reflected back into the camera lens. Lighting and camera must be moved so that hot spots are not visible in the camera finder. Whenever you do see them there, they will appear in the picture itself. With some difficult surfaces you may not be able to direct light on the subject proper at all. This is often true of subjects covered by glass. In such cases, it's possible to reflect the light from large cardboard reflectors well out of camera view.

Films and Filters

In copy work, proper choice of film and filtration are extremely important. In film, use the finest grain film possible. This will probably have a rather low ASA film speed index. In copying, however, this should make little difference since it merely indicates that longer exposures will be necessary. Of course, all copying work should be done from a rigid tripod or copying stand.

Why filters? Panchromatic film, the only type now generally available in 35 mm. black-and-white, does reproduce all the tones of the original photograph in the proper shades of grey. However, in tungsten illumination, which is most often used for copying, red tones are produced much lighter than we actually see them, while blue tones tend to darken more than we may wish. A pale blue filter can offset this tendency and help give you a proper visual balance.

In daylight, blues may tend to become too light. In such cases, a pale green or pale yellow filter will negate the excessive blue sensitivity of the film. Of course, we are assuming that you are copying a coloured subject. For reproduction of a black-and-white page only, no filtration of this type is necessary.

These filtrations suggested are known as colour correction since they simply try to bring back into proper visual balance those colours which will not reproduce on a film as you see them. However, more often a photographer is faced with just the opposite problem—how to increase colour contrasts to separate tonal values to a greater extent than normal. This works in much the same manner as we noted in the chapter on filters—that is, a filter will darken its complementary colour by absorbing it while passing light of its own colour. Suppose you wish to copy a letter which is smudged with blue ink. By using a blue filter the blue ink can be almost if not completely eliminated. If the blue ink was pale and we wished to make it appear more pronounced we could photograph it through a yellow filter.

Some other often-used copying filters are: blue filters for copying a partially faded photograph, yellow filters for copying old photos on a yellow background.

The filters that we have been discussing are, of course, for use with black-and-white photography. When using colour films, simply use the nomograph in the Facts and Figures Section in the back of this book to determine the proper filter for any lighting source and type of film.

Using the Microscope Adapter

We have been discussing close-ups and copying to magnifications of about 3×, the limit of a normal 50 mm. Pentax lens on the Auto Bellows K. Of course, greater magnifications can be obtained either with shorter focal lengths lenses or with more extension—by adding extension tubes to the bellows, for instance. This is the area of macrophotography as we have previously defined it. To produce greater magnification, 10× or more, we must go into photomicrography. Here we will fit the Pentax camera body directly to a microscope by means of the Asahi Pentax Microscope Adapter, which can be used with any microscope having a tube of 25 mm.

The microscope adapter consists of the following parts:

1. Main tube adapter, one end of which has a bayonet mount, to be attached to the lens mount of the camera body. The other end is a bayonet mount. (Note: Models for screw thread cameras have screw thread mounts.)

2. Coupling ring. One side accepts the fastener tube. The other side engages the main tube bayonet adapter.

3. Fastener tube which fits the extension tube of the microscope.

4. Fastening knob.

5. Light sealing tube that prevents interior reflection of light inside the extension tube of the microscope when the eyepiece of the microscope is not in use.

Here's how you mount the microscope adapter and camera:

1. Loosen the knob (4 above) and pull out the light sealing tube (5).

2. Disengage the fastener tube (3).

3. Remove the lens from the camera.

4. Attach the main tube adapter (1) to the lens mount of the camera.

5. Pull out the eyepiece of the microscope.

6. Fit the fastener tube (3) with the coupling ring (2) to the microscope tube.

7. Clamp the fastener tube with the fastening knob by setting the red dot onto the fastener tube.

8. Insert the eyepiece or light sealing tube (5) into the fastener tube (3).

9. Match the red dot of the main tube adapter (1) with the red dot of the fastener tube (3) and the red dot of the coupling ring (2).

10. Put the main tube adapter (1) into the fastener tube (3).

11. Turn coupling ring (2) in direction of arrow to lock it.

12. Insert cable release into cable release socket to prevent camera movement during exposure.

13. Adjust lighting and position of subject while looking through camera finder.

14. Focus microscope correctly while observing focus through camera viewfinder.

15. Determine exposure and shoot picture.

Actual magnification of the image depends greatly upon the optical potential of the microscope used. However, resolving power is generally far more important than magnification. Resolving power can be expressed simply in the ability of the camera, film, microscope combination to separate two close lying microscopic objects. This is actually dependent on the aperture of the microscope objective.

Exposure through a microscope depends upon the illumination source, the microscope optics and the magnification. No hards and fast rule can be given. A through-the-lens meter reading will certainly prove an adequate starting point for determining correct exposure. For early, non-through-lens models, a reading through the finder lens as suggested earlier in this chapter is advisable. Only tests can assure you of correct exposure with your equipment.

SLIDE COPYING

Transparency colour films which are processed into slides for hand viewing or projection are very popular. However, such films do have what may seem at first to be a severe limitation. The very film that you expose in your camera is the one which is turned into the transparency slide. You have, in effect, a single, original, positive picture in colour. With negative films, of course, you have either a black-and-white or colour negative from which you can make any number of equally excellent prints.

While there are commercial services available that will make duplicate slides for you, the cost is rather high and, perhaps more important, the quality is often rather low. Only a few processors can guarantee first-class duplicates. It isn't surprising, therefore, that the word "dupe" has come to mean second rate in terms of quality. Most dupes bear only a slight resemblance to the excellence of the original picture. The dupes usually are much more contrasty, lacking the great tonal and colour gradations of the original. Colour is often washed out. Highlights and shadows don't have the detail in the original picture.

If you learn to duplicate your own slides, however, you can do far better. Not only can you duplicate your original transparency in colour, contrast and sharpness, you can quickly learn to improve transparencies whose original colour didn't quite suit you. You can even recrop your transparency and enlarge portions of it. The cost of such a duplicate is no more than the cost of an original picture made on transparency film—usually less than one-fifth of the cost of a commercially made dupe which may not be one-tenth as good.

Assembling the Slide Copier

The heart of the Asahi slide copying equipment is the Auto Bellows with slide copier attachment. To set up the slide copier, remove the stopper screw at the very end of the bellows track and fasten the slide copier attaching screw into the thread for the stopper screw. Now extend the front plate

USING THE AUTO-BELLOWS K SLIDE COPIER

Here are the features of the Auto-Bellows K Slide Copier:

1. Retainer plate
2. Slide slot
3. Bellows.
4. Bellows retainer plate.
5. Strip film holder.
6. Copier rail
7. Clamp knob.
8. Slide copier attaching screw

To attach the Slide Copier to the Auto-Bellows, remove the stopper screw at the end of the bellows rail and fix the slide copier attaching screw (8) into the thread for the stopper screw. Open the bellows retainer plates (5) on both sides and stretch bellows towards lens in direction of the arrow. Place the copier bellows ring inside the lens rim by pressing in the two grips of the lens mounting ring. Release the grips and the ring will remain fastened to the lens.

When inserting a colour slide to be duplicated into the slot, the view through the camera finder should show the slide right side up and correct right to left.

of the bellows with lens forward on the gear rail. Open the bellows retainer plates on both sides of the slide copier attachment. Pull out the slide copier bellows. Hold the slide copier at the two grips of the lens mounting ring and place the copier bellows ring inside the front of the lens. Release pressure on the grips. (If you're using the lens in reverse position, which is advisable when copying at greater magnifications than 1.2×, put the end ring of the copier bellows into the rear of the front plate in the same way you would mount it to the front of the lens.)

If you're using a 50 mm. *f*1.4 lens, extend the Auto Bellows fully and lock it. When using a 55 mm. lens or 50 mm. Macro, extend it to the red dot on the gear rail instead and then lock it.

Insert the slide to be copied in the slide copier's slot. Look through the camera's viewfinder to make sure the slide is right side up and correct right to left. Note that the copier rod has a magnification scale from 1 to 1.5 for both 50 and 55 mm. lenses. Loosen the copier's bottom knob and move the copier rod holder's red dot to the magnification you want. Extend the Auto Bellows K to the same magnification using the appropriate magnification scale rod. For same size slides, choose 1×. If you want to crop out some of the original slide, choose a somewhat greater magnification, varying it until you get the cropping you wish. Actually this scale is for copying film strips, but it is a good enough approximation for your initial adjustment with mounted slides. For vertical cropping, you can shift the film holder up and down. There's a click position at the central copying point.

If you want to copy a slide or film at a specific magnification, look in the tables accompanying the slide copier or bellows for the amount of lens extension needed for that magnification. Now either extend or compress the bellows as needed, using the magnification rods as a guide until you reach the proper extension. Move the slide copier back and forth on its rode until you get the correct focus through the viewfinder. Then lock it in place. Alternately, however, we think you will find it easier to set the slide copier itself at the wanted magnification, using the slide copier rode as a guide, and then move the camera body itself back and forth using the rear panel knob.

If you have a film strip that you want to copy, unhinge the strip film retainer plate from the slide copier and position the film strip between the diffusing plate and the slide copier. You'll find that the slide copier plate has a grooved slot of the proper width to accept the strip film. Now refasten the retainer plate. It's advisable, however, not to attempt to slide strip film through the copier. Open the copier at the hinge and reposition the picture to prevent film scratching. The film strip holders should be fastened to the slide copier by pushing them on to the support pins. Because the film strip is about 3 mm. further away than slides, the magnification scale position must be adjusted by the same amount in the same direction.

In addition to Slide Copier K, Asahi makes available a budget priced copy device. Slide Holder 1×,K consists of a rigid tube with provision for inserting slides at one end and attachment to a lens at the other. It can be used in conjunction with Auto Bellows K extension tubes plus your normal camera lens or with the Macro 50 mm. $f4$ lens to make slide duplicates at 1× only. No cropping is possible. However, all information on producing duplicates, aside from cropping and greater than 1× magnification, given for the Slide Copier K also applies to Slide Holder 1×,K.

Once you have mastered the mechanics of setting the slide copier for whatever magnification or cropping of your original colour slide that you may want, you are ready to proceed to three other essentials in slide duplication:

1. Choice of illumination.
2. Choice of duplicating film.
3. Exposure.

Light Sources

The most satisfactory slide duplication is generally made using a light source similar to daylight. While daylight itself is certainly the least expensive and the most widely available light source, it varies greatly in quality depending on sky, time and weather conditions. Electronic flash or floodlights balanced for daylight probably make the best illumination sources. Daylight balanced floodlights work quite well with the through lens metering Pentaxes since the continuous light source makes it possible to determine the correct exposure for slide duplication by using the behind the lens meter. For other copying, one of the modern small, inexpensive electronic flash units probably makes the most convenient light source. However, we will cover both types of lighting in conjunction with slide duplication.

Which Film?

Daylight balanced film is the only proper choice if you intend to use daylight or a daylight-balanced light source for duplication. There are more types of daylight films available than tungsten films so the choice of daylight illumination with a daylight balanced film would seem a logical one.

Which of the many brands and types of daylight films is best for slide duplication? High-speed colour films should be eliminated immediately. While these are excellent as prime films to take photographs under difficult lighting conditions, they tend to show excessive graininess and have less colour saturation. The slower, brighter, more fine-grained films are far superior for duplicating purposes.

Still there are many different brands and types of slow colour film. How do you choose the best? Actually you cannot. While some colour films generally will give you good duplicates, the very characteristics of some—more or less contrast, softer colours, finer grain can often help you with specific problem slides.

Generally speaking, a slide duplicate tends to pick up additional contrast and lose in-between tones. Therefore for pictures of average contrast with good range of middle tones, a duplicating film of relatively low contrast but bright colour is preferable.

The same type of duplicating film is also recommended for original slides having low contrast although a duplicating film of average contrast might also do. For original pictures having very high contrast, a very low contrast film should be used. The fact that a film makes excellent colour pictures in a camera is no guarantee that it makes good duplicates. Agfacolor (Agfachrome in the U.S.) produces fine slides yet makes a very poor duplicating film. Some film manufacturing companies make film designed specifically for slide duplication. Your photo dealer can tell you what is available in this line.

Exposure

Once you have loaded your camera and have the slide to be duplicated in place, your big problem with daylight or any continuous light source such as floodlight is exposure. First position your light. With a small flood, place the reflector about three feet in front of and facing the diffuser plate of the slide copier.

Certainly the most convenient and simplest method of determining proper exposure is with a through lens metering Pentax camera. Basically all you need do is to make a reading through the lens as you would for any close-up and shoot the picture. With auto exposure Pentaxes, of course, it's only necessary to press the shutter release and the camera will automatically set the proper shutter speed for the duplicate. We have found by experience, however, that it's advisable to make a few additional exposures at other settings if you are not familiar with duplicating. Give double and half exposure as well as the one which your equipment suggests. Then pick the transparency with the best exposure. With the auto exposure cameras you can do this using the exposure factor control ring at $\frac{1}{2}\times$ and the $2\times$ settings. In addition we've noted that with dense slides additional exposure is often required, while very light slides sometimes need only half the recommended exposure.

While a through lens meter camera is the easiest to use for duplicating with constant light sources, you can get adequate readings with separate meters. If you have a hand-held meter, remove the slide from the copier, hold it up to the light you will use for duplicating, and take a reading through the slide. Replace the slide in the copier and using the magnification scales on the bellows to determine the exposure increase needed. Apply this to the exposure you made through the slide.

In all slide copying it's advisable to use the optimum lens opening, between $f4$ and $f5.6$, varying the exposure by changing shutter speeds when needed. The 50 mm. $f3.5$ SMC Pentax Macro is the best lens for copying.

While we have stressed making three exposures for each slide to be duplicated, one on exposure suggested, one at less and one at more, we feel that with experience you will be able to eliminate the two additional exposures so as to conserve film. Don't expect perfect results immediately. After you have made a number of duplicates and have been able to see the results you should be able to make a very good duplicate in one or at the most two exposures.

There is another method of obtaining correct exposure when using the slide copier. If you have a hand-held CdS silicon or gallium cell exposure meter, you can try taking a reading right through the finder eyepiece with the original slide and light source in place. If using a Pentax clip-on, place the input window of the meter against the viewfinder of the camera. With the meter placed in position, you will be able to read the light that actually exposes the film. However, it's advisable to prevent extraneous light from coming into the input window of your meter and thereby giving you an inflated reading. You can shield the viewfinder window adequately if you slip the correction lens eyepiece over the finder window.

To take a reading, set the film speed calibration ring of your meter to the speed of the film you are using. Turn the switch ring of your meter to "L" since the illumination through the viewfinder is usually dim when copying slides. Now turn the shutter speed dial of your meter so that the black calibration of $f16$ of the meter's scale matches the needle. This black calibration of $f16$ with your meter switched in at the "L" position corresponds to $f1$.

Then read the shutter-speed dial of your meter and use the speed matching the shutter-speed index. Since you are reading the light coming in through the closed-down diaphragm, extended bellows and the prism finder, you don't have to take exposure increase factors into consideration.

If you have a silicon, CdS or gallium cell meter other than the Pentax clip-on, you can take a reading in a similar manner by holding the meter to the eyepiece while the meter scale is in the low light scale level. After setting the meter calculator, read the proper shutter speed opposite the $f1$ aperture setting. This is the proper exposure to use.

We must warn you that the foregoing method is not an exact one. It will, however, furnish you with an approximate exposure. To be more certain that you obtain a satisfactorily exposed duplicate, make a second exposure at half the shutter speed indicated and a third exposure at twice the shutter speed indicated.

Giving specific advice on exposure to the many photographers who do not own a through lens meter camera or modern hand-held exposure meter is rather difficult since it is impossible to measure the illumination from the slide accurately. A series of trial exposures using an ideally exposed test slide will be necessary. Set your camera lens to *f*5.6 and makes a series of exposures from 1 sec. to 1/125 sec. When you get the results back from the processors, you should be able to pick out the properly exposed slide quickly. The data from this slide will then serve for this particular film and lighting set-up with a properly exposed transparency. If you intend to take a duplicate which is slightly larger or smaller than the test duplicate, you can easily compute the proper exposure correction. If the test was made at the same size reproduction, you can make a properly exposed duplicate of $1\frac{1}{2}\times$ by giving $1\frac{1}{2}$ times the exposure. In like manner you can produce the same size duplicate if the test was $1\frac{1}{2}\times$ magnification by giving two-thirds of the exposure.

When you are copying slides which have more density and shadow detail than the test slide, double your exposure. If the slide is rather light without density, halve your exposure. At all times if possible, take a few shots under and over the estimated proper exposure for insurance.

The foregoing procedure was based on maintaining an exact control of the duplication procedure. Once you have established the strength and distance of the illumination source, do not change it or your exposure calculations will be different. Measure the light to copier distance carefully, note the lamp designation and type of reflector. Make sure when duplicating slides that you reproduce the lighting situation exactly.

Using Daylight

You can probably understand by now why daylight is rather unsuitable for duplication. Not only does the strength of the illumination vary considerably day by day and hour by hour, but the colour of the light and the quality also change. If you do duplicate by daylight some slides may be too blue, some too warm, depending upon the quality of the daylight when you make the duplicates.

If you intend to use daylight, it will be almost impossible to guess at exposure. A through lens meter, CdS silicon or gallium cell meter can, as already explained, give you a good indication of exposure. If you have a selenium cell type of meter, you may proceed as follows. Using daylight as an illumination source, make a series of test exposures using a well exposed slide as the original to be copied.

Shoot a series of tests at *f*5.6 using varying shutter speeds from 1 sec. upwards to 1/125 sec. At the same time, take a direct reading of your light source with your meter. When you receive the processed transparencies back, pick out the properly exposed transparency and determine the exposure at which it was made. The next time you duplicate slides by daylight, read the direct illumination again with your meter. If the illumination is exactly the same, you can use the same exposure as you did before. However, if the light proves to be stronger or weaker than the original illumination, you will have to alter the duplicating exposure by the same amount. If your meter indicates that there is but half the illumination, for instance, double your exposure. If the illumination is twice as much as originally, halve the exposure. Of course, you must also adjust your exposure if the slide to be duplicated is not ideally exposed itself.

What type of daylight illumination is best? Since no daylight illumination is ideal for slide duplication, it is more a question of what type of daylight is least harmful. Direct sunlight is almost always too bright. In addition, the brilliancy causes the scattering of light rays producing flare in slide duplication.

Clear north light or blue sky is quite good as an illumination source. However, the scattering of ultra-violet light which causes the sky to be blue will also cause a bluish tinge in your transparency. To correct for this use the proper filter for blue sky illumination which you can find with the filter nomograph at the back of this book.

Using Electronic Flash

Perhaps the best illumination source for slide duplication is the light from an electronic flash unit. Electronic flash is adequately balanced for daylight illumination. The quality is virtually constant. The light is easy to control. You just hold the electronic flash about a foot in front of the slide copier diffuser, and release the shutter. Since many small electronic flash units today have short connecting cords for the camera which are non-detachable, you may have to obtain an extension cord which allows you to remove the flash sufficiently from the camera. A coiled cord extending up to two or more feet is most practical.

In using electronic flash for copying, you must again establish an ideal exposure for a properly exposed transparency. Although it is possible to fix the flash at a non-changeable distance and then change aperture to vary the exposure, it's best to shift the illumination itself to maintain the same most critical lens aperture. You can then vary exposure by establishing a series of different flash-to-copier distances between one foot and three feet.

Again you must make a series of test exposures to establish a norm for your own flash unit. Once you have found the proper illumination placement and aperture, make sure that you jot down all the data so you can duplicate the set-up again whenever you wish to dupe slides.

In duplicating well-exposed slides, you will find that some slides are more difficult to duplicate than others. This is usually caused by the varying characteristics of the slide subjects. If facial tones are of primary importance, you may find that some films used for duplication are not as ideal for facial tones as others. On the other hand, a film which does not reproduce facial tones well, may be extremely good with foliage or some other specific colour. The more experience that you have in duplication, the more films you use for the purpose, the more expert you will become on choosing the right film for each slide.

Correction During Copying

Duplicating slides which you consider excellent is but one copying possibility. Slides which are slightly off colour can not only be duplicated but can be corrected as well.

In duplicating under- or over-exposed slides, vast improvement can be made. However, it is not possible to put back detail in either washed out highlights or unrelieved shadows. You can alter the colour, the contrast and the overall density but you cannot create in the duplicate any detail that was not in the original.

When making a duplicate to correct exposure error, allow less than the "correct" exposure time for an over-exposed original and more for an under-exposed original. The amount of exposure increase or decrease of course, depends upon the error in the original slide. When possible try a number of different corrective measures varying each slightly. To get the perfect dupe make use of the half stops on the Takumar lens.

Colour correction is a fascinating area of slide duplication. Quite often original slides will be off colour. If taken on sunless days or even on a bright day at the beach, a slide may appear bluish. Slides made early in the morning or late in the afternoon may be too warm. The same types of filters used to correct the original picture-taking situations will also work nicely here. We recommend a full set of nine: CC10Y, CC20Y, CC40Y, CC10M, CC20M, CC40M, CC10C, CC20C, CC40C. The filters, incidentally, are available as gelatin squares which can be held in front of the copier diffuser plate. Gelatin squares cost only a fraction of the price of glass mounted filters. Therefore a full set of nine will be less expensive than it might appear at first.

There are no hard and fast rules as to which strength filter will work best. Obviously, if the picture is too warm a bluish filter should be used in copying while a yellow or magenta filter will cut down on the blue in an original.

Making Black-and-White Negatives

Besides making duplicate colour slides, you can use the slide duplicator for another purpose—to make black-and-white negatives from transparencies which will allow you to make black-and-white prints directly.

Actually the making of black-and-white negatives is far simpler than the making of slide duplicates. The exposure latitude of black-and-white film is far greater so that the duplicating exposure is far less critical. In addition, the quality of the illumination is not so critical either. It matters little whether the light is balanced properly for daylight or tungsten film. As long as it's bright and even, it will serve for black-and-white film. Of course, any of the duplicating illumination set-ups we've already described will do splendidly.

Fairly slow black-and-white film having an ASA index between 25 and 50 is recommended for making black-and-white negatives. Since the final black-and-white print will have a combination of the graininess qualities of both the

288

original colour transparency and the graininess of the black-and-white film, you won't want to use a grainier film than is absolutely necessary.

After processing the black-and-white film, you should have a perfectly exposed negative from which excellent black-and-white pictures can be made.

P.W. II—Q

HOW LENSES BEHAVE

Like any other science, optics has its immutable laws, but these laws largely depend on a lens behaving as a "perfect" lens. Unfortunately, the perfect lens has not yet been invented, so the laws of optics have to be bent a little to fit in with the performance to be expected from practical lenses in practical cameras.

That along with a few popular misconceptions, leads to many arguments among photographers on such subjects as focal length, perspective, depth of field and so on. There are different views on how far the laws have to be bent.

As we've seen in preceding chapters, lenses of varying focal lengths have more use than merely to make images smaller or larger from the same camera-to-subject distance. Shorter focal length lenses can cause apparent distortion of perspective by appearing to enlarge close images out of proportion to the parts of the subject further away. Distances in depth appear greater with short focal length lenses. The shorter the lens, the more pronounced the effect.

Longer than normal focal length lenses can produce just the opposite effect if you use them to frame the same picture area. Instead of close objects appearing too large, the same objects appear smaller. Depths seem compressed.

Don't be Misled

Don't be fooled into the notion that it is the focal length of the lens which produces this apparent change in perspective. The focal length of the lens merely changes image size. It is the actual distance from camera lens to subject which creates the extension or compression.

You can prove this to yourself quite easily if you have a long lens and a shorter focal length lens.

First, from about 3 ft. shoot a picture with the short lens of a person holding his hand toward the camera. The hand will appear over large in the resulting picture.

Secondly, replace the short focal length lens with the longer lens and back away from the subject until the subject's body

290

is the same size in the prism finder as it was in the first picture. Shoot a second picture. In this shot you'll see that the hand is much smaller in relation to the rest of the body.

Finally, replace the longer lens with the short lens again and shoot a picture from the same distance as in your second shot. Of course, the image will be much smaller in this third picture because you are using a shorter focal length lens. However, after producing the picture, if you enlarge the *image* to the same size as the *image* in the second picture you will see in your picture that you have exactly the same perspective in the relationship of the size of the hand to the size of the body as you obtained with the longer lens.

This proves that it is distance and not focal length which determines this apparent perspective distortion.

In practical terms this means you should back away from a subject and increase camera-to-subject distance to avoid close image enlargement. You can then vary focal length to increase image size.

Using Perspective Control

Once you have convinced yourself that camera-to-subject distance really controls apparent perspective, you can use this to excellent advantage in controlling your background —provided you have one or more additional focal length lenses.

Suppose you are photographing a person but notice that a large tree seems to be growing out of his head some distance behind him. You could, of course, use a large lens opening to throw the tree out of focus. However, if you do wish a sharp background you can exercise perspective control. Try a shorter focal length lens and approach closer to the person to maintain image size. The shorter lens will tend to increase the apparent depth. This will make the tree appear far smaller in relationship to the person.

If you think the picture can be enhanced more readily by making the tree appear larger, you can try the opposite approach. Use a longer focal length lens and back off to keep the main subject the same size as before. The tree will now appear larger than before.

Backgrounds can therefore be minimised or increased in importance by maintaining subject size but changing focal length and shooting distance.

Understanding Depth of Field

This brings us to a controversial subject—depth of field, which is so easy to define in theory but capable of being much misunderstood in practice. There are various schools of thought on this subject but practical experience leads me to the conclusions outlined below.

The "perfect" lens delivers its sharpest image at a single properly focused flat plane in space. Sharpness falls off in front of and behind that plane. By closing down the lens opening, the degree of sharpness fall-off can be lessened. More depth in the picture appears adequately sharp. However, in theory, still only one single plane in the picture is in sharpest focus.

How do we determine the outer limits of our depth of field? Without going into scientific details, we can explain as follows. If we could focus our "perfect" lens on a point source of light, the light would be reproduced on the film as a pinpoint. When this pinpoint of light is not sharply focused by the lens, it forms a disc on the film. The more it is out of focus, the larger the disc appears. This disc is called the circle of confusion and, in fact, with practical lenses, it always is a disc, even when in sharpest focus. However, by establishing a limit on the size of this circle of confusion we can lay down a criterion of sharpness and thus establish limits to depth of field. The smaller the limit we place on the maximum circle of confusion, the greater we can enlarge a picture and still find sharpness acceptable within the depth of field.

It follows, of course, that depth of field is what we make it. We set our own limit on the size of the maximum circle of confusion according to the type of work we are doing. Where high degrees of enlargement are normal, as in 35 mm. work, the maximum circle of confusion must be kept relatively small. Then, at normal viewing distances, which are likely to be rather shorter than the theoretical "correct", everything within the depth of field should look equally sharp, because, at normal viewing distance, the eye is unable to tell the difference between a point and a disc of a certain size.

Nevertheless, the fall-off in definition is very gradual and, at reasonable shooting distances and apertures, even objects a foot or so outside the theoretical limit may be sharp enough to be acceptable or annoying as the case may be. So, in practical terms, if you want to *use* your depth of field, you com-

FOCAL LENGTH VS PERSPECTIVE

Changing focal length alters image size but not perspective as long as the camera-to-subject distance remains constant.

House and tree behind house are photographed by normal, wide angle and long lens from the same position.

Images produced by three lenses vary in magnification. Long lens creates biggest image, wide angle, smallest image.

If wide angle picture is enlarged and cropped to produce image size equal to either normal or long lens picture, perspective in enlarged wide angle picture will be exactly the same as in shot with longer lens.

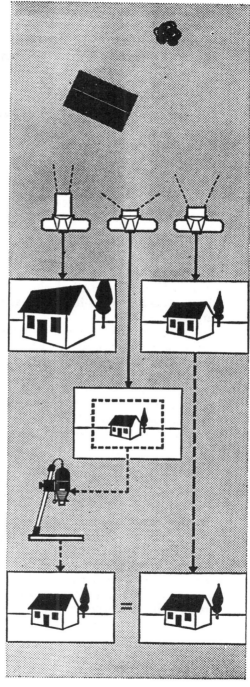

pute it from tables designed specifically for 35 mm. work, such as those in the back of the book. If you want to throw a relatively close background out of focus, you would be wiser to rely on your screen image with the depth-of-field preview lever in use—or open up the lens as fully as possible in the existing circumstances. Depth-of-field is, in practice, entirely subjective. It can only be calculated exactly if various ideals as to film size, enlargement, viewing distance, etc., are all observed.

Depth of Field and Focal Length

From any given distance and at any given aperture, a wide-angle lens gives greater depth of field than a longer focal length lens. This leads many photographers to rely on the wide-angle lens for increased depth sharpness in their pictures. They feel that accurate focus will be less critical and that they can use a larger aperture and still retain greater depth-of-field than they would with a longer lens.

This works out nicely in practical picture taking provided you use the same aperture and shooting distance for each picture. Then, the shot taken with the wide-angle lens always shows greater depth-of-field, even at greater degrees of enlargement.

But suppose you use the wide-angle lens to move in close and get the principal subject the same size on the film as you would with the longer lens and a more distant viewpoint. What happens to your depth-of-field then? Well, in this case, the wide-angle lens does not give greater depth-of-field. Even this does not always apply but you will find in most picture taking situations that when lenses of different focal lengths are used to produce the same size image *on the film*, the depth-of-field is the same when the same aperture is used, regardless of focal length.

All this may seem to be of purely theoretical interest, but it does have practical applications and can help you to avoid some pitfalls into which many a photographer has fallen. For instance, if you purchase a wide-angle lens to achieve a greater viewing angle from any given distance, well and good. However, if you purchase a wide-angle lens with the idea that it will provide greater sharpness in depth than your normal or tele lens, remember that this will not be true if you use the wide-angle lens to give the same size image on the film as the longer lens gives. Only by closing down the

DISTANCE
VS PERSPECTIVE

Changes in perspective can be made with different focal length lenses if you change camera-to-subject distance.

When shooting close portraits with 50 mm. lens, faces tend to elongate and become slim. By using longer lens, such as 135mm. you can shoot at a greater distance, maintain same size face in your finder, yet get much broader facial contours.

When shooting close-ups many photographers mistakenly believe they can get much more depth-of-field with a wide angle lens than with a longer lens at the same aperture and same image size. This is not so. If you vary camera-to-subject distance to maintain image size and you use same lens aperture, you can only vary perspective. With longer lens, depths are compressed, more distant leaves appear larger in relation to pistils. But depth is the same.

Real distortion occurs when a wide angle lens is used fairly close to a subject. Images close to picture edge, much as the end columns here tend to broaden out and look flatter.

aperture of your lens, wide-angle, normal or tele, can you be sure of getting an actual gain in sharpness with images of the same size.

The impossibility of maintaining image size on the film while altering depth-of-field by changing focal length obviates some photographic old wives' tales. One tale suggests you use a wide-angle lens for greater depth in close-ups. This rarely works. If you photograph the same picture area with a long focal length lens, your actual depth of sharpness between objects in the picture is the same at the same aperture.

The conclusion that can be drawn is: choose your focal length lens primarily for image size needed and apparent perspective desired.

Focal Length and Movement

Another misconception which we must put to rest, we've discussed briefly before—the belief that shorter focal length lenses shake less and therefore cause less subject unsharpness than do longer lenses. If you shoot a subject from the same distance with both a short and long focal length lens, then enlarge the shorter lens shot so that the subject image is the same size as in the longer lens shot, you will have the same amount of unsharpness provided you were just as unsteady when holding one lens as the other. Of course, it may be true that the longer focal length lens is simply heavier or harder to hold than the short lens. But then the unsharpness is not an optical phenomenon caused by the focal length. It's a physical phenomenon caused by you.

Let's track down another widely-held belief—that a shorter focal length lens when photographing action will stop movement to a greater extent than will a long focal length lens. If you enlarge the subject made with the short lens, you will have just the same amount of unsharpness as you did before. There are only two sure ways of getting sharper action pictures, use a faster shutter speed or pan with action.

Close-range Distortion

There are two very real distortions which you may discover when using normal or shorter focal length lenses. In shooting close portraits with a normal or shorter focal length lens, you will find that full faces tend to elongate and become narrower. Ears disappear. The reason for this is rather simple. While the centre line of the face is being photographed straight on, the sides of the face towards the cheeks are being photographed at rather an oblique angle. You receive a false impression that the face is really narrower than it actually is. While this may be quite suitable in enhancing the slimness of a pudgy face, it is usually disturbing. Either get further away, photograph the face and then enlarge the facial area if necessary or back off and use longer lenses to increase image size.

With lenses of 28 mm. or shorter, beware of subject matter close to the edges of the picture at moderate distances. For instance, if you photograph a group of people at about 10 ft. that extend from one edge of the picture to the other, you will find that the people towards the edges appear flat and stretched out horizontally, an effect somewhat similar to the very close focusing subject, but the oblique angle of the wide-angle lens picks up extra surface instead of less. The solution is to keep subject matter away from the very edges or back up further and use a less wide angle lens.

USING TELE LENSES

There are few thrills in owning a Pentax camera greater than when you fit a longer than normal focal length lens to your camera and for the first time look through the viewfinder. The longer the lens, the more magnification of the image you achieve and the closer appear the objects at any given distance.

While using long lenses was exciting in the days when such lenses were very heavy and needed tripod support at all times, the possibilities offered by the newer, smaller and lighter optical designs are greater still. Imagine hand-holding lenses up to 400 mm. and still getting acceptably sharp results!

As you begin to use longer and longer focal length lenses, however, various technical difficulties, unforeseen while viewing through the finder, become evident.

Entire areas which appear to be photographic at relatively slow shutter speed of 1/30 or 1/60 sec. become blurred when a singled-out subject is photographed with a longer lens. Seascapes which looked sharp and crisp through the finder yield bluish, hazy transparencies. Photographs of a distant building with a long lens appear to show the straight lines of the building waving like a flag in the breeze.

Some of these inherent difficulties with tele lenses can be overcome directly; others can be avoided. A few are impossible of solution. In this chapter we will try to analyse the telephoto lens problems and help you solve the solvable ones.

Use a Tripod

How do you obtain the sharpest picture with a longer than normal focal length lens? The same way you do with any camera and lens—put the camera and lens on a tripod. No matter what shutter speed you use, focal length lens you employ, aperture you shot through, ability to hold a camera steady you may have, the tripod shot will always be sharpest. However, as images are magnified by longer and longer lenses, the difference between the hand-held shot and the tripod-mounted shot becomes more evident. We, therefore, urge that a tripod be used for all longer than normal focal length lenses except where the tripod proves an inconvenience or hindrance to obtaining a good picture. All efforts to obtain steadier hand-held photos with longer lenses are attempts to approach the tripod-mounted shot's sharpness, but we shall not really equal it.

There are no specific rules as to what long lenses can be safely hand-held with adequately sharp results and which ones cannot. Likewise there are no specific rules as to what shutter speeds must be used with which focal lengths to obtain passable sharpness. The answers to these questions depends on your own ability to hold steady and the degree of unsharpness you might tolerate in a picture. For the average photographer a general rule of 1/30 sec. minimum shutter speed for wide-angle to normal focal length lenses, 1/60 sec. minimum for 85 mm. to 135 mm. lenses, 1/125 sec. for 200 mm. lenses and 1/250 sec. for 300 mm. or over lenses is a good starting guide. However, when shooting, if you can sacrifice depth of field and use a larger lens opening to reach a higher shutter speed, you will usually get sharper results.

When you have your camera and lens mounted on a tripod, of course, your technique can be varied considerably. You no longer need keep a fast shutter speed to minimize camera movement. You can, instead, let the movement of your subject govern the speed and attempt to use a smaller lens aperture when possible for greater depth. To make maximum use of the tripod, the lens should be in perfect balance with the camera, using the tripod mount itself as the fulcrum. You will find that the makers of the Takumar lenses have deliberately positioned the tripod sockets so that proper balance can be maintained on the tripod when the camera is attached to the lens.

It's also advisable when tripod mounting a long lens to use as heavy a tripod as possible. Oddly enough, small 35 mm. cameras really require a heavier and sturdier tripod than do larger cameras. Larger and heavier cameras contribute their own weight to the stability and rigidity of the tripod-camera combination. Light cameras and lenses lacking such weight must make it up by using heavier tripods. In addition when using very long lenses, 500 mm. and upwards, many photographers find it advantageous to dampen vibration by draping a blanket or similar piece of cloth over the top of the lens on the camera.

Needless to say, a cable release should be used when the camera and lens are on a tripod. If you attempt to release the shutter by hand, you may easily undo all the good of the tripod by jarring the camera and lens at the moment of exposure.

Correct Hand-holding

Your stance is extremely important in hand-holding a long lens. With a normal focal length or shorter lens, the primary support is under the camera body. With longer lenses, starting with the 85 mm. *f*1.8 SMC Pentax and going upwards, the primary support should be under the lens.

Holding a long lens and camera properly resembles closely the problems of holding a rifle for offhand shooting. The only difference between camera and rifle is that you can use several body support aids in photography that just aren't allowed in rifle shooting.

In taking up position with a long lens, don't stand square on to your target. Stand at an oblique angle as you would in shooting a rifle. The left side of your body which is closer to the subject will support the lens barrel. This should be your left hand. If you are right handed the position will seem quite natural to you. If left handed, you will have to adopt this stance anyhow since the shutter release is on the right-hand side of the camera body.

Now crook your elbow and support the lens with the entire palm of your left hand. You can use your thumb and middle or forefinger to operate the focusing ring. Bring the camera up to your eye with your right hand. Your right thumb should be on the rapid-wind lever, your right middle or forefinger on the shutter release.

To give your lens maximum steadiness, draw your left elbow into your body so that the point of your elbow digs you in the side, forming a support point. Draw your right arm into your side as far as possible for additional support. Press the camera against your cheek or forehead when steadying yourself before shooting.

This basic position plus a slow, steady release of the shutter with a highly arched finger should work well with all hand-held lenses from 85 mm. up to 400 mm. Dry practice runs will pay off in sharper results later.

Focusing practice is extremely important also. The magnified image and narrow field of view offer little depth even at medium distant shots. For instance, if you were photographing a football game with a 300 mm. Pentax lens and had closed the lens down to $f11$, your depth of field at a 30-ft. distance would only be about $1\frac{1}{2}$ ft.! However, if your main subject is sharply focused on the principal plane of interest (generally the face of a person in a game), the picture will be acceptable to the viewer even if other aspects of the photograph are less sharp.

Problems of Long Lenses

We have now covered the physical considerations of using longer than normal focal length lenses and now must turn to the optical problems involved. At close focusing distances of 100 or so feet, there are no more optical problems than with shorter lenses. However, long lenses are often used for photographing distant objects or scenes. Over such long distances the atmospheric conditions create problems for the photographer.

Unhappily, even on the clearest day, the distance between you and a far subject is not purely of empty space.

The first time you shoot a long-distance shot with a telephoto lens, you'll be amazed to find that the apparently very clear atmosphere has somehow wreaked all sorts of havoc with picture sharpness and colour. Your transparencies are apt to be rather blue. The cause: ultra-violet radiation scattered by water vapour in the air. The best time for picture taking of distant objects is when the atmosphere is the driest. Unfortunately, it's during the summer when relative humidity is apt to be the highest that you'll probably want to shoot your tele pictures.

At 80% relative humidity some of the tiny dust and dirt particles always floating in the air begin to pick up moisture which then develops into tiny water droplets about a millionth of an inch thick. As white light (which contains light of all colours) passes through the air, the tiny droplets scatter the short wavelengths (blue light) very much more than the longer wavelengths (red light). The blue of the sky is scattered and causes the bluish haze which is seen to a greater or lesser degree in all very distant landscapes. As the relative humidity approaches 100%, the size of the water droplets increases and the haze becomes stronger.

This possible haze caused by moisture is only one of the difficulties encountered. But even when the moisture content is low, the air is not perfectly uniform. When warm air is on top and cooler air is below it, the atmosphere is very steady and fine for photography—but this is seldom the case. If the day is sunny, the warmth of the sun hitting the earth causes the earth to heat, thereby warming the adjacent air. The air is warmed underneath but the cooler air remains above. This results in turbulence. How does the turbulence become evident? Usually as heat waves which cause distant images to shake or weave when seen through telescopes, binoculars or telephoto lenses.

Watch out for little puff cumulus clouds. These are a sure sign that atmospheric conditions are far from stable. When such clouds are about, it's not advisable to try distant telephotography. However, a high overcast will increase your chances of seeing long distances. If you have a clear atmosphere under the clouds you have a good chance of getting acceptable telephoto pictures.

The most acceptable conditions for telephotography occur over water, over snow or over land covered with dense vegetation. Here the sun produces little heating of the surface.

If you can manage to take your tele shots at a slight angle up or down, your picture quality should improve and the distant objects should show less unsteadiness. When you shoot at an oblique angle, you are shooting from one stratum of air into another. When you shoot horizontally, you may be shooting directly into the interference between two strata of air causing irregular light refraction.

Astronomical photographers experience less difficulty than you will because most observatories are located on mountains or high hills above the most image-degrading atmospheric conditions. In addition, they don't attempt to shoot pictures horizontally. Their cameras and telescopes are shooting upwards, through the atmospheric layers.

There will be few days on which all atmospheric conditions are perfect for long-distance photography. Early in the morning on a clear day when the sun has not had time to warm up the earth is a good time to try. Directly after a thunderstorm when the air and earth are still cool is another fine time.

Although you must put up with atmospheric conditions, what can you do concerning the haze? On a very clear day, you can cut down the blue in distant shots with a UV filter for colour or black-and-white film. For black-and-white film alone, a medium yellow or light red filter will do a good job of giving you better clarity and sharpness. These two filters will also help with light haze. There is nothing you can do for heavy haze with ordinary colour or black-and-white films.

A useful film for distant black-and-white shots is infra-red film (with a suitable infra-red filter). Infra-red film and filter will allow you to get rid of some scattering of light.

If you use your long lenses on less-distant scenes, you will not run into the same amount of atmospheric problems. However, it's still advisable to keep the UV filter on at all times for colour or black-and-white.

At Longer Range

While the best telephoto pictures are certainly made through long focal length lenses designed specifically for photography, it is quite possible to use ordinary telescopes and binoculars.

Most of these instruments available for home use are not designed with photographic requirements in mind. They have been made for visual observation only. Nevertheless, they can be used for photography.

Why go to the trouble? First, because high-powered binoculars and telescopes produce greater magnification than even the longest lenses available for the Pentax camera. For best astronomical photography, such high magnification is necessary. In addition, many photographers already own binoculars and telescopes and it seems a pity not to make use of them, if possible.

First let's look at some distinct disadvantages of this type of photography. There is a very definite loss in overall sharpness. Binoculars and telescopes do not have the same amount of resolving ability, the same colour correction, the same lack of optical aberrations as do good telephoto lenses. Nor do they have the same amount of light-gathering power. In addition, most maximum apertures are generally rather small, necessitating both fast films and fairly slow shutter speeds. Moreover, binoculars and telescopes are not physically made for attaching to cameras. Connecting them and focusing them can be somewhat of a chore.

Despite these three snags, it is still a great deal of fun to take pictures using such long-range instruments.

With the Pentaxes having behind-lens meter systems, exposure computation isn't even needed with these long teles.

There are three basic methods of shooting pictures through telescopes with your Pentax—Afocal, Prime Lens and Negative Lens Projection.

Afocal Method

This is the simplest method. Focus the telescope by eye, set your camera lens to infinity, hold it as close as possible to eyepiece and shoot the picture. Quite acceptable snapshots can be made in this way but you'll want a more solid, more substantial coupling for best results. Many telescope manufacturing and importing firms have special brackets available. If not, a camera repairman can fabricate a good coupling.

For best results, the camera lens should be about one inch from the eyepiece. Extraneous light between lens and eyepiece should be eliminated with a lens hood or cylinder of dark paper. The normal 50–55 mm. lens is suitable but a slightly longer focal length such as the 85 mm. SMC Pentax is even better.

To calculate approximate length of the combination:

1. Measure actual length of light travel in telescope from front of main glass element (in a standard all-glass refractor telescope) or mirror (in reflecting telescope) to telescope end of eyepiece. Let's say this is 45 in.

2. Check telescope eyepiece for focal length. Usually it's engraved on the eyepiece. Let's say it's 25 mm. or 1 in.

3. Divide focal length found in step 1 by eyepiece focal length of step 2. This is total telescope magnification power. In this telescope example we would have $45 \div 1 = 45$.

4. Multiply total telescope power (of step 3) by focal length of camera lens. This is focal length of combination. Thus in our example, we would multiply 45 by 2 in. (approximate equivalent of 50–55 mm. if you use the standard lens). This give us an effective focal length of about 90 in.

or in millimetres, $90 \times 25 = 2250$ mm. A longer 85 mm. Takumar lens if used instead of the normal 50 or 55 mm. Takumar would yield a total effect of about 4000 mm.

You now have the focal length—and it's impressive. But to make a proper exposure you must have the effective working aperture. If you have a Pentax with a built-in meter, of course, you need only read the exposure right through the telescope and the auto exposure Pentaxes give you correct exposure automatically. However, if you have an earlier Pentax with no built-in meter, here's how you find the aperture:

(*a*) Divide the telescope power of steps 3 above by the diameter of the front telescope lens or mirror. Just take a tape measure or ruler and measure the lens or mirror across the middle. Quite often you will find this step unnecessary since telescopes are usually classified by the diameter of their lenses or mirrors. For instance, a 4 in. telescope indicates that the lens or mirror is 4 in. in diameter. If we had a 4 in. telescope (a common size) we'd divide 45 (from step 3) by 4 and get a little over .11.

(*b*) Multiply figure from step (*a*) by focal length of the camera lens. This would be 11×2 (if a 50 mm. lens) or $f22$.

When examining the results of your tele photography with such an afocal system, one or two dark corners indicates your camera lens isn't properly centred over the eyepiece. Four dark corners indicate that the camera lens was too far from the eyepiece. Light streaks or patches will occur if there is open space between the eyepiece and the lens which isn't properly shaded from an extraneous light.

Prime Lens Method

The above method of taking pictures through a telescope is probably the simplest method but it doesn't yield the best results. You are combining three different lens systems—the main lens of the telescope, the optics of the eyepiece plus the elements of the taking lens of your camera. Perhaps the best method in terms of sharpest results is the prime lens method.

If you take the eyepiece from the telescope and remove the camera lens, you can fit the telescope main lens directly to the camera body. In other words, you use the telescope lens

305

as a giant direct telephoto or more properly, long focal length lens. Again you will have to consult a telescope manufacturer or importer or a camera repairman for the proper fitting. Quite often a short extension tube on the camera can be joined to or slipped within the focusing tube of the telescope.

To find the total focal length of the combination, measure from the refractor lens or reflector mirror to the normal position of the telescope eyepiece. (For instance, a 3 in. refractor measures about 31 in. or 775 mm.) This is the total focal length possible using the telescope as the prime lens. To find the working aperture divide the focal length found by the telescope lens diameter. In the case of a 3 in. telescope already mentioned, this would be $31 \div 3 = f10.3$.

The system has the advantage of good sharpness and fast aperture, but the disadvantage of a relatively short focal length and definite vignetting at the edges and corners of the picture area. Although this prime system is to be used mostly with refractor telescopes, it can also be used with reflectors if the reflecting mirror can be moved upwards in the telescope tube to allow proper focusing.

Negative Lens Projection

While the previous method will undoubtedly produce the best photographs optically, the disadvantages of vignetting and limited focal length are quite real. Perhaps the ideal compromise system is negative lens projection.

When professional astronomers wish to increase telescope power without losing definition they insert into the telescope a negative lens called a Barlow, after the inventor. Average Barlows will produce respectably sharp images. However, first-class coated achromatic Barlows, usually available from telescope supply houses or manufacturers, can yield pictures which are virtually as sharp as with the prime telescope lens alone. By changing the positioning of the Barlow lens in relation to the film plane you can vary the magnification of the Barlow negative lens and telescope combination. The Barlow lens simply slips into the telescope eyepiece tube between telescope and camera.

To find the approximate total focal length of Barlow lens and telescope:

SHOOTING THROUGH TELESCOPES

There are four basic methods of attaching your Pentax to a telescope. In direct objective method the camera lens and telescope eyepiece are removed and the telescope's main objective acts as an ordinary telephoto lens (*left*). Image is seen upright through the finder. In the afocal technique (*second from left*), both the telescope's eyepiece and the camera's own lens are used. The Pentax, in effect, views through the telescope and sees the primary image upside down as you would. In positive projection (*third from left*), the telescope eyepiece is used to project the primary image into the lensless camera body. The image appears upside down in the finder. In negative projection (*far right*), a negative lens element or system is used instead of the telescope's eyepiece to project a right-side-up viewing image into the lensless camera body.

Your Pentax can be adapted to shoot pictures through a monocular or half of a binocular. Actually the monocular or binocular is nothing more than a folded telescope which uses prisms to fold the long telescope length to handier dimensions. Most binoculars or monoculars can be attached to the Pentax using the afocal technique in which the camera's lens sees through the monocular or binocular's eyepiece as you would. Image seen in camera finder is right side up.

1. Measure the light path from refractor lens or reflector mirror to the telescope end of the eyepiece holder. With a 4 in. refractor, this might be about 45 in.

2. Multiply the total telescope length in step 1 by the magnification of the Barlow or negative lens. With a 4× magnification, this would be $4 \times 45 = 180$ in. or 4500 mm.

To find the working aperture:

(a) Divide the total focal length in step 2 by the diameter of your telescope or mirror lens. This would be in our example $180 \div 4 = f45$.

There is yet a fourth method of taking pictures through a telescope—by using the eyepiece of the telescope as a projector lens and actually projecting the image into the lensless camera body. However, the necessary couplings are rather expensive to make and the results are not as satisfying as those which can be obtained by the negative projection method already mentioned.

Avoiding Vibration

When taking pictures through telescopes, great care must be exercised. There are two prime factors involved, steadiness and focus.

One of the difficulties of using any telescope is one of steadiness. Telescopes, because of their very long shape, tend to see-saw and vibrate. Before use, they must be allowed to come to a complete rest. With camera attached this is still very true. The gentle action of the shutter going off can actually cause vibration. You can minimise this by using the fastest ASA index film you can to maintain a high shutter speed. In addition, fasten both camera and telescope securely to a solid tripod. Although it certainly is clumsier, better results can be obtained by mounting camera and telescope on separate tripods and then bringing them together. To minimise and damp the shutter vibration, drape a blanket or similar heavy material over the telescope.

Precise focus is absolutely essential. There is virtually no depth of field when using such long focal lengths, even when shooting at fairly great distances.

When using telescopes for terrestrial photography, don't attempt long-distance shots because of atmospheric conditions which normally prevail. Telescopes can be used for effective medium-range photography such as sports or nature pictures.

In astronomical photography where you can actually shoot upwards through the atmospheric layers instead of across them, you can photograph distant objects. The moon is perhaps the best initial target for would-be astronomical photographers. If you have an interest in this subject, there are several excellent books which can take you further along the line.

Using a Monocular

While telescopes will undoubtedly give you the most spectacular results, you can also adapt a pair of binoculars or a monocular (half a pair of binoculars) to photo use. Binoculars or monoculars, of course, do have the advantage of far more compact size than do the telescopes.

A binocular or monocular can be most expeditiously fitted to the 50–55 mm. Pentax lens by means of a filter adapter ring available from your photo dealer. Many binoculars and monoculars which are convertible to photo use have the proper threads on the eyepieces to allow direct fastening of the camera lens to the monocular.

If not, a camera repairman can easily fabricate such a connection which can be interchanged with the present eyepiece or your binocular or monocular.

To use the binocular or monocular on your camera, open the lens to its widest aperture and set it to infinity; the focal angle of the camera-ocular combination depends upon the focal length of the Pentax lens used and the magnification of the monocular or binocular. On each ocular such numbers as 6×30, 8×50, etc., appear. The first of these pairs of numbers indicates the magnification. To find the equivalent focal length of the camera-ocular combination, multiply the focal length of the camera lens by the magnification of the ocular. For instance, if you are using the 55 mm. SMC Pentax and a 6×30 binocular or monocular, the equivalent focal length would be $55 \times 6 = 330$ mm.

To find the working aperture of the combination, divide the second number of the combination into the total focal length. With our example we would divide 330 by $30 = f11$. However, in actual picture taking you may find that some light is lost due to flare in the system. Therefore it is advisable to allow between $\frac{1}{2}$ stop and 1 full stop additional exposure.

While the best pictures through binoculars and monoculars

can certainly be had with the use of a tripod, the compact size and light weight of the camera-ocular combination makes hand-holding possible at reasonably fast shutter speeds of about 1/125 sec. and over. With today's fast black-and-white and colour films, such exposures should not be hard in reasonably bright outdoor illumination.

While most monoculars and binoculars have but one shooting aperture, some are supplied with extra aperture discs which can be slipped over the main ocular objective lens. These limit the aperture even further, but they help improve sharpness.

Close-up lenses can also be used in conjunction with binoculars and monoculars. These are slipped over or threaded into the ocular's main lens.

Certainly the results obtained with even the finest monoculars or binoculars cannot begin to compare with the excellence of the pictures obtained with long Pentax lenses. However, for many snapshots, such oculars will prove adequate until you're ready for real long lenses.

ARTIFICIAL LIGHT

Photographic lighting is an extremely broad subject. There are many types of lighting—sunlight (and moonlight, too), flashbulbs, flashcubes, electronic flash, various floods, spots, fluorescents, and quartz-iodine lamps plus all the types of lighting you have around your house. There are seldom clear-cut rules which state when one type of lighting is better than another. Often it's a matter of personal taste, of convenience and quite frankly, of what lighting equipment you happen to own. Besides the type of lighting, you have two other factors to consider—the amount of light, the number of lighting units and the proper placement of them.

Since placement of the lights—and number of units used is much the same no matter the type of lighting used, let's first discuss the various types of lighting.

We will rule out sunlight outdoors. This is covered in chapters on exposure, films and shooting various type of pictures. Aside from changing your shooting angle or moving out of the light you have little control over daylight. You must adapt your picture-taking to it.

With all artificial illumination, you are the artist in control—except for artificial existing light shots where you are simply shooting in whatever lighting happens to be available.

Let's examine the assets and liabilities of the type of artificial lighting most familiar to beginning photographers— light from flashbulbs.

Flashbulb and Flashcube Pros and Cons

The advantages of flashbulbs are numerous—even though today electronic flash is far more important to most Pentax owners. The modern flashbulb or cube is tiny—many can be carried in a pocket. The flashgun and reflector for these tiny bulbs are compact and often can also be carried in a pocket. They fit easily on the camera and do not get in the way of camera operation. Bulbs or cubes produce an amazing amount of light when compared to their modest size. They allow you to shoot pictures in surprisingly large areas with the light of just one flash.

Now let's look at the disadvantages. Because flash is an instantaneous light, you have no sure way of determining just what effect it will have on the subject—where the highlights will be, how the shadows will appear. There is also an expense factor. You can only use a bulb once. Each bulb is fairly inexpensive—but if you shoot many pictures, expense begins to add up. Also, you cannot measure proper exposure for flash accurately. You must use simple tables based on your shutter speed, your lens opening and the distance of your subject. Lastly, flashbulbs must be changed after each shot, a decided inconvenience.

Nevertheless, the bulb or cube, because of size and convenience factors, remain extremely important light sources not only for amateurs but professionals who want the assurance that wherever they go they can always pull out a tiny flash reflector plus bulb, or just a cube, and be assured of pictures.

For amateurs who don't shoot too many artificial light pictures, flashbulbs or cubes are the ideal answer when they are needed.

What is a flashbulb? Basically it is a small glass envelope —much like a tiny electric light bulb. Inside is a highly inflammable wire which is connected to the negative and positive poles of the bulb. When a current passes through the bulb, the wire lights quickly and brilliantly—just long enough to illuminate the subject while the shutter is open. Often various gases are used alone or in combination with the wire to heighten the brilliance and hasten the burning.

Flash Synchronization

The electrical circuitry in a focal plane shutter single-lens reflex is cleverly designed to make the most of the bright light of a flashbulb. The camera must work in such a way that the flash circuit is closed before the shutter is released, since it does take a fraction of a second, called the delay, for the bulb to reach near peak illumination. Because the focal plane shutter on Pentax cameras consists of a slit travelling over the film itself, the flashbulb must remain evenly lit during the entire travel of the slit. If it doesn't, part of the picture may be well lit while other parts may be much under-exposed.

To simplify matching the flash to the right shutter speeds, we've included flash synchronization tables in the Facts and Figures Section in the back of the book to show which flash-bulbs should be used at what speeds. There are special focal plane bulbs which do allow flash synchronization at all shutter speeds with some Pentaxes. These would seem the best all around choice, but they are rather more expensive than the ordinary AG1, PF1, M2, flashcube, etc., which can generally only be used at shutter speeds of 1/30 sec. or slower, but work with all cameras. This makes them a distinct liability in terms of obtaining sharp, motion-free photographs if there is an appreciable amount of other light in the scene.

You'll note from the synchronization table that your flash unit must be connected to the X (or FP terminal, if it has one) on the front of your camera (or directly to the hot sync shoe atop the prism of modern Pentaxes. If not using the hot shoe, check that you have the synchronization cord securely attached. Make certain that you are using a recommended speed. It's best to use the fastest speed your bulbs (and exposure necessities) allow.

For black-and-white photography, you can use either clear white flashbulbs (if available) or blue tinted flashbulbs. For colour films, use blue bulbs only or your pictures will have a reddish-orange coloration.

Flash Exposures

Determining approximate flash bulb exposure is usually easy. Examine the carton or sleeve of flashbulbs when you buy them. The correct flash guide number for your film is often printed on the back or side. Make sure you look for the instructions for focal-plane-shutter cameras. You'll see that the guide numbers are listed in terms of the film's speed. Find the right guide number of your film. Note the suggested shutter speeds. The rest is simple. Divide this guide number by the distance of your subject from the direct flash. The resulting figure is the right lens aperture. Shoot at this open-ing and the shutter speed allowed for that bulb. For instance, if the guide number of your flashbulb is 160 and you plan on shooting a subject at 10 ft., you'd just divide the 160 by 10 and come up with an ƒ16 shooting aperture.

Sometimes your division may come out with a number between actually marked lens apertures. Then use the in-between click aperture markings on your Takumar lens.

Note that we've stressed direct flash and flash-to-subject distance. If you point the flash anywhere but directly at the subject, your guide number calculations have to be modified.

Electronic Flash

Closely allied to the flashbulb is the electronic flash unit. The electronic flash unit uses a tube filled with gas. When a very high voltage electric current is passed through the tube the gas produces a brilliant but extremely brief light.

The great advantage of electronic flash over the flashbulb is the flashtube's ability to fire again and again—perhaps 25,000 to 50,000 times without wearing out. The flashbulb can only fire once.

Small electronic flash units have become quite common. To make the gas light up so brilliantly it's necessary to feed a very short burst of high-voltage electricity into the tube. The power can come from house current or from various types of accumulators or batteries—wet cells like those used in automobiles, dry cells which must be thrown away after some use or the rechargeable nickel cadmium batteries which can be charged from house current after their power has been exhausted. The power passes through a relatively complicated circuit of transformers and capacitors to build up the required high voltage. This takes a certain amount of time, known as the unit's recycling time. A small pilot light indicates when the unit is again fully charged and ready to fire. Flashguns which work off household current or have large power packs may recycle in less than 5 sec., while the recycling time of the smaller, more compact, battery-powered guns is likely to be in the region of 6–10 seconds. The recycling time increases rapidly as the battery nears exhaustion.

Remarkable strides have been made in recent years in electronic flash design. The small units slip right into the accessory shoes of the cameras and, with the cameras having shoes with built-in sync contact, making connection directly through the accessory shoe itself with no need for a separate sync cord. While the units, if used regularly, will more than pay for themselves, compared with individual flashbulb costs, flashbulbs remain far more powerful in illumination. Before

314

buying an electronic flash, make certain that its specifications are sufficiently powerful for the film you intend to use, the aperture you would like to shoot at and the farthest distance you intend to photograph with the flash. You might ask yourself, too, how long it would take you to use the flashbulbs you could buy for the same money.

We now have a large selection of automatic-exposure electronic flash units. Besides allowing you to use the flash manually, they have sensing cells, usually CdS, on their front plates which measure the light reflected by the subject during the actual exposure. They cut off the flash when proper exposure is reached. These are quite handy, but it is necessary for you to shoot at a specified aperture only (or sometimes with a limited choice) and the distance ranges on automatic exposure are somewhat restricted. Flash units with an energy-saving circuit not only cut off the flash when sufficient illumination has been reached but also return the energy to the flash unit to be used again, thus producing more flashes and faster recycling. Many of the modern auto electronic flash units provide bounce flash. The CdS sensor reads the flash from the subject even when the flash reflector is pointed towards the ceiling or wall. In some units a checklamp tells you whether there has been sufficient light for a proper exposure.

Electronic Flash Practice

Unlike the flashbulbs, which must be dyed blue for use with daylight colour films, the flash emitted from electronic flash units has much the same qualities as daylight in terms of practical photography. If you own an electronic flash unit, you can use daylight colour film exclusively with no need for any filters.

Since the duration of the electronic flash is quite short—usually 1/500 or 1/1000 sec. or less—the problems of synchronizing electronic flash to your camera are quite different from those of flashbulbs. There is no delay needed to allow the gas in the flashtube to reach maximum intensity. It flashes almost instantaneously. On the shutter speed dial of your Pentax there's a red X mark which indicates the proper shutter speed to use with electronic flash. At this speed, the entire shutter is fully open so that the whole film area can be exposed to this instantaneous flash of light. Do not use faster speeds or part of your picture will be unexposed.

Your electronic flash synchronization cord must be plugged into the X socket on your camera—or, if has a hot shoe sync connection, slid into a hot shoe atop the camera. X-sync provides virtually no delay between the time the shutter is open completely and flash goes off.

While the very high speed of the electronic flash can be of great help in freezing all action and so ensuring sharp pictures, this very quick flash does present a problem, too. The electronic flash must be used at fairly slow shutter speeds. On many Pentax cameras the X settings usually represent either 1/45 or 1/60 sec. shutter speeds. If you are using your film in an area which has some reasonable amount of existing light already, there is danger of producing a second or ghost exposure—primary exposure from the flash but a ghost from the light already in the room. To avoid such a ghost image, keep the light level in the room well below the level of the flash illumination.

Calculation of correct electronic flash exposure for non-automatic exposure flash units is much the same as for flash-bulbs. Practically every electronic flash manufacturer provides a calculator on the electronic flash unit which indicates the proper flash guide number to use with various films. Before actually shooting an important subject, however, try a practice roll using the guide number suggested by the unit's maker. Also shoot a few pictures using a guide number slightly greater and slightly less than the maker's suggested guide number. Quite often you will find that some slight alteration in guide number will produce better pictures. This is often true in colour photography.

Bounced Flash

Why point the flash away from the subject? Many advanced amateurs and professionals have found that they can get more pleasing flash results by pointing the flash at the ceiling or wall. The light reflected on to the subject is then more diffused, even and pleasant. Such light appears very natural and it is difficult to tell that flash was used at all. When flash is pointed at a ceiling half-way between the camera and subject, the entire surrounding area is quite well lit by the reflected light.

LIGHTING

Direct flash or flood at camera is most convenient but often creates unpleasant results. Lighting on subject' is harsh, two dimensional. Shadows appear right behind subjects.

By directing the light from camera position on to ceiling or wall, soft, even illumination can be produced. But exposure is often hard to determine and coloured bounce surfaces can alter colour picture results.

Best direct flash or flood can be obtained by using light some distance away from camera. Shadows now fail to one side.

Two very convenient types of indoor lighting units are the quartz iodide lamps (left) and the self-contained reflector floods (right).

The picture no longer has the characteristic flash shadows directly behind the subject plus the marked light fall-off.

When bounce flash is used, however, exposure calculation becomes a very risky business indeed—unless you have a flash meter or an electronic flash unit offering automatic exposure with bounce flash. Without these, you must take into consideration the height of the ceiling plus its reflective ability. You can usually make a fairly good estimate of practical bounce exposure by calculating the distance from the flash to the reflecting surface plus the distance from the reflecting surface to the subject. Add these two distances together and use them as the flash-to-subject distance. Then allow one or perhaps two more *f*-numbers exposure to compensate for the light lost in actually reflecting from the surface of ceiling or wall. With very white surfaces, one *f*-number more exposure will be enough. However, with cream or other light coloured surfaces, allow two more *f*-numbers.

Bounce flash works best for black-and-white photography. With colour materials there is the danger of having off-white or coloured bounce surfaces add coloration to the colour picture. Use bounce flash with colour only if you have a very white surface or you are willing to tolerate off-colour pictures in return for more even illumination.

Off-the-camera Flash

Although most electronic and bulb flashguns are designed to be used on the camera, this can be a bad place for them unless you're using bounce flash. Direct camera flash has very little to recommend it except expediency. Flash-on-camera tends to flatten out the subject. When photographing people or animals head-on, you will get bright reflections of the flash in the pupils of their eyes.

While this is sometimes acceptable in black-and-white photography, it is most annoying in colour where these highlights in the pupils may show as two glowing red spots—interesting if you are photographing lions but not so desirable with other subjects. This is the so-called "red-eye effect" typical of on-camera flash technique.

How can you avoid these unfortunate on-camera flash results? By removing your flash from the camera. Although some flash units do have fairly long synchronization cords which would permit the removal rather easily, most modern flash units have very short ones. You can obtain an extension for this cord from your photo dealer.

When removing the flash from your camera for better results, you can either hold the flash yourself or attach it to a light stand, a tripod or other convenient unit. Since the entire purpose of using flashbulbs is one of convenience, you will probably wish to hold the flash yourself. Holding the camera in one hand while holding the flash in the other does take some agility. It's wise to practice a bit before attempting to use off-camera flash technique.

One of the best places to hold the flash is about two feet above the camera and slightly to the side. This will give you some three-dimensional modelling caused by off-camera shadows. It will also prevent the extreme shadows that flash far off to one side or another can cause.

If your flash gets fairly far from the camera, you will not be able to use camera-to-subject distance for calculating exposure. Remember that you must calculate flash-to-subject distance, not camera-to-subject distance.

You can judge the effect at different flash positions by holding a photoflood lamp in a reflector or even a table lamp in the same position you intend to use with the flashbulb or electronic flash. Note the effect on the subject. This is approximately the same effect that you will get when you use the flash.

You can also use a single flood to give you an indication of just how much light you will lose if you use bounce flash instead of direct flash. Just point your flood directly at the subject and take an exposure meter reading. Now point your flood at the spot on wall or ceiling from which you intend to bounce the light. Take another reading from your subject. The amount of light loss in percentage is approximately the same amount of light loss you will get when you use bounce flash as opposed to direct flash. If the light loss is two f-numbers with flood, when using bounce flash try using two f-numbers more exposure than the guide number calls for.

Quite often in comparing the exposure directions that come with a flashbulb unit against the recommendations on the flashbulb package you will note a discrepancy of one or perhaps even two f-numbers. Flashbulb makers give guide numbers for the average flash unit. Manufacturers of flash units, however, are in a far better position to give precise information on guide numbers for a specific flash unit. The manufacturer knows the reflector's contours, the surface and its reflecting ability plus the angle of coverage of the reflector. Some reflectors concentrate a very bright beam for normal focal length lenses such as the 55 or 58 mm. Takumars or longer. Other flash unit makers deliberately design shallower reflectors which spread the light further thus covering the angles of view for wide-angle lenses such as the 35 mm. Takumars. When wider angles of light are produced, the light spread is necessarily greater, but the concentration of brightness is less and a lower guide number must be used. Always follow the suggestions of the flash unit maker first. Better, shoot a trial set of pictures first to make sure the guide numbers advocated are correct.

At one time it was quite fashionable to use multiple flashbulbs for special lighting effects. While it is possible to link up many flashguns with extension flash reflectors, it is seldom done today. Most photographers whose work requires such extensive flash use now have turned to electronic flash for multiple work. The cost of shooting two or more bulbs to get one picture quickly mounts up to the point where the initially higher cost of electronic flash quickly equals the cost of the flashbulbs.

Multiple Flash

Multiple lighting setups for photoflood lamps are discussed on page 263. The enterprising user of flash who is willing either to make the moderate purchase of additional flashbulbs or the less moderate purchase of extra electronic flash units can also achieve more flexibility in this way. Check carefully with your photo dealer to make certain that you have the right connections between units and your camera. It is possible to mismatch units and cause damage to your camera's flash contacts. To determine exposure, use the guide number of your main light source when the other units are used only as fill-in and background lights.

With flashbulb or electronic, it is no longer necessary to have sync cords attached to all your supplementary lighting units. Small cable-less slave units are available with photo cells which fire automatically when the main light goes off. These are much more convenient to use than the older, wired accessory flash units.

With compliments

LEAMINGTON CAMERA EXCHANGE LTD.

G8, Regency Arcade, The Parade, Royal Leamington Spa, CV32 4BQ.
Telephone: Leamington (0926) 886166

When shooting in your home, you can save valuable accumulator or battery life by operating from house current. If you have a rechargeable battery electronic flash unit and want to get the most flashes from each charge, try this: whenever the unit has been stored for over a day, attach it to house current before you use it. Here's why. When the unit isn't in use, the current which has been stored up in the capacitors by the batteries drains away. By attaching the unit to house current briefly you refill the capacitors without draining the batteries.

Continuous Light Sources

While the two types of flash—electronic and flashbulb—have certainly gained great acceptance, continuous forms of lighting are still very important in photography. By continuous forms of lighting we mean the lighting most familiar—illumination which goes on at the touch of a switch and stays on with even brightness. Compared to flashbulb or electronic flash, continuous light is generally less expensive even if bright and unnatural. Of course, it does need to be connected to house lines. However, it has very important assets. You can see just what effect it has on your subject before you shoot. That's why skilled portraitists, still-life photographers and other careful workers often use it in preference to flash.

Floods and spots for photography come in all forms, shapes and sizes from the simple housebulb-sized lamp to giant arc lights for professional use. We'll confine our discussion to the most practical types of lighting for general 35 mm. use.

Photoflood Lamps

The two most common types of small tungsten lights for photography are the photoflood lamps which must be used with separate reflectors, and the reflector floods and spots which have reflectors already built in. If you plan on using them with colour films, consult the colour filter nomograph in the Facts and Figures section at the back of the book.

All special bulbs for photographic use have one feature in common—they are short-lived. In order to produce great quantities of light, the filaments must be so designed that they burn more brightly than standard filaments. Flood and spot

P.W. 11—S

bulbs often have their estimated life span printed on the container.

The plain No. 1 and No. 2 reflectorless floods are the least expensive types of illumination. However, you will need to purchase metal reflectors plus a clamp-on socket or simple light stand to use them. The reflector floods are usually more efficient and compact, but they do have their own reflectors which must, of course, be thrown away with the bulb when the bulb burns out. The reflector floods and spots are therefore higher in cost. There are several reflector flood types and sizes. Consult your photo dealer concerning the proper fittings and holders for them.

Quartz-iodine Lamps

Perhaps the most efficient continuous light is the quartz-iodine (or tungsten-iodine) lamp. Although originally designed primarily for motion picture work, quartz-iodine lamps were soon adapted to still photography.

What is a quartz-iodine lamp? It's a quartz glass sealed small tube a few inches long with a tungsten filament, an inert gas and iodine. When current is turned on, vaporized tungsten combines with the gaseous iodine in the lamp to form tungsten iodine. The tungsten iodine then recycles back to the filament and tungsten particles are returned to the hottest part of the filament in a continuous cycle. There are no black deposits on the glass envelope as there are with ordinary bulbs, so colour temperature remains constant no matter how many hours the bulbs are used. A 30-hour life—far greater than the life of floodlamps—is not unusual.

These small quartz-iodine tubes are generally used in very carefully designed reflectors. As a result of the extreme efficiency of the tube plus the efficiency of the reflector, such tubes can produce as much light as up to 4 regular reflector floods. They are primarily designed for use with Type A or B colour films, but many manufacturers offer filter accessories for them for use with daylight colour films.

These quartz-iodine lamps are so efficient and convenient that they may replace all standard floods eventually. They are available in many different models to mount on your camera, on light stands or tripods. The lamps also come in several sizes and brightnesses. Since overloaded house current lines are always a problem when using more than one floodlamp, the quartz-iodine lamp lessens the danger of blown fuses. You get more light for less wattage. Consult your photo dealer for the latest quartz-iodine units available.

While one flashgun or electronic flash unit is usually used by 35 mm. camera owners, the ease of checking results and making exposure readings allows continuous light enthusiasts to try multiple setups. Three lights—two floods and a spot—can make up an excellent at-home or small studio system capable of handling most requirements. While we will take up the lighting of various subjects when we discuss each subject, we feel that experimenting with various lighting setups using two and then three lights will probably teach you more about lighting than most lighting diagrams. However, it's advisable to use one flood fairly close to your subject as a main light, another flood at a distance to lighten the shadows somewhat of the first flood, and the spotlight to brighten the background or furnish a toplight. Exposure? Use your meter carefully.

If you do use quartz-iodine lamps, please remember that they tend to build up a great deal of heat. Not only the bulbs but the housings themselves can cause severe burns. It is not advisable to use them around children where there is any possibility that the child could possibly get close to them.

PICTURES OF PEOPLE

Pictures of people present an extremely wide range of possibilities for your camera. Subjects may vary from the simple (but satisfying) family snapshot to the posed formal portrait, to candids taken on the street or in theatres, to photojournalistic stories such as those which appear in leading news magazines. Your camera is more than capable of handling all of them. Without any accessories it can do a splendid job. With various aids such as interchangeable lenses it is capable of results that cannot be surpassed by other equipment, professional or amateur.

Since we will study candid pictures and night photography in other chapters, here we'll concentrate on informal pictures of individuals and small groups. We'll start with the simplest and most common type of photography: the pictures of family or friends near home.

The Family Snapshot

No matter how poor a family snapshot is—blurry, badly exposed, awkward in pose—it will be treasured and loved by mothers, fathers, sisters and brothers. Such pictures are the most common products of cameras throughout the world today. And although you can shoot such pictures with virtually any camera, including the most inexpensive, it's surprising how many of these photographs are made with superlative equipment—like the Pentax.

With proper technique, your camera can produce far better photographs which can also be admired for their artistic ability as well as their family appeal. You can also put each subject's best foot forward, bringing out each person's good features while minimizing the less admirable.

In learning to photograph people, it's wise to start with readily available subjects who expect to be photographed and will be ready and willing to aid you. They will not expect miracles of photography immediately—even if you do own fine equipment. Once you have mastered some of the basics with your home-grown subject material, you'll be ready to pass on to the more difficult subject.

The family portrait is probably the most important type of picture made. Most are dreadful. A very self-conscious child standing too far away from the camera blinks bravely into a brilliant sun right behind the photographer. The subject's face is washed out by the sun while deep eye shadows are formed by the direct light. Quite often the low angle of the sun causes the photographer's shadow to become visible on the ground right in front of the subject. Let's see how we can improve this picture.

The average poor photograph of a person which we justify by terming a "snapshot" is a product of a self-conscious subject and an unschooled photographer. As awkward as the pose may look, it is a posed picture—except that the subject does not know how to pose and the photographer doesn't know how to pose the subject.

Professional photographers often have a great deal of difficulty eliciting the proper pose and expression even from professional models. Small wonder that an amateur, beginner or expert, may have difficulties with a subject who has no schooling in posing.

The best "snapshots" and often the best serious photographs are unposed. Luckily, the Pentax, with its easy to focus lenses, fast shutter speeds and ease of operation, is an ideal camera with which to capture unposed photographs.

Get Out of the Sun

Let's go back to that awkward-looking subject and try again. First we must find a better photo environment. Bright sunlight is hard to control. While the old rule of keeping the sun over your shoulder was adequate in the days of very slow film, the harsh nature of bright sunlight makes the rendition of pleasing facial tones quite difficult. What subject can face a sun and not squint? And why suffer the deep shadows under the eyes or increase the chance of highlighting wrinkles with direct sunlight?

Instead, let's find a picture area in bright shade—perhaps underneath a large tree or within the shadow of a building. Suddenly the subject is no longer faced with the sun's glare. The harsh contrasty light is gone and is replaced with a more even overall lighting. If there were wrinkles and furrows before, notice how the absence of pronounced sunlight minimizes them.

Improve the Pose

Your subject, however, is still just standing there, looking directly into the camera. This won't do at all. What we want is a natural expression, easily recognizable as being characteristic of the subject. First, how do we get the subject to relax? We must find a natural pose. Seating the subject on a rock or in a chair is commendable. Asking the subject to lean against a tree or a doorway is a useful alternative. The subject may also be asked to stand, sit or kneel in a natural position. Now move in with your camera. Don't keep waste space in that viewfinder. The bigger your subject appears in the finder, the larger the image will be on the negative and the sharper and crisper will be your final picture. Keep moving in until you have a very tight composition with just the minimum amount of surrounding scenery.

How is the background? If it's distant, you will have little trouble since it will probably be outside the depth of field when you focus on your main subject. If the background appears close and cluttered, plan on using a fairly large lens opening to throw the clutter out of focus when you shoot. Better still, move the subject or change your own shooting angle to improve the background.

Now we have a relaxed, more natural pose, a tight camera-to-subject distance, an appropriate background and have set the exposure properly for the camera.

Your subject is still looking stone faced, right at you. Start a conversation, If you know his or her interests, fine. If not, discuss what your subject is wearing, the weather—anything but the camera. The subject must really become interested. Continue the conversation but start looking through that viewfinder. See the expression you want? Release the shutter.

Still not quite certain of the pose? While talking to your subject, suggest a change. Want his or her hands folded in the lap? Suggest it. How about a man lighting a pipe? Need a profile? Ask your subject to look at a specific object in the direction you wish, but keep up the conversation.

Obviously this technique of conversation plus photography will require practice. All the technical aspects must be out of

PEOPLE OUTDOORS

Despite the old advice that it's best to photograph people with the sun over your shoulder, don't do it. Direct sunlight is harsh and subject will have to squint in order to open eyes at all.

Bright shade is excellent light, produces soft even illumination in which your subject will appear far more at ease. Bright overcast days are also good.

Watch those backgrounds. If they are confusing and distract from subject, use larger aperture and correspondingly greater shutter speed. Large aperture shortens depth of field, blurs background, thus making it less distracting.

Use camera angle to control background. At left, picture shot on level contains annoying tree. By increasing camera height and shooting downwards, you can eliminate tree and get small brook as background instead.

the way first—distance, choice of film, exposure settings, proper focus, background angle—so that you can concentrate on the subject only with occasional need to refocus.

The foregoing technique works with almost every adult subject, whether a friend, relative or absolute stranger. But it seldom works on children. With children you need some diversion—a book for them to read, a kite to fly, an ice cream cone to eat, a ball to play with. The list of diversions is endless. If you haven't had much practice in following an active child with a camera, find some stationary diversion to keep the child in one place.

Dealing with Groups

Photographing two people or a small group should hold no fears either. How much worse can a group picture be than the traditional album pictures you've seen of two or more people standing in line facing the camera? Instead, get them into a naturally arranged discussion group. Standing groups (unless you are taking formal pictures of a school graduation) should be avoided. Try seating your subjects if possible. However, a small group of people leaning on a bridge or stair railing can make an interesting picture. You must use your ingenuity and imagination to make the most of natural props at hand.

With groups, you can often get conversation started among the individuals. Then let them carry on while you change angle and subject distance for different pictures. If you want all the subjects to look at you, just interrupt the conversation. But shoot just as soon as all heads turn in your direction or your subjects will lose their naturalness.

So far we have only attempted to improve the basic snapshot and make it into a more acceptable photograph. However, there are many more techniques you can use to improve picture taking of people further. With a single-lens reflex many of the most common mistakes made when photographing people can be easily avoided, since you can actually see just what effect you are achieving by watching your viewing screen.

Choose the Right Angle

From what angle should you shoot subjects? This depends on the subject to some extent. However, it's more advisable to shoot at a downward angle than from lower than a subject's eyes. If you do shoot from a low angle you will emphasize the size of the chin and the nostrils at the expense of the really essential features of the face such as the eyes. Usually you will achieve the best results by shooting at the same level as your subject's eyes. If your subject is seated, it may be advisable to seat yourself at the same level. You can often improve your background by shooting down from a higher level. If you do, make sure you have your subject look upwards so that you get the face fairly parallel to the camera film plane. Incidentally, many a double chin will disappear as if by magic if you ask your subject to raise his or her head.

In shooting pictures of children, many photographers take the easy way and shoot downwards from adult height. This produces a dwarf effect—largish heads and tiny feet. Children are best photographed from their own level. To check this statement, try looking at a child from your height and then from the child's height. You can see the difference immediately on your finder screen.

Baby pictures suffer even more because of poor picture taking angles. Far too many are photographed from on high. Faces are lost and backs of head and bodies favoured. With a crawling or walking baby, you will often find the best shot can be made if you lie flat on the ground and aim right at the baby. Of course, excellent pictures of children are possible by having the parents or parent hold the child. If you take such a picture, don't allow the mother and child to stare at the camera. Ask the mother to attract the child's attention. A parent looking at the child and the child looking at the parent does offer a far warmer and more satisfying picture possibility. And remember to get as close to your subject as you can without actually cutting off valuable subject material around the main subject.

From what angle should you shoot pictures of people? Full face, head-on portraits are often the most flattering. Few people have sufficiently good profiles for profile pictures. Three-quarter pictures are difficult, since a three-quarter photograph does show the cheekline and shape of the nose quite acutely. If these features are fine, you will have few problems. If the nose is large and the cheek contour poor, full-face photography is to be preferred.

What can you do with very round faces to minimize them? There are two possibilities. You can slim a full face by split lighting. If it's possible to create a slight highlighted area on one side of the face and slight shadow on the other, you will find that the face does appear narrower. However, this is difficult outdoors where the directional lighting for such a picture—the sun—is largely uncontrollable. Directional sunlight can also throw unfortunate shadows across the nose and mouth.

A second method slimming the face when shooting pictures outdoors is to focus closely with a normal 50–55 mm. Pentax lens which, as we've seen, does have a tendency to elongate the face.

However, you will probably best ignore the problems of a round face and attempt to lead the viewer from the roundness by having the subject rest his or her head in his hand, by asking the subject to tilt his or her head or any other pose which breaks up the symmetrical roundness of the face.

Watch the Background

What is the ideal background? Either it should be as simple as possible to prevent it from detracting from the subject— a sky is usually fine, for instance—or it should be a background which has some personal connection with the subject —the subject in front of his or her house, for instance, would be a correct use of background. The subject standing in front of a brick wall or a timber yard would be incorrect use of background—unless the subject were a bricklayer or carpenter. When a background is unsuitable, first attempt to find a suitable one. If you can't find one, you must use your technical ability to blur the background by placing it outside the depth of field as previously explained.

When on vacation or when travelling, a detailed background can become an essential part of any good snapshot. The background itself becomes a vacation or travel scene while the person within it establishes the fact that he or she was there.

Controlling the Light

So far we have restricted your picture taking to a bright but shaded area to simplify lighting and posing problems. Unfortunately, you will often be unable to find such ideal spots.

You may be forced to shoot with technically inconvenient lighting. However, even here good results can be obtained when care is exercised.

If the sun is still fairly high on a bright sunlit day, and you find your subjects squinting, and the shadows unflattering, try doing just the opposite to what most photographers advise. Instead of standing with the sun at your back, have the subjects stand (or sit) with the sun behind them. This, in effect, immediately removes the sun from their eyes and produces much the same lighting situation in terms of frontal rendition as you had with bright shade. Be sure, however, to make a fairly close exposure meter reading of the subject's face so that you will not be led astray by the brighter background.

Sometimes, however, you may have no choice concerning the direction of the lighting. You will be forced to take pictures with your subject looking into harsh bright sunlight.

It's often suggested that you use a large white cardboard or crinkled aluminium foil pasted to a large board as a reflector in which to catch the sunlight and reflect it back to the subject. This does lighten the shadows and works quite well in practice. The effect of it can readily be seen through the viewfinder.

However, few photographers keep such reflector material handy at all times when taking pictures.

It is possible to lighten shadows by using synchro-sunlight, either flash or electronic flash in combination with daylight. However, the difficulties of balancing the daylight with artificial light are rather great because of the mechanical complications of the single-lens reflex's focal plane shutter.

If your subject must face a bright sun, ask him to keep his eyes shut until the moment you are ready to shoot. When you are ready, ask the subject to open his eyes for just an instant. Shoot immediately.

Exposure for facial tones in extremely bright sunshine can be very tricky. As we've seen in the chapter on exposure, most black-and-white films have the ability to reproduce the brightness range of about 7 f-numbers, but printing papers cannot encompass such a range unless some amount of printing manipulation—burning-in heavily exposed areas and dodging lightly-exposed areas—is attempted. With colour films, the difficulty of reproducing colours accurately when the brightness range is stretched makes compromise necessary. You must decide which colours are most important. A compromise exposure half-way between the proper exposure for highlight and the proper exposure for shadow is often the best answer. But on a bright day, the brightness range almost invariably exceeds the limits of colour film. In such a case most photographers expose for the highlights and let the shadows go dark. The reason: deep undetailed shadows are acceptable in a picture, but bright washed-out highlights are not acceptable.

Shooting Indoors

Many photographers connect indoor picture taking automatically with some type of added artificial illumination. But some of the very best indoor photographs in both black-and-white and colour are actually made with daylight or room light.

Professional studio photographers today use more and more daylight. Many build giant skylights and huge windows into their studios to facilitate such photography. Some have even installed huge overhead banks of lights in an attempt to simulate daylight if and when there is no daylight available.

As an amateur photographer, you can choose your time and type of daylight for indoor photography. While you may not have the elaborate skylights and giant studio windows, you do have windows in your own home or apartment or flat which let in light. If they let in light, they will be usable for indoor picture taking.

Your Asahi Pentax is the ideal 35 mm. camera for shooting pictures indoors by windowlight. With its large maximum lens aperture it can make the most from even weak illumination. And, of course, you can see just what effect the daylight streaming in through the window will actually produce.

Advantages of Daylight

Why is daylight so ideal for indoor picture taking? First, because it's natural. It lights your house interior and the people therein as you see them each day.

Since the lighting is natural, subjects are apt to be at their ease and less self-conscious. You can photograph often then, at your and their leisure. A person is seldom as stiff and awkward in his own home as when facing a camera in a strange location.

332

USING WINDOWLIGHT

Effective indoor pictures can be made easily using only the light coming through the windows in your home. To get light on your entire subject, place camera close to window. To achieve a half lit subject with partial shadow area, place camera at right angle to window. For a silhouette or backlit picture, place subject between camera and window.

Some windows shed better light than others. North light which never has direct sunlight is fine all day and is preferred by professional photographers. South light is equally good. East and West windows can also be used but you must pay attention to the sun's position. Direct sunlight on an indoor subject should be avoided unless you deliberately wish harsh, contrasty results.

N

Good Light All Day

Fair A.M.   Harsh A.M.

W   SUN TRAVEL   E

Harsh P.M.   Fair P.M.

Good Light All Day

S

Daylight is also a vast economizer of equipment. You will be expending no bulbs, trying to connect no lights, waiting for no electronic flash unit to recycle. All you need is your camera, film and a subject.

Perhaps the most cogent reason to use daylight indoors is actually the very nature of daylight itself. It can produce all sorts of effects depending on how and where you use it.

With east and west oriented windows through which the sun actually streams into the house or interior during the day, you have very harsh dramatic lighting on sunny days. On north and south windows with no sun, or with any window on a bright overcast day, you have soft delicate light which best brings out pleasing facial contours.

By using today's rather fast black-and-white and colour films, you will not experience any difficulty in producing well-exposed indoor pictures using daylight.

The greatest amount of illumination, of course, is right at the window. Illumination falls off rapidly in brightness as you move away from the window. The interior of your room also affects the amount of light available. Dark-panelled, curtained rooms with rugs (which absorb light) certainly won't be as bright as when the same amount of sunlight enters a white-walled, light-floored room (which reflects light).

If you want even illumination on your subject, you must stay between your subject and the window. From this camera position your entire frontal subject area will be lit by windowlight. As soon as you let the subject get between you and the windowlight, you create shadows. These can be interesting if properly handled. For instance, if daylight is hitting the side of a face toward the window and the other side of the face is in shadow, you can produce a dramatic picture.

To make silhouettes, just move to a point where you can face the window. Your subject should be between you and the window. If you expose for the daylight behind the subject you will have a silhouette.

Exposing indoors with daylight requires much the same technique as outdoors. For black-and-white, try a compromise exposure between the highlight and the lowlight reading. With colour, expose for the highlights if the brightness range is over $1\frac{1}{2}$ or 2 stops.

334

Using Household Lamps

Available light picture taking not only means shooting indoors using daylight by day; it also indicates using only the household illumination to shoot indoors during the sunless hours.

If a house or interior is suitably lit for reading, it is also usually suitably lit for much black-and-white photography and some colour photography. As with daylight indoors, one of your biggest assets is the naturalness you can preserve.

Before attempting to shoot pictures in your own home by available house lamps and lights, run an exposure test. Pick the most likely spots where you'll want to take pictures—near a reading lamp, at the piano, around the coffee table. Take an exposure meter reading from the palm of your hand held in the light which would normally be illuminating a subject at one of these locations.

You will then learn where you do and where you don't have enough light for picture taking.

If you find that several key places have insufficient illumination, don't give up. Simply replace the bulb with a stronger one.

What about colour photography under existing house lamps? Since artificial-light colour transparency films are balanced for specific types of floodlamps, you might be reluctant to expose them with ordinary house lamps. However, you will be surprised at the reasonable quality of the colour rendition you can achieve with house lamps and Type A or Type B colour films. Careful tests indicate that filtering is not absolutely necessary. You will be quite pleased with filterless results.

A word of warning, however. The colour of the lampshades can seriously affect the colour of your transparency. White or cream coloured shades are best. Avoid any tint or stronger colour. If you are photographing with the aid of a ceiling, wall fixture or any type of lighting which reflects light from the ceiling or walls, the wall or ceiling colour may affect your colour pictures. White or near-white ceilings and walls, of course, produce the best colour.

Since colour films do have such a very limited exposure latitude and ability to encompass a broad brightness range (as we've seen), it's essential that you keep your subjects quite close to the light source and that you expose carefully for that part of the face or body close to the light. Shadow areas will simply go dark.

How should people be posed indoors? If possible, they should not be posed at all. Within the walls of their own house or a house familiar to them, they should be allowed to assume natural positions. They should read, write, listen to music, sew—do whatever they would normally. You should then try various camera angles and heights while cropping the picture carefully in the viewfinder until all extraneous picture material has been removed. When you're ready to shoot, you can either photograph your subject concentrating on whatever he's doing or you can call him or her by name. As they look up, snap the picture.

The secret of photographing anyone, indoors or out, colour or black-and-white, daylight or tungsten, is to maintain or re-establish naturalness. If you bend your best efforts towards removing the stone faces, the stares, the awkward, self-conscious poses of your subjects, you will be well on the way to successful photography of people.

Formal Portraits

In formal portraiture the prime aim is to idealize the subject. The tools to be used are: pose, camera and lighting.

Perhaps the most flexible tool is lighting. If you think of light areas of a print coming forward and dark areas receding, you can begin to see the possibilities in the alteration of light. There are five main areas which govern modelling: forehead, nose, chin and both cheeks. By changing the lighting on these five areas many different portrait effects can be achieved.

However, the problem of lighting for portraiture is often not only one of attempting to idealize the subject. It may be even more essential to hide actual facial defects—a jutting chin, a thin face, a long nose.

The Main Light

In formal portraiture—or any portraiture for that matter—one light source should predominate and all other illumination should be secondary. For this reason the placement and direction of the primary light source in formal portraiture is of prime importance. There are three main lighting placements based on achieving three different results:

FORMAL PORTRAITS

Broad lighting: The side of the face turned toward the camera is illuminated fully. Such a light is used primarily to help widen thin or narrow faces.

Short lighting: The side of the face turned away from the camera is now illuminated fully. This is a good light for the average face since it emphasizes facial contours well. However, it does tend to narrow plump faces and can thus be used correctively if needed.

Butterfly lighting: When the main light is placed directly in front of the subject, it casts a shadow underneath the nose. This is a good type of illumination for glamour pictures of attractive girls.

Try to build your lighting set up in three successive steps. First establish your main light.

Now add your secondary fill-in light and adjust distance to achieve proper balance with main light.

Lastly add third light illuminating background to the required degree.

1. *Broad lighting* places the main light so as to illuminate fully the side of the face nearest the camera. Such lighting tends to broaden faces which are too thin.

2. *Short lighting* places the main light so as to illuminate the side of the face furthest from the camera. Such lighting narrows oval or too broad faces. It is also useful as a strong or low key light for portraits of men.

3. *Butterfly lighting* places the main light in front of and slightly higher than the face, in line with the nose. Such lighting is excellent for normal faces. It tends to delineate good cheekbone lines, but it does light up prominent ears and is therefore seldom used on male subjects, whose ears are not usually hidden by hair.

Now for light placement. The main floodlamp should be placed slightly higher than the seated subject's head, about 45° to either side of the camera and about 3 ft. from the subject. This main light should cause a reflection in the pupils of the subject's eyes. Don't move the main light too high or the shadow underneath the nose will begin to lengthen and become objectionable.

The best main light is a soft flood. A diffuser over the front often proves helpful. While the three types of lighting already mentioned will give you a general guide in fitting the lighting to the face, keep in mind that a narrow face should be lit as completely as possible while a broad face should be illuminated as little as possible with as many broken up areas of light as is feasible.

Background and Secondary Lighting

A background light should be positioned behind the subject, between the subject and background. Make sure that no part of the lamp or its cable can be seen in the viewfinder. The purposes of this light are many. It can serve to separate the subject from the background. It can provide an even lighting over the background for high-key shots. It can even put a pattern or subtle shading on the background if you put a suitable screen or other object in front of the light.

The secondary light is called the fill-in light. Generally a lesser-powered, rather diffused light is used from a position close to the camera or on the opposite side of the camera from the main light. If no lower powered illumination is available, use the same power illumination as the main light but at a greater distance—perhaps six feet instead of three.

The fill-in light's purpose is to control the degree of difference between the highlight and the shadow areas of the portrait. However, there are some dangers in using a fill-in light. If the subject wears glasses, watch out for unwanted reflections. If you notice them from camera position, move the fill-in light until they no longer appear. Also watch out for a second set of light reflections in the eyes. If they appear, you will have to spot them out on the final print.

Often a third light, called a hairlight or top light, is used. This is usually located behind the subject at somewhat of a height but directed downward to illuminate the subject's hair.

Portraiture Problems

The problems besetting the formal portrait photographer and their solutions are many. Herewith a few difficulties which may arise and how to solve them.

Reflections from glasses: Tilt the lenses slightly downwards if possible without altering the characteristic appearance of the subject. Alternatively, alter the angle of the subject's gaze or the position of the offending light. Check the result in the viewfinder. The reflex viewing system is your insurance that if the reflections don't show in the viewfinder, they won't show in the picture.

Long Nose: Minimize it by taking a full-face picture with the nose pointing right at the camera but don't shoot from too close in.

Prominent Ears: Use ¾ view with one ear hidden. Keep the other ear in shadow.

Baldness: Lower camera angle, blend top of head with background tone, avoid lighting on top of head.

Double chin: Tilt chin upwards or use a higher camera position.

Heavy subject: Use short, low key lighting. Have subject dressed in dark clothes.

Wrinkles in face: Used diffused lighting, ¾ pose.

These, of course, are but a few of the problems and solutions. As far as camera technique is concerned, make full use of the fixed subject position to employ a tripod and cable release for complete camera steadiness. Use a fairly small aperture for maximum sharpness in depth. A fairly slow, fine-grained colour or black-and-white film is preferable for quality and biggest enlargement with full detail. If you have one, use an 85 mm., 105 mm. or 135 mm. lens to minimize apparent perspective distortion of close facial or body features appearing too prominent in pictures.

When actually shooting, compose and focus carefully through the viewfinder. Then move away from the finder and take the picture with a cable release while directing your subject. While you are actually focusing through the finder you may find that your subject will appear most apprehensive and stiff in pose. By moving away from the camera, even if you still are holding a cable release, you can often get a subject to relax somewhat.

THE CANDID APPROACH

The words "candid photography" were once almost synonymous with 35 mm. The first 35 mm. cameras set the photographer free from long exposures and posed subjects. With a small camera and a fairly fast lens, a photographer was able to depict people and events as he saw them. He became the unobtrusive observer able to preserve a "slice of life" whenever and wherever he pleased—provided, of course, that there was sufficient light to expose his rather slow film.

Today, candid photography has become more or less the standard method of shooting with a 35 mm. camera. The term "candid" is generally used to distinguish the approach as opposed to "studied" or "posed". The candid photographer is always ready and capable of shooting pictures as they occur—at home, on vacation, in world events, in sports. As you can readily see, candid photography is practised by the photojournalists who shoot pictures for magazines and newspapers as well as the amateur photographer who plans little else than good representative photographs of his friends and family.

Overcoming Timidity

Although the Pentax camera makes excellent candid photographs and is actually used for this purpose by many professional photographers, there are many owners of this superb instrument who have never made a really candid picture. The reason is generally one of timidity. The photographer is psychologically unprepared to point the camera in the direction of a subject who is not expecting to be photographed.

You can see such photographers near any vacation spot. They may even have their cameras out and ready. But whenever they wish to take a photograph, they purposely wait until everyone passes by and then take a picture of the scenery with no human subject matter visible. Quite often such photographers talk themselves into believing that such pictures *are* really better with no human beings. However, this is simply not true. Every camera owner must overcome timidity, shyness or aversion to taking candids. The world is full of people and your pictures will be the better for the proper ones in the right position.

You can, of course, avoid the whole problem by photographing people only from the back, when they couldn't possibly see what you are doing. However, such pictures certainly do not have the interest of those made with people's faces showing.

Basically there are two candid approaches to photography. You can keep your Pentax out of sight until the subject appears and then quickly take a picture before the subject has a chance to react to the presence of the camera, or you can keep the camera in constant sight and take pictures with no regard as to whether the subject notices the camera or not. There are good reasons for both approaches. Which you use depends on your subject. But first, how do you overcome the timidity of photographing people you don't know?

There is but one way. Go ahead and shoot. It is akin to diving off a high board into a pool for the first time. The first time *is* the hardest. The more you think and agonise, the more difficult taking the picture becomes.

There is another interesting aspect of candid photography which is extremely important. If you take pictures with no hesitation, many subjects will find no reason to object. However, if you appear unsure as to whether you dare take a photograph, your hesitation and lack of purpose is immediately transmitted to the subject. This gives him or her an opportunity to make objections even if no such objections were originally planned.

Surprisingly enough, people don't normally bite. If you are not invading their privacy, taking pictures of them in awkward positions or otherwise making fun of them, people are usually found co-operative subjects.

Prove this to yourself by going out on the street and taking pictures.

Approaching the Subject

Now back to the two methods of making candid pictures. The first is to hide the camera until you're ready to shoot. This technique is often necessary with children, who will start to overact, to freeze, to "mug" for the camera. If you are around

342

CARRYING YOUR CAMERA FOR CANDIDS

If you don't want your camera seen but wish to have it ready at all times, attach neckstrap to caseless camera, wrap strap around wrist to prevent accidental dropping, and keep camera hand behind your back.

When you see subject, bring hand around, lift camera to your eye and shoot. Have shutter speed, aperture, focusing distance preset. Check depth-of-field scale to see actual possible zone of adequately sharp shooting. Think of this as a circular doughnut around you (A). Anywhere within, you can shoot and be sure of getting good results.

If carrying a camera in full view isn't a drawback to the taking of candids, hang bare Pentax (or Pentax in back half of carrying case only) around neck with short neck-strap so camera rests on chest. It takes only a split second to grab camera, raise it to your eye and shoot.

the children often enough and they can become used to your camera, it may not be necessary for you to hide the camera when shooting pictures. But if the children are new to your camera and you to them, they will probably be more natural if they do not realise you are trying to take pictures of them.

There are subjects who are camera shy—a wife who freezes whenever her husband shows up with a camera, for instance. There are others who really do not want their pictures taken if asked but who will not object if you do not ask. In some tourist vacation spots where tourists have been lavish with tipping money, any native seeing a camera will immediately demand a tip and then pose frozen faced because he thinks that this is what is expected of him. There are those who may be engaged in some interesting job until they see you and the camera. They will then stop and watch you.

You must decide upon the subject approach. But there is nothing to be ashamed of in hiding a camera before you are ready to use it. You are simply making certain that you will have natural unspoiled picture material.

When can you walk around with your camera in full view? Whenever your subjects are completely engrossed in some event and are taking no notice of you. Examples: spectators at a sports event, people watching a parade.

Quick-shooting Methods

If you intend to keep your camera out of sight, you will have to practice drawing and firing like learning to draw and shoot a pistol or revolver quickly. Where can you hide a camera as handy as the Pentax? First, remove the front of the case if you can. If you cannot, you will have to take the camera out of its case and carry it by the neckstrap attached to the camera by lugs.

Wrap the strap around your right wrist so that most of the strap "play" is removed. Then grasp the camera in your right hand with your right forefinger on the shutter release and your right thumb on the rapid-wind lever.

You should be able to hold the camera securely in one hand whether at your side or behind your back. The strap is a safety device in case you lose your grip on the camera itself.

Practice bringing the camera quickly to your eye, focusing and firing. The more you can preset the Pentax, of course, the easier it will be to shoot quickly. Whenever you arrive at the place where you intend to take pictures, make an exposure meter reading and set your camera accordingly. Keep in mind that you want a fairly good depth of field so that any mistakes in focus will not ruin your photo possibilities.

If you are to photograph in two lighting conditions, calculate two exposures, one for each condition. Be prepared to shift your camera controls from one condition to the other quickly, depending on where you find your subject.

Although it is sometimes possible to find the time to focus your camera accurately once you have the Pentax at your eye, it is still advisable to preset not only exposure but focus too. Try to predetermine just how far away your subject is likely to be or just how close you are likely to approach. Learn to estimate distances fairly accurately, but as explained, allow yourself some room for error by using an aperture producing a fairly extensive depth of field (zone of sharp focus). Allow your subject to reach this range before you shoot.

If you do keep your camera in full view, carry it around your neck, not over your shoulder. Although an over-the-shoulder carry is quite sufficient for carting a camera from one picture-taking situation to another, a camera over the shoulder is not near shooting position. You would have to unsling the camera, then bring it up to eye level.

Most of the camera carrying straps, including the Pentax straps, are too long. You may have to put an additional hole in the strap to shorten it. A Pentax should be carried not at stomach level but at chest level.

Although you may be carrying the camera in clear sight you may still be able to achieve a good element of total surprise. People noting a camera around the neck do not immediately expect that you may raise it and shoot swiftly. You should be able to get the camera to eye level and shoot before the subject realises what is happening. In addition, the slow methods by which less practised photographers take pictures are in your favour. Most people do take a long time, getting the camera ready, setting it, focusing it and finally taking the picture. Few of the subjects will believe the speed at which you can operate. You will have already perhaps taken three pictures before your subjects realise you are even ready to take the first one.

When to Shoot

In shooting candids you should develop a very definite approach as do professionals. When should you take the picture? As soon as you see it. It is worthwhile waiting to see if the subject gets better or the composition improves? It seldom is. Instead shoot immediately to make sure you do not miss the picture. If you wish then to find a better position, background or change angle or height, do so.

Shoot a picture as soon as it intrigues you. Then move in towards your subject, tightening the composition. As soon as you feel you have improved the picture, don't hesitate to see whether it will get or can be made even better. Shoot again. Then attempt further improvement. Each series of photographs should be a small picture story beginning when you first spot the subject and continuing until it becomes impossible for you to better the picture.

Of course, there are exceptions to this rule. There will be many once-in-a-lifetime subjects which will allow no possibility of a retake. Also, once the subject is aware of the camera, the whole appeal of the photograph may disappear.

Using Lenses

Since the Asahi Pentax accept a large variety of interchangeable lenses, both wide-angle as well as long lenses should be used where they can be of advantage.

In close quarters such as a marketplace, the wide-angle lens, either the 35 mm. or 28 mm. lens, will be best. With these you can shoot general scenes and groups. You will have little focusing trouble since the overall depth of field is considerable.

The longer lenses, particularly the 85 mm., 105 mm., 135 mm. or zoom lenses, are excellent for candids. Since the lenses are quite small in physical size, many subjects don't realise that you are actually taking close-ups. These longer lenses do allow you to remain further away from subjects.

For indoor work the fast speed of the 85 mm. $f1.8$ SMC Pentax is extremely helpful. Outdoors the 105 mm. $f2.8$, 120 mm. $f2.8$, 150 mm. $f4$ or 135 mm. SMC Pentaxes are good performers.

Film choice is important in candid photography. Use fairly fast films from Group 3. These will allow fairly fast shutter speeds and allow sufficient depth of field. For colour, try films with fairly high ASA indexes.

Candid photography requires all your abilities—physical co-ordination, will power, technique, quick thinking, ability to judge distance, ability to anticipate the moves of your subject. Aside from some memorable formally posed portraits of famous statesmen, practically all the best known and great pictures made in recent years by amateurs and professional alike were the results of candid photography.

OUT AND ABOUT

Your camera can travel with you to a variety of locations. Holiday and business trips are obvious occasions when interesting shots may present themselves. But even in your ordinary leisure time, at the theatre or circus, or even at home by the TV set, you can still find plenty of opportunities to add to your photographic record.

The Travelling Camera

It isn't our purpose here to examine where you might travel. That will be your own personal preference. We can, however, make some suggestions about equipment and approach to subjects. First the equipment.

If you take only colour or only black-and-white film you will have little trouble in deciding which film to carry, although the type and speed needed will make some choice necessary. If you like both colour and black-and-white pictures, you do have a problem if you have only one camera body. The ideal answer, of course, is to have two bodies—even if you have but one lens. You can swiftly shift from one camera to the other to cover subjects in both colour and black-and-white.

If you do have two camera bodies, there are two possible alternatives. You can shoot some of the time in colour and some of the time in black-and-white. Of course, this does mean that if you are travelling in a hurry and cannot revisit a spot, you will not be able to duplicate all your subjects in both colour and black-and-white. Here's another possible solution, although it is not possible to make accurate colour pictures from black-and-white film, surprisingly good black-and-white enlargements can be made from colour transparency and negative originals. If you choose a fine-grained colour transparency film, you can use a slide copying device or have a photofinisher make a black-and-white negative of any transparency on fine grain black-and-white film. This black-and-white negative can then be used to make black-

and-white enlargements in the usual manner. It would be foolish to suggest that such black-and-white copies are always as good as those made from original black-and-white negatives, but they can approach quite close.

Films to Take with You

What film should you take and how much? Make a careful investigation of film purchases (and prices) where you are going. If you are certain of picking up good fresh film with which you are familiar at reasonable prices, there is little sense in lugging film with you. But it is poor economy if you must rely on a foreign brand of film with which you have had no previous experience. If you plan on being away for over a week, make provision for having your colour film processed. Once colour film has been removed from its hermetically sealed container, its worst enemy, humidity, gets at it. The sooner it is processed the less chance of any annoying shifts in colour. In selecting a lab., don't trust services that are untried. If the pictures are valuable make sure they are processed by people with whose work you are familiar.

Should you carry fast or slow black-and-white and colour film? The choice depends on the type of subject material with which you will contend. A landscape photographer who plans all shots from a tripod need not take anything but slow fine-grained materials. However, for nearly everyone else a fairly fast black-and-white emulsion with an ASA index between 200 and 400 should suffice for low light shots while a slow or medium slow emulsion from ASA 25 to 160 will take care of other exigencies.

In colour, two films, one fine grained with good colour at ASA 50 or less and another with a speed of between 160 and 200 for emergencies, should be carried. If you plan on shooting indoor colour by low available light you might want to consider using only tungsten balanced film (with a proper correction filter outdoors). You will find this technique more convenient that that of using daylight-balanced film with a filter for indoor shots. This latter combination yields very low film speeds.

Filters? Close-up equipment? Only necessary if you really expect to use them. A tripod? Quite a bother but often a big help. Accessory lenses? If you have them, by all means take them along. Besides making many an impossible picture possible, they will add variety to your composition. Now what do you put all this equipment in?

A carryall bag is a great aid but too large a bag is as bad as none at all. Don't get a bag which is so large that you must find things to put into it. If anything, get a bag slightly too small, which will make you selective in carrying equipment. And remember that bags become heavier and heavier the longer and farther they are carried.

Avoid the Picture Postcard

When travelling, most people photograph scenes much like those in postcards. Make a simple rule. If there is a postcard scene which is identical to the picture that you intend to take, don't take the picture. In any scene try to inject individuality. If you are travelling with someone, have the person included in the scene—not staring into the camera, but examining a building's ornamentation, or waving while riding the tramcar. People must fit into the scene, not look as if they were stuck on like figures atop a wedding cake.

If you are travelling alone, quite often you will be able to get some photographer passing by to take a shot with you in the picture.

How do you take pictures of people that you don't know when travelling? The answers are as varying as people are. In some areas, people don't mind having their picture taken. In others, every snapshot is considered a distinct invasion of privacy. In some areas heavily travelled by tourists, the natives expect to be paid whenever you take their pictures.

For the best possible natural pictures, shoot quickly. Even if people are willing to pose later, the pictures look posed. You will probably find that your most effective pictures are made with unposed subjects.

The automatic diaphragm of the Takumar lenses will allow you to get pictures quickly and easily. Be sure that you keep your camera set with the proper exposure at all times. After you have seen a picture possibility, it is too late to start worrying about exposure. Exposure must be preset.

Lenses for Travel Shots

The 35 mm. $f2.8$ and $f2$ SMC Pentaxes are excellent travelling companions for general scenes. However, make sure that you do not try to include so much distant detail in your picture or all the subject material will appear minute. Never use a wide-angle lens on distant scenics. Invariably you will be disappointed in the diminutive size of the picture components.

Be selective. If you do have a choice of lenses, use the longest one possible and the tightest cropping you can. With no longer lens at your command, use your feet and approach each subject as closely as possible. Try to maintain some continuity to your pictures. Good magazine and newspaper photographers realise that every picture cannot be a masterpiece. Many pictures must be functionally descriptive bridging shots. If you try to make all your pictures individual works of art, you will have a rather disjointed series of photographs. Think of the pictures as you might show them later. Don't miss any important points even if, aesthetically speaking, they don't appeal to you at the time.

A small electronic flash unit makes an extremely valuable accessory—particularly for interiors. More and more places—even churches—allow electronic flash. The small modern units have rechargeable batteries and charging units which can recharge the cells on virtually any current on earth. There is really very little excuse today for the picture that got away indoors because there wasn't sufficient light.

Scenics

The Pentax camera is one of the best instruments for shooting scenics. Perhaps the scenic requires the most practised eye, the most ability to see individual elements of the picture. The life-size viewing and focusing image allows all elements to be analysed and controlled.

What is a scenic? We'll define it as any photograph in which the setting dominates the picture. This might be a landscape, a seascape, a city scape. But we certainly don't wish to imply that these dominating picture areas must be peopleless. Far from it. The right human or animal subjects positioned in just the right place in the picture area can quite often add just the extra bit of seasoning that's needed to make a scenic come alive.

How should the picture be framed? Where should the people, if any, be placed? What should be in focus or out of focus?

Composing the Picture

Many rules have been made for scenic photography. By following these rules you are supposed to arrive at the proper composition for landscapes. While most rules were based on the general methods of composition used by academic painters, following them too stringently can cripple the creative ability of photographers. As many good scenics are shot by disregarding the rules as are made by sticking to the rules.

Every scenic must have a focal point of interest—that part of the picture to which your eye is drawn. It may be a distant mountain, the façade of a building, a boat on the sea. It may be quite small, but it must be there. Too often photographers shoot scenics in which there is no focal point. Often the mountains in the background are too small because a wide angle lens is used, or the sea trails off into nothing but water. Your eye seeking a centre of interest simply wanders away to infinity. The picture defeats itself in its inability to hold your interest.

Whatever the main subject, it should be of sufficient size to be readily recognizable. Of course, there are some exceptions to this. When you are attempting to reproduce the hugeness and grandeur of a scene, you will deliberately make your subject small in relationship to his or her surroundings. How can you control image size in a landscape? To some extent by moving back and forward yourself if the main subject is not too distant. If your main subject is a distant mountain, you will have a difficult and long walk to alter its size in your picture area. In this case, a change in focal length lens will produce the required image reduction or enlargement.

If your main subject area contains people, you can, of course, place them nearer or further away from the camera to achieve different size images.

Just how big should the central image be? To some extent this must be dictated by circumstance. An ocean liner cutting through the water toward you should be large and overpowering. Two seated figures in a vast woodland area can be quite small. An impressive mountain seen across a lake can be medium sized to allow you to frame it tastefully.

Placement is also important. Impressive dynamic objects can often be centrally located. Medium size landscape images should be placed off centre, but not at the very picture edge.

Can a landscape have more than one main subject? Yes

352

COMPOSITION OF SCENICS

While hard and fast compositional rules seldom work at all times in practice the following technique of improving a scenic may be helpful.

Scenic with distant houses and horses is pleasant but rather static. Can it be improved?

We've come in closer to make images larger, but, alas, we've chopped off part of tree without improving overall picture much.

Let's get even closer and eliminate the distracting tree at left. The images are large enough to be striking but we need some framing device.

By moving to the right and thus changing camera angle we can keep image size, pick up the tree at right for framing and also include the tree in the left distance to complete the composition.

it can. You can have people in a scenic who are looking at a distant mountain. The viewer's eye should first pick up the small figures, then shift to the same subject that the small figures are viewing—the mountain.

Dynamic, large central subjects often don't require framing, but other landscape subjects usually do. Without some framing, the main subject at a distance appears lost on the enlarging paper or projection screen.

Foremost framing device is foliage, usually tree branches in both the top left- and top right-hand corners of the picture area. If these do not actually exist they can be printed in later on black-and-white prints. An arch or doorway also serves as a useful frame. The frame simply channels your viewing eye into the picture and towards your main subject.

It's quite important in scenic photography that you render both frame and subject in sharp focus. An out-of-focus frame can be extremely disturbing. You can generally rely on a quick check of your lens's depth-of-field scale. The depth of field can sometimes be shifted if necessary in case the depth of field does not appear to get both foreground and main subject in good sharpness

The illusion of depth is most important in scenic photography. Certainly the framing accounts for at least one additional plane of depth. However, other planes should be recorded. With each subject or framing at a different plane of depth you can add to the picture's ability to hold the viewer.

Contrasting colour plays an extremely important part in scenic photography. A bright red, blue or yellow jacketed subject carefully placed within a landscape can spice a dullish scenic. Of course, persons with such bright colouring should be kept at an appropriate distance within the picture frame or they will take over and dominate the entire picture.

Using Filters

In black-and-white scenic work, the proper use of filters can help produce better scenics. Even if you do not use filters, some differential between clouds and sky will be recorded on film. However, the clouds may not be visible in a standard print. The clouds and sky will need special, additional print manipulation. You can make the clouds easily printable by using a medium yellow filter for average cloud effects, or dark red filter for very dramatic dark sky and white cloud effects.

A green filter helps scenics with foliage. The green filter lightens foliage and also provides some darkening of the sky to enhance clouds.

In taking scenics be careful to keep your camera as level as possible—don't point it up too far to include a tree or the entire façade of a building. If you do, you will create apparent perspective distortion. The trees and buildings will appear to be falling over backwards.

While this fault can be overcome to some extent by tilting the enlarging easel when making a black-and-white enlargement, there is little that can be done to aid a colour transparency. The closer your viewpoint the more apparent distortion you will create if you tilt the camera upwards or downwards.

Exposing the Scenic

Although we have examined exposure problems in a full chapter, the special difficulties of obtaining good exposure of a scenic requires additional mention.

A meter reading from camera position will usually produce a sufficiently accurate exposure. This is particularly true if the scene is fairly evenly lit and the highlight areas do not overpower the shadow areas. If there is a very great difference in size between highlight and shadow areas, you will have to read the light from the bright area and shadow area, average them and use the mid-way reading.

In many scenics it will not be possible for you to approach the various areas in the picture to take an accurate highlight and shadow area reading. In such cases you must make what is called a substitute reading. This means that you must find some subject material close at hand which appears to be in approximately the same light as your more distant subject. You must then take readings from these substitute subjects and calculate the exposure from them. If no actual subject is available, try holding the palm of your hand in the light and take readings from it.

When making overall readings of a scene with a great deal of sky area, always point the meter down slightly. This will prevent the bright sky from dominating the picture area and giving you an erroneous, underexposure calculation.

Scenics, like pictures of your family and friends, can be simply dull snapshots or good photographs. Much depends on the time and effort that you put into it.

Architecture

When using the Pentax camera for architectural photography there are some cardinal rules which will aid you in obtaining more acceptably accurate pictures. Always keep your film plane parallel to the subject. If the plane of your subject is parallel to the film plane of your Pentax, there will be no linear distortion. In other words, if you are photographing a building, don't point your camera up or down. Point it straight ahead and all lines will be parallel, all right angles true. If you cannot get all the required subject material within the finder, back off until you can. If you cannot increase camera-to-subject distance, you will have to use a wider angle lens. If you do not have one or still find that the subject is insufficiently covered, you will have to point your camera upwards or downwards and risk linear distortion. In black-and-white printing these lines can sometimes be restored to linearity by tilting the enlarger easel in the opposite direction from which the camera was tilted until the lines again appear parallel on the easel.

If possible, try to work with just the normal lens of your camera. It produces a pleasing perspective and, at most shooting distances, an acceptable illusion of three-dimensional depth. When using wide-angle lenses be careful that you do not exaggerate distances of near and far objects—unless you want to. Certainly there is no better way to create the effect of spaciousness in a room that is less than really spacious than to use a wide-angle lens. On the other hand, the more distant viewpoint of a long lens produces foreshortening distortion. Distances in depth appear abbreviated. Here, too, the effect may be useful or it may damage the accuracy of your picture.

When photographing buildings be sure that you get good separation between the building and the sky area. If the building is fairly light in colour and you wish to have a sharp building line delineation, use a deep yellow or red filter to darken the sky, but remember the effect such filters have on other colours in the scene.

When an interior is inadequately lit, you do have a prob-

BUILDINGS
AND INTERIORS

If you photograph a tall building you will get correct linear perspective only if you keep the camera's film plane parallel to building. To keep whole building in picture, however, you may tilt camera upwards—unless you can back away far enough or change to a sufficiently wide angle lens. If you do point the camera upwards your resulting picture will show the buildings converging and falling towards you. In printing, this can be corrected either by tilting the enlarger head, the baseboard or both.

Beware of buildings whose tone blends into sky. A filter, particularly a yellow or orange filter outdoors can separate building from sky.

When photographing interiors with a normal lens, you may not be able to cover the entire room. However, a 35 mm. or wider lens will allow you to take in a far greater angle from the same camera position. In addition, a wide angle lens tends to increase the apparent depth between objects, making the room appear bigger.

lem which is possibly insurmountable. In large interiors where you cannot use a tripod and must take the pictures while others are in the building there seems little that can be done. However, if you can put your camera on a tripod and use a floodlamp, you can try a technique which works for many photographers. Set your shutter to "B" and use the smallest lens opening possible. Now "paint" the interior of your picture area with light by travelling around with the lamp on an extension cord, lighting the shadow areas. Make sure you do not throw any light on yourself and that no part of you or the lighting equipment comes between the cast light and the camera lens. Otherwise blurred traces will appear in the picture.

Flashbulbs or electronic flash can be similarly used to lighten the shadows in interiors but you must take care not to overpower existing lighting. If room lights are on, they should appear natural. The exposure has to be carefully calculated so that the flash or flood exposures are weaker than the existing lighting, which will be receiving rather long exposure while the shutter is set on "B". If strong daylight is entering and will be included in the picture area this method is not suitable, for windows and daylight parts of the room will be far too heavily overexposed.

Shots in the Night

Your camera should not retire at nightfall merely because there is no more outdoor illumination or because flash, floods, or even natural room-light are no longer available. Excellent outdoor photographs are still possible with street lights, the illumination coming from houses, theatre marquees, moonlight, advertising signs, car headlamps—the list is virtually endless. Your camera need never go to sleep.

Obviously the amount of light available for such picture taking does vary. To be safe, choose fairly fast films—colour or black-and-white. Films with ASA indexes of 400 or over are preferable in black-and-white. In colour, films with indexes between 160 and 200 are obtainable. Strangely enough, many professional photographers prefer to use daylight-type colour films for outdoor night shots rather than the tungsten types which you might imagine would better match the artificial illumination prevalent at night. The warmish coloration of daylight films when used with tungsten lighting is

358

often more pleasing for night shots than the rather coldish results obtainable with tungsten-balanced colour films.

Subject matter is wide indeed—particularly in a large city. Many buildings are well lit, fountains are meticulously illuminated. Lighting under movie theatres is quite good and well illuminates passersby. Store windows can be fascinating with the people passing in front of them in silhouette. Most cities have specific colourful areas which only come alive at night and make excellent hunting grounds for you and your camera.

After rain, streets shine and reflect the street and theatre lighting. Interesting reflection patterns can be photographed in both colour and black-and-white. The tracery of head-lamps and tail-lamps of cars also forms interesting patterns. Any busy street at night will give you a bewildering criss-cross of headlamps. A time exposure will record many of these and also allow the headlamps to light up considerable portions of the surrounding scenery.

Exposure in Low Light

Naturally, exposure is somewhat of a problem with such diverse sources of illumination. Both the clip-on meter and the Spotmatic camera with meter behind the lens are sensitive enough to make readings of such scenes with good accuracy. The question, of course, is: what do you read and where you do read it from?

When photographing people under fairly bright light outdoors, take a reading as you normally would. Read for the highlight areas predominantly in colour photography and for the shadow areas in which you wish to hold detail if you are shooting in black-and-white.

Store windows can be read by your meter. Just point the meter inwards at the displays. If you wish to use the passers-by as silhouettes, stand some distance away from the window and let the people pass between you and the window. If you expose for the window only the people will be in silhouette.

Neon signs, street lights and automobile headlamps are perhaps the most confusing subjects to expose for properly. With any lights in which the light itself plays the most important part, you need do no more than approach fairly close to the illumination source, point your meter and take a reading. You can then retrace your steps back to the more distant position from which you wished to take the picture and shoot according to the close-up reading.

Such an exposure, however, will only show off the signs or lights themselves. If you wish the lights to illuminate some of the surrounding area, you will have to give additional exposure. If there is some specific subject which is illuminated—a person under a street lamp, for instance, make your reading from this subject rather than the lighting itself. When photographing lighting alone, it is often advisable to allow slightly more exposure than the meter calls for. While the meter reading will give you a perfectly exposed light, the light will not seem real. By overexposing the light will produce some natural appearing flare.

Moving Lights

Pictures made by the tracings of automobile headlamps and tail-lamps are really quite easy to take. If you point your camera up any street on which there is traffic, the oncoming cars will show bright white headlamps while only the red tail-lights will glow from the other lane of traffic—provided the street is a two-way thoroughfare. For such pictures a tripod or other support is needed. The exposure can be as long or as short as you wish depending on the number of light tracings you wish and the brightness of the picture you intend to create. If the street is a busy one and you keep the camera shutter open on "B" for a minute or so, the whole picture area will be rather bright. For such pictures, a meter is of doubtful value. Only experimentation with various amounts of exposure time will yield answers as to what re-results you can expect. Don't forget about depth of field, however. Make sure your entire subject area lies within the zone of sharp focus. If your camera is on a tripod and you are taking a time exposure, there is no reason to use the widest lens opening. Use the proper lens opening for the subject material and then increase exposure time to compensate for it.

Exceedingly long time exposures at night· on a busy thoroughfare can be quite interesting, because people and cars hurrying by will not be visible. Only subjects who remain in one place for any length of time will show up in the picture.

Night out of Town

City life is not the only type which offers possibilities of making night photographs. Moonlight shots in the country or at the seashore with the moon reflecting from the water can be very dramatic indeed. The moon, incidentally, is brighter than you might think. You can usually get a rather accurate reading of the moon itself using the behind lens meter of your Pentax. You can also use a separate meter. If not, try exposures of 1/30 at f2.8 with fairly fast black-and-white film for the moon itself. To make sure of your picture, take a few additional frames at more and less exposure. An exposure of 1/30 sec. is usually sufficient to stop the movement of the moon itself relative to the earth.

For landscapes or seascapes lit by the moon, you will have to rely on judgment. If you have had no experience in guessing such exposures, take a number of photographs at varying time exposures up to a few minutes. Check the results and use the data when you're ready to try a moonscape again.

Fireworks

Fireworks can easily be captured in both black-and-white or colour. Certainly the most interesting results are those in colour. Firework pictures should be made with your camera on a tripod. Use an f4 to f8 aperture and fast colour film with an ASA index of 100 or over. Before the individual display goes off, open your shutter by turning the shutter dial to "B" and maintaining pressure on a cable release. Keep the shutter open until the entire individual display is over—the complete flight and bursting of a skyrocket, for instance. Then close the shutter. You will have thus photographed the entire pattern and path of the skyrocket. For most spectacular effects, you can leave the shutter open to record a number of different displays on the same film frame.

At the Theatre

In many theatres you will not be allowed to photograph from your seat. In some countries the stagehands' or actors' unions have specific instructions against allowing such pictures to be taken. Still many people do take such photographs, rules or no rules.

Taking pictures of stage presentations, circuses, ice shows and similar entertainments isn't really difficult. Most such events are lit by powerful arc lamps allowing you to use daylight colour films which generally have higher ASA indexes than the slower tungsten types.

With your through lens reading meter you can take accurate meter readings. A fairly long interchangeable lens helps, because you can use it to make a close-up reading of the subject from your seat. If your reading still takes in too much of the brighter stage area around your subject, allow between ½ and 1 stop extra exposure to compensate for the darker subject. However, with no metered camera or Spot Meter you will not be able to make an accurate reading of the actual lighting available. In such cases some intelligent guessing will be necessary.

Serious stage plays are fairly easy to judge. The lighting is usually good and not coloured. With a moderately fast film having an index of between 160 and 200, exposures of 1/30 sec. at f2.8 or larger should produce good results. This is for average stage lighting. If a bright spotlight is used, of course, cut down exposure. Low-key dramatic scenes are generally impossible to photograph from audience position.

Musical shows and reviews are more difficult to photograph. The colour and brightness of the lighting is constantly changing. While 1/30 sec. at f2 or f1.8 is a good usual exposure, it is almost impossible to expect consistently good results unless you've had a good deal of practice in stage photography.

Amateur plays and shows do offer the average photographer a better chance to get good pictures. During dress rehearsal the photographer can get to the stage to make a correct reading right from the subjects.

Circus performances also offer a great challenge to serious photographers in terms of subject choice and timing. While you should use the fastest shutter speed possible to stop action, you can still get crisp photographs at 1/60 sec. if you can anticipate events and catch performers at the peak of the action when there is the least motion. Generally, however, large apertures, accurate focus and fast shutter speeds produce the best circus results. If you are sitting fairly close to the arena or rings, you can make good meter readings from the performing area itself.

At the Cinema

Pictures from motion picture screens tend to be very disappointing in terms of quality. The movie when watched seems quite sharp, yet the individual still pictures shot from the screen lack this very sharpness. Actually the motion picture itself is seldom as sharp as it looks during a showing. The movie is made up of 16 to 24 individual frames per second projected in rapid sequence. Frames showing motion are often blurred. You do not notice this any more than you notice the momentary blanks between the individual pictures. But when you photograph the screen with a still camera you remove the action and expose the blur. Nevertheless, taking a still picture from a movie screen does represent a rather simple method of obtaining an adequate still snapshot from a movie without going through the elaborate techniques of direct printing from the film itself.

You can make quite respectable still snapshots with high-speed black-and-white film using a shutter speed no faster than 1/30 sec. Actually 1/15 sec. is better to avoid the possibility of catching the film during one of its intermittent periods of darkness between frames. Most movie projectors running at 16 or 24 frames per second have shutters working at about 1/30 to 1/50 sec. The Pentax shutter speed therefore should be slower. A good exposure on a fairly bright screen would be 1/15 or 1/30 sec. at f2. Naturally, exposure will depend greatly on the brilliance of the projected image. To get the sharpest picture possible, wait until action ceases on the screen. Then shoot. The finer the screen surface, the better the still picture possible. Take a number of exposures of each scene as insurance.

Television Stills

Quite akin to taking pictures from a motion picture screen is photographing from your own TV set. Here the production of the image is somewhat different from that of movie screen. In movies complete pictures are intermittently flashed on the screen. The TV picture is composed by a single spot travelling back and forth across the tube at phenomenal speed. Owing to a certain amount of afterglow existing on the tube face and the natural phenomenon known as persistence of vision it appears to form a complete picture made up of horizontal lines.

These lines are formed interlace fashion, the spot covering the whole picture area in 1/50 second but forming only half the lines. It then shoots back to the start position to fill in the gaps between the lines. Thus the complete picture is formed in 1/25 second. These figures apply to the British 50 Hz system. The picture takes 1/30 sec. from the American and other 60 Hz domestic electricity supply.

Since the total shutter curtain travel of the Pentax is far longer than 1/25 or 1/30 sec., a complete image can only be guaranteed if you use a shutter speed no faster than 1/8 sec.

The aperture required will naturally vary with the brightness of the picture but a few experiments with a reliable exposure meter, taking readings directly from a mid-tone on the screen, will soon provide the answer. That is likely to be somewhere around $f5.6$ with a 200 to 400 ASA film. There is no point in using fine-grain material. Even with the smallest screens, the lines making up the picture are far more destructive of definition than the grain of the film. Colour sets generally require an aperture of $f2$–2.8 on a 64–80 ASA film. A CC40R filter is advisable to bring out the reds properly.

Line your camera up squarely with the tube face and focus on the finest visible detail. Take care that there are no reflections on the protective screen from windows or room lights. If you turn up the brightness control a little, you will increase the illumination and cut down the contrast.

SPORTS AND PASTIMES

Twenty or so years ago, the 35 mm. single-lens reflex would have been the last camera any serious photographer would have suggested for taking sports or action pictures. The camera was just too slow in operation. By the time you focused your subject, made the decision to take a picture and then closed down your lens aperture manually to the proper opening, the decisive, climactic instant of the action was over. Should you somehow capture the picture, the view-finder went black the moment after the picture was taken because the interior mirror flipped up out of the way of the light path—and stayed up.

Today the 35 mm. single-lens reflex has moved to the very forefront of those cameras judged ideal for sports and action photography. The automatic diaphragm of the Pentax lenses solves the problem of closing the lens down after you decide to take the picture. You need only press the shutter release and the lens closes to any preselected opening and re-opens to full aperture automatically. The rapid return mirror provides virtually continuous viewing and focusing. You do not lose sight of the action after the shutter is released. A photographer can shoot, wind, refocus if necessary and shoot again without removing the camera from his eye.

However, modern Pentax cameras offer further assets to the photographer wishing to photograph action. The auto-winders and motors make it possible to take pictures in split-second sequence, a built-in meter system or automatic exposure provides proper exposure. And a wide series of lenses allows the photographer to pick the exact picture area he wishes to cover for any photograph. The Pentax zoom lenses introduce even greater flexibility. Suddenly the photographer has an infinite choice of focal lengths. The action can be followed and the picture area varied constantly as the photographer wishes.

The 35 mm. single-lens reflex has grown to become the leading camera type used today.

Balancing the Variables

Whether you are a professional photographer assigned to cover games or events, or an amateur sitting in a fixed position in the stands, you must tackle three important variables in sports photography; lighting, distance and focal length of the lens. These three factors plus all the other usual variables of camera operation govern your success or failure technically in action photography.

Lighting is of extreme importance. When you expect to halt action, more lighting is called for than if you are taking quiet pictures around your home. Seldom will you have the advantages of creating your own lighting as you would at home, particularly if you are an amateur. Professionals, of course, can and do use flash, mostly electronic today, when they are sufficiently close to the action. At outdoor events, there is generally enough lighting for either colour or black-and-white—particularly with today's modern faster film emulsions. Indoors, however, lighting is usually just barely adequate.

Distance is a factor in sports photography because most games require the photographer—amateur or professional—to remain on the sidelines, off the playing field. The spectator has an even greater distance problem since there is an additional distance from sideline to seat. In local or amateur events, the amateur photographer has a far better chance of operating right at the sidelines close to the field.

Choice of lens focal length is the opposite side of the coin from distance. If you cannot get sufficiently close to the action, the only possible alternative is to make the action come to you by drawing it in with a longer than normal focal length lens. But while many sports pictures are made with long lenses, a normal or even wide-angle lens is needed to record large areas close to the camera. The amateur, often further away, must make use of even longer lenses to achieve the same subject area size on his negatives or transparencies.

The battle over focal length has been in progress for some time—ever since modern optical science made the long lens or even a zoom a rather small, fairly easy-to-hand-hold instrument. Photographers too often find it more convenient to remain aloof from the sports or action and to draw it close with a long lens. Other photographers feel that the long lens produces a sense of remoteness from the subject. They explain that proximity is most important to "feel" the action. Simplifying the problem a bit, this is the difference between a photographer close to a pole vaulter, pointing his short focal length lens upwards from the ground at the vaulter high in the air, as opposed to the photographer at a great distance photographing the same jump but with his long lens more or less level with the subject. It's evident that the most dramatic and compelling picture will be made by the photographer close to the action. Generally, you will get better pictures if you get closer than if you rely on the long lens to bring the action closer.

There are as many different techniques in photographing sports and action as there are different types of games and sports. Photographing any of them, of course, is an excellent test of your reflexes, judgment and quick thinking. There is no time to rethink a problem either technically or in terms of subject composition. Every action from setting the exposure to determining the proper moment to press the shutter release must be almost automatic. Balancing what you see in your viewfinder against your technical limitations—top shutter speed available because of lighting conditions and maximum depth available for this particular exposure—is all part of the challenge of sports photography.

Catching the Action

One of the keys to any sports picture is mastering the moment of peak action. If you analyse any athletic motion, you will see that there are certain climaxes when the action reaches a dramatic point and is actually moving at a much slower pace than usual. For instance, a hurdler going over a hurdle seems to float without moving a muscle for a brief instant as he clears the hurdle. A pole vaulter seems to remain virtually suspended in air at the moment he clears the bar. These moments not only are the most dramatic, but are the best photographically since they epitomise the action and allow you to capture the instant with the slowest possible shutter speed.

Panning with the motion, one of the most effective ways to portray action, can be used with some types of action and sports events, yet oddly enough does not seem to work well with others. At track meets or other events where the action's direction and general speed can be predetermined to some extent, panning is certainly the best method of obtaining a sharp image against a blurred background. The background blur heightens the feeling of motion in the picture.

Panning is really quite a simple technique. With your feet apart to give you good balance and your Pentax held firmly, simply twist the upper half of your body slowly and evenly while following the action in your viewfinder. At the best picture-taking instant, as determined through the finder, take the picture while still twisting. Then continue panning in a follow-through motion. A good panning technique can help you take a number of photographs in one pan provided you can advance film quickly and continue to pan after your first shot.

Team games and team events are more difficult to photograph with pan action since much of the action usually involves broken field running and attempts to elude pursuers. In such instances, you can follow the action in the finder, shifting focus quickly as the action shifts, shooting at whatever moments you can. If you learn to move your camera smoothly by rotating at all times from your waist you may sometimes be able to take advantage of brief pans.

What speed should you use to photograph action? If you can pan, you can often cut down the shutter speed considerably. Runners, hurdlers, even sports cars can be stopped at an amazingly slow 1/125 sec. However, other actions which must be spot shot will require 1/500 sec. The safest general rule is to use the fastest shutter speed available that will still give a reasonable shooting aperture. For action, $f4$ is about the largest aperture you should consider. While it is possible to get a sharp figure in motion at $f2.8$ or even larger apertures, the extremely shallow depth-of-field at these apertures plus the moving subject makes the possibility of focusing errors too dangerous.

Electronic flash is an ideal subject-stopping light source. Most units work at 1/500 sec. or even faster quite independent of the shutter speed set. There is, however, owing to the comparatively slow shutter speed necessary, a danger of secondary or ghost images from any existing daylight or strong artificial light. The lighter the subject the greater the danger of such secondary images.

368

WHAT SPEED
FOR ACTION?

Is there one speed which will assure complete sharpness when shooting a moving subject? Usually not. Subjects in motion generally have different parts travelling at different speeds. Obviously the runner's hands and legs are moving faster and require a higher speed than his body. Solution: Use the fastest shutter speed possible.

When using speeds of 1/125 sec. or slower, most subjects in action will appear blurred if you hold camera steady.

If you pan with the action and move your camera in the same direction as the subject you can get a sharper picture of the moving subject, but your background will now be blurred.

When action is coming towards you, movement is not as noticeable as when action is moving at right angles. Here a slower shutter speed can be used.

Choosing the Viewpoint

Proper picture taking angle is an essential part of sports and action photography. Quite often the angle will be dictated by your position or the type of action. However, when you can pick and choose your vantage point, height and angle, do so. The most striking position for nearly every action is right in front of it. This is not usually possible. Sometimes it is possible but unwise as in sports car racing. However, the next best angle would be as close to directly in front as possible. In the sports car field it would be right at the edge of the track or road where the cars could be pictured at less than a 45-degree angle.

Camera height has a great deal to do with dramatic impact of action pictures. Usually a low angle will emphasise speed and power. Care must be taken, however, not to distort the subject inadvertently. If your viewpoint is too close, parts of the subject close to the camera will appear larger than those further away. In some instances, however, this increase in close mass plus subject elongation adds to the effect of action. In recent years, many photographers have actually turned to lenses of 20 mm. or even wider to achieve this deliberate distortion.

Photography Under Water

With the advent of skin diving as a hobby within recent years, the possibilities of underwater photography as a companion hobby have become quite evident. Here is a beautiful world of different landscapes, colours and creatures. They can be photographed by a swimmer with but a simple face mask and camera projector or by a practised diver using underwater breathing equipment and the most expensive of underwater cameras and housings.

We cannot take the time and space to examine underwater diving itself, but we can discuss the practicalities of using the Pentax for underwater photography.

Taking pictures under water represents quite a challenge, since the problems to be encountered are like nothing on earth. But before we discuss the technique of taking pictures we had better find a safe, watertight case for the Pentax.

Surprisingly, one of the easiest, most convenient and practical housings is also the least expensive. This is the simple rubber or plastic bag with glass face plate through which you take the picture. You take off the face plate, insert the camera loaded with film, refasten face plate, and you're ready to go. Almost all the camera controls can be operated right through the soft rubber housing. You can check changes in shutter speed, aperture and focus by looking at the camera controls through the face plate. Unfortunately there is no way to use the prism reflex system either for viewing or focusing underwater. You just point the camera in the direction of the subject.

The soft rubber housing and face plate work remarkably well in shallow water to 10 ft. or so of depth. Below this, the camera controls and housing become increasingly difficult to use. There is also some danger of the housing leaking. For deeper and/or more serious work, a solid underwater case is needed. While Asahi does not make its own case, many underwater camera housing manufacturers produce cases which can be suitably adapted. Housings are of either plastic or metal. The plastic housings are usually less expensive and allow you to see the camera clearly through the plastic so you can check control settings. Clear plastic or brass gear rings are fastened to the camera controls and these, in turn, are controlled by knobs or levers which extend through the housing. The Pentax cameras offering auto exposure systems can be a great convenience underwater, since the auto exposure systems generally provide as good an exposure under water as above. However, with cameras allowing the owner to set the aperture and the camera to set the shutter speed there is the danger of too slow a speed being set to stop underwater action. Therefore, fairly large apertures should be used to keep shutter speeds as high as possible.

The housing is usually kept watertight with rubber "O" rings which resemble giant rubber bands. These fit into grooves around the lid of the housing. As water pressure increases the housing lid presses further against the "O" ring and housing back, thus keeping water out.

Before using any underwater housing, test it carefully for leaks. A Pentax is an expensive camera to ruin by inadvertent submission inside a leaky case. To test, take your empty camera case underwater as far down as you will probably photograph. Look for tell-tale air bubbles escaping. If there are bubbles, you have a leak. Check closures to find the leak.

If the housing itself is at fault, don't attempt repairs yourself. Return the housing to a competent expert in underwater housings.

While plastic housings are practical and less expensive, they are brittle and subject to damage. All-metal housings are far more expensive and do not let you see the settings of the camera itself. However, they are more durable than plastic. Both the metal and plastic housings can easily be equipped with a large open sight which frames your picture area.

Housings should have a strap which you can hang around your neck (made of plastic or nylon cord). When in the water a housing should have slight negative bouyancy—that is, the housing plus camera should neither bounce to the surface nor sink quickly. When left alone in the water, it should almost stay put or sink very slowly. If the housing sinks rapidly, weight must be pared from it or small air containers must be fitted to it. If the housing bounces to the surface there is too great an air space within. Either it must be pared down or lead weights added inside or outside the housing.

Which Focal Length Lens?

As you probably already know, the refraction of light rays in water causes all objects under water to appear $\frac{1}{3}$ closer to you than they actually are. This is the enlarging effect of water, which also increases the effective focal length of your lens by a third. That's why wide-angle lenses of 35 mm. or 28 mm. are preferred by underwater photographers.

There is another reason why long lenses are not used underwater. Water is about one thousand times less transparent than air even at its clearest. The further away you are from an underwater subject the more danger of losing both sharpness and picture contrast. Therefore a wide-angle lens used as close as possible will yield the best results. A 35 mm. Pentax lens becomes a 47 mm. lens underwater, while the 28 mm. elongates to about 37 mm. Luckily, there is no alteration in aperture.

Focusing Problems

The problem of setting correct footage is not as great as it would seem. If you simply set your lens for the *apparent* distance underwater instead of the *actual* measured distance, the subject will be correctly focused. Of course, you can no longer use the depth-of-field scale on your lens, since the lens, for practical purposes, is $\frac{1}{3}$ longer in focal length. However, you can adapt the scale safely if you allow about two stops error. In other words, instead of trying to read the footage scale between $f8$ markings, read the scale between the two $f4$ markings.

For exposure, you can make your readings as you would normally, getting as close to the subject as you can. However, light does fall off the deeper you dive. Unless the water is spectacularly clear, and the sun bright, photographs should be taken within 15 ft. of the surface.

As very few housings allow a clear sight of the meter needle, many Pentax owners will probably want to use an accessory meter for underwater photographs. While photographers used to place hand-held meters in watertight pickle jars for underwater use, there are now both expensive and inexpensive hand-held meters, plus moderately priced underwater housings to accommodate the most popular exposure meters. These are far easier to use and less liable to leak.

Underwater Flash

While many good underwater pictures are made by sunlight, the most brilliant are made with flash, either electronic or bulb. Many different flash housings are available, usually made by the same companies producing the underwater camera housings. The use of flashbulbs or cubes underwater presents no problems, provided the flashgun itself is completely waterproof and safe against shocks.

You can carry a load of bulbs in a mesh bag. While bulbs may not explode underwater, implosions, or the crushing of bulbs by water pressure after exposure, has been known to occur at depths.

Because of the tiny dust and dirt particles in all water, it is essential that the flash be placed as far from the camera as possible. If direct on-camera flash is used, the tiny particles act as direct reflectors and bounce the light right back at the lens, causing loss of contrast, increased flare and reduction of sharpness. Most flash units have rigid and long extension arm brackets which allow the flash to be used some distance from the camera and at an angle.

Electronic flash units must be encased in watertight housings similar to the camera housings. They, too, must be removed from the line of direct flash.

Flash can give the skin diver the advantage of a consistent light suitable for colour work. As soon as you can work out your own flash number for your gun and flashbulbs underwater, you will be able to set exposure exactly. You may want to use clear flashbulbs rather than blue ones with colour films to counteract the bluish tint of the water. Similarly you might need to use a filter with electronic flash.

Electronic flash has the additional advantage of a very short-duration light which freezes all motion. When photographing rapidly moving fish or in turbid water where it is difficult for the photographer to remain in the same position, electronic flash is most convenient.

It isn't possible to offer additional information on flash exposure since much depends on the clarity of the water. Medium fast and fast black-and-white and colour films seem to work best underwater.

NATURE AND WILDLIFE

The single-lens reflex camera design and the necessities of flower photography seem virtually wedded together. In no photographic field is the advantage of through-the-lens focusing and viewing better adapted to the subject material.

Actually flower photography can cover a vast number of different approaches—from the photography of entire fields of blossom to photomicroscopy of tiny segments. However, here we'll take up the more common types: general photography for horticultural use and the photography of flowers for artistic purposes.

Equipment for Flower Photography

The Pentax is particularly suitable for flower photography. In its basic form with normal lens, it can focus to less than two feet, making it possible to shoot many flower pictures with no more equipment than the camera plus nomal lens. Quite often you will not be able to get close enough with just the normal lens. The Close-Up Lens can then be threaded in front of the nomal lens. However, a close-up lens, in effect, shortens the focal length of your normal lens slightly. This means that you must get closer to your subjects. Since apparent perspective distortion (the enlargement of closer objects in relationship to more distant ones) increases with closeness to the subject, close-up lenses are not the best solution.

An extension tube set is an excellent alternative to close-up lenses. When out shooting you can easily pocket the extension tubes and then thread those needed to the camera lens when you're ready to shoot. The bellows units allow continuous focusing to $1\times$ magnification and beyond, but they are rather more cumbersome when out shooting in the field.

Both extension tubes and bellows unit allow you to maintain a greater camera-to-subject distance than the close-up lens, thus avoiding apparent perspective distortion to a greater extent.

A 105 mm. lens seems to furnish a close-to-ideal perspective at a good shooting distance. The 105 mm. SMC Pentax with the extension tube set will handle just about any flower situation you may encounter.

If you do intend to do much close-up work, it will be well worthwhile for you to consider the 100 mm. $f4$ SMC Pentax M Macro. Optically it has been designed for best results at close range and it can furnish focusing from infinity to $\frac{1}{2}\times$ and is therefore ideal for flower photography. The shorter 50 mm. $f4$ SMC Pentax is also most useful but, because of its shorter focal length, is not as suitable for three dimensional subjects such as flowers.

Surprisingly there is a great disparity in requirements for flower pictures for horticultural purposes and flower photos for artistic use. Horticulturists are mostly interested in the clearest, sharpest delineations of flowers. They require the petals, pistils, stamens, stems, buds and leaves all to be crystal clear. Slight backlight is generally needed to provide petal translucency. Most flower photographs which satisfy the needs of the flower expert will not impress you as beautiful photographs.

Choosing the Flowers

For best possible non-artistic but technically satisfying flower pictures, you must pick your flowers with care.

What type of flowers do you intend to photograph? Probably the most universal type are those which are domesticated and grown in a garden. These pictures then become a documentary of each flower type or arrangement. Entire gardens, of course, can also be photographed and provide enjoyment for gardeners during the winter months when the flowers themselves are not available.

The author, however, prefers to photograph wildflowers. Hiking in the fields and woods while keeping a sharp eye peeled for the smallest new blossoms presents a real challenge. A large collection of wildflower photos taken over a year's span offers beauty, colour and variety.

Wild flowers seem to offer the greatest possibility for artistically satisfying pictures.

If you do intend to photograph wildflowers and know little of them, a good wildflower field guide is a must. Make sure that the guide covers the flowers in your region.

Wildflowers chance from country to country, area to area. Names also change; characteristics change. Make sure that the illustrations—usually drawings in colour—are clear and explicit. If you are not yourself an enthusiast, ask someone who is to recommend the best pocket guide on the subject. In searching out wildflowers, begin in early spring. Wildflowers blossom then. Unfortunately, many wildflowers have only a brief blossoming period, so check your field or woods often.

It's almost impossible to suggest any specific areas in which to look for wildflowers. There are different types in fields, in the woods, in marshes, near streams. Some are large and easily spotted. Others are amazingly tiny. And remember, practically every plant—even grass—has blossoms which can be photographed.

The flowers should be physically perfect with no blemishes. At least one leaf should be showing in the photograph. If possible a yet unopened bud should also be included. When sharpness and complete delineation of the entire flower is necessary, an extremely small aperture should be used, coupled with, of course, a slower shutter speed. A small table top tripod with a fairly large universal head is an almost necessary acquisition. Some large tripods have reversible centre-posts which allow the heads to be reversed for close ground work.

When using a slow shutter speed, even the slightest breeze can cause unsharpness. To overcome it, use a cardboard sheet upwind of the flower to protect the flower from wind movement. Some photographers prefer a build a small cylinder of cardboard and drop it over the flower. They can then photograph from above and use the cardboard itself as a separating background. When using a small aperture, the background plays a very important part in the picture. If you photograph the flower against the background as you find it, you may have a dreadfully complicated tangle of leaves, grass blades and flower. If you do not use the protective cylinder already described, a coloured cardboard can be tried behind the flower. A light blue or brown cardboard generally will produce sufficient separation.

Exposure and Lighting

For most accurate exposure meter readings, make the reading

from a standard grey card held just before the subject. This provides quite accurate exposure for most flowers except those which are white or very pale or those which are extremely dark. For very light flowers, one half stop less exposure is preferable. For dark flowers, a half stop additional exposure should take care of the problem.

If you have an old Pentax without a through lens meter, remember to allow the additional exposure required by the bellows or extension tubes as well. With a behind-the-lens meter, you can simply take a reading right through bellows or tube without any additional exposure increase calculations. But, as already discussed, use a grey card and adjust exposure depending on the deepness of the flower colour.

Quite often the lighting of the flower will not be all that it might be. In such cases you can aid it by using a white cardboard reflector or a cardboard on which you've pasted crumpled aluminium foil. Many photographers find that a small shaving mirror makes an excellent reflector to redirect light to small flowers.

Usually, lighting to the side and slightly behind the flower shows the flower to best advantage. Such illumination has the advantages of cross lighting to delineate detail and also provides you with sufficient trans-illumination through the petals. However, with judicious use of reflectors, such light can often be simulated if it isn't actually available.

Artistry with Flowers

The most enjoyable wildflower photography forsakes the quest for overall sharpness and instead seeks to produce a photographic work of art. The delicacy and beauty of a wildflower isn't necessarily contained in sharpness. It is rather in the overall visual illusion created. Within recent years, there has been a serious re-examination of nature and flower photography. Many important new books of wildflower photographs have appeared with pictures which would have shocked photographers of a generation ago. In these books, wildflowers are shown in which only a small portion of the flower —usually the pistils and stamens is sharp. The background is a blur of green, and the stem and petals swiftly fade into unsharpness. Yet many flower experts admit they do get more of the feeling of the wildflower from these softer delineations than from the more accurate, technically correct, supersharp photos of the same flowers.

I have personally found that if I used the entire Pentax extension tube set with a 105 mm. Pentax lens, $f5.6$ was about as small an aperture as I wished for best results with the "new" flower photography. Quite often even larger apertures of $f4$ were better.

Of course, the large lens openings do allow a much faster shutter speed. Consequently I now find that it is relatively unnecessary to take a tripod along on my woodland trips. A speed of 1/125 sec. or faster can usually stop any camera or flower movement. Most of my flower pictures are made flat on my stomach with both elbows resting on the earth. Even when there is a slight breeze, I can often pick the instant when the breeze lets up and the flower remains still. I shoot most easily without a cable release. Somehow a cable release slows up my ability to release the shutter at the precise instant that I wish.

With a large lens openings it isn't necessary to use background material. The large lens opening throws all the confusing natural background into a pleasing out-of-focus green blur which is, of course, really more natural than an artificial background.

Preparing a wildflower for its portrait can take patience. When you have what you feel is the best angle, don't automatically take an exposure meter reading and shoot. Look around the picture area through the finder. Often there will be distracting grass blades or weeds near or even in front of the flower. Remove all annoying additional vegetation, but don't disturb the plant you are photographing.

For very small flowers, even the 105 mm. lens and bellows or extension tubes may offer insufficient magnification. In such cases the normal 50 mm., 55 mm. or macro lens can be used. Since the flower itself is so small, the depth of the flower will be less and the danger of apparent perspective distortion from the shorter focal length lens will not be so acute.

While the entire concept of taking flower pictures at a large aperture when working so close may seem rather odd to you at first, do make some comparison shots. Shoot the same flowers at a large aperture and then repeat the same photographs of the same flowers from the same angle but at a small aperture. When the pictures have been processed, compare the results. I think you'll like the larger aperture pictures better.

A word about choice of colour films. Pick a film which offers the softest colours and best reproduction of subtle changes of hues. In flower photography you will really be able to tell differences between colour film capabilities! Try to avoid those colour films which produce bluish greens, orangy yellows and reds. Purple is often a most difficult colour for a film to render properly. You may need to do some experimenting with films before you find the proper one for flower photography—and it may not be the film that you generally prefer for ordinary photographic work.

Bringing Birds to the Camera

Bird photography is probably one of the most rewarding areas of picture taking. It represents a challenge—the hand must be quicker than the bird. It also can furnish valuable ornithological data and will, of course, give you a record of all the species in your own neighbourhood. In addition, you will also acquire excellent photographs.

Most people think of photographing birds as roaming the fields with a giant telephoto lens. This is seldom practical. You can either approach a known bird nest carefully or make the bird come to you.

Oddly enough, making the bird come towards the camera is the easiest technique. All that is required is a bird feeder fastened to a window and some bird seed. If you then open your window, place your Pentax on a tripod and wait, inevitably you will have your chance at a bird or birds. Even the normal 50 or 55 mm. lens can be used. Since it's necessary to approach closer than 3 feet to the bird for a good sized image on the film, focus your camera at some specific area of the bird feeder. Sit further away yourself and trip the shutter with a long cable release.

The normal lens of the camera does have a disadvantage, of course. To advance film, you must get to the camera (unless you have an auto winder or motor drive which can be controlled at a distance). This can scare away the birds. However, if you leave your window open constantly and the birds see that they aren't being harmed, they will become bolder and ignore your actions. Quite soon you will find that the various bird species have personalities. Some are bold and will allow you to approach quite closely. Other will only be lured to the feeder after many weeks. And any movement inside the house will scare them off again.

A 135 mm. lens will certainly prove far more convenient for photography than a 50 mm. or 55 mm. lens—not to get closer to the birds, but to allow the camera to be further from the window. With small birds a short extension tube may be needed to produce a sufficiently large sized image. However, with a long lens you can keep the camera in your own hands, release and advancing film whenever you wish.

For a beginning, use daylight and a rapid colour film—it would seem such a shame to shoot birds in black-and-white. Be careful of the lighting. If the light is coming towards the camera you will have near silhouettes. Top or sidelight is best. Wait until the bird has actually landed or you will find a natural blur on your film. Since most bird feeders are not too photogenic, you may wish to adapt your bird feeder to photography. Small branches and twigs can make excellent perches for the birds between actual feedings. You can then shoot them right on the branch or twig perches and crop out the feeder itself in the viewfinder. The pictures will show the birds perching on a tree branch. Make up a number of different branches so that it won't appear that all your bird pictures were made on the same branch.

The advantage of the perched-on-branch bird is the ease with which you can get sharp pictures at fairly slow shutter speeds. With regular daylight you will often have to shoot at 1/30 or 1/60 sec. which is far too slow to capture any bird in motion.

While these basics will do nicely if you don't intend to get thoroughly enmeshed in bird photography, you can increase the variety of birds and therefore the variety of pictures. Where should the feeder be put? If you are in the country, place it on a windowsill next to some outside shrubbery or a tree. The shrubbery or tree affords the birds some protection in case of danger. Use a good birdseed mixture. Some of the most interesting bird pictures are made in the winter with the snow on the ground. Colourful birds contrast beautifully with the snow. If you start feeding birds towards the autumn every day, many will stay around all winter giving you good photographic companionship. However, since they will depend on you for a good supply, don't stop feeding them. Within one day, they can starve to death. If you plan on being away from your home for any length of time, make certain that you make proper arrangements for someone to come in and feed your birds.

Not all birds, of course, will eat from a feeder. As food is dropped by the birds at the feeder, others will sit patiently on the ground below and pick over the leavings. During the winter you can scatter birdseed in the snow and catch these ground feeders against a tastefully plain background.

Birds in Flight

Inevitably the possibilities of photographing still birds will begin to bore you. Actually you can photograph birds in flight with much the same set-up plus a small electronic flash unit.

Set up a small flash unit with the light directed on to the added branch of the feeder. Connect the flash to the camera with a long lead. You're now set up for taking frozen-action (or at least near frozen) pictures of the birds. You may find that the flash scares some birds at first, but they soon get used to it.

When do you actually snap the shutter? Where do you point the camera? Keep the camera trained on the same branch. Try to prejudge the birds' action. You will see that birds generally repeat their flight habits. They may travel from a nearby bush or tree to the branch, back to the feeder, back to the branch and then return to the distant tree. I found that I could just about catch a bird landing with wings outstretched if I pressed the shutter release as the bird left a nearby branch to attempt a landing on my pre-rigged branch.

When using flash with a focal plane shutter camera, care must be taken to avoid the formation of a secondary or ghost image by the available light. To minimize the possibility, try shooting against a dark background. This tends to absorb the secondary image, which is usually underexposed and dark-toned, even if the subject is light-coloured.

Mobile Bird-watching

While taking bird pictures through your own window is

certainly the easiest way, only certain birds will approach a feeder. Many larger birds must be sought out. This can be a time and energy consuming proposition.

Without getting involved in the many complicated techniques such as the hides used by professional bird photographers—there are some hints that might help you in the field. A longer lens is essential—the longest lens you can safely hand-hold at speeds of 1/125 sec. or faster.

You may get good results actually stalking through the fields, but an automobile makes good mobile camouflage. It's also not too difficult to adapt a simple camera support which fastens to the car's window channel. You can then cruise up and down slowly looking for birds and often shoot them from the car.

Wild Animals, too

Photographing domesticated animals—cats, dogs, etc.—presents no more difficulties than photographing the more human members of a family. They, too, are best caught unaware.

Photographing animals in the wild is entirely another matter. Serious animal photographers have gone to extraordinary lengths to bring down the quarries, building elaborate and time-consuming hides. Generally speaking, whatever can be shot with a rifle can be photographed—and a good picture of deer or other game animal is often a more difficult but more lasting prize to bring home than the dead animal is to the hunter.

The problems of nocturnal animals, which require the uses of special tripping devices and remote flash units, is too specialized a subject for this book. But stalking wild animals in daylight merely requires the presence of the animals, the right equipment, technique and patience.

Like any good hunter, the photographer must attempt to get downwind of the animal where the human smell and the noise of the photographer's movements are not as likely to be communicated to the animal. Clothing which blends into the foliage is helpful. When animals are present, move only when absolutely necessary. Many animals have poor eyesight, but they can detect movement. It is advisable to use a fairly long lens which is easily hand-holdable: the 200 mm.,

300 mm. and 400 mm. Pentax lenses are superb for animal photography. Medium fast film will allow you a fairly rapid shutter speed of 1/125 sec. or better at maximum apertures.

Most animals in the wild must be photographed before they are alarmed and take flight, so movement of the subject is seldom the problem. The shallow depth-of-field at maximum aperture also aids the separation of the animal from the background. Focus on the animal's eyes when possible. If the animal is facing away, you may have to chance it and make a slight noise to attract its attention in your direction for that instant before it takes flight. Be prepared to shoot quickly. You will often not get a chance at a second shot. Even the shutter noise may cause animals to bolt.

CAMERA MAINTENANCE

Camera equipment only works properly if it is treated well. What constitutes good treatment and what constitutes bad, however, is not often as clear as one might like.

Camera Cases

The safest place for any camera is in its case—the sturdier and more cushioned the better. However, the sturdier the case, the more difficult it often becomes to use the camera. For instance, the hard everready case undoubtedly offers the greatest camera protection, but it is bulky and does take time to open and shut. Photographers instead often prefer the soft leather case, which is more supple and easier to open but does not offer the same amount of protection.

There are also many photographers who feel that any case whatsoever is a restriction which takes up room and causes the loss of valuable time in opening and closing. These photographers often use no case at all but merely fasten the camera to a neck strap by the eyelet lugs at the camera ends.

Maintenance in terms of carrying the camera safely to protect it against bumps, abrasions or even dropping it is a matter of personal preference. Most amateurs do keep their cameras in cases at all times when the cameras are not in actual use.

Lens Protection

There are three important protective items for camera lenses. When lenses are not in use, both ends should be covered by lens covers, front and rear. When the lens is on the camera, the front cap alone, of course, is sufficient. The rear cap should only be removed at the time you intend to place the lens on the camera. The front cap should remain on except when actually taking pictures. If the camera body is to be left for any time at all with no lens, a camera body cap should be threaded into place to prevent dust, dirt or other foreign matter from entering the mirror box.

When taking pictures, your lens should have one of two protections or perhaps both. A Pentax lens hood is designed specifically for each focal length lens to prevent extraneous light from hitting the lens and causing flare. However, the lens hood also furnishes excellent physical protection against fingermarks on the lens or the accidental contact of the front lens surface with other objects. The hood further protects against flying sand or moisture at the beach or against raindrops in stormy weather and snow during the winter. Therefore, even if there is no sun and no optical reason for a lens hood, use it for lens protection.

The front lens element is quite delicate. There will be much less cause to clean it if you keep a skylight filter permanently threaded into the front of the lens mount. The skylight filter eliminates some types of haze and also gives a warmer (tendency towards red) rendering at most colour pictures. However, it will also serve as further lens protection. Dust, dirt, moisture and fingerprints can be cleaned from a filter far more conveniently than from the camera's own lens. Since the skylight filter requires no additional exposure and can never harm a photograph, there is no reason why the skylight filter can't be used over your Takumar lens at all times.

Cleaning Lenses

Inevitably, lens surfaces do get dirty. Even if you avoid touching them, some amount of dust will be attracted by the glass surface and adhere to it. If the lens surface exhibits dust only, don't feel that you have to clean the glass thoroughly. Instead, concentrate on removing the dust. This can be done in two ways—by using a small brush to flick it off or by blowing the dirt off with a stream of air.

To remove the dust with a brush, either buy a small pocket brush specially made for photo use or purchase a good sable brush. Avoid inexpensive paint brushes. These often contain some oil to help hold the shape of the brush. While this oil is relatively harmless to paintings, it can come off on the front element of your lens. An inexpensive brush is apt to cause more trouble than it solves.

When using the brush, hold your camera up side down with the lens pointings to the floor. If the lens faces upwards, you simply do what many a maid does with a feather duster—

PROTECTION
AND CLEANING

When carrying a lens on camera or in gadget bag, reverse lens hood, place lens cap over it. When ready to shoot, take off lens cap, place in pocket or gadget bag, reverse lens hood.

To clean lens properly with lens tissue, fold as shown, tear folded tissue in half, place torn halves together, use torn edges to clean lens surface. Work from outer edges in towards centre.

Small specks of dust can be flicked off lens with clean brush.

Cotton swab on toothpick cleans finder window nicely.

To clean dust from mirror, remove lens, hold camera upside down so dust won't resettle as you flick it off with tip of brush.

stir up the dust, which then settles again right back where it came from. By holding the camera with the lens pointing downwards, the dust or dirt will quit the glass when dislodged by the brush and continue its progress downwards out of harm's way.

Start cleaning with a circular stroke from the outside of the lens. If you start from the inside and attempt to clean outwards, much of the dust and dirt dislodged at the centre might be massaged into the edges underneath the manufacturer's identification rims. If you start at the lens circumference, you can work the dirt inwards. When you get it in the middle, you can remove it with one final swipe.

Most dust and dirt on lenses should be readily removable with a small brush. However, to avoid touching the soft glass surface too often, you should try a small air blower such as an ear syringe. With it you may be able to blow much of the dust and dirt from lenses without actually touching them.

When even a gentle touch with a brush is insufficient to dislodge a particular speck or spot, you must resort to lens tissue.

Most photographers do not know how to use lens tissue properly. You are not supposed to take a sheet and massage the front of the lens with the flat of it. This can grind the impurity into the front element and cause damage. Instead, try following this technique.

Take one sheet of lens tissue. Roll it up like a cigarette. Now tear the "cigarette" in two. Holding one of the outside edges of the paper, use the rough edge on the glass as you would a brush. Massage in the same outside-to-inside circular motion. Do not apply any more pressure against the lens than you can exert from the end of the rolled up lens tissue.

Under no circumstances use ordinary eye glass tissue on a camera lens. Such tissues usually are treated with silicone materials, an abrasive composition which not only scratches the front of lens elements but also reacts chemically with the anti-reflection coating of the lens. This chemical reaction can build up a heavy deposit which causes loss of definition and colour balance.

Fingerprints are a primary and constant source of trouble. No matter how hard you try, sooner or later you will inadvertently place a finger on the lens leaving a small grease spot. These grease spots are by no means easy to remove. Here's one possible way, however.

Roll a lens tissue and tear in two as indicated above. Now breathe heavily on the front element surface. Before the moisture has a chance to evaporate, begin to clean the front element with the torn lens tissue as already explained. If some grease streaks still remain, repeat the cleaning operation.

There will be times when your very best efforts at lens cleaning will not avail with grease spots. Purchase a reliable fluid lens cleaner from your camera dealer and follow directions carefully. Don't use too much lens cleaner. Often the cement between lens elements is soluble in liquids quite similar to those used for lens cleaner. The amount of lens cleaner therefore should be minimal.

The rear viewfinder window can be cleaned in a similar manner to the front and rear of the lens. However, it is often difficult to clean the outer edges of the finder window. For edge cleaning, try some cotton swabs on a toothpick (called a Q-Tip in the U.S.).

Cleaning the Camera Body

The rest of the outer camera body should also be attended to regularly. A small brush can be used to clean the dust and dirt from nooks and crannies, particularly on or around the setting controls. The outer leather-like material needs no attention, but a very slightly damp cloth can help maintain the lustre of the chrome.

A great deal of dust does settle within the camera body and can deposit itself on your film, causing small unexposed spots. To prevent this, establish a regular series of maintenance operations perhaps twice a month. Open the back of the camera and examine thoroughly. Sometimes, small bits of film leader snap off. These bits can easily get into the shutter speed mechanism and cause trouble. Clean them out. Then go after the dust. Hold the camera open with the lens facing upwards and flick out all dust with a small brush. Gravity will make sure it doesn't resettle in the same place. Avoid touching the shutter blinds. A small low-powered vacuum cleaner makes an excellent camera interior cleaning tool. Do not use a high-powered cleaner!

After cleaning the lens and the camera back thoroughly, remove the camera lens and clean the interior of the mirror box with a brush. Again hold the camera face downwards so that dislodged dust can exit through the lens mount. Pay particular attention to the underside of the focusing screen. Quite often small particles of dust will become stuck there. These particles can usually be seen in the finder. While holding the camera to your eye, insert the brush carefully and locate the spot on the focusing screen. Then flick it off.

For this cleaning, use nothing but a good-quality, long-handle painter's brush. Most photo brushes are too stubby and round. Such brushes could conceivably damage the mirror when you are attempting to reach the underside of the focusing screen.

The mirror is another major settling area for dust and dirt. While the dust and dirt there do not affect camera sharpness, a large amount can cause deterioration of the focusing image. In addition, it is quite easy for this dust on the mirror to redeposit itself on the underside of the focusing screen when the mirror flips upwards out of the way during exposure.

The mirror, however, is probably the most delicate exposed mechanism in a single-lens reflex. Unlike the mirrors you have at home in which the silver reflecting surface is underneath glass and is therefore protected, the silver surface of the rapid return mirror in the Pentax and similar single-lens reflexes is on the top. Top surface mirrors prevent doubles images which are difficult or impossible to focus accurately.

When cleaning the mirror, use only the lightest strokes from a brush or from your rolled-up lens tissue. Don't attempt to dislodge grease or fingermarks. There should, of course, be no fingermarks or other smudges on the mirror. If there are, leave them there until you can send the camera to an authorized Pentax repairman for mirror replacement. The replacement cannot be done by the camera owner.

Lubrication

Your camera is carefully lubricated when it leaves the Asahi factory in Japan and should require no further treatment or lubrication for many years. Various parts use different lubricants which are designed to allow the camera to operate even in extreme temperatures. However, if you are visiting locations where temperatures of far below zero are commonly encountered, consult your importer or distributor on the advisability of having your camera winterized. Such winterization usually requires that the ordinary lubricants be removed and special high viscosity lubricants substituted in some places and all lubricants removed from others. The camera should only be operated in this condition when absolutely necessary. As soon as it is returned from cold temperatures, the original lubricants should be replaced.

Under no circumstances attempt to use any oil or grease on the camera or equipment yourself. And do not take the camera to any but an authorized repair firm for service and lubrication. While other technicians can probably "lubricate" the camera, they may not have exactly the right lubricants. You may then find that the camera tends to become sluggish when the weather gets cold or run too swiftly if the weather is hot.

When the camera is not going to be used for some time, it's advisable to untension the shutter. Make it a practice to keep the Pentax shutter unwound whenever you are not using the camera. Only wind to the next exposure, thus also winding the shutter, when you are reasonably sure you will be taking additional pictures. Keeping the shutter tensioned for a time will not harm it, but constant tension over a long period of time may cause a loss of shutter curtain travel speed.

Exercising the Camera

If you are not using your camera regularly, take it out once every week or so and operate the shutter at all speeds. Also operate the self-timing mechanism and the lens diaphragm at all apertures to keep them from getting sluggish.

If your camera is still loaded with film and you don't want to waste the remainder of the frames during this procedure, try this: Make a careful note as to which frame number you are on. Now rewind the film carefully. Watch the small red dot on the bottom of the rewind button. When the red dot ceases to turn, the film has left the take-up spool. Stop rewinding immediately. You can then remove the film cassette from the camera with a length of film leader protruding. If you continue to rewind after the red dot has ceased to turn, the film will be wound completely into the cassette.

With the cassette removed, exercise the camera as already explained. Afterwards, replace the cassette in the camera, re-thread the film and with the lens cap in place so you do not fog the film, advance the film by alternately pressing the shutter release and winding the film until you again reach the same frame number. As insurance, you might advance the film one additional frame. You will have then lost one frame only.

Camera maintenance depends greatly on your own thoughtfulness and attention. Many early model Pentaxes are still around in perfect condition optically, mechanically and visually, because the owners were careful. Others, used hard and not so carefully looked after, show the effects of hard wear and neglect much earlier. Pride of ownership should be important to the careful owner. It's always a pleasure to own and use a Pentax in perfect condition. And your pictures will show the difference, too.

PRACTICAL HINTS

Reading about the basic principles of equipment and its use represents just the beginning of learning to enjoy the possession of your Pentax camera and accessories. The rest will come in applying the knowledge and reaping the reward of the pictures themselves. Certainly much will be learned by trial and error, as it always is with every photographer and his equipment. However, after spending many a year with single lens reflexes of many makes—with special emphasis on the Pentax—I would like to pass on some of the hints and tips that I have found of help in taking pictures.

Bags and Cases

First, let's discuss the carrying of equipment. Every-ready cases that chew up time between the instant you see the subject and the instant you are ready to photograph it, annoy me, but most people still keep the cameras in their cases. If you must, at least keep the case open or, if the front snaps off, keep the camera at the ready without the front.

Suppose you have accessories, what then? For a few accessories—even an additional lens and some film—an expensive gadget bag may look imposing but it isn't necessary. A soft leather pouch with top zipper and over-the-shoulder carrying strap will do just as nicely and will be less conspicuous.

I do not recommend keeping lenses or any accessories in the nicely made individual leather cases in which they inevitably come. These cases are bulky and take time to open. Instead, remove the lenses and accessories and place them in small plastic bags similar to those used for keeping food in refrigerators. The lens or accessory drops down into the bag nicely and the bag can then be rolled up like a cocoon. It can be opened just as quickly. Because it's transparent, you can always see what's inside. Keep lens caps on both front and rear of all lenses not in actual use.

When you begin to accumulate enough accessories to make a small leather pouch rather a jumble in which you cannot put your hands instantly on what you want, it's time to investigate the possibilities of a real camera gadget bag. Personally, I don't like huge heavy leather ones with all sorts of odd outside pockets. Equipment is heavy enough to carry without adding the weight of a heavy case. Avoid cases with oval zippered tops. The zippers can stick either open, shut or half-way. Things are forever getting caught in them. Instead, search for a bag with a single snap lock and hard top. With a flip of the lock and top you can open the case, extract or replace what you wish and close the case again— all in seconds. At the beach or in bad weather you'll appreciate that fast operating snap top.

To prevent individual items of your equipment from banging together, some sort of compartmentation is quite essential. Those cases which offer the most flexibility in changing the shape and size of each compartment are probably the most useful. You can alter compartments as your equipment changes. Each compartment should be sufficiently large to allow you to drop the camera, lens or other accessory in with no trouble. If it is the slightest bit difficult to fit a piece of equipment in, think of how frustrating the case may become when you are taking pictures and you're in a hurry to change equipment!

Try not to buy a case larger than you really need. The smaller the case, the easier it is to carry. And there's little sense in buying a large impressive case which you then feel obligated to fill.

It is not necessary to get a case which can hold two camera bodies if you have two. You can always carry one camera at the ready outside the case. Make sure there is sufficient room for film. The amount of room needed depends on your own shooting tastes. You will obviously need more room if you are a prolific shooter than if you are a slow, careful shooter.

Handling Film

In placing film in a carrying bag, there is no real purpose in keeping it in the individual cardboard box. The box must be thrown away anyhow. When you're shooting pictures you can lose valuable time opening film boxes. Keep the film in the metal or plastic foil sealed containers, however, since these have been sealed against moisture and humidity.

394

After exposure, replace the film in the container. If you are taking pictures in a hot and humid climate, place the film containers in a plastic refrigerator bag along with some oven-dried bags of silica gel. After shooting the film, get it into the containers and into the bag as quickly as possible. The silica gel will absorb the moisture (which actually is a far greater enemy of film than heat).

Having loaded Pentax cameras more times than I can remember, I have finally decided that it is not safe simply to thread the film leader only into the take-up spool. Quite often the film simply will not advance. You will find that you have no trouble if you keep the camera back open and advance film until the full width of the film winds on to the take-up spool and both sets of sprocket teeth on the sprocket wheel are engaging the sprocket holes of the film. Then you can close the camera with assurance that the film will advance properly.

In rewinding film, don't attempt to see how fast it can be done. Exceedingly fast rewinding with any camera can, under certain conditions, cause static electricity marks to form on the film. Take a little longer to rewind film and avoid the marks.

Viewing and Focusing

In using a central microprism grid for focusing, you will find that it snaps images in and out of focus with medium focal length lenses more efficiently than with either wide-angle or extremely long lenses. Of course, maximum focusing aperture also has much to do with it. However, you will find it more difficult to focus long lenses on a tripod than hand-held long lenses. The tiny prisms which make up the microgrid cause shattering and shimmering of the subject when out of focus, to a greater degree if the subject or camera moves slightly. Therefore, if you do have some trouble with exact focus when using a long lens on a tripod, remove the lens and focus hand-held. Then you can put the lens back on the tripod for greater rigidity.

Contrary to what you may have read or been told, the Pentax viewfinder does not show exactly what the lens records on the film. In fact, it shows about 10 per cent less. In addition, wide angle lenses actually produce a slightly larger picture area on the film than larger lenses because the edge rays from a wide angle lens "creep" under the focal plane picture frame at an acute angle. This means that you actually have available a larger picture area than you thought you had when you pressed the shutter release. In practical picture taking terms, this 10 per cent or so additional area is essential. Most cardboard mounts for 35 mm. transparencies use up about 10 per cent of the total picture area in fastening the transparency edges to the mount. Many glassless negative carriers do the same with black-and-white negatives. However, you can use the extra area to reposition the negative or transparency slightly if a tiny bit of the picture appears nipped off when mounted or enlarged.

In actual shooting, make your entire picture frame work for you. Before you take a picture, look around all four sides carefully. Is there any part of the picture area that isn't essential? If so, you haven't framed your picture tightly enough. Move in until the subject material fills the frame so perfectly that there isn't any space that could be sliced off.

Always crop in your viewfinder. In colour you won't have another equally good chance unless you copy and enlarge the slide. In black-and-white you can, of course, exert considerable control during printing. But the less cropping you do, the less magnification you need and the better quality will be your enlargement.

Not coming close enough to the subject is one of the most frequent mistakes of all photographers. Except for vast sweeping landscapes, most subject material benefits from a close approach. A large dominating image has more detail, is easier to see and provides more impact. It's surprising how many camera users will photograph vertical subjects while holding the camera horizontally. They seldom think about taking a vertical-format picture which would allow them to get closer to the subject and provide a better image on the film.

The key to good cropping is to carry a built-in viewfinder within your head. You should learn to view a scene and know with fair exactness just how much will be recorded with each different focal length lens you own.

Every mechanical operation concerning the camera and accessories must become practically automatic, requiring you to give little thought to it. Finding picture material and recording it should occupy most of your time. The less time spent worrying about the operation of the equipment, the better will be your final pictures.

Essential Equipment

What equipment is essential and what equipment is not? Naturally it would be delightful to own every single piece of equipment and then to pick and choose just those items needed for specific purposes. However, we are limited by what we can afford and what we can carry. Probably the essential outfit would include a normal lens, 35 mm. lens and 105 or 135 mm. lens. If you shoot both black-and-white and colour transparency films, you will probably eventually need two camera bodies. A UV filter, medium yellow filter and perhaps a green filter would be a good small collection. A small electronic flash which can fit into your gadget bag will be handy.

Lens hoods are often considered a must. I have found modern lens coatings such as used on the SMC Pentaxes to be so effective that I've yet to find an instance where a lens hood would produce a better picture optically than without one. Lens hoods, however, do keep dust, dirt and fingers away from the lens. In poor weather they keep out rain and snow. If for nothing else but protection, you should have them.

The extension tube set or close-up lens would round out the equipment we would suggest for an initial kit of equipment.

There are some odds and ends which you will find useful to have in your gadget bag. A small jeweller's screwdriver will keep all tiny equipment screws tight. Don't use a larger-bladed screwdriver than necessary or you can ruin the tiny screw heads.

A roll of adhesive tape and knife or scissors will serve as a labelling kit. You can stick tape labels on a camera and on it write the name of the film contained or note how many exposures are left in half-used film cassettes. A ball pen usually writes nicely on adhesive tape. Some photographers prefer a roll of paint masking tape since it peels off more neatly than the ordinary adhesive tape.

A word about tripods. A compact folding job that just about fits into your hip pocket can actually be worse than no tripod at all. A tripod, to be any use, must hold the camera rigidly during exposure. Many light tripods actually vibrate when the shutter is released. Hand-held pictures, in which the camera action is cushioned by your body, can provide sharper pictures than such a tripod.

If you need a tripod, get the traditional good sturdy one. Testing a tripod is quite easy. Load the camera with a fairly fast film and place it on the tripod. Photograph a pinpoint source of light such as a torch bulb shining through a tiny pinhole in a piece of metal foil. Use shutter speeds from 1/30 sec. downwards to the slowest speeds you have. If the tripod is steady, each negative should show a light pinpoint. If you have a streak instead, the tripod's not good enough. Oddly enough, short focal length lenses often need a sturdier tripod than heavier, longer ones. The weight of the longer lenses often acts as an extra damping factor on shutter vibrations. In addition, long lenses add more weight to the tripod camera combination.

Storing Negatives

What do you do with your negatives after they have been developed? Is it necessary to have every one enlarged to see what they're about? How do you store these long rolls? These same questions have been asked about film ever since the advent of 35 mm. photography. Fortunately, there are some practical answers to the questions.

It isn't necessary or even advisable to have every black-and-white picture you take enlarged. If you must watch expenses, you will only be able to afford the poorest quality photofinishings if you insist on a print from each negative. If you do your own work, so much printing will easily wear you out and turn the fun of photography into a dreadful drudge.

Once you have the negatives they should be cut up into strips of 5 or 6 frames and filed either in a single business envelope or better still in glassine sleeves that are available from photo dealers in nearly every country on earth. While many people once did keep their film in one long roll and store in the metal can, the film grating against itself often scratched. A tiny grain of dust or dirt could cause some very unpleasant gouges.

To check your negatives' sharpness you will need a 10×

HANDLING NEGATIVES

Don't store negatives in long, curled-up strips within a film can. The emulsion may become scratched and the film itself curly and hard to handle. Instead, buy glassine negative folders from your photo store. Cut your long negative strips into smaller strips of 5 or 6 pictures and insert them into folders as shown. You can examine negatives through semi-transparant glassine material.

To check negatives for proper exposure, look through negative at white surface with backlight reflecting from surface as illustrated.

Have made (or make yourself) a same size identification contact sheet from each roll of negatives. You can use a low powered magnifier to check sharpness. With a grease pencil, mark any necessary cropping or printing instructions for yourself or a commercial processor.

magnifying glass. In an emergency you can use the normal Pentax lens as a magnifier. Just unscrew it from the camera. Place a sheet of white paper on a table. Shine a bright light on the white paper and view your negatives against this white paper. With such a technique you will be able to see whether your negatives are sharp and whether you have captured all the subject material that you wished. Unless you have had many years of experience, however, you will not be able to interpret the negatives and tell whether or not they are good photographs. You must make them into print positives first.

The simplest and least expensive way to make prints is to have a contact strip or sheet made from the negatives or make one yourself. Take an 8 × 10 piece of plate glass. Place an 8 × 10 sheet of contact printing paper on it, face up. Arrange the strips of negatives across the enlarging paper so that they do not overlap. Sandwich negatives and paper with another glass sheet. Expose a print by holding the strips to light as in ordinary contact printing. You can, of course, use the enlarger baseboard instead of the bottom sheet of plate glass and use the enlarger lamp as illuminant. Then it is relatively easy to standardise on the exposure required.

After development you will have a complete record of your entire roll of pictures. You can examine the individual picture frames with a magnifier and pick out the compositions and expressions which please you. Since the negative numbers of the film frames also print through, it will be easy to identify each frame. Mark the frame with a red grease pencil. Try cropping the frame with edges of white paper to enhance the picture composition. Outline the area to be enlarged with a red grease pencil. This will serve as a guide when you are doing the enlarging or giving the printer instructions to do it for you.

In filing your negatives, you can place each set of strips with the matching contact sheet, or keep the contact sheets in a separate file to avoid too much handling of the negatives. If you give a number to each set of negatives and the same number to each contact sheet, there will be less danger of losing track of either. Whenever you want additional prints, leaf through the contact sheet and select the necessary matching negative.

Storing Colour

If you shoot colour negative pictures, you can use the same black-and-white contact sheet technique for picking pictures and for filing instead of going to the expensive waste of having colour prints made of everything immediately.

The problem of storing colour transparencies is more complicated. If you have a projector—and it makes little sense shooting colour transparencies unless you do, or have one available to you—examine the slides by projection as soon as they are returned from the processor. Throw away the bad duplicates and failures immediately. Store the shots you intend to keep in whatever type of slide magazine your projector uses. If your projector does not have a magazine, use the container in which the processor returned the slides to you, or buy a slide storage box.

Mark the transparency mounts so that you can easily project them correctly. To do this, hold the slide up to the light so that as you look through it, the picture is right way up and right way round. Then place a prominent dot or sticker on the bottom left-hand corner of the mount. As the slide goes into the projector, this dot should then be in the top right-hand corner facing you as you stand behind the projector.

401

FACTS AND FIGURES

ASA	Din	Relative Exposure Needed
800	30	1
640	29	1.3
500	28	1.6
400	27	2
320	26	2.5
250	25	3.2
200	24	4
160	23	5
125	22	6.3
100	21	8
80	20	10
64	19	13
50	18	16
40	17	20
32	16	25
25	15	32
20	14	40
16	13	50
12	12	63
10	11	80
8	10	100
6	9	125
5	8	160
4	7	200
3	6	250
2.5	5	320
2	4	400

Exact ASA-DIN conversion is not possible but these figures are accurate for all practical purposes and are those used by most film manufacturers.

FEET-METRE
CONVERSION

Feet/inches to metric units		Metric units to feet/inches	
$\frac{1}{8}$ in.	0.32 cm.	0.5 cm.	$\frac{3}{16}$ in.
$\frac{1}{4}$ in.	0.64 cm.	1 cm.	$\frac{3}{8}$ in.
$\frac{1}{2}$ in.	1.27 cm.	2 cm.	$\frac{13}{16}$ in.
1 in.	2.54 cm.	3 cm.	$1\frac{3}{16}$ in.
2 in.	5.08 cm.	4 cm.	$1\frac{9}{16}$ in.
3 in.	7.62 cm.	5 cm.	$1\frac{15}{16}$ in.
4 in.	10.2 cm.	6 cm.	$2\frac{3}{8}$ in.
5 in.	12.7 cm.	7 cm.	$2\frac{3}{4}$ in.
6 in.	15.2 cm.	8 cm.	$3\frac{1}{8}$ in.
7 in.	17.8 cm.	9 cm.	$3\frac{1}{2}$ in.
8 in.	20.3 cm.	10 cm.	$3\frac{15}{16}$ in.
9 in.	22.9 cm.	12 cm.	$4\frac{3}{4}$ in.
10 in.	25.4 cm.	15 cm.	$5\frac{7}{8}$ in.
11 in.	27.9 cm.	20 cm.	$7\frac{7}{8}$ in.
1 ft.	30.5 cm.	25 cm.	$9\frac{13}{16}$ in.
2 ft.	61.0 cm.	30 cm.	$11\frac{3}{4}$ in.
3 ft.	91.4 cm.	40 cm.	$15\frac{3}{4}$ in.
4 ft.	1.22 m.	50 cm.	$19\frac{3}{4}$ in.
5 ft.	1.52 m.	60 cm.	$23\frac{3}{8}$ in.
6 ft.	1.83 m.	80 cm.	$31\frac{1}{2}$ in.
7 ft.	2.13 m.	100 cm.	$39\frac{1}{2}$ in.
8 ft.	2.44 m.	1.5 m.	4 ft. 11 in.
9 ft.	2.74 m.	2 m.	6 ft. 7 in.
10 ft.	3.05 m.	2.5 m.	8 ft. 3 in.
15 ft.	4.57 m.	3 m.	9 ft. 10 in.
20 ft.	6.10 m.	4 m.	13 ft. 2 in.
30 ft.	9.14 m.	5 m.	16 ft. 5 in.
40 ft.	12.20 m.	10 m.	33 ft. 0 in.
50 ft.	15.24 m.	15 m.	49 ft. 2 in.
100 ft.	30.48 m.	20 m.	66 ft. 0 in.

One metre is actually a little over 3 ft. $3\frac{1}{4}$ in. This table is calculated on 3 ft. $3\frac{1}{2}$ in. and the error is of little consequence in practical photography.

Here's a quick way of adjusting your exposure properly to compensate for extension tube or bellows extension when shooting close-ups if you do not have a Pentax with through-lens meter.

1. Focus on your subject at close range. Turn this book on its side and use scale at subject distance across the horizontal length of picture area. Align zero mark with left hand edge of picture as seen through viewfinder.

2. Read required exposure increase at right edge of picture area in finder. Either use multiplying figure to adjust exposure or increase exposure by indicated number of stops.

PENTAX SPOTMATIC

ASA	B	I	$\frac{1}{2}$	$\frac{1}{4}$	$\frac{1}{8}$	$\frac{1}{15}$	$\frac{1}{30}$	$\frac{1}{60}$	$\frac{1}{125}$	$\frac{1}{250}$	$\frac{1}{500}$	$\frac{1}{1000}$
	Shutter Speeds											
20												
·25												
32												
·40												
·50												
64												
·80												
100												
·125												
·160												
200												
·250												
·320												
400												
·500												
·640												
800												
·1000	B											
·1250												
1600												
3200												

A

PENTAX SPOTMATIC II

ASA	B	I	$\frac{1}{2}$	$\frac{1}{4}$	$\frac{1}{8}$	$\frac{1}{15}$	$\frac{1}{30}$	$\frac{1}{60}$	$\frac{1}{125}$	$\frac{1}{250}$	$\frac{1}{500}$	$\frac{1}{1000}$
	Shutter Speeds											
20,25												
50												
100												
200												
400												
800												
1600												
3200												

A

PENTAX K1000, KM

Sec. / f	2	2.8	4	5.6	8	11	16	22
1	B							
$\frac{1}{2}$								
$\frac{1}{4}$								
$\frac{1}{8}$								
$\frac{1}{15}$								
$\frac{1}{30}$					A			
$\frac{1}{60}$								
$\frac{1}{125}$								
$\frac{1}{250}$								
$\frac{1}{500}$								
$\frac{1}{1000}$								B

METER RANGES

Black area A indicates operating range of Spotmatic. Shaded B area indicates range where needle will move and speed index window is black but meter will not operate properly. The meter range on early models was slightly more restricted. ASA range of Spotmatic extends to 1600.

PENTAX KX

Sec. \ f	1.4	2	2.8	4	5.6	8	11	16	22
1									
$\frac{1}{2}$									
$\frac{1}{4}$									
$\frac{1}{8}$									
$\frac{1}{15}$									
$\frac{1}{30}$				A					
$\frac{1}{60}$									
$\frac{1}{125}$									
$\frac{1}{250}$									
$\frac{1}{500}$									
$\frac{1}{1000}$									B

PENTAX MX

SHUTTER SPEED		1	$\frac{1}{2}$	$\frac{1}{4}$	$\frac{1}{8}$	$\frac{1}{15}$	$\frac{1}{30}$	$\frac{1}{60}$	$\frac{1}{125}$	$\frac{1}{250}$	$\frac{1}{500}$	$\frac{1}{1000}$
ASA	25											
	50											
	100											
	200											
	400											
	800											
	1,600											

As exposure measurements made at 1/1000 sec. with 25 ASA film will not be accurate, exercise caution. When using the 50mm f/1.4 lens, accurate exposure measurement at the points found in the striped area in the above table can be guaranteed only when using up to f/16 (f/1.4~f/16).

PENTAX ME

SHUTTER SPEED		8	4	2	1	$\frac{1}{2}$	$\frac{1}{4}$	$\frac{1}{8}$	$\frac{1}{15}$	$\frac{1}{30}$	$\frac{1}{60}$	$\frac{1}{125}$	$\frac{1}{250}$	$\frac{1}{500}$	$\frac{1}{1000}$
ASA	12														
	25														
	50														
	100														
	200														
	400														
	800														
	1,600														

PENTAX CLOSE-UP LENSES

●Type	●SMC Pentax Lens	●Lens-to-subject distance range	●Magnification
S40	50 mm. f/1.7, 50 mm. f/1.4, 55 mm. f/1.8, 40 mm. f/2.8	48.0 ~ 27.0 cm. (with 50 mm. f/1.7 lens)	1/7.6 ~ 1/3.5 (with 50 mm. f/1.7 lens)
S25	50 mm. f/1.7, 50 mm. f/1.4, 55 mm. f/1.8, 40 mm. f/2.8	32.6 ~ 22.0 cm. (with 50 mm. f/1.7 lens)	1/4.8 ~ 1/2.7 (with 50 mm. f/1.7 lens)
T80	85 mm. ~ 150 mm.	91.6 ~ 50.5 cm. (with 85 mm. f/1.8 lens)	1/9.4 ~ 1/4.2 (with 85 mm. f/1.8 lens)
T160	100 mm. ~ 150 mm.	175.0 ~ 89.5 cm. (with 135 mm. f/3.5 lens)	1/11.9 ~ 1/4.9 (with 135 mm. f/3.5 lens)
T95	135 mm. f/2.5, 200mm. f/4	114.0 ~ 84.0 cm. (with 200 mm. f/4 lens)	1/4.8 ~ 1/2.6 (with 200 mm. f/4 lens)
T183	135 mm. f/2.5, 200 mm. f/4	202.0 ~ 113.0 cm. (with 200 mm. f/4 lens)	1/9.1 ~ 1/3.8 (with 200 mm. f/4 lens)

PENTAX KM

SHUTTER SPEED		$\frac{1}{1000}$	$\frac{1}{500}$	$\frac{1}{250}$	$\frac{1}{125}$	$\frac{1}{60}$	$\frac{1}{30}$	$\frac{1}{15}$	$\frac{1}{8}$	$\frac{1}{4}$	$\frac{1}{2}$	1	B
ELECTRONIC FLASH	X												
FLASH BULB	FP	FP CLASS											
	X						M · MF · FP CLASS						

PENTAX KX

SHUTTER SPEED		$\frac{1}{1000}$	$\frac{1}{500}$	$\frac{1}{250}$	$\frac{1}{125}$	$\frac{1}{60}$	$\frac{1}{30}$	$\frac{1}{15}$	$\frac{1}{8}$	$\frac{1}{4}$	$\frac{1}{2}$	1	B
ELECTRONIC FLASH	X												
FLASH BULB	FP	FP CLASS											
	X						M · MF · FP CLASS						

Shaded areas indicate usable shutter speeds.

PENTAX K2, K2 DMD

SHUTTER SPEED		$\frac{1}{1000}$	$\frac{1}{500}$	$\frac{1}{250}$	$\frac{1}{125}$	$\frac{1}{60}$	$\frac{1}{30}$	$\frac{1}{15}$	$\frac{1}{8}$	$\frac{1}{4}$	$\frac{1}{2}$	8	4	2	1	B
ELECTRONIC FLASH	X															
FLASH BULB	FP		FP CLASS													
	X						M · MF · FP CLASS									

Shaded areas indicate usable shutter speeds.

PENTAX MX

SHUTTER SPEED		$\frac{1}{1000}$	$\frac{1}{500}$	$\frac{1}{250}$	$\frac{1}{125}$	$\frac{1}{60}$	$\frac{1}{30}$	$\frac{1}{15}$	$\frac{1}{8}$	$\frac{1}{4}$	$\frac{1}{2}$	1	B
ELECTRONIC FLASH	X												
FLASH BULB	FP	M, FP CLASS											
	X						M, MF, FP CLASS						

Shaded areas indicate usable shutter speeds.

Note: Pentax ME has X-sync only for electronic flash at 1/100 sec.

OLDER PENTAXES

Dark areas indicate useable shutter speeds for each type of flash synchronization.

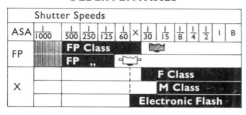

ASA	$\frac{1}{1000}$	$\frac{1}{500}$	$\frac{1}{250}$	$\frac{1}{125}$	$\frac{1}{60}$ X	$\frac{1}{30}$	$\frac{1}{15}$	$\frac{1}{8}$	$\frac{1}{4}$	$\frac{1}{2}$	1	B
FP		FP Class										
		FP ,,										
X				F Class								
				M Class								
				Electronic Flash								

SPOTMATIC PENTAXES

Shutter Speeds

ASA	$\frac{1}{1000}$	$\frac{1}{500}$	$\frac{1}{250}$	$\frac{1}{125}$	1/60 X	$\frac{1}{30}$	$\frac{1}{15}$	$\frac{1}{8}$	$\frac{1}{4}$	$\frac{1}{2}$	1
FP	FP Class &										
	M Class										
X	F Class										
	M Class										
	Electronic Flash										

PENTAX SPOTMATIC F

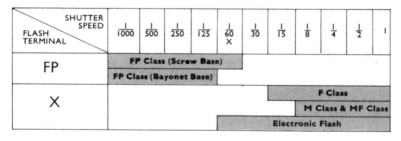

FLASH TERMINAL / SHUTTER SPEED	$\frac{1}{1000}$	$\frac{1}{500}$	$\frac{1}{250}$	$\frac{1}{125}$	$\frac{1}{60}$ X	$\frac{1}{30}$	$\frac{1}{15}$	$\frac{1}{8}$	$\frac{1}{4}$	$\frac{1}{2}$	1
FP		FP Class (Screw Base)									
		FP Class (Bayonet Base)									
X							F Class				
							M Class & MF Class				
						Electronic Flash					

PENTAX ES, ES II

SHUTTER SPEED		$\frac{1}{1000}$	$\frac{1}{500}$	$\frac{1}{250}$	$\frac{1}{125}$	$\frac{1}{60}$
FLASH BULB	FP					
ELECTRONIC FLASH	X					

PENTAX K1000

SHUTTER SPEED		$\frac{1}{1000}$	$\frac{1}{500}$	$\frac{1}{250}$	$\frac{1}{125}$	$\frac{1}{60}$	$\frac{1}{30}$	$\frac{1}{15}$	$\frac{1}{8}$	$\frac{1}{4}$	$\frac{1}{2}$	1	B
ELECTRONIC FLASH	X												
FLASH BULB							MMMF · FP CLASS						

Extension tube combination	Subject size	Film-to-subject distance	Magnification	Exposure factor

With 35 mm. lenses

Distance scale set 1 ft. 6 in. (.45mm.)

Extension tube combination	Subject size	Film-to-subject distance	Magnification	Exposure factor
Not used	$10\frac{1}{4} \times 1-7\frac{1}{4}$ (26 × 49 cm.)	1–6 (45 cm.)	0.1	1.2
1	$2\frac{1}{4} \times 4$ (6.6 × 10 cm.)	7 (18 cm.)	0.4	1.9
2	$1\frac{1}{2} \times 2\frac{1}{4}$ (3.8 × 5.7 cm.)	6 (15 cm.)	0.6	2.7
3	$1 \times 1\frac{1}{2}$ (2.6 × 4 cm.)	$5\frac{1}{2}$ (14 cm.)	1.0	4.0
1+	$\frac{3}{4} \times 1\frac{1}{4}$ (2 × 3 cm.)	$5\frac{1}{2}$ (14 cm.)	1.2	4.7

With 55 mm. lenses

Distance scale set 1 ft. 6 in. (.45 m.)

Extension tube combination	Subject size	Film-to-subject distance	Magnification	Exposure factor
Not used	$5\frac{1}{2} \times 8\frac{1}{4}$ (13.9 × 20.8 cm.)	1–6 (45 cm.)	0.2	1.4
1	$2\frac{3}{4} \times 4$ (6.9 × 10.4 cm.)	$11\frac{1}{2}$ (29 cm.)	0.3	1.8
2	$1\frac{3}{4} \times 2\frac{3}{4}$ (4.6 × 6.9 cm.)	$9\frac{1}{2}$ (24 cm.)	0.5	2.3
3	$1\frac{1}{2} \times 2$ (3.5 × 5.2 cm.)	9 (22.8 cm.)	0.7	2.9
1+3	$1\frac{1}{4} \times 1\frac{3}{4}$	$8\frac{3}{4}$ (22.1 cm.)	0.9	3.5
2+3	$1 \times 1\frac{1}{2}$	$8\frac{3}{4}$ (22.1 cm.)	1.0	4.0

With 85 mm. lenses

Distance scale set 2 ft. 9 in. (.85 c.m)

Extension tube combination	Subject size	Film-to-subject distance	Magnification	Exposure factor
Not used	$7\frac{1}{2} \times 11\frac{1}{4}$ (18.9 × 28.4 cm.)	2–9 (85 cm.)	0.1	1.3
1	4×6 (10.1 × 15.1 cm.)	$1-9\frac{3}{4}$ (55 cm.)	0.2	1.5
2	$2\frac{3}{4} \times 4$ (6.9 × 10.3 cm.)	$1-5\frac{1}{4}$ (44 cm.)	0.3	1.8
3	2×3 (5.2 × 7.8 cm.)	$1-3\frac{1}{2}$ (39 cm.)	0.5	2.1
1+3	$1\frac{3}{4} \times 2\frac{1}{2}$ (4.2 × 6.3 cm.)	$1-2\frac{1}{2}$ (37 cm.)	0.6	2.5
2+3	$1\frac{1}{2} \times 2$ (3.5 × 5.3 cm.)	1–2	0.7	2.8
1+2+3	$1\frac{1}{4} \times 1\frac{3}{4}$ (3 × 4.5 cm.)	$1-1\frac{1}{2}$ (34.4 cm.)	0.8	3.2

These tables are mathematically calculated and are intended for guidance only. Each individual lens may give fractionally different results when working at such close range. In many cases the figures have been rounded off. The metric figures are the more accurate. In practical work, further rounding off is possible, especially when the exposure factors are applied to black-and-white work. In such circumstances, there is no practical difference for example, between 1.8 and 2.0. Measurements are given in feet and inches with metric figures in brackets, i.e. 1–6 denotes 1 ft. 6 in.

Close-up Table I

SMC Pentax Lens	Magnifi-cation	Tube length	Distance scale on lens (m.)	Picture area (mm.)	Film-to-subject distance (mm.)	Exposure factor (X)
35 mm. f/2.8	0.76		∞	31.6 × 47.4	159	2.3
	0.93	Shortest	0.30	25.9 × 38.8	157	2.7
	1.33		∞	18.0 × 27.0	159	3.6
	1.50	Longest	0.30	16.0 × 24.0	162	4.1
35 mm. f/3.5	0.76		∞	31.7 × 47.5	152	2.5
	0.89	Shortest	0.35	27.0 × 40.5	149	2.8
	1.33		∞	18.1 × 27.1	152	4.0
	1.46	Longest	0.35	16.4 × 24.7	154	4.4
40 mm. f/2.8	0.64		∞	37.6 × 56.4	177	2.3
	0.83	Shortest	0.60	28.9 × 43.4	170	2.8
	1.12		∞	21.4 × 32.1	169	3.6
	1.31	Longest	0.60	18.3 × 27.4	171	4.2
50 mm. f/1.4	0.52		∞	46.0 × 69.0	219	1.9
	0.67	Shortest	0.45	35.9 × 53.9	205	2.2
	0.91		∞	26.3 × 39.4	197	2.8
	1.06	Longest	0.45	22.6 × 34.0	197	3.1
50 mm. f/1.7	0.51		∞	47.0 × 70.5	229	2.2
	0.66	Shortest	0.45	26.2 × 54.3	213	2.6
	0.89		∞	26.8 × 40.2	205	3.4
	1.05	Longest	0.45	22.9 × 34.4	204	3.9
55 mm. f/1.8	0.47		∞	51.4 × 77.2	258	2.1
	0.64	Shortest	0.45	37.5 × 56.3	235	2.6
	0.82		∞	27.8 × 41.8	224	3.2
	0.99	Longest	0.45	24.2 × 36.3	223	3.9
85 mm. f/18	0.31	Shortest	∞	77.2 × 115.8	450	1.9
	0.44		0.85	55.0 × 82.5	382	2.3
	0.55	Longest	∞	44.0 × 66.0	352	2.7
	0.67		0.85	35.4 × 53.7	334	3.2
100 mm. f/2.8	0.27		∞	90.0 × 135.0	601	1.9
	0.39	Shortest	1.00	61.0 × 92.0	492	2.4
	0.47		∞	51.5 × 77.3	459	2.8
	0.59	Longest	1.00	40.5 × 60.8	426	3.4
105 mm. f/2.8	0.25		∞	95.0 × 142.5	663	1.9
	0.36	Shortest	1.20m	66.5 × 99.7	549	2.4
	0.44		∞	54.2 × 81.3	504	2.8
	0.55	Longest	1.20	43.5 × 65.3	469	3.3
120 mm. f/2.8	0.22		∞	108.7 × 163.0	822	1.9
	0.35	Shortest	1.20	68.7 × 103.0	638	2.5
	0.39		∞	62.0 × 93.0	608	2.7
	0.52	Longest	1.20	46.5 × 69.3	547	3.4
135 mm. f/2.5 and f/3.5	0.20	Shortest	∞	121.7 × 182.5 (122.3 × 183.4)	996 (991)	1.8 (1.7)
	0.31		1.50	77.5 × 116.3 (77.9 × 116.8)	764 (757)	2.4 (2.21)
	0.34	Longest	∞	69.4 × 104.1 (69.7 × 104.6)	723 (716)	2.5 (2.4)
	0.46		1.50	52.4 × 78.5 (52.6 × 78.9)	643 (635)	3.2 (3.0)
M135 mm. f/3.5	0.20		∞	122.0 × 183.0	1041	1.0
	0.31	Shortest	1.50	76.0 × 115.0	801	2.6
	0.34		∞	69.0 × 104.0	765	2.8
	0.46	Longest	1.50	52.0 × 78.0	682	3.7
150 mm. f/4	0.18		∞	135.8 × 203.8	1229	1.9
	0.28	Shortest	1.80	85.3 × 128.0	928	2.5
	0.31		∞	77.5 × 116.2	844	2.7
	0.41	Longest	1.80	57.9 × 86.9	777	3.4
200 mm. f/4	0.13		∞	181.0 × 271.5	2007	1.7
	0.27	Shortest	2.00	90.4 × 135.6	1227	2.5
	0.23		∞	103.3 × 154.9	1378	2.3
	0.37	Longest	2.00	65.7 × 98.5	1091	3.3

Note 1: In the case of the 35 mm. or the 40 mm. lens, it is recommended that you do not use a magnification ratio of more than 1× because it might cause image distortion.

Note 2: In the case of the 135 mm. lens, the upper box refers to the f/2.5 lens and the lower to the f/3.5.

CLOSE-UP TABLE 2

SMC Pentax Lens	Magnification	Tube Length	Picture area (mm.)	Film-to-subject distance (mm.)	Exposure factor (X)
28 mm. f/2	3.04	Shortest	7.9 × 11.8	198	12.2
	3.74	Longest	6.4 × 9.6	216	17.5
28 mm. f/2.8	2.71	Shortest	8.8 × 13.2	160	10.8
	3.42	Longest	7.0 × 10.5	178	16.0
28 mm. f/3.5	2.83	Shortest	8.5 × 12.7	176	11.9
	3.53	Longest	6.8 × 10.2	194	17.3
30 mm. f/2.8	2.71	Shortest	8.8 × 13.2	169	10.7
	3.37	Longest	7.1 × 10.6	187	15.4
35 mm. f/2.8	1.94	Shortest	12.4 × 18.6	172	6.9
	2.51	Longest	9.5 × 14.3	188	10.2
35 mm. f/3.5	2.16	Shortest	11.1 × 16.7	171	8.5
	2.73	Longest	8.8 × 13.2	187	12.2
40 mm. f/2.8	1.24	Shortest	19.3 × 29.0	170	4.2
	1.72	Longest	13.9 × 20.9 mm.	181	6.4
50 mm. f/1.4	1.29	Shortest	18.7 × 28.0	200	4.1
	1.68	Longest	14.3 × 21.4	211	5.8
55 mm. f/1.8	0.85	Shortest	28.3 × 42.5	225	3.3
	1.20	Longest	20.0 × 30.0	225	4.7
Macro 50 mm. f/4	1.33	Shortest	18.1 × 27.1	212	5.8
	1.72	Longest	14.0 × 21.0	223	7.8

414

CLOSE-UP REFERENCE TABLE

TABLE 1: 35 mm. f/3.5

(Distance scale at ∞)

Magnification	Bellows Extension (mm.)	Area to be Photographed (mm.)	Film-plane-to-Subject distance (mm.)	Exposure factor
0.92	32	26 × 39	149	× 2.9
1.14	40	21.0 × 31.5	150	× 3.5

TABLE 2: 55 mm. f/1.8

(Distance scale at ∞)

Magnification	Bellows extension (mm.)	Area to be photographed (mm.)	Film-plane-to-subject distance (mm.)	Exposure factor
0.56	32	43 × 64	242	× 2.4
0.70	40	34 × 51	230	× 2.9
0.88	50	27 × 41	224	× 3.4
1.06	60	22.7 × 34	223	× 4.1

TABLE 3: 85 mm f/1.8

Distance scale at ∞)

Magnification	Bellows extension (mm.)	Area to be photographed (mm.)	Film-plane-to-subject distance (mm.)	Exposure factor
0.38	32	64 × 96	408	× 2.1
0.47	40	51 × 76.5	371	× 2.4
0.59	50	41 × 61	345	× 2.9
0.70	60	34 × 51	330	× 3.4
0.82	70	29 × 43.5	323	× 3.9
0.94	80	25.6 × 38.4	320	× 4.5
1.06	90	22.7 × 34.1	320	× 5.1

TABLE 4: 105 mm. f/2.8

(Distance scale at ∞)

Magnification	Bellows extension (mm.)	Area to be photographed (mm.)	Film-plane-to-subject distance (mm.)	Exposure factor
0.31	32	79 × 118	597	× 2.1
0.38	40	63 × 94.5	536	× 2.5
0.48	50	50 × 75	491	× 2.9
0.57	60	42 × 63	464	× 3.4
0.67	70	36 × 54	448	× 4.0
0.76	80	31.5 × 47	438	× 4.6
0.86	90	28 × 42	433	× 5.2
0.95	100	25.2 × 37.8	431	× 5.9
1.05	110	23 × 34.5	431	× 6.6

TABLE 5: 120 mm. f/2.8 (Distance scale at ∞)

Magnification	Bellows extension (mm.)	Areas to be photographed (mm.)	Film-plane-to-subject distance (mm.)	Exposure factor
0.27	32	90 × 135	734	× 2.1
0.33	40	72 × 108	652	× 2.4
0.42	50	57 × 86	590	× 2.8
0.50	60	48 × 72	552	× 3.3
0.58	70	41 × 61.5	528	× 3.8
0.67	80	36 × 54	512	× 4.4
0.75	90	32 × 48	502	× 5.0
0.83	100	29 × 43	496	× 5.6
0.92	110	26 × 39	493	× 6.3
1.08	130	22.2 × 33.3	493	× 7.7

TABLE 6: 135 mm f/2.5 and f/3.5 (Distance scale at ∞)

Magnification	Bellows extension (mm.)	Area to be photographed (mm.)	Film-plane-to-subject distance (mm.)	Exposure factor	
				f/2.5	f/3.5
0.24	32	101 × 151.5	880	× 2.0	× 1.9
0.30	40	81 × 121	774	× 2.3	× 2.2
0.37	50	65 × 97	693	× 2.7	× 2.5
0.44	60	54 × 81	642	× 3.1	× 2.9
0.52	70	46 × 69	610	× 3.6	× 3.4
0.59	80	40 × 60	586	× 4.1	× 3.8
0.67	90	36 × 54	571	× 4.6	× 4.3
0.74	100	32 × 48	560	× 5.2	× 4.8
0.89	120	27 × 40.5	551	× 6.4	× 5.9
1.02	137	23.7 × 35.5	548	× 7.6	× 6.9

TABLE 7: 150 mm. f/4 (Distance scale at ∞)

Magnification	Bellows extension (mm.)	Area to be photographed (mm.)	Film-plane-to-subject distance (mm.)	Exposure factor
0.21	32	112 × 168	1088	× 2.1
0.27	40	90 × 135	956	× 2.4
0.33	50	72 × 108	853	× 2.8
0.40	60	60 × 90	788	× 3.3
0.47	70	51 × 77	745	× 3.8
0.53	80	45 × 67	714	× 4.4
0.60	90	40 × 60	693	× 5.0
0.67	100	36 × 54	678	× 5.6
0.80	120	30 × 45	661	× 7.0
0.91	137	26.3 × 39.4	654	× 8.3

TABLE 8: 200 mm. f/4

Magnification	Bellows extension (mm.)	Area to be photographed (mm.)	Film-plane-to-subject distance (mm.)	Exposure factor
0.16	32	150 × 225	1753	× 1.8
0.20	40	120 × 180	1511	× 2.1
0.25	50	96 × 144	1321	× 2.4
0.30	60	80 × 120	1197	× 2.8
0.35	70	68.5 × 103	1112	× 3.2
0.40	80	60 × 90	1051	× 3.6
0.45	90	53 × 80	1005	× 4.0
0.50	100	48 × 72	971	× 4.5
0.60	120	40 × 60	924	× 5.5
0.69	137	35 × 52.6	900	× 6.4

TABLE 9: 300 mm. f/4

Magnification	Bellows extension (mm.)	Area to be photographed (mm.)	Film-plane-to-subject distance (mm.)	Exposure factor
0.11	32	217 × 325	3529	× 1.8
0.14	40	173 × 260	3033	× 2.0
0.17	50	139 × 208	2623	× 2.3
0.21	60	115 × 173	2354	× 2.7
0.24	70	99 × 148	2164	× 3.0
0.28	80	87 × 130	2024	× 3.4
0.31	90	77 × 115	1918	× 3.8
0.35	100	69 × 104	1834	× 4.2
0.41	120	58 × 87	1714	× 5.1
0.47	137	50.7 × 76.1	1645	× 6.0

*Using the Auto-Extension Tube No. 3 with the SMC Pentax Macro 50 mm. f/4 lens gives you magnification of 1× (life-size); both the automatic diaphragm and full-aperture metering capability is retained. For close-ups up to life-size, use of the Auto-Extension Tubes is recommended.

TABLE 10: Macro 100 mm. f/4

Magnification	Bellows extension (mm.)	Area to be photographed (mm.)	Film-plane-to-subject distance (mm.)	Exposure factor
0.82	32	29 × 43	405	× 3.8
0.90	40	26.6 × 39.8	402	× 4.1
1.00	50	24 × 36	401	× 4.6
1.10	60	21.7 × 32.6	402	× 5.1

BELLOWS UNIT K LENS REVERSED

TABLE 11: 28 mm. f/3.5

Magnification	Bellows extension (mm.)	Area to be photographed (mm.)	Film-Plane-to subject distance (mm.)	Exposure factor
3.02	32	7.9 × 11.9	180.7	× 13.3
3.30	40	7.3 × 10.9	188	× 15.5
3.66	50	6.6 × 9.9	197	× 18.3
4.01	60	6.0 × 9.0	206	× 21.5
4.36	70	5.5 × 8.3	216	× 24.9
4.71	80	5.1 × 7.6	225	× 28.5
5.41	100	4.4 × 6.6	244	× 36.5
6.12	120	3.9 × 5.8	264	× 45.5
6.72	137	3.6 × 5.4	280.5	× 53.9

TABLE 12: 35 mm. f/3.5

Magnification	Bellows extension (mm.)	Area to be photographed (mm.)	Film-plane-to subject distance (mm.)	Exposure factor
2.32	32	10.4 × 15.5	175	× 9.4
2.55	40	9.4 × 14.1	182	× 10.9
2.83	50	8.5 × 12.7	190	× 12.9
3.12	60	7.7 × 11.6	199	× 15.0
3.40	70	7.1 × 10.6	208	× 17.3
3.69	80	6.5 × 9.8	217	× 19.8
4.26	100	5.6 × 8.5	236	× 25.2
4.83	120	5.0 × 7.5	255	× 31.2
5.31	137	4.5 × 6.8	271.5	× 36.5

TABLE 13: 50 mm. f/1.4

Magnification	Bellows extension (mm.)	Area to be photographed (mm.)	Film-plane-to subject distance (mm.)	Exposure factor
1.40	32	17.2 × 25.8	202	× 4.5
1.55	40	15.5 × 23.2	207	× 5·2
1.75	50	13.7 × 20.6	213	× 6.1
1.95	60	12.3 × 18.5	220	× 7.1
2.14	70	11.2 × 16.8	227.6	× 8.2
2.34	80	10.3 × 15.4	235.6	× 9.4
2.73	100	8.8 × 13.2	252.5	× 12.0
3.12	120	7.7 × 11.5	270	× 14.8
3.46	137	6.9 × 10.4	285.6	× 17.5

TABLE 14: 55 mm. f/1.8

Magnification	Bellows extension (mm.)	Area to be photographed (mm.)	Film-plane-to-subject distance (mm.)	Exposure factor
0.95	32	25.4 × 38.1	223	× 3.7
1.09	40	22.1 × 33.2	224	× 4.2
1.26	50	19.0 × 28.5	226	× 5.0
1.44	60	16.7 × 25.0	231	× 5.8
1.61	70	14.9 × 22.3	236.5	× 6.7
1.79	80	13.4 × 20.1	243	× 7.6
2.14	100	11.2 × 16.8	258	× 9.7
2.49	120	9.6 × 14.4	274	× 12.0
2.79	137	8.6 × 12.9	288.6	× 14.2

TABLE 15: Macro 50 mm. f/4

Magnification	Bellows extension (mm.)	Area to be photographed (mm.)	Film-plane-to-subject distance (mm.)	Exposure factor
1.44	32	16.7 × 25.1	214	× 6.3
1.59	40	15.1 × 22.6	219	× 7.1
1.78	50	13.5 × 20.2	225	× 8.2
1.98	60	12.1 × 18.2	232.5	× 9.2
2.17	70	11.1 × 16.6	240	× 10.5
2.37	80	10.1 × 15.2	248	× 11.8
2.75	100	8.7 × 13.1	265	× 14.6
3.14	120	7.6 × 11.5	283	× 17.8
3.47	137	6.9 × 10.4	298.3	× 20.6

TABLE 16: Macro 100 mm. f/4

Magnification	Bellows extension (mm.)	Area to be photographed (mm.)	Film-plane-to-subject distance (mm.)	Exposure factor
0.96	120	25.1 × 37.7	401.1	× 4.8
1.06	130	22.7 × 34.1	401.2	× 5.3
1.13	137	21.3 × 32.0	401.5	× 5.6

AUTO BELLOWS K, LENS UNREVERSED

TABLE 1: 50 mm. f/1.7 (Distance scale set to ∞)

Magnification	Bellows extension (mm.)	Area to be photographed (mm.)	Film-plane-to-subject distance (mm.)	Exposure factor
0.73	38	33 × 50	209	× 2.8
0.77‡	40	31 × 47	208	× 3.0
0.96†	50	25 × 37	204	× 3.6
1.15†	60	21 × 31	205	× 4.3

TABLE 2: 55 mm. f/1.8 (Distance scale set to ∞)

Magnification	Bellows extension (mm.)	Area to be photographed (mm.)	Film-plane-to-subject distance (mm.)	Exposure factor
0.67	38	35.9 × 53.8	233	× 2.7
0.70	40	34.1 × 51.1	230	× 2.8
0.88‡	50	27.3 × 40.9	224	× 3.4
1.06†	60	22.7 × 34.1	223	× 4.1

TABLE 3: 85 mm. f/1.8 (Distance scale set to ∞)

Magnification	Bellows extension (mm.)	Area to be photographed (mm.)	Film-plane-to-subject distance (mm.)	Exposure factor
0.45	38	53.8 × 80.7	378	× 2.3
0.59	50	40.9 × 61.4	345	× 2.9
0.82	70	29.2 × 43.8	323	× 3.9
1.06	90	22.7 × 34.1	320	× 5.1

TABLE 4: SMC Pentax-M 100 mm. f/2.8 (Distance scale set to ∞)

Magnification	Bellows extension (mm.)	Area to be photographed (mm.)	Film-plane-to-subject distance (mm.)	Exposure factor
0.38	38	63 × 95	499	× 2.4
0.50	50	48 × 72	448	× 3.0
0.70	70	34 × 51	411	× 4.0
0.90	90	27 × 40	399	× 5.3
1.10	110	22 × 33	398	× 6.7

TABLE 5: 105 mm. f/2.8 (Distance scale set to ∞)

Magnification	Bellows extension (mm.)	Area to be photographed (mm.)	Film-plane-to subject distance (mm.)	Exposure factor
0.36	38	66.3 × 99.5	548	× 2.4
0.48	50	50.4 × 75.6	491	× 2.9
0.67	70	36.0 × 54.0	448	× 4.0
0.86	90	28.0 × 42.0	433	× 5.2
1.05	110	22.9 × 34.4	431	× 6.6

TABLE 6: 120 mm. f/2.8 (Distance scale set to ∞)

Magnification	Bellows extension (mm.)	Area to be photographed (mm.)	Film-plane-to-subject distance (mm.)	Exposure factor
0.32	38	75.8 × 113.7	669	× 2.3
0.42	50	57.6 × 86.4	590	× 2.8
0.58	70	41.1 × 61.7	528	× 3.8
0.75	90	32.0 × 48.0	502	× 5.0
0.92	110	26.2 × 39.3	493	× 6.3

TABLE 7: 135 mm. f/2.5 and f/3.5. (Figures in brackets for f/3.5 lens)

(Distance scale set to ∞)

Magnification	Bellows extension (mm.)	Area to be photographed (mm.)	Film-plane-to-subject distance (mm.)	Exposure factor f/2.5	Exposure factor f/3.5
0.28	38	84.9 × 127.3 (85.3 × 127.9)	801 (795)	×2.2	×2.1
0.37	50	64.5 × 96.7 (64.8 × 97.2)	699 (692)	×2.7	×2.5
0.45	60	53.7 × 80.6 (54 × 81)	649 (641)	×3.1	×2.9
0.52	70	46.1 × 69.1 (46.3 × 69.4)	616 (607)	×3.6	×3.4
0.59	80	40.3 × 60.5 (40.5 × 60.8)	594 (585)	×4.1	×3.8
0.67	90	35.8 × 53.7 (36 × 54)	579 (570)	×4.6	×4.3
0.74	100	32.2 × 48.4 (32.4 × 48.6)	569 (559)	×5.2	×4.8
0.82	110	29.3 × 44.0 (29.5 × 44.2)	562 (553)	×5.8	×5.3
0.97	130	24.8 × 37.2 (24.9 × 37.4)	557 (547)	×7.1	×6.5
1.04	140	23.0 × 34.5 (23.1 × 34.7)	557 (547)	×7.8	×7.1

TABLE 8: SMC Pentax-M 135 mm. f/3.5

(Distance scale set to ∞)

Magnification	Bellows extension (mm.)	Area to be photographed (mm.)	Film-plane-to-subject distance (mm.)	Exposure factor
0.28	38	85 × 128	845	×2.4
0.37	50	65 × 97	742	×3.0
0.44	60	54 × 81	691	×3.5
0.52	70	46 × 69	657	×4.1
0.59	80	40 × 60	635	×4.7
0.67	90	36 × 54	620	×5.4
0.74	100	32 × 48	609	×6.1
0.82	110	29 × 44	603	×6.9
0.96	130	25 × 37	597	×8.5
1.04	140	23 × 34	597	×9.4

TABLE 9: 150 mm. f/4

(Distance scale set to ∞)

Magnification	Bellows extension (mm.)	Area to be photographed (mm.)	Film-plane-to-subject distance (mm.)	Exposure factor
0.25	38	94.7 × 142.1	983	× 2.3
0.33	50	72.0 × 108.0	853	× 2.8
0.40	60	60 × 90	788	× 3.3
0.47	70	51.4 × 77.1	745	× 3.8
0.53	80	45.0 × 67.5	71	× 4.4
0.60	90	40 × 60	693	× 5.0
0.73	110	32.7 × 49.1	668	× 6.3
0.87	130	27.7 × 41.5	656	× 7.7
1.00	150	24 × 36	653	× 9.3
1.07	160	22.5 × 33.8	654	×10.2

TABLE 10: 200 mm. f/4

Magnification	Bellows extension (mm.)	Area to be photographed (mm.)	Film-plane-to subject distance (mm.)	Exposure factor
0.19	38	126.3 × 189.5	1561	× 2.0
0.25	50	96 × 144	1321	× 2.4
0.30	60	80 × 120	1197	× 2.8
0.35	70	68.6 × 102.9	1112	× 3.2
0.40	80	60 × 90	1051	× 3.6
0.45	90	53.3 × 80.0	1005	× 4.0
0.55	110	43.6 × 65.5	944	× 5.0
0.65	130	36.9 × 55.4	908	× 6.0
0.75	150	32 × 48	887	× 7.2
0.85	170	28.2 × 42.4	876	× 8.4

TABLE 11: 300 mm. f/4

Magnification	Bellows extension (mm.)	Area to be photographed (mm.)	Film-plane-to subject distance (mm.)	Exposure factor
0.13	38	182.9 × 274.4	3141	× 2.0
0.17	50	139.0 × 208.6	2623	× 2.3
0.21	60	115.9 × 173.8	2354	× 2.7
0.24	70	99.3 × 149.0	2164	× 3.0
0.28	80	86.9 × 130.3	2024	× 3.4
0.31	90	77.2 × 115.9	1918	× 3.8
0.38	110	63.2 × 94.8	1768	× 4.7
0.45	130	53.5 × 80.2	1671	× 5.6
0.52	150	46.3 × 69.5	605	× 6.7
0.59	170	40.9 × 61.3	1559	× 7.8

TABLE 12: Bellows 100 mm. f/4

Magnification	Bellows extension (mm.)	Area to be photographed (mm.)	Film-plane-to- subject distance (mm.)	Exposure factor
0.02	40	1198 × 1797	5187	× 1.0
0.12	50	199.7 × 299.5	1044	× 1.3
0.22	60	108.9 × 163.4	676	× 1.6
0.32	70	74.9 × 112.3	545	× 1.9
0.42	80	57.1 × 85.6	481	× 2.2
0.52	90	46.1 × 69.1	445	× 2.6
0.72	110	33.3 × 49.9	412	× 3.4
0.92	130	26 × 39	402	× 4.3
1.12	150	21.4 × 32.1	402	× 5.3
1.32	170	18.2 × 27.2	409	× 6.4

AUTO BELLOWS K, LENS REVERSED

TABLE 13: 28 mm. f/2.8

(Distance scale set to ∞)

Magnification	Bellows extension (mm.)	Area to be photographed (mm.)	Film-plane-to-subject distance (mm.)	Exposure factor
2.61	56	9.1 × 13.7	158	× 10.2
5.22	130	4.5 × 6.8	226	× 33.6
5.92	150	4.0 × 6.0	246	× 42.3
6.63	170	3.6 × 5.4	265	× 51.9

TABLE 14: 28 mm. f/3.5

(Distance scale set to ∞)

Magnification	Bellows extension (mm.)	Area to be photographed (mm.)	Film-plane-to-subject distance (mm.)	Exposure factor
2.66	70	9.0 × 13.5	172	× 10.8
3.36	90	7.1 × 10.7	189	× 15.9
4.07	110	5.9 × 8.9	208	× 22.0
5.12	130	5.0 × 7.5	227	× 29.1
5.47	150	4.4 × 6.6	246	× 37.2
6.18	170	3.9 × 5.8	266	× 46.3

TABLE 15: 30 mm. f/2.8

(Distance scale set to ∞)

Magnification	Bellows extension (mm.)	Area to be photographed (mm.)	Film-plane-to-subject distance (mm.)	Exposure factor
2.57	63	9.3 × 14.0	166	× 9.8
2.80	70	8.5 × 12.8	172	× 11.3
3.47	90	6.9 × 10.3	190	× 16.2
4.13	110	5.8 × 8.7	208	× 21.9
4.79	130	5.0 × 7.5	227	× 28.6
5.45	150	4.4 × 6.6	247	× 36.1
6.11	170	3.9 × 5.9	266	× 44.5

TABLE 16: 35 mm. f/2.8

(Distance scale set to ∞)

Magnification	Bellows extension (mm.)	Area to be photographed (mm.)	Film-plane-to-subject distance (mm.)	Exposure factor
1.90	62	12.6 × 18.9	171	× 6.6
2.12	70	11.3 × 16.9	177	× 7.9
2.41	80	10.0 × 14.9	186	× 9.6
2.70	90	8.9 × 13.4	194	× 11.4
2.98	100	8.0 × 12.1	203	× 13.4
3.27	110	7.3 × 11.0	212	× 15.6
3.84	130	6.2 × 9.3	230	× 20.5
4.41	150	5.4 × 8.1	249	× 26.0
4.98	170	4.8 × 7.2	268	× 32.1

TABLE 17: 35 mm. f/3.5

(Distance scale set to ∞)

Magnification	Bellows extension (mm.)	Area to be photographed (mm.)	Film-plane-to-subject-distance (mm.)	Exposure factor
2.01	58	12.0 × 18.0	166	× 7.6
2.34	70	10.2 × 15.4	176	× 9.6
2.63	80	9.1 × 13.7	184	× 11.5
2.92	90	8.2 × 12.4	193	× 13.5
3.20	100	7.5 × 11.2	209	× 15.7
3.49	110	6.9 × 10.3	211	× 18.1
4.06	130	5.9 × 8.9	230	× 23.2
4.63	150	5.2 × 7.8	248	× 29.1
5.20	170	4.6 × 6.9	268	× 35.6

TABLE 18: 40 mm. f/2.8

(Distance scale set to ∞)

Magnification	Bellows extension (mm.)	Area to be photographed (mm.)	Film-plane-to-subject distance (mm.)	Exposure factor
1.32	45	20.0 × 30.0	170	× 4.1
1.34	50	18.0 × 27.0	172	× 4.6
1.58	60	15.0 × 23.0	177	× 5.7
1.82	70	13.0 × 20.0	184	× 6.9
2.06	80	11.6 × 17.4	191	× 8.2
2.30	90	10.4 × 15.6	199	× 9.7
2.78	110	8.6 × 12.9	216	× 12.9
3.27	130	7.3 × 11.0	233	× 16.6
3.75	150	6.4 × 9.6	252	× 20.8
4.23	170	5.7 × 8.5	271	× 25.4

TABLE 19: SMC Pentax-M 50 mm. f/1.4, 50 mm. f/1.4

(Distance scale set to ∞)

Magnification	Bellows extension (mm.)	Area to be photographed (mm.)	Film-plane-to-subject distance (mm.)	Exposure factor
1.10*	(M) 60	21.7 × 32.6	197	× 3.3
1.18*	64	20.3 × 30.5	198	× 3.6
1.30†	70	18.5 × 27.7	200	× 4.1
1.50‡	80	16.0 × 24.0	205	× 4.9
1.69	90	14.2 × 21.3	211	× 5.9
1.89	100	12.7 × 19.1	218	× 6.8
2.09	110	11.5 × 17.3	225	× 7.9
2.48	130	9.7 × 14.5	242	× 10.3
2.87	150	8.4 × 12.5	259	× 12.9
3.26	170	7.4 × 11.0	276	× 15.9

424

NOTES:
*The optimum aperture for subjects in a flat plane is f/16 or smaller.
†The optimum aperture for subjects in a flat plane is f/11 or smaller.
‡The optimum aperture for subjects in a flat plane is f/8 or smaller.

TABLE 20: 50 mm. f/1.7   (Distance scale set to ∞)

Magnification	Bellows extension (mm.)	Area to be photographed (mm.)	Film-plane-to-subject distance (mm.)	Exposure factor
0.90†	56	26.6 × 39.9	205	× 3.4
1.17†	70	20.5 × 30.7	205	× 4.5
1.36‡	80	17.6 × 26.4	209	× 5.3
1.56	90	15.4 × 23.1	214	× 6.2
1.75	100	13.7 × 20.6	221	× 7.2
1.94	110	12.3 × 18.5	228	× 8.3
2.32	130	10.3 × 15.5	243	× 10.7
2.71	150	8.8 × 13.3	260	× 13.3
3.09	170	7.7 × 11.6	278	× 16.3

NOTES:
*The optimum aperture for subjects in a flat plane is f/16 or smaller.
†The optimum aperture for subjects in a flat plane is f/11 or smaller.
‡The optimum aperture for subjects in a flat plane is f/8 or smaller.

TABLE 21: 55 mm. f/1.8   (Distance scale set to ∞)

Magnification	Bellows extension (mm.)	Area to be photographed (mm.)	Film-plane-to-subject distance (mm.)	Exposure factor
1.08†	80	22.2 × 33.3	224	× 4.2
1.26‡	90	19.1 × 28.7	226	× 5.0
1.61	110	14.9 × 22.4	236	× 6.6
1.96	130	12.2 × 18.4	250	× 8.6
2.31	150	10.4 × 15.6	266	× 10.8
2.67	170	9.0 × 13.5	282	× 13.2

TABLE 22: Macro 50 mm. f/4   (Distance scale set to ∞)

Magnification	Bellows extension (mm.)	Area to be photographed (mm.)	Film-plane-to-subject distance (mm.)	Exposure factor
1.23	77	19.5 × 29.2	210	× 5.3
1.49	90	16.2 × 24.2	216	× 6.5
1.87	110	12.8 × 19.2	229	× 8.7
2.26	130	10.6 × 15.9	244	× 11.1
2.65	150	9.1 × 12.5	261	× 13.9
3.04	170	7.9 × 11.9	278	× 16.9

AUTO EXTENSION TUBE SET K
EXTENSION TUBE SET K
WITH LENS UNREVERSED

CLOSE-UP REFERENCE TABLE

● Figures in bold face are for the Auto Extension Tubes, regular weight figures in parentheses are for the Extension Tubes. (—) indicates that the preceding bold face figures also apply to Extension Tubes.

TABLE 1: 28 mm. f/2, f/2.8 and f/3.5   (Distance scale at 0.3 m.)

Magnification	Tubes to be used	Area to be photographed (in mm)	Film-to-subject distance (in mm)	Exposure factor
0.13 (—)	Not used	179 × 269 (—)	302 (—)	× 1.2 (—)
0.56 (0.47)	1	43 × 65 (51 × 77)	152 (160)	× 1.8 (1.7)
0.80 (—)	2	30 × 45 (—)	144 (—)	× 2.3 (—)
1.05 (—)	3	23 × 34 (—)	142 (—)	× 2.7 (—)

TABLE 2: 35 mm. f/2 and f/3.5   (Distance scale at 0.35 m.)

Magnification	Tubes to be used	Area to be photographed (in mm)	Film-to-subject distance (in mm)	Exposure factor
0.13 (—)	Not used	183 × 274 (—)	350 (—)	× 1.2 (—)
0.47 (0.40)	1	51 × 76 (59 × 89)	169 (180)	× 1.8 (1.7)
0.68 (—)	2	36 × 54 (—)	154 (—)	× 2.3 (—)
0.88 (0.95)	3	27 × 41 (25 × 38)	150 (149)	× 2.8 (2.9)

TABLE 3: 35 mm. f/2.8   (Distance scale at 0.3 m.)

Magnification	Tubes to be used	Area to be photographed (in mm)	Film-to-subject distance (in mm)	Exposure factor
0.17 (—)	Not used	142 × 213 (—)	300 (—)	× 1.2 (—)
0.51 (0.44)	1	47 × 70 (55 × 82)	173 (182)	× 1.8 (1.7)
0.71 (—)	2	34 × 51 (—)	161 (—)	× 2.2 (—)
0.91 (0.98)	3	26 × 39 (24 × 36)	157 (—)	× 2.6 (2.8)

TABLE 4: 40 mm. f/2.8   (Distance scale at 0.6 m.)

Magnification	Tubes to be used	Area to be photographed (in mm)	Film-to-subject distance (in mm)	Exposure factor
0.08 (—)	Not used	295 × 443 (—)	600 (—)	× 1.1 (—)
0.37 (0.31)	1	65 × 97 (77 × 116)	213 (232)	× 1.7 (1.6)
0.54 (—)	2	45 × 67 (—)	185 (—)	× 2.1 (—)
0.71 (0.77)	3	34 × 51 (31 × 47)	173 (171)	× 2.5 (2.6)
0.83 (0.77)	1 + 2	29 × 43 (31 × 47)	170 (171)	× 2.8 (2.6)
1.00 (—)	1 + 3	24 × 36 (—)	168 (—)	× 3.3 (—)
1.17 (1.23)	2 + 3	21 × 31 (20 × 29)	169 (170)	× 3.8 (4.0)

426

As the 50mm. f/1.4 and 50mm. f/1.2 lenses are not suitable for ultra close-ups (larger than life size) unless the Reverse Adaptor is used, the table lists only a few examples of when to use which tubes. However, a combination of No. 1, 2 and 3 tubes is possible.

TABLE 5: 50 mm. f/1.2, f/1.4 and f/1.7
(Distance scale at 0.45 m.)

Magnification	Tubes to be used	Area to be photographed (in mm)		Film-to-subject distance (in mm)	Epxosure factor
0.15 (—)	Not used	158 × 237 (—)		450 (—)	× 1.3 (—)
0.38 (0.34)	1	63 × 94	(72 × 108)	256 (273)	× 1.9 (1.7)
0.52 (—)	2	46 × 69	(—)	228 (—)	× 2.2 (—)
0.65 (0.75)	3	37 × 55	(34 × 51)	214 (211)	× 2.6 (2.8)
0.75 (0.70)	1 + 2	32 × 48	(34 × 51)	209 (211)	× 2.9 (2.8)
0.88 (—)	1 × 3	27 × 41	(—)	205 (—)	× 3.4 (—)
1.02 (1.07)	2 + 3	23 × 35	(23 × 34)	204 (204)	× 3.8 (4.0)
(1.25)	1 + 2 + 3		(19 × 29)	(207)	× (4.7)

TABLE 6: 55 mm. f/1.8
(Distance scale at 0.45 m.)

Magnification	Tubes to be used	Area to be photographed (in mm)		Film-to-subject distance (in mm)	Exposure factor
0.17 (—)	Not used	139 × 209 (—)		449 (—)	× 1.4 (—)
0.38 (0.34)	1	63 × 94	(70 × 105)	279 (302)	× 1.9 (1.8)
0.51 (—)	2	47 × 71	(—)	251 (—)	× 2.2 (—)
0.63 (0.68)	3	38 × 57	(35 × 53)	236 (240)	× 2.6 (2.7)
0.72 (—)	1 + 2	33 × 50	(—)	230 (—)	× 2.9 (—)
0.84 (—)	1 + 3	29 × 43	(—)	225 (—)	× 3.3 (—)
0.97 (1.01)	2 + 3	25 × 37	(24 × 36)	223 (231)	× 3.8 (3.9)
(1.18)	1 + 2 + 3		(20 × 30)	(225)	× (4.6)

TABLE 7: 85 mm. f/1.8
(Distance scale at 0.85 m.)

Magnification	Tubes to be used	Area to be photographed (in mm)		Film-to-subject distance (in mm)	Exposure factor
0.13 (—)	Not used	191 × 287 (—)		839 (—)	× 1.3 (—)
0.27 (0.24)	1	90 × 135	(101 × 151)	492 (542)	× 1.7 (1.7)
0.35 (—)	2	69 × 103	(—)	424 (—)	× 2.0 (—)
0.43 (0.46)	3	56 × 84	(52 × 78)	384 (388)	× 2.3 (2.6)
0.49 (—)	1 + 2	49 × 74	(—)	365 (—)	× 2.5 (—)
0.57 (—)	1 + 3	42 × 63	(—)	347 (—)	× 2.8 (—)
0.65 (0.69)	2 + 3	37 × 55	(35 × 53)	335 (333)	× 3.2 (3.6)
0.71 (—)	50 mm	34 × 51	(—)	330 (—)	× 3.4 (—)
(0.79)	1 + 2 + 3		(30 × 45)	(324)	× (3.8)

TABLE 8: 100 mm. f/2.8

Magnification	Tubes to be used	Area to be photographed (in mm)	Film-to-subject distance (in mm)	Exposure factor
0.13 (—)	Not used	190 × 285 (—)	1000 (—)	× 1.4 (—)
0.25 (0.22)	1	97 × 146 (108 × 162)	628 (671)	× 1.8 (1.7)
0.32 (—)	2	76 × 114 (—)	545 (—)	× 2.1 (—)
0.39 (0.41)	3	62 × 93 (58 × 87)	495 (482)	× 2.4 (2.5)
0.44 (0.41)	1 + 2	55 × 82 (58 × 87)	470 (482)	× 2.7 (2.5)
0.51 (—)	1 + 3	47 × 71 (—)	446 (—)	× 3.0 (—)
0.58 (0.60)	2 + 3	42 × 62 (40 × 60)	429 (424)	× 3.4 (3.5)
0.63 (—)	50 mm	38 × 47 (—)	420 (—)	× 3.6 (—)
(0.70)	1 + 2 + 3	(34 × 51)	(411)	× (4.0)
1.13 (—)	100 mm	21 × 32 (—)	399 (—)	× 6.9 (—)

TABLE 9: 120 mm. f/2.8

Magnification	Tubes to be used	Area to be photographed (in mm)	Film to subject distance (in mm)	Exposure factor
0.13 (—)	Not used	187 × 281 (—)	1202 (—)	× 1.5 (—)
0.23 (0.21)	1	105 × 158 (115 × 173)	805 (853)	× 1.9 (1.8)
0.29 (—)	2	84 × 126 (×)	705 (—)	× 2.2 (—)
0.35 (0.37)	3	69 × 104 (65 × 98)	641 (623)	× 2.5 (2.6)
0.39 (—)	1 + 2	62 × 93 (—)	609 (—)	× 2.7 (—)
0.45 (—)	1 + 3	54 × 81 (—)	575 (—)	× 3.0 (—)
0.50 (0.53)	2 + 3	48 × 72 (46 × 69)	551 (544)	× 3.3 (3.5)
0.55 (—)	50 mm	44 × 66 (—)	538 (—)	× 3.6 (—)
0.96 (—)	100 mm	25 × 37 (—)	492 (—)	× 6.7 (—)
(0.60)	1 + 2 + 3	(40 × 60)	(523)	× (4.0)

TABLE 10: Zoom 45 mm. ∼ 125 mm. f/4

Magnification	Tubes to be used	Area to be photographed (in mm)	Film-to-subject distance (in mm)	Exposure factor
0.04 (—)	Not used	651 × 976 (—)	1501 (—)	× 1.0 (—)
0.28 (0.19)	1	87 × 130 (126 × 189)	340 (418)	× 1.3 (1.2)
0.42 (—)	2	57 × 86 (—)	287 (—)	× 1.5 (—)
0.56 (0.57)	3	43 × 64 (42 × 63)	264 (263)	× 1.7 (1.8)
0.66 (—)	1 + 2	37 × 55 (—)	255 (—)	× 1.9 (—)
0.80 (—)	1 + 3	30 × 45 (—)	249 (—)	× 2.1 (—)

TABLE 11: 135 mm. f/2.5 and f/3.5

(Distance scale at 1.5 m.)

Magnification	Tubes to be used	Area to be photographed (in mm)	Film-to-subject distance (in mm)	Exposure factor
0.11 (—)	Not used	215 × 322 (—)	1499 (—)	× 1.4 (—)
0.20 (0.18)	1	119 × 179 (132 × 198)	977 (1045)	× 1.7 (1.7)
0.25 (—)	2	95 × 143 (—)	846 (—)	× 2.0 (—)
0.30 (0.32)	3	79 × 118 (74 × 111)	762 (740)	× 2.2 (2.3)
0.34 (—)	1+2	70 × 105 (—)	719 (—)	× 2.4 (—)
0.39 (—)	1+3	61 × 92 (—)	673 (—)	× 2.7 (—)
0.45 (0.46)	2×3	54 × 81 (52 × 78)	640 (631)	× 2.9 (3.0)
0.48 (—)	50 mm	49 × 74 (—)	622 (—)	× 3.2 (—)
(0.53)	1+2+3	(45 × 67)	(602)	× (3.5)
0.85 (—)	100 mm.	28 × 42 (—)	551 (—)	× 5.6 (—)

TABLE 12: SMC Pentax-M 135 mm. f/3.5

(Distance scale at 1.5 m.)

Magnification	Tubes to be used	Area to be photographed (in mm)	Film-to-subject distance (in mm)	Exposure factor
0.12 (—)	Not used	206 × 308 (—)	1500 (—)	× 1.5 (—)
0.21 (0.19)	1	117 × 175 (128 × 192)	1012 (1074)	× 2.0 (1.9)
0.26 (—)	2	93 × 140 (—)	886 (—)	× 2.3
0.31 (0.33)	3	77 × 116 (73 × 110)	805 (783)	× 2.6 (2.7)
0.35 (—)	1+2	69 × 104 (—)	764 (—)	× 2.8 (—)
0.40 (—)	1+3	60 × 90 (—)	720 (—)	× 3.2 (—)
0.45 (0.47)	2+3	53 × 80 (51 × 77)	688 (678)	× 3.6 (3.7)
0.49 (—)	50 mm	49 × 74 (—)	670 (—)	× 3.9 (—)
(0.54)	1+2+3	(44 × 67)	(650)	× (4.3)
0.86 (—)	100 mm	28 × 42 (—)	600 (—)	× 7.3 (—)

TABLE 13: 150 mm. f/4

(Distance scale at 1.8 m.)

Magnification	Tubes to be used	Area to be photographed (in mm)	Film-to-subject distance (in mm)	Exposure factor
0.11 (—)	Not used	229 × 344 (—)	1802 (—)	× 1.5 (—)
0.19 (0.17)	1	130 × 195 (144 × 216)	1193 (1278)	× 1.9 (1.8)
0.23 (—)	2	104 × 156 (—)	1036 (—)	× 2.2 (—)
0.28 (0.29)	3	86 × 129 (82 × 123)	934 (908)	× 2.5 (2.6)
0.31 (—)	1+2	77 × 116 (—)	882 (—)	× 2.7 (—)
0.36 (—)	1+3	67 × 101 (—)	826 (—)	× 3.0 (—)
0.41 (0.42)	2×3	59 × 89 (57 × 85)	785 (773)	× 3.4 (3.5)
0.44 (—)	50 mm	55 × 82 (—)	761 (—)	× 3.6 (—)
0.77 (—)	100 mm	31 × 47 (—)	663 (—)	× 6.7 (—)
(0.49)	1+2+3	(50 × 75)	(735)	× (4.0)

P.W. 11—AA

TABLE 14: 200 mm. f/4

Magnification	Tubes to be used	Area to be photographed (in mm)	Film-to-subject distance (in mm)	Exposure factor
0.13 (—)	Not used	181 × 271 (—)	2001 (—)	× 1.7 (—)
0.19 (0.18)	1	124 × 186 (133 × 199)	1546 (1615)	× 2.0 (2.0)
0.23 (—)	2	105 × 158 (—)	1394 (—)	× 2.3 (—)
0.26 (0.28)	3	91 × 137 (87 × 131)	1284 (1252)	× 2.5 (2.6)
0.29 (—)	1+2	83 × 125 (—)	1223 (—)	× 2.7 (—)
0.32 (—)	1+3	74 × 111 (—)	1155 (—)	× 3.0 (—)
0.36 (0.37)	2+3	67 × 101 (65 × 97)	1101 (1085)	× 3.2 (3.3)
0.38 (—)	50 mm	63 × 94 (—)	1069 (—)	× 3.4 (—)
0.63 (—)	100 mm	38 × 57 (—)	913 (—)	× 5.8 (—)
(0.42)	1+2+3	(57 × 86)	(1033)	× (3.7)

TABLE 15: 300 mm. f/4

Magnification	Tubes to be used	Area to be photographed (in mm)	Film-to-subject distance (in mm)	Exposure factor
0.09 (—)	Not used	255 × 382 (—)	3996 (—)	× 1.7 (—)
0.14 (0.13)	1	177 × 265 (189 × 283)	3070 (3212)	× 2.0 (1.9)
0.16 (—)	2	150 × 225 (—)	2754 (—)	× 2.2 (—)
0.18 (0.19)	3	131 × 196 (125 × 187)	2523 (2455)	× 2.4 (2.5)
0.20 (—)	1+2	119 × 179 (—)	2393 (—)	× 2.6 (—)
0.23 (—)	1+3	107 × 160 (—)	2246 (—)	× 2.9 (—)
0.25 (0.26)	2+3	96 × 144 (93 × 139)	2128 (2092)	× 3.1 (3.2)
0.27 (—)	50 mm	90 × 135 (—)	2059 (—)	× 3.3 (—)
0.44 (—)	100 mm	55 × 82 (—)	1682 (—)	× 5.5 (—)
(0.29)	1+2+3	(83 × 124)	(1975)	× (3.6)

TABLE 16: Macro 50 mm. f/4

Magnification	Tubes to be used	Area to be photographed (in mm)	Film-to-subject distance (in mm)	Exposure factor
0.50 (—)	Not used	48 × 72 (—)	234 (—)	× 2.3 (—)
0.73 (0.68)	1	33 × 49 (35 × 53)	213 (215)	× 3.2 (3.0)
0.86 (—)	2	28 × 42 (—)	209 (—)	× 3.7 (—)
1.00 (1.05)	3	24 × 36 (23 × 34)	208 (208)	× 4.3 (4.5)

TABLE 17: Macro 100 mm. f/4

Magnification	Tubes to be used	Area to be photographed (in mm)	Film-to-subject distance (in mm)	Exposure factor
0.50 (—)	Not used	48 × 72 (—)	450 (—)	× 2.5 (—)
0.62 (0.60)	1	39 × 58 (40 × 60)	424 (428)	× 2.9 (2.5)
0.69 (—)	2	35 × 52 (—)	415 (—)	× 3.2 (—)
0.76 (0.79)	3	31 × 47 (31 × 46)	408 (407)	× 3.5 (3.9)
0.81 (—)	1+2	29 × 44 (—)	405 (—)	× 3.7 (—)
0.88 (—)	1+3	27 × 41 (—)	402 (—)	× 4.0 (—)
0.95 (0.98)	2+3	25 × 38 (25 × 37)	401 (401)	× 4.3 (4.9)
1.0 (—)	50 mm	24 × 36 (—)	401 (—)	× 4.5 (—)
(1.07)	1+2+3	(22 × 33)	(401)	× (4.9)

AUTO EXTENSION TUBE SET K
EXTENSION TUBE SET K
TABLES FOR LENS ATTACHED REVERSED

TABLE 18: 28 mm. f/2.8

Magnification	Tubes to be used	Area to be photographed (in mm)	Film-to-subject distance (in mm)	Exposure factor
1.78 (—)	Not used	**13.5** × **20.2** (—)	**139** (—)	× **5.6** (—)
2.20 (2.11)	1	**10.9** × **16.3** (11.3 × 17.0)	**148** (146)	× **7.7** (7.3)
2.45 (—)	2	**9.8** × **14.7** (—)	**154** (—)	× **9.2** (—)
2.78 (2.70)	3	**8.6** × **12.9** (8.9 × 13.3)	**162** (160)	× **11.3** (10.7)
2.87 (—)	1+2	**8.3** × **12.5** (—)	**164** (—)	× **11.9** (—)
3.12 (—)	1+3	**7.7** × **11.5** (—)	**170** (—)	× **13.7** (—)
3.45 (3.36)	2+3	**6.9** × **10.4** (7.1 × 10.7)	**179** (177)	× **16.2** (15.5)
3.79 (—)	1+2+3	**6.3** × **9.5** (—)	**188** (—)	× **19.1** (—)

TABLE 19: 28 mm. f/3.5

Magnification	Tubes to be used	Area to be photographed (in mm)	Film-to-subject distance (in mm)	Exposure factor
1.90 (—)	Not used	**12.7** × **19.0** (—)	**154** (—)	× **6.4** (—)
2.32 (2.23)	1	**10.4** × **15.5** (10.8 × 16.1)	**164** (162)	× **8.7** (8.2)
2.56 (—)	2	**9.4** × **14.0** (—)	**169** (—)	× **10.2** (—)
2.81 (2.90)	3	**8.5** × **12.8** (8.3 × 12.4)	**175** (178)	× **11.8** (12.4)
2.99 (—)	1+2	**8.0** × **12.1** (—)	**180** (—)	× **13.1** (—)
3.23 (—)	1+3	**7.4** × **11.1** (—)	**186** (—)	× **14.9** (—)
3.48 (3.57)	2+3	**6.9** × **10.3** (6.7 × 10.1)	**193** (195)	× **16.9** (17.6)
3.90 (—)	1+2+3	**6.2** × **9.2** (—)	**204** (—)	× **20.5** (—)

TABLE 20: 35 mm. f/2.8

Magnification	Tubes to be used	Area to be photographed (in mm)	Film-to-subject distance (in mm)	Exposure factor
1.18 (—)	Not used	**20.4** × **30.6** (—)	**158** (—)	× **3.5** (—)
1.52 (1.45)	1	**15.8** × **23.7** (16.5 × 24.8)	**163** (162)	× **4.9** (4.5)
1.72 (—)	2	**13.9** × **20.9** (—)	**167** (—)	× **5.8** (—)
1.99 (1.92)	3	**12.0** × **18.0** (12.5 × 18.7)	**174** (172)	× **7.2** (6.8)
2.06 (—)	1+2	**11.6** × **17.4** (—)	**176** (—)	× **7.5** (—)
2.26 (—)	1+3	**10.6** × **15.9** (—)	**181** (—)	× **8.7**(—)
2.54 (2.46)	2+3	**9.4** × **14.2** (9.7 × 14.6)	**189** (187)	× **10.4** (9.9)
2.81 (—)	1+2+3	**8.5** × **12.8** (—)	**197** (—)	× **12.2** (—)

TABLE 21: 35 mm. f/3.5

Magnification	Tubes to be used	Area to be photographed (in mm)	Film-to-subject distance (in mm)	Exposure factor
1.40 (:—)	Not used	**17.1 × 25.7** (—)	**153** (—)	× **4.7** (—)
1.74 (1.67)	1	**13.8 × 20.6** (14.3 × 21.5)	**160** (158)	× **6.3** (5.9)
1.94 (:—)	2	**12.3 × 18.5** (—)	**165** (—)	× **7.3** (—)
2.14 (2.22)	3	**11.2 × 16.8** (10.8 × 16.2)	**170** (172)	× **8.4** (8.8)
2.29 (:—)	1+2	**10.5 × 15.7** (—)	**174** (—)	× **9.3** (—)
2.49 (:—)	1+3	**9.6 × 14.5** (—)	**180** (—)	× **10.5** (—)
2.69 (2.76)	2+3	**8.9 × 13.4** (8.7 × 13.0)	**186** (188)	× **11.9** (12.4)
3.03 (:—)	1+2+3	**7.9 × 11.9** (—)	**196** (—)	× **14.4** (—)

TABLE 22: 40 mm. f/2.8

Magnification	Tubes to be used	Area to be photographed (in mm)	Film-to-subject distance (in mm)	Exposure factor
1.06 (—)	2	**22.6 × 33.9** (—)	**169** (—)	× **3.5** (—)
1.29 (1.23)	3	**18.6 × 27.9** (19.5 × 29.3)	**171** (170)	× **4.4** (4.1)
1.35 (—)	1+2	**17.8 × 26.7** (—)	**172** (—)	× **4.7** (—)
1.52 (—)	1+3	**15.8 × 23.7** (—)	**176** (—)	× **5.4** (—)
1.75 (1.69)	2+3	**13.7 × 20.6** (14.2 × 21.3)	**182** (180)	× **6.5** (6.2)
1.98 (—)	1+2+3	**12.1 × 18.2** (—)	**188** (—)	× **7.7** (—)

TABLE 23: 50 mm. f/1.4

Magnification	Tubes to be used	Area to be photographed (in mm)	Film-to-subject distance (in mm)	Exposure factor
1.00 (0.95)	1	**24.0 × 36.0** (25.2 × 37.8)	**197** (197)	× **3.0** (2.8)
1.14 (—)	2	**21.1 × 31.6** (—)	**198** (—)	× **3.5** (—)
1.28 (1.33)	3	**18.8 × 28.2** (18.1 × 27.2)	**200** (201)	× **4.0** (4.2)
1.38 (—)	1+2	**17.5 × 26.2** (—)	**202** (—)	× **4.4** (—)
1.51 (.—)	1+3	**15.9 × 23.8** (—)	**206** (—)	× **5.0** (—)
1.65 (1.70)	2+3	**14.5 × 21.8** (14.1 × 21.2)	**210** (211)	× **5.7** (5.9)
1.89 (—)	1+2+3	**12.7 × 19.1** (—)	**218** (—)	× **6.8** (—)

Magnification	Tubes to be used	Area to be photographed (in mm)	Film-to-subject distance (in mm)	Exposure factor
1.00 (0.95)	**3**	**24.1 × 36.1** (25.3 × 38.0)	**204** (204)	× **3.7** (3.6)
1.04 (—)	**1 + 2**	**23.0 × 34.5** (—)	**204** (—)	× **3.9** (—)
1.18 (—)	**1 + 3**	**20.3 × 30.5** (—)	**206** (—)	× **4.5** (—)
1.31 (1.31)	**2 + 3**	**17.6 × 26.4** (18.3 × 27.4)	**209** (208)	× **5.3** (5.1)
1.54 (—)	**1 + 2 + 3**	**15.5 × 23.3** (—)	**214** (—)	× **6.2** (—)

TABLE 25: 55 mm. f/1.8

Magnification	Tubes to be used	Area to be photographed (in mm)	Film-to-subject distance (in mm)	Exposure factor
1.05 (—)	**1 + 3**	**22.8 × 34.3** (—)	**223** (—)	× **4.1** (—)
1.17 (1.22)	**2 + 3**	**20.4 × 30.7** (19.7 × 29.6)	**225** (226)	× **4.6** (4.8)
1.39 (—)	**1 + 2 + 3**	**17.3 × 25.0** (—)	**229** (—)	× **5.5** (—)

Caution: It is meaningless to reverse the Macro 100mm. f/4 lens and use it with the three extension tubes, No. 1, No. 2 and No. 3, for greater magnifications. In this case, you will obtain a magnification of less than 1X.

TABLE 26: Macro 50 mm. f/4

Magnification	Tubes to be used	Area to be photographed (in mm)	Film-to-subject distance (in mm)	Exposure factor
1.05 (1.00)	**1**	**22.9 × 34.4** (24.0 × 36.0)	**208** (208)	× **4.5** (4.8)
1.18 (—)	**2**	**20.3 × 30.4** (—)	**209** (—)	× **5.1** (—)
1.32 (1.37)	**3**	**18.2 × 27.3** (17.6 × 26.3)	**212** (213)	× **5.7** (6.0)
1.42 (—)	**1 + 2**	**17.0 × 25.4** (—)	**214** (—)	× **6.2** (—)
1.55 (—)	**1 + 3**	**15.5 × 23.2** (—)	**218** (—)	× **6.9** (—)
1.69 (1.74)	**2 + 3**	**14.2 × 21.3** (13.8 × 20.7)	**222** (224)	× **7.6** (7.9)
1.92 (—)	**1 + 2 + 3**	**12.5 × 18.8** (—)	**230** (—)	× **9.0**

EXTENSION TUBE DATA for S-3 type extension tubes.

Extension tube combination	Subject size	Film-to-subject distance	Magnification	Exposure factor
With 105 mm. lenses		Distance scale set 4 ft. (1.2 m.)		
Not used	8¾×1–1¼ (22.4×33.6 cm.)	4–0 (120 cm.)	0.1	1.2
1	4¾×7¼ (12.1×18.2 cm.)	2–6 (76 cm.)	0.2	1.4
2	3¼×5 (8.3×12.5 cm.)	2–0 (60 cm.)	0.3	1.7
3	2½×3¾ (6.3×9.5 cm.)	1–9 (53 cm.)	0.4	1.9
1+3	2×3 (5.1×7.7 cm.)	1–7 (48 cm.)	0.5	2.2
2+3	1¾×2½ (4.3×6.4 cm.)	1–6 (46 cm.)	0.6	2.4
1+2+3	1½×2¼ (3.7×5.5 cm.)	1–5¼ (44 cm.)	0.7	2.7
With 135 mm. lenses		Distance scale set 6 ft. 6 in. (2 m.)		
Not used	1–0×1–6 (30.6×45.9 cm.)	6–6 (200 cm.)	0.1	1.2
	6¼×9½ (16.1×24.2 cm.)	4–0 (120 cm.)	0.15	1.3
2	4¼×6½ (11×16.5 cm.)	3–0 (92 cm.)	0.2	1.5
3	3¼×5 (8.3×12.5 cm.)	2–6 (78 cm.)	0.3	1.7
1+3	2½×4 (6.7×10 cm.)	2–3 (69 cm.)	0.35	1.8
2+3	2¼×3½ (5.6×8.4 cm.)	2–1 (64 cm.)	0.4	2.0
1+2+3	2×2¾ (4.8×7.2 cm.)	2–0 (61 cm.)	0.5	2.3
With 200 mm. lenses		Distance scale set 8 ft. (2.5 m.)		
Not used	9¾×1–2¾ (25×37.5 cm.)	8–0 (245 cm.)	0.1	1.2
1	6½×10 (16.7×25.3 cm.)	6–0 (182 cm.)	0.15	1.3
	5×7½ (12.6×18.9 cm.)	4–10 (149 cm.)	0.2	1.4
3	4×6 (10×15 cm.)	4–3 (129 cm.)	0.25	1.5
1+3	3¼×5 (8.4×12.6 cm.)	3–10 (116 cm.)	0.3	1.7
2+3	2¾×4¼ (7.2×10.8 cm.)	3–6 (107 cm.)	0.35	1.8
1+2+3	2½×3¾ (6.3×9.5 cm.)	3–3 (100 cm.)	0.4	1.9

These figures are approximate.

Extension tube combination	Subject size	Film-to-subject distance	Magnification	Exposure factor
With 300 mm. lenses				
		Distance scale set 18 ft. (5.5 m.)		
Not used	1–3 × 1–11 (39 × 59 cm.)	18–0 (550 cm.)	0.05	1.1
1	10¼ × 15½ (26 × 39 cm.)	12–6 (380 cm.)	0.1	1.2
2	7½ × 11½ (19 × 29 cm.)	9–10 (300 cm.)	0.1	1.3
1 + 2	6 × 9 (15 × 23 cm.)	8–6 (260 cm.)	0.15	1.3
1 + 3	5 × 7½ (13 × 19 cm.)	7–6 (230 cm.)	0.2	1.4
2 + 3	4¼ × 6¼	6–6 (200 cm.)	0.2	1.5

Extension tube combination	Subject size	Film-to-subject distance	Magnification	Exposure factor
With 35 mm. lenses				
		Distance scale set 1 ft. 6 in. (0.45 m.)		
Not used	10½ × 1–3¾ (27 × 40 cm.)	1–6 (45 cm.)	0.1	1.2
1	3 × 4½ (7.7 × 11.6 cm.)	7¾ (19.5 cm.)	0.3	1.7
2	1¾ × 2¾ (4.6 × 6.9 cm.)	6 (15.5 cm.)	0.5	2.3
1 + 2	1¼ × 2 (3.2 × 4.9 cm.)	5½ (14.3 cm.)	0.7	3.0
3	1 × 1½ (2.5 × 3.8 cm.)	5½ (14 cm.)	1.0	4.0
1 + 3	¾ × 1¼ (2.1 × 3.2 cm.)	5½ (14.1 cm.)	1.2	4.7

Extension tube combination	Subject size	Film-to-subject distance	Magnification	Exposure factor
With 55 mm. lenses				
		Distance scale set 1 ft. 9 in. (0.55 m.)		
Not used	7¼ × 11 (18.5 × 27.7 cm.)	1–9 (55 cm.)	0.1	1.3
1	3½ × 5½ (9.2 × 13.8 cm.)	1–1 (33.3 cm.)	0.3	1.6
2	2½ × 3½ (6 × 9 cm.)	10½ (27 cm.)	0.4	2.0
1 + 2	1¾ × 2½ (4.4 × 6.6 cm.)	9½ (24.2 cm.)	0.5	2.4
3	1½ × 2 (3.6 × 5.4 cm.)	9 (22.9 cm.)	0.7	2.8
1 + 3	1¼ × 1¾ (3 × 4.5 cm.)	8¾ (22.2 cm.)	0.8	3.0
2 + 3	1 × 1¼ (2.5 × 3.8 cm.)	8½ (22 cm.)	1.0	4.0
1 + 2 + 3	¾ × 1¼ (2.2 × 3.3 cm.)	8½ (22 cm.)	1.1	4.3

These figures are approximate.

EXTENSION TUBE DATA for S-1 type extension tubes.

Extension tube combination	Subject size	Film-to-subject distance	Magnification	Exposure factor
With 85 mm. lenses		Distance scale set 2 ft. 9 in. (0.85 m.)		
Not used	7¼×11 (18.5×27.7 cm.)	2–9 (85 cm.)	0.1	1.3
1	4¼×6½ (10.9×16.4 cm.)	1–11 (58.3 cm.)	0.2	1.5
2	3×4¾ (8×12 cm.)	1–6¾ (47.6 cm.)	0.3	1.7
1+2	2½×3½ (6.2×9.2 cm.)	1–4½ (42 cm.)	0.4	1.9
3	2×3 (5×7.5 cm.)	1–3¼ (38.8 cm.)	0.5	2.2
1+3	1¾×2½ (4.2×6.3 cm.)	1–2½ (36.8 cm.)	0.6	2.5
2+3	1½×2¼ (3.6×5.5 cm.)	1–2 (35.5 cm.)	0.7	2.7
1+2+3	1¼×2 (3.2×4.9 cm.)	1–1¾ (34.7 cm.)	0.75	3.0
With 105 mm. lenses		Distance scale set 4 ft. (1.2 m.)		
Not used	8½×1–1 (21.8×32.7 cm.)	4–0 (120 cm.)	0.1	1.2
1	5¼×8 (13.3×20 cm.)	2–8 (81.6 cm.)	0.2	1.4
2	3¾×5¾ (9.6×14.4 cm.)	2–2 (65.6 cm.)	0.25	1.6
1+2	3×4½ (7.5×11.3 cm.)	1–10½ (57 cm.)	0.3	1.7
3	2½×3½ (6.2×9.2 cm.)	1–8½ (51.8 cm.)	0.4	1.9
1+3	2×3 (5.2×7.8 cm.)	1–7 (48.5 cm.)	0.45	2.1
2+3	1¾×2½ (4.4×6.7 cm.)	1–6¼ (46.2 cm.)	0.5	2.4
1+2+3	1½×2¼ (3.9×5.9 cm.)	1–5½ (44.7 cm.)	0.6	2.6
With 135 mm. lenses		Distance scale set 5 ft. (1.8 m.)		
Not used	10½×1–4 (27×40.5 cm.)	5–0 (180 cm.)	0.1	1.2
1	6¾×9¾ (17×25 cm.)	4–0 (120 cm.)	0.15	1.3
2	4¾×7 (12×18 cm.)	3–1 (94 cm.)	0.2	1.4
1+2	3¾×5½ (9.5×14 cm.)	2–9 (81 cm.)	0.25	1.6
3	3×4½ (7.7×11.5 cm.)	2–4 (57 cm.)	0.3	1.7

These figures are approximate.

Extension tube combination	Subject size	Film-to-subject distance	Magnification	Exposure factor

With 135 mm. lenses—contd.

Distance scale set 5 ft. (1.8 m.)

Extension tube combination	Subject size	Film-to-subject distance	Magnification	Exposure factor
1+3	2½ × 3¾ (6.5 × 9.8 cm.)	2–2 (51 cm.)	0.35	1.9
2+3	2¼ × 3¼ (5.7 × 8.5 cm.)	1–11 (46 cm.)	0.4	2.0
1+2+3	2 × 3 (5 × 7.5 cm.)	1–10 (42 cm.)	0.5	2.2

With 200 mm. lenses

Distance scale set 8 ft. (2.5 m.)

Extension tube combination	Subject size	Film-to-subject distance	Magnification	Exposure factor
Not used	9¾ × 1–2½ (25 × 37 cm.)	8–0 (250 cm.)	0.1	1.2
1	7 × 10½ (18 × 27 cm.)	6–6 (192 cm.)	0.13	1.3
2	5½ × 8¼ (14 × 21 cm.)	5–3 (160 cm.)	0.17	1.4
1+2	4¾ × 6¾ (12 × 17 cm.)	4–8 (140 cm.)	0.2	1.5
3	4 × 6 (10 × 15 cm.)	4–2 (126 cm.)	0.25	1.6
1+3	3 × 5 (8 × 13 cm.)	3–10 (116 cm.)	0.28	1.6
2+3	2¾ × 4¼ (7 × 11 cm.)	3–7 (109 cm.)	0.32	1.7
1+2+3	2½ × 4 (6.7 × 10 cm.)	3–6 (103 cm.)	0.36	1.8

With 300 mm. lenses

Distance scale set 18 ft. (5.5 m.)

Extension tube combination	Subject size	Film-to-subject distance	Magnification	Exposure factor
Not used	1–3½ × 1–11 (39 × 59 cm.)	18–0 (550 cm.)	0.06	1.1
1	11 × 1–4½ (28 × 42 cm.)	13–7 (410 cm.)	0.09	1.2
2	8¾ × 1–0½ (22 × 32 cm.)	10–10 (330 cm.)	0.1	1.2
1+2	7 × 10¼ (18 × 23 cm.)	9–2 (280 cm.)	0.14	1.3
3	6 × 8¾ (15 × 22 cm.)	8–2 (250 cm.)	0.16	1.35
1 × 3	5 × 7½ (13 × 19 cm.)	7–6 (230 cm.)	0.2	1.4
2+3	4½ × 6¾ (11 × 17 cm.)	6–11 (210 cm.)	0.2	1.45
1+2+3	4 × 6 (10 × 15 cm.)	6–2 (190 cm.)	0.25	1.5

These figures are approximate.

EXTENSION BELLOWS DATA FOR BELLOW II AND AUTO BELLOWS

As with the extension tube data, these figures are rounded off expressions of mathematically calculated data. Exact figures cannot be given to cover every individual lens, owing to the normal slight variations in actual focal length as compared with the nominal or marked focal length. Data are given here only for the minimum ($1\frac{1}{2}$ in). and maximum (7 in.) extensions of the bellows. There is, of course, a wide range of settings between these limits. Measurements are given in inches with metric figures in brackets.

Bellows extension		Subject size	Film-to-subject distance	Magnification	Exposure factor
With 35 mm. lenses					
Minimum	$1 \times 1\frac{1}{2}$		$5\frac{3}{4}$	1.0	4.0
	(2.4×3.6 cm.)		(14.9 cm.)		
Maximum	$\frac{1}{4} \times \frac{1}{4}$		$10\frac{1}{2}$	5.2	38.0
	($.7 \times .5$ cm.)		(26.6 cm.)		
With 55mm. lenses					
Minimum	$1\frac{1}{2} \times 2\frac{1}{4}$		9	0.7	2.7
	(3.7×5.5 cm.)		(22.9 cm.)		
Maximum	$\frac{1}{3} \times \frac{1}{2}$		12	3.2	17.5
	($.8 \times 1.1$ cm.)		(30.4 cm.)		
With 85 mm. lenses					
Minimum	$2\frac{1}{4} \times 3\frac{1}{4}$		$15\frac{1}{2}$	0.4	2.0
	(5.5×8.2 cm.)		(39.6 cm.)		
Maximum	$\frac{1}{2} \times \frac{1}{2}$		15	2.1	10.0
	(1.6×1.1 cm.)				
With 105 mm. lenses					
Minimum	$2\frac{3}{4} \times 4$		$21\frac{3}{4}$	0.4	2.0
	(6.8×10.1 cm.)		(55.3 cm.)		
Maximum	$\frac{1}{2} \times \frac{3}{4}$		18	1.7	7.5
	(2.1×1.3 cm.)		(46.2 cm.)		
With 135 mm. lenses					
Minimum	$3\frac{1}{2} \times 5\frac{1}{2}$		32	0.3	1.5
	(8.7×13.7 cm.)		(80.7 cm.)		
Maximum	$\frac{3}{4} \times 1$		22	1.3	5.5
	(1.8×2.7 cm.)		(56.2 cm.)		
With 100 mm. Bellows-Takumar					
Minimum			∞		1.0
Maximum	$\frac{3}{4} \times 1$		$16\frac{1}{4}$	1.4	6.0
	(1.7×2.5 cm.)		(41.4 cm.)		

FILTER EQUIVALENTS

Various manufacturers label filters differently. Those in the left column above are used in the Nomograph on page **439**; the others listed are *approximate* equivalents.

Accura Enteco Kodak Tiffen Walz	Ednalite	Harrison and Harrison	Enteco Hasselblad Lifa Rollei Tiffen	Gevaert
85B	Chrome B	C-5	R13	
85	Chrome A	C-4	R11	CTO8
85C	Chrome F	C-2	R8	
81EF	CTY6	C-1	R5	CTO4
81D	CTY5	C-$\frac{1}{2}$	R4	
81C	CTY4	C-$\frac{1}{4}$	R3.5	
81B	CTY3	C-$\frac{1}{4}$	R3	CTO2
81A	CTY2	C-$\frac{1}{8}$	R2	
81	CTY1	C-$\frac{1}{8}$	R1	CTO1
Skylight	Chrome Haze	U.V.-Haze	R1 or 1.5	
82	CTB1	B-$\frac{1}{8}$	B1	CTB1
82A	CTB2	B-$\frac{1}{4}$	B2	CTB2
82B	CTB3	B-$\frac{1}{2}$	B3	
82C	CTB4	B-$\frac{1}{2}$	84.5	CTB4
80C	80C	B-2	B8	
80B	80B	B-4	B11	CTB8

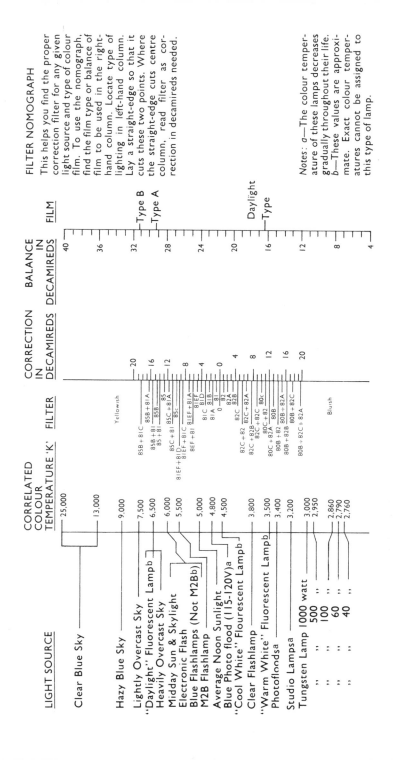

FILTER NOMOGRAPH

This helps you find the proper correction filter for any given light source and type of colour film. To use the nomograph, find the film type or balance of film to be used in the right-hand column. Locate type of lighting in left-hand column. Lay a straight-edge so that it cuts these two points. Where the straight-edge cuts centre column, read filter as correction in decamireds needed.

Notes: *a*—The colour temperature of these lamps decreases gradually throughout their life. *b*—These values are approximate. Exact colour temperatures cannot be assigned to this type of lamp.

FILM

- 40
- 36
- 32 — Type B
- — Type A
- 28
- 24
- 20 — Daylight
- — Type
- 16
- 12
- 8
- 4

BALANCE IN DECAMIREDS

CORRECTION IN DECAMIREDS

- 20
- 16
- 12
- 8
- 4
- 0
- 4
- 8
- 12
- 16
- 20

FILTER

- Yellowish
- 85B + 81C
- 85B + 81 / 85B + 81A
- 85 + 81 / 85B
- 85C + 81 / 85C + 81A
- 85C
- 81EF + 81D / 81EF + 81C
- 81EF + 81 / 81EF + 81A
- 8EF + 81 / 81EF
- 81C / 81D
- 81A / 81B
- 0 / 81
- 82
- 82A
- 82B
- 82C + 82 / 82C + 82A
- 82C + 82B
- 82C + 82 / 80c
- 80C + 82A / 80B
- 80B + 82 / 80B + 82A
- 80B + 82B / 80B + 82C
- 80B + 82C + 82A
- Bluish

CORRELATED COLOUR TEMPERATURE 'K'

- 25,000
- 13,000
- 9,000
- 7,500
- 6,500
- 6,000
- 5,500
- 5,000
- 4,800
- 4,500
- 3,800
- 3,500
- 3,400
- 3,200
- 3,000
- 2,950
- 2,860
- 2,790
- 2,760

LIGHT SOURCE

- Clear Blue Sky
- Hazy Blue Sky
- Lightly Overcast Sky
- "Daylight" Fluorescent Lamp *b*
- Heavily Overcast Sky
- Midday Sun & Skylight
- Electronic Flash
- Blue Flashlamps (Not M2B *b*)
- M2B Flashlamp
- Average Noon Sunlight
- Blue Photo flood (115-120V) *a*
- "Cool White" Flourescent Lamp *b*
- Clear Flashlamp
- "Warm White" Fluorescent Lamp *b*
- Photofloods *a*
- Studio Lamps *a*
- Tungsten Lamp 1000 watt
- ,, ,, 500 ,,
- ,, ,, 100 ,,
- ,, ,, 60 ,,
- ,, ,, 40 ,,

Filter	Wratten No.	Application	Exposure Factor

For Monochrome Films

Filter	Wratten No.	Application	Exposure Factor
U.V., Haze	1A	Many filters are sold under these and similar description. Their main function is to absorb ultra-violet radiation that is invisible to the human eye. They reduce distant haze.	1
Light Yellow		Absorbs excess blue and emphasises difference between blue sky and white clouds.	1.5
Medium Yellow		Stronger effect than light yellow.	2
Yellow-green		Similar effect to medium yellow but some photographers prefer it for outdoor portraits with sky background.	2
Orange		Stronger absorption of blue to give dramatic skies. Useful for marine scenes, aerial photography, some architecture and copying.	3
Red		Very strong absorption of blue for maximum sky/cloud contrast and similated night scenes by underexposure. Strong haze cutter. Excellent for copying blueprints.	6

For Daylight Type Colour Reversal Films

Filter	Wratten No.	Application	Exposure Factor
U.V., Haze, Skylight	1A	See above. Particularly suitable with colour film to remove blue cast in mountain views, scenes over water, sunlight snow scenes, pictures in open shade, etc.	1
Cloud	81A	Stronger effect than haze or U.V. type. Sultabe for use on cloudy days to "warm up" colours that might look too blue.	1.5
Morning and Evening	82A	Within two hours of sunset and sunrise, the light tends to contain a higher proportion of red. This filter prevents too much red light getting through to the film.	1.5
Flood	80B	In emergencies, you can use this filter to bring photoflood lighting into balance with daylight film. It is not recommended for general use, both on account of the compromise colour rendering and the loss of film speed.	3

These are the principal uses of filters with monochrome and colour film. It must be remembered, however, that few natural colours are pure. A coloured filter may have some effect on all the colours in a scene.

*The exposure factors given here are approximate. Experiments must be made to find the correct factor of any particular filter.

INDEX

444